RUNNING WITH FIRE

RUNNING WITH FIRE

THE TRUE STORY OF 'CHARIOTS OF FIRE' HERO
HAROLD ABRAHAMS

MARK RYAN

The Robson Press

First published in 2011 by JR Books, 10 Greenland Street, London NW1 0ND

This edition published in Great Britain in 2012 by
The Robson Press (an imprint of Biteback Publishing Ltd)
Westminster Tower
3 Albert Embankment
London
SE1 7SP
Copyright © Mark Ryan 2011

ISBN 978-1-84954-289-0

10 9 8 7 6 5 4 3 2 1

A CIP catalogue record for this book is available from the British Library.

Set in Electra
Cover design by Namkwan Cho

Printed and bound in Great Britain by
CPI Group (UK) Ltd, Croydon, CR0 4YY

DEDICATION

To my son Luca, source of such joy. And to the children and staff at Kimbolton St James' C.E. Primary School in Herefordshire, who also provided great inspiration during the writing of this book.

Contents

Part III Bannister To Chariots

I came to know Harold Abrahams when I was invited to become President of the British Amateur Athletic Board in 1952. He served as both Chairman and Treasurer of the Board between 1946 and 1975. I never played an 'executive' part in the activities of the Board, but I had many discussions with Harold Abrahams about the state of British athletics and the many hideous problems involved in trying to administer such a diffuse collection of fiercely independent athletic disciplines. His dedication to the efficient administration of British athletics and his commitment to the welfare and development of individual athletes was complete.

The period in history during which Harold Abrahams was involved in British athletics, both as a highly successful competitor and as an administrator, covered the evolution of both national and international athletic competition. The pioneers were amateurs, but the growing popularity of athletics, both as a sport and as a spectator event, created massive strains for the administrators as they endeavoured to cope with the transition from amateur status to 'assisted competitor' status which allowed all talented athletes to compete on equal terms.

I very much welcome this book which is a timely tribute to one of the most influential figures in the creation and development of athletic competition as we know it today.

PROLOGUE

Usain Who?

September 12, 2009, Hotel Capsis – Thessaloniki, Greece

Usain Bolt, fastest man in the world, strolls out of the first-floor restaurant holding some golden track shoes. They're a far cry from the springy old pair of spikes preferred by the hero of this book. But Bolt is the latest golden boy, he has the shoes to match, and they glitter in the sunlight streaming through the hotel windows.

Now is the moment. I approach the great man and explain that I'm writing the biography of Harold Abrahams, the sprinter from *Chariots of Fire*.

Usain looks blank.

'Some people call him the father of modern sprinting,' I explain.

Bolt seems happy enough to listen. He isn't making a break for the nearby escalator. If he did, that would be it. No point trying to catch him. He stays, but it's a one-way conversation; and after letting me ramble for a while, he starts to see the funny side.

'I've got no idea what you're talking about, man,' he smiles.

'Well,' I tell him, 'Harold Abrahams was an Olympic 100 metres champion – just like you.'

'Oh yeah, what year?' asks Bolt, a little more interested.

'In 1924,' I reply.

Usain's eyeballs drift northwest as if to say, 'Ancient history, man, no wonder I've never heard of the guy.'

But history can help a modern athlete. The London 2012 Olympic chief, Lord Coe, explains, 'Smart athletes understand the history of their sport, the genesis of the event and evolution. That helped me during the big moments of my career.'

Seb isn't taking a pop at Bolt, they just think differently. The Jamaican doesn't have much appetite for a history lesson on the day we meet, which is a little ironic, because Greece is definitely the right country for Olympic history. This is where it all began and Harold Abrahams, a true student of his sport, wrote about the first race of the 'modern' era. It was the 100 metres – and Usain Bolt would have been tickled by the winning time if nothing else.

Harold wrote:

On Easter Monday, April 6, 1896, just over 1,500 years after the Emperor Theodosius had abolished the Olympic Festival, said to have been held since 776 B.C., the First Modern Olympic Meeting began with a heat of the 100 metres. The description of this historic occasion contained in an account of the 1896 Games is as follows:

'The champions for the first race made their entrance by a subterranean passage; they were lightly attired in a flannel shirt, short under-garments and light canvas shoes . . . The interest of the public was fully excited when the Champions entered the lists. After they had arranged themselves in a straight line, ready to bounce forward, a pistol shot gave the signal for starting. Onwards they ran, Mr Lane an American arrived first at the goal, having run the race in 12⅕ sec.

Forty years later, I watched the first race of the 1936 Games, also a heat of the 100 metres. It was won in 10.7sec, while about half an hour after, Jesse Owens won the twelfth heat and equalled the Olympic record of 10.3sec . . .'

Bolt knows all about Jesse Owens, whose granddaughter, Marlene Dortch, presented Usain with his gold medal at the 2009 World Championships in Berlin. But Harold Abrahams, a champion Owens respected and befriended, remains a mystery to him. It's a pity in a way, because Bolt became a global icon partly due to men like Harold Abrahams, who pioneered the broadcasting of athletics events, and brought the excitement of races into homes around the world.

I ask Bolt something straight out, and the question is a little provocative. 'Do you think the old Olympic champions should be respected?'

'Of course we should respect them,' Usain says without hesitation. Then he reflects for a moment – and this is the first time he is really engaging in the conversation. 'I'm going to be an old Olympic champion one day, and I will want to be respected.'

Somehow Bolt is maintaining a healthy perspective on what is happening to him in this, his most extraordinary of years. At the time of our brief exchange, he has just brought the 100 metres world record down to 9.58. The record books say he is over a second faster than Harold Abrahams ever was. His speed seems to know no limits, the whole planet loves him. My 4-year-old son Luca kisses his face when it pops up on the TV screen, and there are kids like Luca all over the world. From these youngsters will come the next generation of great athletes – and somewhere among them is the next Usain Bolt.

Yet here he is, the man of the moment, at the height of his fame, suddenly contemplating old age and the distant possibility of an era when people might not know who the hell he is either. 'Yes, I'll want to be respected too. So it's important to respect past champions,' he repeats.

He looks thoughtful, as if pondering obscurity. Not too long after we meet, Bolt asks fellow track legend Michael Johnson what it feels like to retire. Usain might have been interested to know that when Abrahams retired he was only twenty-five; and the overwhelming emotion was relief. He was able to embark on new adventures, some of them every bit as dramatic as the old.

The Abrahams story didn't stop at the 1924 Olympics in Paris, though his running days alone were dramatic enough to be immortalised in a film called *Chariots of Fire*. Harold's desire to attend Hitler's Berlin Olympics of 1936, and the controversy that caused, were just as remarkable. A Jewish broadcaster with underlying psychological problems, Abrahams ignored his critics to broadcast for the BBC with a defiant bias. Did that represent a triumph for humanity, for lovable imperfection, over the Nazi concept of a superhuman race? Or did it expose a troubled man who ignored his roots to put ambition first? Make up your own mind.

At the time of our meeting, Usain Bolt hasn't seen *Chariots of Fire* and he hasn't heard of Harold Abrahams. No crime in that, but it seems to have got him thinking. One day there'll be a reigning Olympic 100 metres champion who has never heard of Usain Bolt. Then maybe someone will make a beautiful movie based on what Bolt achieved on the track too.

There were understandable distortions of the truth in *Chariots of Fire*; but Harold never knew about them. He died when the project was still in its infancy. His fiancée from way back during his running days, Christina McLeod Innes, was still alive when the film came out in the early 1980s. She went to see it as quickly as a woman pushing eighty could. Lord

Puttnam – the movie's producer – was pleased when he heard about that in 2010. 'The film would have been a thin brew without Harold Abrahams,' he added.

Chariots of Fire, I remind Bolt, before we part company. 'That's the movie. You might enjoy it.'

The sheer thrill of running fast is what started Abrahams on the road to glory. And that thrill hasn't changed too much down the years.

PART I

GIFTED, ABUSED,
ENGAGED AND CROWNED

CHAPTER ONE

LEFT FOR DEAD

It is three o'clock on Monday afternoon, July 7, 1924. This is the Colombes Stadium, Paris, and Harold Abrahams is out on the track at the Games of the Eighth Olympiad. His face looks gaunt, as if the enormity of the moment has just hit him. He has always been highly strung, and a few weeks ago he almost broke down completely before a big race. This race is much bigger. He comes across as arrogant, but he is also insecure and perhaps too intelligent for his own good. His high forehead and deep-set eyes make him look older than his twenty-four years. His lips, plump when relaxed, are thin with tension. Sport has a habit of distorting him, just as it has always made him feel special.

'Crack-a-Jack and twinkle-footed', his coach Sam Mussabini calls him. His enemies prefer 'conceited and big-mouthed' but they don't know how kind and generous he can be. Harold is full of contradictions; gloomy one moment, so happy the next that his smile can light up a room and his blue eyes sparkle like the sea on a summer's day.

There will be no smiles today, not this side of the tape anyway. And even if he safely negotiates the Olympic semi-final, there will be no reward – except the certainty of an even tougher ordeal that evening. Harold feels a little sick. He describes it as a sinking feeling, just as if his stomach were taking a walk up to his mouth and leaving a vacuum behind it. He always feels sick before a race, and he is trying not to let the occasion get to him. 'Avoid fussing like the plague,' coach Mussabini always tells him. 'If you are becoming increasingly worried, it is a good idea to sit down quietly, close your eyes, and relax all your muscles for about ten minutes.'

There isn't time for that now. But he must master his fear of failure; the fear that he will make a fool of himself in front of thousands of spectators. Most seem to be packed into the covered stand hugging the straight. Harold can hear them, a buzzing mass, the tone rising as the noise grows more persistent. They can't contain their excitement and soon the starter will need to calm them down again. But Harold's excitement is tenfold, the sensation hard to control. Abrahams intends to use this extra nervous energy to his advantage. He is determined not to let the sinking feeling get the better of him. Otherwise it will give rise to panic. Surprisingly, considering that he is about to take part in an Olympic semi-final, he manages to settle. This could be a good day.

Harold is still wearing his blazer over his white vest, which sports the image of a neat Union Flag waving in the wind. The vest, which looks like a twenty-first-century T-shirt, is just the way he likes it; not too high in the neck, a snug fit but not too tight. Harold's broad shoulders and powerful torso can live comfortably inside this one. The number 419 has been pinned across his belly and he has memorised it. If the starter or stadium announcer mentions 'quatre cents dix-neuf', Abrahams knows they are talking about him. He wears his own pair of shorts, roomy and loose. His legs are toned and unusually long, as if specifically built for extreme speed. In these shorts his legs can move freely to create short, rapid paces.

He looks down at his running shoes. He has rejected a recently purchased pair in favour of some springy old shoes. The decision has been taken after advice from Mussabini. Both pairs were made to measure, much like the shorts he is wearing. But by now the older track shoes fit like a second skin. Each shoe hides six strategically placed, half-inch spikes below. They are designed to give maximum grip on a cinder track.

He surveys his lane, a private kingdom defined by straight lines of string tied to shin-high pegs. He is still waiting to begin his pre-race ritual, hoping it will compose him for the second semi-final of the 100 metres. His captain and roommate in the British team's hotel, Philip Noel-Baker, has come to watch the race. He too feels the tension of the moment, because he knows that semi-finals carry a greater risk of oblivion than finals:

> To a sprinter, an Olympic final is the supreme moment of his athletic life. In all probability, it comes to him just once. To a sprinter's friends, a semi-final is even more exciting, in the strain it imposes on

their emotions and their nerves. If their man goes through, he joins the immortal ranks of the first six finalists in the Olympic Games. If he fails, his name may be forgotten, and he himself feel the sharp, though temporary, bitterness of defeat . . . I was sharing Harold's bedroom in our Paris hotel, and I knew at first hand the intensive training, with its minute attention to every detail, which he had done. I had seen, and I had tried to help with his psychological preparation. As he himself says, no wise man will venture a firm prediction on Olympic victories.

Down on the starting line, Harold is ready to dig his footholds with a trowel. He can almost hear his coach, Mussabini whispering in his ear, 'Be careful about the measurements of those holes to the fraction of an inch.' Each hole must be big enough to contain the ball of the foot, and yet not too wide. If the foot has room to move around then stability is lost. The athlete will be unsteady at the first stride. The fit has to be snug, and then there are the angles to consider. The front wall must slant forward to remove the sharp edge. Otherwise the toe is apt to catch as the foot comes through for the completion of that all-important first stride. The back wall presents the opposite challenge. It has to be sloped at such an angle that Harold's foot can fit firmly against the wall in the 'set' position. 'The back wall of the rear hole should be slanting at 75 degrees,' Harold always tells himself.

Abrahams works diligently. He seems pleased with his efforts. Now he takes a piece of cord out of his blazer. It is just less than three feet long. He places one end of the cord on the starting line in the centre of his lane, and marks the spot where the cord finishes. Then he takes that point and draws a line parallel with the starting line. That is where his first stride will land. The first stride will either reinforce the poise of the runner or throw him slightly off balance. Get it wrong and it is almost impossible to recover. Harold's first stride is always just under three feet when he gets it right. The cord should help him achieve his customary precision.

Such intricacies are lost on the French crowd, who rioted in the same Colombes stadium just a couple of months earlier, when their rugby heroes somehow managed to lose the gold medal game to a rag-tag bunch from the USA. The Parisians have packed the Stade Colombes to support the Frenchman, Maurice Degrelle. An eyewitness account tells how 'the loud-speaker had to appeal for silence among the clamorous, gesticulating crowd'. In this environment, composure doesn't come

Digging for victory: Clearly visible is the amount of work Harold has done with his trowel to create his 'starting holes'. A yard ahead of his 'dry-run' start-line is another line, where his first full stride will land.

easily. There were three false starts prior to the first semi-final, eventually won by the Boston Bullet, Jackson Scholz. Degrelle was the offender in each case and now he has been eliminated.

As Harold removes his jacket for the second semi-final, Philip Noel-Baker can suddenly sense the massive potential for something to go wrong. 'I felt a growing, urgent tension as he and his five opponents stripped and went to their marks. My instinct was not mistaken. What really happened, only Harold – and perhaps the starter – can say.' Beyond dispute is the fact that a false start further delayed proceedings.

No wonder the competitors are jumpy as they are called again. 'A *vos marques*,' says the starter, Dr Moir from Manchester, in the best French accent he can muster. Harold knows how important it is that Dr Moir, in his long white coat and summer hat, shows composure too. 'I have always felt that what counts more than anything else with starting is the personality of the starter, who above all must inspire confidence in the competitor. It must, of course, be conceded that there are some people who deliberately attempt to "beat the pistol" but they are few and far between and a starter who knows his job will have them "stone cold" every time.'

Abrahams and the other athletes, who are waiting a few yards behind the starting line, walk forward again purposefully. A hush finally falls across the stadium. Harold recalled the scene, 'I had to face the two Americans, Charley Paddock and Chester Bowman, "Slip" Carr of Australia and Cyril Coaffee, the Canadian champion. I was in fact sandwiched in between Carr and Coaffee, with the two Americans on my extreme right.' Giovanni Frangipane of Italy is on the inside.

Harold reaches for his footholds in the cinder track and places his right foot in its temporary home first. Then he puts his left in the front hole. His running shoes nestle snugly like rockets on launch pads. Now his hands are on the starting line, the width of his body apart. His thumbs point inward, his index fingers touching the line itself. The other fingers spread out just short of the line. Harold looks down his lane again. Each lane is separated from the next by stretches of string connected to low posts. That should help to focus the mind. It's what you do that matters, not the next man. It's all down to you. This is it.

'Run a sprint race as if you were the only competitor.' That is what Harold always tells others, because that is what Mussabini has told him. But it is easier said than done. Harold's rivals are real enough, and they want to destroy his dreams, just as he must try to destroy theirs. Harold is aware of a longing; 'the enormous amount of hope one concentrates in ten brief seconds', as he puts it. He feels the adrenalin coursing through his veins. Yet he must achieve calm, so that his muscles are relaxed, his position comfortable. He must not hurry unduly and he must not let the starter or anyone else fluster him. Nothing must distract his attention one iota. If he feels irritated by a speck of grit on his right knee he must brush it away while he has time. If he feels something is wrong, he is entitled to stand up and call the starter's attention to it. On this occasion there is no need. All is well.

'*Prêt!*' calls the starter with urgency, preparing to pull the trigger right behind the racers. Harold and the others raise their bodies, predators ready to hunt. He remains in the set position for what seems an eternity, yet his control over his body is total. Senses are magnified. For the rest of his life Harold will 'remember every millimetre of the semi-final'.

His whole world should now be focused on the starter's gun and his first stride. His head is down yet his eyes are glued to the spot where that first stride must land. He sees the mark he has made. No margin for error. The sound of the gun is coming, he knows it. Harold is used to holding this position for ten or twenty seconds at a time. It is second nature; he practises it in his bedroom every night before he goes to sleep. Poised, sharp, patient; Harold later boasted, 'I spent many hours perfecting starting, and am proud to record that during the whole of my athletic career, I never once caused a false start.'

Since reaching Paris, Abrahams has been taught an old French proverb, *C'est peu de courir; il faut partir a point*. He translates it like this: There is nothing in running; the real trouble is to start at the right moment. Many sprint races are won and lost in the first second after that pistol has been fired.

Something suddenly invades Harold's peripheral vision. Later he revealed:

> Slip Carr was immediately on my right, and he had the reputation of being faster off the mark than any man alive. Before the pistol was fired, I saw him out of the corner of my eye. I definitely saw Carr on the move. 'Bang!' went the pistol, and for a fraction of a second I did not react, believing there would assuredly be a recall.

His sense of precision, his quest for perfection, demands similar standards of others.

He knows the starter will call the others back; he will soon stand up and walk around again, maintaining his focus. He thinks he knows. Harold recalled, 'Dr Moir was a very good starter indeed; but in Paris I think he was a little overawed with the occasion – and who would not be?'

Dr Moir does not call the others back. In those same dreadful fractions of a second there is a grim realisation. Moir has ruled the start legitimate. The others have gone. The race to reach the Olympic final has started without him. The moment stayed with Harold forever. 'I waited for the second gun, but none came. There was no recall. In front of me I could see three backs. To my horror, I was at least one-and-a-half yards behind the others. For a fraction of a second I began to panic.'

Similarly horrified, Harold's captain, Philip Noel-Baker looked on helplessly. 'Certain it is that he was "left" – "left" by a yard and a half – a yard and a half that might have been two yards. Who could give so great a start to sprinters good enough to reach the semi-final?'

The next few seconds would be definitive, not just for the race but for the rest of his life. The world waited to see whether Harold Abrahams was a fighter.

CHAPTER TWO

BORN TO RUN

For a man who never made a false start in his entire sprinting career, Harold Abrahams showed a remarkable lack of discipline at birth. In fact he was so impatient that he almost didn't survive his opening minutes at 30 Rutland Road in Bedford, England. Harold insisted on joining his three brothers and two sisters so prematurely on a mid-December Friday in 1899 that it was almost the end of him. To be born a few weeks early is sometimes acceptable. To be born in the wrong century is asking for trouble.

'I ought to have been born in February 1900 because I was a seven-month baby and weighed three-and-a-half pounds. I oughtn't to have stayed very long, I'm told.' Somehow he escaped the ultimate punishment for jumping the gun, and sounded quite proud of the way he had broken the rules. 'I wasn't disqualified for a false start,' he explained. But it was touch and go for quite a while. 'He was not expected to live,' said Harold's adopted daughter Sue Pottle more than a century later. 'His mum Esther and his sister Dorothy fed him milk on a "drip" by soaking it through cotton wool. He survived – so he showed plenty of fighting spirit from the start.'

Harold probably inherited that grit from one of the most brutish men in Bedford at the time – his father Isaac. The sprinter's nephew, Tony Abrahams, explained that Isaac, normally flint-hearted, became uncharacteristically emotional about the little baby's struggle for survival, and always retained a soft spot for his youngest son. 'He was extremely sentimental about Harold, because he was not much more than three pounds when he was born.' There is a photo of Isaac holding Harold as a baby, the first picture of the future Olympic hero. The infant has clearly won his fight for life by then and put on a few more pounds. The pride with which Isaac shows off his youngest child for the camera does suggest that he possessed a warmer side of sorts. But those who knew Isaac might have been surprised to hear him described as 'sentimental' or 'warm' about anything. A tough refugee who couldn't speak English, he didn't put being nice high on his list of priorities. Finding a way to make money came first.

Isaac Klonimus was born in Vladyslovovo in Suwalki, Lithuania, or Russo-Poland as it was then. Klonimus proclaimed himself a Lithuanian Jew and escaped to Britain to avoid persecution. He arrived virtually penniless as a 15-year-old and changed his name to Abrahams, in recognition of his father – Abraham Klonimus.

It didn't take Isaac long to meet Harold's mother, Esther Isaacs, a distant cousin who was born in Merthyr Tydfil in Wales. Her father Samuel had been born in Poland but had emigrated to Britain, living briefly in Wales before setting up in Birmingham as a bedding manufacturer.

The eldest of eight siblings, Esther was introduced to Isaac as her family helped the newcomer to find his feet in the Midlands. He too began to make a living in Birmingham, but didn't like the place enough to want to stay. He took a shine to Esther, though, and the young couple married there in 1880. Then they headed for South Africa, where Isaac began to demonstrate his extraordinary ability for making money out of just about anything. Tony explained, 'They sold ostrich feathers and whisky to the natives for a while. Adolphe, Harold's eldest brother, was born in South Africa. Aged one, he and my grandparents came back to Britain.'

It took Isaac a while to put down fresh roots. He and Esther stayed in Birmingham at first, and then moved to Brighton. That's where another of Harold's brothers was born, Sidney (Tony's father – also known as Solomon or 'Solly'). They finally settled in Bedford, where the remaining four children – Lionel, Dorothy, Ida and Harold – completed the line-up. The three eldest boys – Adolphe, Sidney and Lionel – were educated at Bedford Modern, while Harold went to Bedford School, which was regarded as the better of the two. (Dorothy was at Bedford High and Ida was at Roedean, just outside Brighton).

Harold's father could barely speak English and he certainly couldn't write it – not even his name. So his rise was remarkable, as his grandson Tony Abrahams explained. 'He showed a good deal of native wit. He was very shrewd. He made a lot of money.' Isaac had a stall in Bedford market, where he sold tobacco and certain precious stones. He gradually began to lend money to selected people, including minor Bedfordshire aristocracy. At this stage, business was done at home or in the market; there was no pawnbroker's shop. As he succeeded, he took as collateral the houses or businesses of his debtors. He opened an office. Then he opened several – in Bedford, Luton, Ipswich, Watford and London. They made him richer still, and by the time the twentieth century was into its stride he had founded the Bedfordshire Loan Company.

Harold was sixteen years younger than Adolphe, and fourteen years younger than Solly. By the time Harold went into education, his father felt rich enough to call himself a 'financier and jeweller'. Yet behind the scenes Isaac was still renewing his pedlar's licence, almost as if he feared waking up one day to find that his astonishing success had been a dream. The fact that he was still classified as a foreigner – a Russian – couldn't have made him feel any more secure. Even when he became a British national later, Isaac was still something of an outsider; a feeling that Harold would come to understand later in life, albeit to a lesser extent.

As a small boy, Harold discovered that he had little else in common with his father, though they did share one passion. Harold's nephew, Tony, revealed:

> The Gilbert and Sullivan interest came first from Harold's father, who sang with a very thick Jewish accent any 'G and S' he could get hold of. The rest of the family were thus brought up on the 'G and S' operas. Otherwise Harold's father was a bit of a swine. There is no evidence of any athleticism – I don't know if the 'Old Man' was fast – he was very portly and not very tall. One of my colleagues once told me, 'I remember your grandfather at his stall – a funny little chap, very fat.'

But there was nothing funny about Isaac when he drank, because he became abusive and violent. Fortunately, as Tony pointed out, 'There were enough older siblings to protect Harold. I think his mother Esther and his sister Dorothy would protect Harold against the Old Man. He was a brute and they definitely feared him. I don't think Harold was beaten by his father in terms of really being clouted, though.'

Harold may have feared his father and found him hard to love, but he still appreciated the opportunities Isaac's success afforded his sons. 'My father couldn't write a letter until the day he died, but he could sign a cheque. It was through his efforts that we were given such a fine chance in life.' The problem, as Harold's brother Solly put it when reflecting on their childhood, was this: 'We had comfort but no happiness'.

There were six Jewish families in Bedford at the time. They were not persecuted but they would, according to Tony Abrahams, have felt 'set apart', simply because they were different from the majority. Since they weren't subjected to anti-Semitism in Bedford, Harold's family didn't seem to mind this feeling of being different. And when Isaac wasn't around, the athlete wasn't a complete stranger to fun. For example, a photo survives from this period which can be said to show Harold's first race – even though his legs weren't doing the running. The older children are hurdling over garden obstacles with the younger ones on their backs. Everyone concerned seems ready to collapse with laughter, yet there is also a competitive edge. Harold, who looks more like a girl with his long, curly locks, is clinging to Lionel's back in the 'middle lane' and clearly loving every moment.

No wonder Harold was able to reflect later, 'I was almost born sprinting!' And he was delightfully unpretentious when asked much later why he had taken up running as a boy. 'Well certainly in the early days . . . it's just exciting moving fast, you know? In my earliest days I wanted to run. I was plunged into athletics almost from the start.'

Sibling rivalry was part of the equation and always would be. Harold added:

> One of my brothers [Sidney] was a Cambridge Blue in the long jump and British Champion, and another [Adolphe] was a good all-round athlete, inter-hospitals champion and a doctor. Their interest in athletics meant that almost literally from my cradle I was guided and encouraged to perform. I was surrounded by this atmosphere of running. Sidney and Adolphe used to train me when I was tiny – even six years old. Whether they knew I'd got a lot of ability I don't know.

Harold was used as a pacemaker during Sidney's training. 'He used to give me half a minute's start in the quarter-mile and woe betide me if I glanced behind in the straight,' the youngest brother recalled.

Whatever recriminations he suffered, Harold had already decided the pressure was a price worth paying for the thrill of a race and the distant hope of a fancy jacket. He revealed later:

> My brother Sidney got his 'Blue' in 1904. I liked the Blue blazer very

much and I determined – I should think at the age of six – that I was going to wear one as soon as I could get it. I saw this pale-blue blazer and I thought how terribly good I'd look in it. Already at six, seven, eight, I lived athletics – I used to ask my brothers to let me run. I suppose I also resented their athletic fame and was determined to do better. As a very tiny boy I would, I suppose, have been described as a phenomenon.

Adolphe and 'S.S.' (Sidney Solomon) weren't about to let that talent go to waste. Tony Abrahams knew how hard his uncle had been pushed. 'The moment Harold started showing great athletic ability, the brothers would make him run everywhere. Their favourite game was to make him run around the houses in Bedford, and they would give him a time to beat and if he didn't make it they would hit him over the head with rolled newspapers.' Harold's adopted son Alan observed later, 'It sounds a little bit like Michael Jackson, being thumped over the head by his brothers if he didn't achieve the right levels of performance.'

Though Harold respected all his brothers, it seems that 'S.S.'was his favourite. And by the age of six, he must have sensed the excitement as Solly prepared for the biggest athletic event of the century so far. 'S.S.' competed in the 100 metres and the long jump in the Olympic celebration at Athens in 1906. But frustratingly for Harold, it was another brother, Lionel, who accompanied Solly to Athens, where he came fourth in the semi-final of the 100 metres in a time of 11.8sec.

A reporter for the *Sportsman* newspaper later recalled, 'I remember seeing Lionel in Athens in 1906. If only he had kept up athletics like his brother 'S.S.' he would very likely have succeeded in Championship honours. At Bedford his form in sprinting was very fine and on two occasions he won the public school race against Bedford County School.'

But Lionel lacked the kind of obsessive dedication that was necessary if you wanted to be the best. And after an emergency operation for appendicitis he didn't pursue his athletics dreams any further. Harold, on the other hand, was determined to become the best; and he was barely seven when he first experienced the thrill of victory in an organised event.

The first prize I ever received, for winning a fifty yards race on the sands at Hunstanton, was a copy of *The Pilgrim's Progress*. I was given a long start, because I looked such a miserable little fellow. They never saw me for sand. I came home with *The Pilgrim's Progress*, and I never looked back from that moment until I was lucky enough to run in the Olympic Games some thirteen years later.

When Harold was eight the Olympics first came to London, and a passionate coach named Sam Mussabini trained a young South African called Reggie Walker to the 100 metres gold medal. Harold would have to wait his turn to work with Mussabini, who was already causing controversy because of his professional approach to sport. Before they could team up, Abrahams had to negotiate his early school days in Bedford, where his father's growing wealth gave Harold a better start than his brothers. He explained, 'I went to the Bedford Junior School – known as the "Incubator" – of what was then the Bedford Grammar School for £5 a term. The Grammar subsequently became Bedford School.'

Harold enjoyed life in 'the 'Incubator', not least because it offered him stability at a time when his father's behaviour became erratic. Tony Abrahams explained, 'Isaac was a heavy drinker and a womaniser. He slept with anyone he could get hold of and he was a bully.'

With so much tension at home, athletics also offered a welcome escape. Harold won a handsome mug, his prize for winning an Under-10 440 yard race at school. Bedford's sporting community already knew it was nurturing a special talent. Elsewhere in England, that talent sometimes came as a nasty surprise.

Harold used to visit Brighton, where he had relations, and he tasted success in another race there. His daughter Sue explained, 'Again they gave him a head start because he was smaller than the others. He ran off and that was it. No one caught him. I still have the mug he won – it says "1910 Quarter-Mile. Over-Ten. First – Abrahams."'

Soon Harold was ready for his first big race in a recognised athletics arena, one which is now more famous for football. He recalled, 'I won my first gold medal at ten at Stamford Bridge. It was 1910 and it was an event called the Lotinga Cup, which was for the sons and brothers of members of the London Athletic Club. They gave you so many yards per year that you were under fifteen. I think I got 31¼ yards start that first time.'

A photograph survives of that summer event, which was run over 150 yards. A skinny Harold, legs bent, almost appears to be jumping at the tape in his huge shorts. In second place trails a much smaller boy who looks no more than six.

The organisers didn't forget the way events unfolded that day. Harold remembered, 'The next time I did that race, in 1911, I was penalised seven yards for winning and it worked out that I got seventeen yards' start.' It made no difference to the result. Abrahams confirmed, 'I was the first person to win it twice.'

Aged eleven, Harold won his school 100 yards in a time of 14sec. But a more important race was the traditional dash from the playing fields back to the main school building. It was measured at 300 yards, and Harold won the 1911 race in 47.4sec.

Victories soon became less spectacular, much to the disappointment of his demanding brother Adolphe, who wrote later, 'As a little boy, up to the age of ten, H.M. Abrahams was really remarkable: "the little fellow ran like a man".' But later in boyhood and early adolescence he was of hardly more than average ability.'

Academically he was also unexceptional, though his classics teacher described his work as 'quite promising'. English was 'very fair', mathematics 'satisfactory', French 'handicapped by absence', natural science 'satisfactory' and drawing 'moderate'. He was rated fourteenth out of twenty-two boys in his class overall. Hardly the stuff of a future Cambridge University student.

All the time he longed to emulate Solly, the family Olympian. Instead he was excluded from his brother's sporting adventures, and never forgot the feeling of frustration. He explained, 'I was at Bedford up to the age of twelve . . . I can remember my mother, my sister and my two brothers going to Stockholm for the 1912 Olympic Games, and I desperately wanted to accompany them.' This time Solly only competed in the long jump; and although he was still unable to win a medal, at least he had been part of it. And Harold hadn't even been able to watch.

Three Olympic Games had passed Harold by. He intended to put that right one day; but for the moment there was only upheaval. He recalled, 'I came away [from Bedford] for four terms in order to go to a Jewish Prep School at Brighton to be confirmed. Then I went back to Bedford and did one term in the Upper School.' Tony Abrahams explained later, 'Harold was Bar Mitzvahed at the appropriate age, but joined no congregation.' Sent back and forth between schools of contrasting cultures, these were the first in a series of unsettling moves. Later he claimed they created within him a tendency to leave things unfinished in his life.

An even more destabilising event was just around the corner. Tony explained, 'Something happened between his parents and they separated. I don't know if it was a civilised separation or not, but Esther established the new family home in Fulham Palace Road, West London.' Isaac left Bedford for London too, and moved into a flat in Rodney Court, Maida Vale. Before long, his daughter Dorothy was getting an allowance to look after him.

With the new family home in Fulham Palace Road came a new family dynamic. Harold's elder brothers were often out working, or living the lives of adults in their prime. So Harold was sometimes left to play the 'man' of the house as his mother adapted to the separation. That must have brought a fresh set of pressures – and as a new boy at school he was the outsider again.

At least sport provided some comfort. Abrahams chose not to mention the domestic and emotional upheavals behind the scenes when he looked back. 'After Bedford Upper School I moved in 1913 to London, where I went to St Paul's in Kensington as a day-boy for a year. At St Paul's I did a certain amount of rugger and a certain amount of athletics.' Harold also excelled at shooting, and won a trophy which had been donated by the Old Paulines of Bengal.

Meanwhile Sidney 'Solly' Abrahams claimed an even greater prize; he won the long jump title at the Amateur Athletic Association Championships in 1913. Harold felt proud and jealous of his brother in the same moment.

Abrahams began to frequent a track at Herne Hill in South London. There, in 1913 he came into contact with two men who would leave a deep impression on him. 'I met Sam Mussabini, who was going to play a very great part later in my running. He was training Applegarth.' Willie Applegarth had taken the 200 metres bronze medal at the Olympic Games of 1912. 'I was a great admirer of Applegarth,' Abrahams said later.

Mussabini, forty-six years old with a big grey moustache, intense eyes and exotic name had been working his magic down at Herne Hill for so long that he was almost part of the furniture. When Harold met him, he was being employed two evenings per week as the Polytechnic Harriers' senior coach. He lived in a house almost overlooking the track – at 84 Burbage Road. 'I think Harold's brothers introduced them' said his friend Rosemary Warne much later. In the fullness of time, Harold Abrahams and Sam Mussabini would be linked forever in athletics history. Back then the wily old coach sometimes went by the name of 'Sam Wisdom'. That pseudonym said as much about his character as anything. But once he had mastered the mouthful, Harold always referred to his coach as Mussabini or 'Old Sam'.

Though Sam must have known all about the Abrahams' family pedigree, Harold didn't exactly shine at that tricky stage in his physical development. He found his new, adolescent body was strange and awkward. Nevertheless Mussabini saw enough to know that Harold and his long legs might hold some promise for the future. So Sam began to keep an eye on him too, and offered the occasional tip.

No one can say for sure that Mussabini's influence helped Harold to return to winning ways in 1914 at St Paul's. But it happened and Abrahams said, 'I was the long-jump champion there with 15ft 3in.' He also won the 100 yards in 11.8sec, a decent time for a 14-year-old who hadn't done any serious running for two years. Harold came second equal in the 300 yards and second in the high jump, to show that he had the ability of an all-rounder.

And all the while, Harold's sprinting role model continued to inspire him. 'As a schoolboy, on July 4, 1914, I visited my first AAA Championship meeting. I well remember the thrill of seeing Willie Applegarth in the inside string tearing round the bend on a banked track at Stamford Bridge. He equalled the world's 220 yards record in 21.2sec, his strides following one another with incredible rapidity. Applegarth beat Vic D'Arcy, another great sprinter, by four yards.'

What kind of superman would Mussabini have made of Harold too, had the outbreak of World War One not caused a parting of ways? We will never know, and Abrahams would have to wait nine long years for his turn to work intensively under the studious gaze of the magician with the Midas touch.

For the moment, however, all the talk was of war. Like many adolescents, Harold wondered what he could do to help his country. Sue Pottle tells a story about her father trying to run away to war aged fourteen – only to be caught in London's docks as he tried to board a troop carrier. Harold was certainly a good enough shot to have held his own alongside most soldiers. But his nephew Tony doubted whether he was ever steely enough for warfare. He spoke of Harold affectionately but admitted, 'I wouldn't regard him as a courageous man in that sense.

Whatever the truth, Harold's father decided to put him out of harm's way at a boarding school a good distance from the English Channel. Abrahams talked later as though he had been given a say in that traumatic move. He said, 'I felt that a day school wasn't really as good for me as a boarding school would be, so I went to Repton, actually, just after the outbreak of war.'

CHAPTER THREE

A JEW AT REPTON

Repton was grim, though not as appalling as the prospect of fighting on the battlefields of northern France. Many unfortunate boys moved swiftly from one to the other, their young lives obliterated in an instant. At least the anti-Semitism Harold had to face at Repton wasn't life threatening.

In every sense, Repton was a long way from the life Harold Abrahams knew. The school still dominates a little village in Derbyshire, where the Midlands meets the North of England. Harold was given a place there because his brother Adolphe had the right contacts. Through his doctor's practice, the eldest sibling had come to know a top Liberal politician called Sir John Simon. Adolphe was physician to Lady Simon, who was a campaigner against persecution of any kind, whether of Jews or black slaves. She knew the staff at Repton and used her connections on Harold's behalf.

In 1914, the outgoing head was William Temple, who became Archbishop of Canterbury. He was succeeded by Geoffrey Fisher, who was just twenty-seven years old when he became headmaster. Unsurprisingly, Fisher was keen to show that he was already tough enough for the task. He would also go on to become Archbishop of Canterbury, though not before his regime had scarred Harold with some of his least pleasant memories.

Abrahams later claimed that he had been rejected by one Repton boarding house because he was the son of a moneylender. Though he was accepted by another – Old Mitre House, which had played host to the Sherlock Holmes actor, Basil Rathbone, a few years earlier – it didn't save him from discrimination. Luckily Abrahams had a way to fight back. 'As a schoolboy, at my public school, I think that I used athletics for covering up that sense of inferiority. I was determined to demonstrate my superiority over others. And what better way than in athletic distinction?'

The irony was that Abrahams had no great desire to defend the Jewish faith and didn't wish to be defined by it. He once joked, 'I lost my Jewishness the first time I smelt bacon and eggs at Repton.' In reality, he never entirely lost his Jewishness – partly because others would not let him.

There is no doubt that Harold was hurt by anti-Semitism as a teenager, because he referred to it so consistently in later interviews. On another occasion he reflected:

> I was good at athletics even at Repton, and found an opportunity, really for self-expression. I wanted something to justify myself. 'There was quite a deal of anti-Semitism at schools in those days and I had to find something where I could score off people. And by running of course you can do it, you can get first and you can win and I was determined to do so.

Before he had the chance to show his athletic prowess, Harold had to play football. Unfortunately he had more speed than skill. Harold admitted later, 'I was moderate at other games – I played soccer for the house and I got into Second XI at outside right. But I can't really say I was any good at soccer.'

He had to wait before he could show the bigots what he was really made of. By then he had developed a burning anger at the prejudice he was suffering on a regular basis. 'There was much more anti-Semitic feeling in those days and it provided one with the driving force to succeed in athletics. I never sought grievances, it was more a question of "this animal is dangerous when attacked". And I was attacked a few times.'

Some of the 'attacks' may have been more than verbal. Harold had to find a way to survive in a world where the absence of girls reduced the options for boys seeking sexual expression. Unable to escape the homosexual advances of a stronger, older boy, Harold succumbed. Much later he told his nephew about the incident. Tony explained delicately, 'The question as to whether we had any homosexual experience came up. And he said there had been an occasion at Repton when a more senior boy had sexual experience with him one night. But Harold certainly wasn't homosexual.'

That incident probably took place in the Old Mitre House itself, a three-storey building and former pub which can still be seen when you look out through the ancient, arched school entrance, in the direction of the village shops. Harold's temporary 'alliance' with the older boy may have earned him protection – or simply invited further abuse. To an extent the law of the jungle applied, and if you were weak you had to become strong quickly. Only then could you determine your own path as you progressed through the school.

When the chance to show his strength finally came, Harold took it. He was a better long-jumper than a runner in his mid-teens; and on Sports Day in March 1915, he produced a leap to be proud of. It also started a numbers game in Harold's head, one that would continue for his entire athletics career. Harold explained, 'When I was just fifteen years old, I managed to long-jump 18ft 1½in. My age (within a few days) runs conveniently with the years, and I resolved that I would set my ambition as a long-jumper to keep for as long as possible ahead in feet of the date.'

He had until 1919 to jump in excess of 19ft, a good four years to build up more strength. But the prospect of future physical maturity wasn't necessarily comforting, because it meant war.

Many a young man felt obliged to join up and fight even before he was fully grown. Others waited in trepidation for their turn to face the German guns. Harold braced himself for the ghastly conveyor belt of war, just like everyone else in his school. He was part of the Repton School Officer Training Corps, and in October 1916 he learned the art of 'Signalling', proud to join those who had 'qualified for their flags'.

Harold wrote to his mother on Bonfire Night that year to tell her, 'We had a very good field day last Friday against Shrewsbury. I was a signaller and did very well indeed.' But war games were a reminder of what might be waiting across the English Channel. It was scary; death didn't seem far away. No wonder Harold was grateful for any small luxury Esther sent him. On one occasion after receiving a parcel he wrote, 'My darling mother, not many people have such good and kind mothers as I have I am sure.'

But Harold's mother couldn't stop the war or its impact on his education. Abrahams reflected later:

> I started off with Classics. And here is another thing which would recur again and again, you see one of the things I had a disadvantage

that I found early on was that I went to so many schools – Bedford, Brighton, Bedford, St Paul's. I then went to Repton in war time, with no future ahead of us because the war was on and we were all – I certainly was – extremely frightened of the future. So that I never really felt I had to finish anything. And you get that time and time again that one doesn't go thoroughly into things. I think that has something to do with the fact that I never had to exert myself to the utmost. We had no exams at all at Repton during the war.

The wholesale slaughter left a strain on the educational system. Besides, there was little point in putting teenagers through exams when they probably wouldn't live to benefit from their academic success. A former Classics classmate called Donald McLeod Innes, whose sister Harold would soon know so well at Cambridge, lost his brother Patrick to that war in April 1917. So many Repton boys had to suffer similar news of lost loved ones.

Donald McLeod Innes came to terms with his grief by writing the following haunting poem – preserved even now in Repton history.

The Young Dead

Those whom we loved are gone; and at their going
We, who so ill could spare them needs must stay.
They were our best and brightest: it was they
On whom our hopes were builded, all unknowing
The destiny that was theirs; we watched them growing,
Learning where joy is found, and day by day
Happier, worthier. Now – they are fled away,
They are blotted out, beyond all human showing.

The skies grow dark: dead is the western gold:
Across the starlit heaven the grey clouds creep,
Yet know we, though the immortal stars are hidden,
They are not dead; soon, when they are bidden –
A puff of wind, and they'll wake from sleep
Nobler, serener, purer, than of old.

Tragically, Donald was to join 'the young dead' in the final year of that same war, before he could reach the sanity and serenity of Cambridge.

Like his brother, he had earned a place at Trinity College, and would never have the chance to go.

This was the sort of sadness that threatened to engulf Repton in Harold's final years there, as he heard what he described as 'seemingly endless roll-calls' of the fallen. As it turned out, Harold would feel the loss of Patrick and Donald McLeod Innes acutely, through the sister they left behind.

For the moment, Abrahams clung to any sense of normality that sport could offer. Athletics provided the escape from all things ugly. It always had, it always would. And after a couple of mediocre years, Harold's speed had returned with a vengeance, because he won the 100 and 220 yards at Repton in 1917. His time for the 100 yards was a searing 10.8sec, while he took a respectable 25sec for the 220 yards. Looking back on this period of Harold's life, his brother Adolphe wrote with a scarcely suppressed excitement, 'At about the age of seventeen a change became evident.'

By his final year, Harold had overcome most of his difficulties, and there were no older boys left to intimidate him. He moved from House Prefect to Head of House and School Prefect. He was also a Sergeant in the Corps. And his growing authority was built in no small measure on his athletic prowess, a highly respected commodity in such a competitive environment.

But Abrahams still felt his religious roots unfairly restricted his role within the school. His nephew Tony explained:

> Harold disliked the headmaster, Fisher, who was an anti-Semite. Harold was irritated when the headmaster picked him out early to become a prefect but then said he wasn't allowed to read the prayers. The Headmaster made him Head of House; but as for reading in assembly, he wasn't allowed to read the lesson. He was only allowed to read various items of administration.

The sticking point was the fact that the Jewish faith does not consider Jesus to be the Son of God. The headmaster decided that Harold was therefore unfit to utter the words 'through Jesus Christ our Lord, Amen'. Feeling that he was going to be discriminated against whatever solution he found, Harold approached the problem with a humour that only thinly masked his exasperation. Tony added, 'Harold told the headmaster that he was quite prepared to read prayers in the normal way but end them by saying "through Jesus Christ YOUR Lord".' The headmaster declined his offer.

Abrahams focused on the Repton Sports Days of 1918 instead. They were to provide a fitting symbol for the way Harold had risen above the abuse he had suffered, without entirely leaving it behind.

Harold remembered, 'I had an interesting experience in the long jump because [for a pit] they used to take just the turf off the top to jump into. And the distance from the take-off board to the end of the pit was 22ft and I landed on the grass! And I sat back and my measured jump from my bottom was 20ft 5½in.'

He still had some jumping to do before he could claim to be in the same league as C.B. Fry, an Old Reptonian who had set a new world record for the long jump in 1893 with a leap of 23ft 6½in. Fry later claimed that Abrahams had 'obliterated' his Repton school record. In fact the meagre dimensions of the pit had prevented Harold from making any kind of school history.

Despite that setback, Abrahams ended the school sports on a high with victories in the 100 and 220 yards. He could go to the 1918 Public Schools Championship at Stamford Bridge feeling confident, and sure enough claimed two big prizes there too. The *Sportsman* newspaper's correspondent, well aware of all four Abrahams brothers, wrote:

> The last of the athletics quartet, Harold, who by winning the 100 yards public schools title at Stamford Bridge on a heavy track in 11sec, and the long jump with 20ft 3¾in, proved himself to be a worthy holder of dual honours. He has excellent nerve, judgement and steadiness for one so young and if some day he secures the titles that his brother S.S. once held, and with an even better performance to his credit, I for one shouldn't be surprised.

But E.A. Montague, portrayed in the film *Chariots of Fire* as Aubrey, the narrator and steeplechaser, remembered souring his rival's moment of glory. Harold's future friend explained:

> It was a weak year, and each of us won two events without much trouble. In the dressing room afterwards Harold and I eyed each other with interest and, in Harold's case, with a touch of bitterness, for I had done his school, Repton, out of the championship cup. In those days only first places counted towards the cup, or second in the case of a tie. His two victories and mine made Repton and Rugby equal, but Rugby had also gained second place in the mile, and Harold had only managed third in the quarter.

Abrahams had an important consolation. He explained, 'At the Public Schools Sports in 1918 Sir John Simon came with my brother to watch me.' Harold was in awe of the politician, who had already been Home Secretary and went on to become Chancellor of the Exchequer, Foreign Secretary and finally Lord Chancellor. Simon asked Harold what he intended to do for a living. Still undecided over the path he should follow, the schoolboy suddenly made up his mind. 'He [Sir John] had been Attorney General and I suppose partly one tries to imitate people. My father was a moneylender and I didn't want to go into that. I wanted to go to Cambridge and I had to select something to read so I chose law. '

Harold's athletic prowess and his father's money virtually assured him a place at Cambridge, whatever he studied. When Sir John Simon invited him to watch some real-life legal cases unfold in London before he went up to start his studies, Harold believed he had chosen well. He would have the chance to follow the same challenging career path as two of his siblings. His brother Solly had joined the Colonial Service to become a Town Magistrate in Zanzibar, and later went on to become Chief Justice of Ceylon. Another of his brothers, Lionel, had become a practising solicitor not far from Cambridge. So it was clear to Harold that a degree in law offered a variety of options further down the road.

But before anyone could look to the future, they had to survive the war. Indeed that Public Schools Championship could have been one of Harold's last races. He explained, 'I went from Repton to a Cadet Battalion in the First War and I won some events and represented the Army for the long jump against the Americans.' Mercifully, he didn't have to fight because the war ended. He knew just how lucky he was; and he reckoned the army was lucky too. 'I'd have been an incredibly bad soldier,' he once said. 'Hated it.'

Abrahams was demobilised at the end of 1918; but just when he thought he had cheated death, it almost claimed him. He contracted Spanish flu, which went on to kill more young Brits than the war itself. Regaining his strength after his brush with death, Harold was able to enjoy life to the full again. By May 1919 he was well enough to relax at Sir John Simon's country mansion, Fritwell, where he played tennis with the politician's teenage daughters, Margaret and Joan. He took photographs of them; and another of Sir John on a beautiful white stallion. These were peaceful, happy times, sweetened by sheer relief. Not only had he beaten his illness, but the carnage across the English Channel was over; the fear of joining 'the young dead' in battle gone forever.

Harold began to train with other sprinters on a track in Paddington, West London. That summer he took part in the first post-war AAA Championships. 'I ran a very long way behind W.A. Hill in the furlong [220 yards],' he recalled. However, in late August 1919, shortly before going up to Cambridge, Harold had the chance to race against his boyhood hero, Willie Applegarth, the sprinter Mussabini had trained to an individual 200 metres bronze medal and relay gold in the 4 × 100 metres at the Stockholm Olympics in 1912. Applegarth had lost none of his pre-war confidence, and acted like a master ready to dish out a harsh lesson to his pupil. Abrahams was still only nineteen, his body hadn't yet taken on the power of an adult. Applegarth was twenty-nine, but his pace was legendary. With times to his name of 10.6sec for the 100 metres and 9.8sec for the 100 yards, Willie's reputation alone was enough to worry most opponents.

It was the veteran against the kid, a straight showdown. Though Applegarth was keen to remind Abrahams of the pecking order, he didn't want to embarrass his protégé too much. So Willie offered Harold what amounted to a head start. Since the race was to be decided over 100 yards, he gave his Herne Hill apprentice two yards.

It had been Harold's habit since childhood – whether racing on the beaches of Brighton and Hunstanton or on the hallowed cinders of Stamford Bridge – to make people regret having given him a head start. This one was probably the least generous he had ever been given; but that wasn't the point. Was Applegarth trying to humour him, to patronise him and psyche him out of the race before it had started?

The starter's pistol signalled the commencement of hostilities. Using all his experience, Applegarth set about trying to eat away Harold's slender advantage, like a greyhound chasing a rabbit. Surprisingly, however, the master failed to make much impression on the pupil he was stalking. The gap stayed at two yards. Then, to everyone's astonishment, Abrahams started to pull away. Three yards, four; then five, as a shocked Applegarth tightened. When Harold hit the tape, he was six yards ahead. Harold Abrahams had come of age.

He still had plenty to learn, though – and not just about sprinting. Harold prepared for university – and life beyond – by taking up Sir John Simon's offer to watch him at work in the law courts of London. He recalled, 'I listened to cases even before I went up to Cambridge; a very famous court case called Isaacs against Hobhouse in which [Sir John Simon] was taking part. I was thrilled to look at the papers and to be there and to feel terribly important, sitting behind one of the leading advocates of the day.'

Sir John asked for something in return – Harold's support in the general election. Abrahams obliged, though his heart wasn't entirely in his work. He confessed, 'I think there again I wasn't genuinely drawn towards politics but I was asked to help him in the elections. I took part in the 1918 election – Walthamstow. There was also a by-election in 1919 in Spen Valley, in which I took part, canvassing, beginning to speak, though my speeches were not very profound.'

Having lost his seat in 1918, Sir John was trying to get himself elected back into Parliament a year later at Spen Valley. Harold played his campaign role as enthusiastically as he could, and though he didn't fall in love with politics, he did rather like the attention. He recalled, 'My capacity or incapacity for "punning" was evident very early. I remember in the 1919 election, somebody saying, "Mr Lloyd George is a great artist," and I remember saying, "Ah yes, but we want the country governed, not the House of Commons decorating," and I was very pleased with myself because people laughed. I got a lot of election experience.'

Sir John Simon still lost to Labour. As for Harold Abrahams, the political ladder wasn't to prove sufficiently inviting. What he wanted above all was a light-blue blazer, the one he had seen his brother Solly wearing during his Cambridge days. A symbol of sporting excellence, a very fine colour, something the 6-year-old Harold had decided would suit him very nicely. In thirteen long years, Harold's opinion hadn't changed. He was determined to get his hands on one.

CHAPTER FOUR

THE CAMBRIDGE FRESHMAN

If Harold Abrahams was trying to follow in the footsteps of his brothers at Cambridge, the plan seems to have encountered a hitch even before he reached the university.

His nephew Tony said, 'Something funny happened because two of his elder brothers had been up at Emmanuel but he didn't go to that college. And there was a rumour that Emmanuel had not accepted him. At any rate, Harold went to Gonville and Caius.'

Caius wasn't as spectacularly beautiful as nearby King's or Trinity; but it was cosy and atmospheric all the same. Harold's task, in time, was to progress through the symbolic Caius gates – the Gate of Humility, the Gate of Wisdom, the Gate of Virtue; and finally the Gate of Honour, the little wooden door through which students still pass to receive their degree at the Senate House. The journey would not be without its trials and tribulations, especially for a Jew like Abrahams.

Lord Puttnam insisted that there was an unsavoury undercurrent at Caius. He maintained:

> One of the reasons I had problems filming at Caius was that anti-Semitism had been rife during Harold's time. It was probably evident in all of Cambridge and Oxford for all I know, but certainly in Caius College. It is a fact. And Caius got very, very neurotic about us filming there, because they thought we would go further in our portrayal of the anti-Semitism. Caius were hypersensitive. I remember a phrase was, 'We don't want all that being dragged up again.'

An article for the college magazine of Harold's era, *The Caian*, reflects the pervading anti-Semitism of the age. Entitled 'Shylock the Jew', it salutes Shakespeare's portrayal of the central character in *The Merchant of Venice*. But the reason Shakespeare has been so brilliant, the college magazine seems to argue, is that he has suspended a natural loathing for the worst characteristics of Jews. The writer, who signs himself only 'MJO', says of Shylock:

> He is not there, so that the British public may indulge themselves in a few minutes' quiet hate and contempt, so that they may become flattered into a comfortable belief in their own virtue and in the degradation of others . . . In the character of Shylock, Shakespeare has accomplished the feat of putting himself in complete sympathy with a personality some aspects of which he must have loathed with an wholesome loathing.

If such views formed the backdrop to Harold's time at Caius, he could at least be grateful that Cambridge students considered themselves too well bred to exercise that prejudice blatantly. He would not be physically attacked or verbally abused for being a Jew, or even prevented from climbing most social ladders at the university. Neither, on the other hand, would he often find an enthusiastic audience when he described his Jewish father's rise to financial power from nothing. Harold remained grateful nevertheless.

As his great friend Norris McWhirter recalled, 'He would sometimes tell of the astonishing story of a father who arrived all but penniless from Eastern Europe without a word of English – but whose burning conviction about higher education propelled his sons through Cambridge.'

So Abrahams didn't want to betray his father; nor did he want to be restricted or disadvantaged by his Jewish roots, for which he felt no great passion. No wonder he suffered such insecurity and angst about his identity and the way others perceived him. He must have sensed that an open-minded approach to Christianity would help him at Cambridge. And when he signalled that open-mindedness to others, it sparked a fierce battle for his soul.

Like other freshmen, Harold became an instant target for recruitment by various religious groups and societies within the university. And he was ready to take part in a post-war Cambridge search for a way to avoid the carnage of recent years. The loss of a bright young generation cried out for a formula to prevent future wars. Religion was 'in'.

The Cambridge Inter-Collegiate Christian Union – or CICCU – was the group most determined to capture the souls of freshmen. One CICCU member at the time wrote: 'It was looked upon as a disgrace to hear a CICCU sermon on Sunday evening, without at least one "fish" in tow! If you could walk in with a whole string of 'captives', it was very difficult to maintain due humility!'

Rivals to the evangelical CICCU were the more moderate Student Christian Movement, which endeavoured to combine in one association those who are seeking and those who find.

Overtures from the likes of CICCU and the SCM sparked something inside Harold. Perhaps it was here in his first year that he took his initial steps towards Christianity. Realising that actions speak louder than words, he did what he could to live a 'Christian' life at Cambridge. Writer A.J. Wallis, later said of Harold, 'He devoted much of his time while at Cambridge to a group of young working men who had not had an undergraduate's advantages in life. He ran in their sports, wrote for their magazine, and helped them to produce a play. This eagerness to help those less fortunate than himself has remained throughout his life.'

He was referring to the Caius Mission in Battersea, South London, where boxing, football and athletic clubs thrived, and Cambridge students visited whenever time allowed. Harold maintained his links with the Mission until long after he left the University. He served on the Caius Mission London Committee at the height of his fame in 1924. And he was still serving on that same committee, for the benefit of those less fortunate than himself, nearly ten years later. The place clearly impressed him from the first time he saw it as a student.

Despite the pervading religious zeal, Harold still found time for more indulgent societies and clubs. Tony Abrahams explained, 'Harold chose the Pitt Club – which was political with a small "p"– because he was clubbable.' He also helped to establish the Gonville and Caius Law Club. The idea was to hold a debate on key legal issues of the day and invite a guest speaker to attend dinners.

Harold polished up his own public speaking too, with one eye on the future. He revealed, 'I took lessons in elocution for the Bar at Cambridge. It's very important to avoid saying "er" every few seconds.' It would help his athletics commentary later in life, too. In fact this was a key decision, and not just for the fluency of his speech. Elocution lessons effectively guaranteed the removal of any Jewish intonation in Harold's delivery, giving him the opportunity to mix with the Cambridge social elite with less fear of prejudice. Outwardly at least, those lessons would give him the vocal authority of an upper-class student from an established British family.

Norris McWhirter later recalled a conversation he had with Abrahams about his smooth exterior. 'I remember saying on a journey with him, "The trouble with you, Harold, is you are so effortlessly superior." He replied, with that ever-youthful twinkle reserved for confidences, "Effortlessness has nothing to do with it." That was the remark of a man of consummate modesty and gentleness.' It may also have been the remark of a man who was remembering his elocution lessons as a Cambridge student.

University opened up a whole new world after the bleak years at Repton. Harold explored it with relish and marvelled at the opportunities he had to meet colourful characters. He said later, 'I enjoyed the freedom, I enjoyed the people I met up there.'

Harold was still interested in politics, even if he had already realised that he didn't want to become a Member of Parliament. He realised that his connections in that sphere were a means to the social acceptance he secretly craved. With his election experience, he joined the Cambridge Liberal Club not long after he went up, and was soon on the committee.

The *Cambridge Daily News* of 30 January 1920, carried a story which read more like an advertisement:

OPEN-MINDED UNDERGRADS

University Liberal Club and the New Order
   A new type of undergraduate has risen in Cambridge: the man with the open mind on political questions, the unprejudiced man, who wants to learn the facts. It is to this kind of Varsity man that the revival of Cambridge University Liberal Club is making a special appeal; the liberal, as well as the Liberal, will be welcomed within its ranks.

Harold met John Maynard Keynes, the famous economist and Liberal. Keynes had been sent to the Versailles Peace conference as the senior Treasury Official in the British delegation. He was so opposed to the crushing reparations imposed on Germany by the treaty that he wrote a book – *Economic Consequences of the Peace* – which warned they could lead to another war in time. If only enough powerful figures had listened to him – particularly in France.

On one occasion Abrahams showed his Liberal colours on the University's most formidable intellectual stage. He recalled:

> I went to the [Cambridge] Union a lot, and I was a member of the Committee of the Liberal Club at Cambridge, but the only time I spoke at the Union was when I was asked to open a debate on capital punishment. And therefore I would say that in the pattern – giving one a specific subject to work out – I would take infinite trouble over days to get to the bottom of it and then produce a quite reasonable speech, (but) I did an awful lot of things at Cambridge and none of them very well.

That may have been true, were it not for his sporting prowess. And he did quickly add, 'I think I did athletics quite well.'

It was only a matter of time in that first year before Harold exploded onto the university track and field scene. After all, as he pointed out, 'I lived athletics in the sense that if I were going along the street and there was an entry to a yard about fifteen feet wide, I would always jump across.'

The recognised venue for such demonstrations of athletic prowess was Fenners. The ground still plays host to the university cricketers, though in Harold's day they had to share it with the athletes. The track is long gone, but during the summer it tries to return like a ghost from the past. When the ground is dry, the old cinder outlines rise to the surface, almost as though athletes long forgotten wish to push their achievements into the present. 'The cinder track comes back, even though we filled it in with soil,' confirmed the head groundsman, John Moden in 2010. 'It's fascinating.'

Even in its heyday, the Fenners track was a peculiarity. Harold later explained:

> For reasons I have never been able satisfactorily to draw, the running tracks at Oxford and Cambridge have since time immemorial (or very nearly) been 586⅔ yards in circumference, that is to say, three laps to the mile. I strongly suspect that my university was responsible, since Fenners was built long before Oxford's Iffley Road, and was three laps, probably to allow full play to the cricketers.

Harold's first challenge at tree-lined Fenners was to make a big impact at the Freshman's Sports, held in his first term. To do that, he would have to blaze down the 100-yard stretch of track which hugged tightest to a row of horse-chestnut trees. With spectators pressing in on the other side of the track, competitors ran the gauntlet in an atmosphere of passionate intensity. Undaunted, Abrahams fed off that pressure to win his first big race in 10.2sec. He also jumped an impressive 21ft 3in and ran 52.8sec for the quarter-mile.

A prestigious clash between Cambridge University and the Amateur Athletic Association was next on the calendar. Harold was one of the stars of the show. Evelyn Montague explained, 'When at the end of his first term he beat W.A. Hill, the reigning AAA Champion, in 10.2sec over 100 yards, there could no longer be any doubt that a future champion had arrived.'

One newspaper talked of 'the promise of future excellence given in the revived encounter between AAA and CUAC at Fenners, where H.M. Abrahams and [another rising talent, the powerfully built Guy] Butler were among the heroes of the meeting.'

The *News of the World* clearly thought that Cambridge University's coach, Alec Nelson, was even better than the famous Sam Mussabini. Nelson, the newspaper's correspondent suggested, was just the man to take Harold to Olympic standard, along with Butler. On January 4, 1920, the newspaper's correspondent argued:

Nelson is, in my opinion, the greatest athletic coach we have in England, and the knowledge he will be able to impart to G.M. Butler, English quarter-mile champion, and H.M. Abrahams, CUAC sprinter and long jumper, should put them among the finalists in the 400 and 100 metres races at the Olympic Games this year. The added sprinting ability that Abrahams will gain at Nelson's hands will develop his long-jumping prowess.

In fact Harold wasn't very impressed with Nelson's sprint coaching. 'Thanks to my brothers, I knew far more about it than he did. He was a good chap for jollying you along.' Whatever Nelson's abilities, the conceited Abrahams didn't think he could be taught much about sprinting by anyone. He felt he already knew it all; and later he freely admitted that as a young man he could hardly have been cockier. 'I would say that an enlarged head is much more common in youth than an enlarged heart,' he said of his early Cambridge days. Harold certainly wasn't as modest about his stunning triumphs and rave reviews as convention demanded at the time. But then what was the point in pretending that he wasn't good when he clearly was? The problem lay in the fact that his honesty gave jealous rivals and the anti-Semitic element ammunition with which to snipe at him.

Even if he had been the modest type, Harold's talent alone would probably have antagonised those around him. As Harold's future friend Norris McWhirter put it in the Dictionary of National Biography (DNB): ' If the road to popularity at university lies in never inculcating a sense of inferiority into one's contemporaries, Abrahams stood little chance of being popular.'

It wasn't just his enviable talent or big mouth that antagonised others, but the way he took his sport so very seriously. Bevil Rudd, a brilliant South African all-rounder who was at Oxford before and after the First World War, described the acceptable training ethic of the day: 'I belonged primarily to the pre-war era, when training was essentially casual, and competition very occasional. We conformed to a traditional training schedule which, while it kept us fit, in no way tested our individual abilities or polished our style. A faulty style was regarded as a fascinating idiosyncrasy, and misplaced energy as a sign of guts.'

It would be a while before Harold Abrahams ironed out his own style with the help of the brilliant Sam Mussabini. But even during his first year at Cambridge, he must have seemed rather too intense in his sporting ambitions to fit in with the prevailing ethos of the day. In November, for example, Abrahams had written, 'A man or boy should never be out of training. "The sports are over for now" seems to be a most repulsive attitude . . . Take a cold bath every morning (winter and summer) . . . Do some exercises before retiring to bed at night for about ten minutes – press-ups, etc. . . . Lead a clean life; always be in training.' But to some this 24/7 commitment to sporting excellence was cheating, pure and simple.

Sport was still amateur, sport was for fun. Harold and his new athletic intensity were on collision course with Rudd and his old-style courage. As Abrahams breezed through the Cambridge Inter-Collegiate Championship, he didn't realise how soon Rudd would be waiting for him. Harold seemed to be sweeping all before him. His college magazine, The Caian, revealed delightedly during that first year how 'In the Inter-Collegiate Championship, Caius defeated Jesus in the semi-final by 60 points to 40.'

Leap of faith: Long-jumping at Fenners, Cambridge University. Sandwiched between trees on one side and spectators on the other, Harold ran the gauntlet and hoped the take-off board would hold firm before launching into mid-air.

Despite having suffered a bout of flu earlier in February, Harold still managed to win five events – including the high jump. He repeated the feat against Emmanuel, his brothers' old college, in the final. Abrahams won the 100 yards in 10.2sec and the 120 yards hurdles in 18sec, took the quarter-mile in 53sec, cleared 5ft 5in to claim the high jump, and completed his one-man show by leaping 21ft 11½in in the long jump. The college magazine added, 'In the final Caius defeated Emmanuel with almost equal ease. The College thus secured the Rouse Ball Challenge Cup for the first time.'

The impact Harold had made in February was not restricted to Cambridge alone. Evelyn Montague remembered, 'I met [Harold] for the second time early in 1920; I was then at Oxford, and his college team, Caius, came over to run against mine.' The contest, hosted at Iffley Road by Oxford's Magdalene College on February 5, 1920, was an historic occasion. It was the first meeting between athletes of Oxford and Cambridge since the end of the First World War. The track was reported to be 'very heavy, thanks to overnight frost and bright sunshine'. That didn't bother Harold, who was described in one write-up as 'a tower of strength'.

Montague's wry account conveyed a blend of shock and admiration. He wrote, 'Caius had a curious team; it seemed to consist almost entirely of Abrahams and Henry Stallard. Harold won most of the events, and Henry won the rest.' Caius actually won 7–3, though Montague emphasised, 'Harold at that time was potentially a great all-round athlete, and I have always thought what a wonderful decathlon man he would have made. Without any special knowledge whatever he could high-jump 5ft 6in, put the weight 34ft and run 120 yards hurdles in 18sec.'

Harold had the potential to become the Daley Thompson of his era. But the decathlon was still evolving; and even though it had featured at the 1912 Olympics, its complicated scoring system made it less than appealing. 'The decathlon is often called the most gruelling human activity,' one wit claimed during Harold's era. 'It isn't. The most gruelling is compiling the table used for scoring the decathlon.' Despite his versatility, Harold was only ever truly passionate about two disciplines in athletics – sprinting and long-jumping. And he knew they would provide the ticket to his 'Blue', if only he could impress at Cambridge University Sports in March 1920.

Under blue skies, surrounded by as many fanatical spectators as Fenners could take, Abrahams went about his task like a man on a mission. A report explained:

> The afternoon turned out beautifully fine, but the very strong, gusty wind which blew against the sprinters and hurdlers disposed of any possibilities of records being broken . . . Chief credit must go to H.M. Abrahams, the Repton freshman, who had the distinction of being the only man to win two evnts. He just beat G.M. Butler in the hundred in 10.2sec, and then carried off the long-jump with a wonderful leap of 22ft . . . The jumpers were at a decided disadvantage owing to the encroachment of the crowd.

Harold didn't care, he just loved the attention. He was a star; and more important he had guaranteed himself the Light Blue jacket he had coveted since he had been just six years old. Mighty fine he looked in it, too.

CHAPTER FIVE

FROM QUEEN'S
TO ANTWERP

The Queen's Club in West Kensington, London, beckoned for the big Varsity showdown against Oxford. The athletics rivalry between the universities dated back to 1864. Harold's rivalry with his brothers didn't go back quite that far, yet journalists understood its influence.

The *Sunday Times* wrote, 'In spite of the coaching H.M. Abrahams had received at the hands of his brothers, I don't think he will do 10sec [for 100 yards] this year; but he is a racer and Queen's will probably not ruffle him. He must borrow the speed of his brother's famous shutter camera to do "evens".' As for the long jump, it wasn't so much Adolphe's love of photography as Solly's athletic pedigree that might provide the inspiration. 'With the record of his brother S.S. to act as a beacon, he should have his tail up and do 22ft 4in.'

The race venue – now famous for tennis – wasn't for the faint-hearted. It drew so many fans from Oxford and Cambridge that they could have filled the little stand closest to the newly constructed cinder track twice over. A report explained, 'The revival, after the suspension during the war, of the inter-Varsity sports drew a large and enthusiastic assembly of spectators. Indeed, at 1 o'clock, over an hour before the first contest, the ground was well filled.'

Harold's race was the very first, scheduled for 2.15 p.m. The crowd pressed so close to the athletes that the runners must have heard almost every whisper, and smelt the cigarette smoke as they prepared for their big moment. Weather conditions were far from ideal. One report mentioned an 'adverse wind' for the '100 yarders'. Another claimed the wind was 'certainly not helping' the runners. Harold could deal with the wind. But the atmosphere, both intimidating and exhilarating, was new. The clamour of an all-Cambridge crowd was one thing. The claustrophobic effect of this Varsity mix at the start of the biggest race of Harold's career was quite another. And to make matters worse, Abrahams had drawn the lane closest to the stand.

Later he claimed, 'I know of no other greater ordeal than the sensation – fear and joyful anticipation mixed – as one goes to the start of a race at Queen's Club. Somehow, the fact that one is representing a great University with centuries of traditions is both terrible and wonderful.'

Harold would carry the hopes of the Cambridge fans, just as he drew the hostility of Oxford's. In a way this was the future racing the past. His chief rival was going to be Bevil Rudd, the veteran who favoured the amateur ethos of the pre-war era. Born in Cornwall but educated mainly in South Africa, Rudd had been a war hero. He returned to Oxford with a Military Cross, and knew better than most why sport should never be regarded as a matter of life and death. That didn't mean he wasn't keen to beat Abrahams, the young upstart from the rival university. What greater sporting pleasure could there be than to put in their place someone who was arrogant and rumoured to train too hard?

Sure enough, Harold felt untouchable. He thought Rudd had spread himself too thin, and simply wouldn't be in his league any more. He recalled:

My Oxford opponents were Bevil Rudd and R. Stapledon. Bevil, who had already beaten 51sec for the 440 yards and 1 minute 59.0sec for 880 yards before he was nineteen years old, and incidentally done 10.4sec for 100 yards at the age of seventeen, had represented Oxford against Cambridge in 1914. Four years' active service in the war had not diminished his enthusiasm for athletics and he was selected to compete against Cambridge in 1920 in no fewer than four events. I remember we at Cambridge thought this was rather a sign of Oxford's weakness.

Being very young, with absolutely no doubt how good I was (the doubts came with more maturity), I felt supremely confident of victory. Rudd had been right through the war, and though he had been credited with fast times at Oxford, I thought of him more as a quarter-miler taking part in the sprint because there was nobody better.

The start, of course, was everything. It had to be right. For Abrahams, it wasn't. The little Queen's Club stand was packed to the rafters as the pistol cracked and Rudd, Oxford's President, tore through the air like a bullet. The shorter man's, compact arms were already pumping furiously as Harold's arms still flailed loosely. In this instant the crowd went wild and students of Oxford were strident.

Harold recalled, 'I received a rude shock. I got a good start, but Bevil had a better one. Bevil gave me the fright of my sweet young life . . . After thirty yards he was perhaps half a yard ahead. Time seemed to stand still.' Harold explained, 'Ten seconds is not after all very long, but it can seem an eternity on occasions, and this was one of such. Thirty yards from the tape I was still perhaps six inches to the bad.'

An onlooker, surely a Cantabrigian, confessed, 'H.M. Abrahams pleased me greatly in the manner he wore Rudd down when the latter looked all over a winner.' If the contest had been down to style alone, Harold would have continued to struggle. *The Times* said of Harold, 'He is certainly not a graceful runner, with so very marked and curious a roll. But he runs low, with a fine stride, and his body well forward, and any amount of dash and resolution.'

As they neared the tape, it seems that Rudd thought he had the edge in all departments. He raised his arms, perhaps in triumph; but in that moment the joy turned to anguish as he realised that Abrahams, pushing out his torso, may have broken the tape first. Now it was the turn of the Cambridge fans to go wild.

Harold said, 'He led me for 80 yards of the 100, and but somehow I just managed to thrust myself ahead in the last stride or two to win by a very, very short six inches.' Given the conditions, the time was as extraordinary as the sheer drama of it all. One report claimed, '[Abrahams] won a clear, though very narrow, victory. [His] hundred in 10sec dead, with the wind certainly not helping him, was a fine achievement.'

When Abrahams looked back on his life, he saw those ten seconds at Queen's as make-or-break moments in his climb towards the top. The two protagonists knew straight away that their tussle had been something special. Whatever their preconceptions, they had won each other's lasting respect. Harold explained, 'My exciting race with Bevil was the beginning of a friendship which lasted until he died. Had I lost that race, my whole athletic career might have been different. And it is no exaggeration to say that a victory in an inter-Varsity contest means more to its proud possessor than a world's championship.'

Adrenalin and gritty determination had seen Harold through. But what would the effort cost him when it came to the long jump? One reporter commented later, 'It appeared to me that Abrahams put rather too much into his last few strides on the cinders, and that this might account for the lack of what I may perhaps term elasticity in his leaping.' And another reflected, 'H.M. Abrahams is not an elegant jumper, but 22ft 7in is well over the average jump.'

It was also the winning jump, and three inches further than the *Sunday Times* had predicted. Harold had seen off Oxford in the long jump too. Evelyn Montague, running for the 'enemy' in his first Varsity, later conceded, 'Harold jumped straight into the limelight.' He had more than earned his 'Blue' in both the 100 and long jump.

Bevil Rudd at least saw to it that Abrahams didn't finish on the winning side. Harold explained, 'He ran a dead-heat with Guy Butler, (AAA Champion the year before) in the 440 yards in 49.6sec, [then] won the last event of the afternoon, the half-mile. Oxford won by 5½ events to 4½ and their success was very largely due to that one great athlete.'

Abrahams was still the toast of Cambridge, though. And ordinarily, his heroics would have earned him an invitation to join one of the university's most prestigious organisations – the Hawks Club. After his Varsity triumph, Hawks members would doubtless have debated his suitability, if not for immediate nomination then for the following academic year, as was the norm. You could only join if you were a sports-man who had won a 'Blue' by representing Cambridge against Oxford. On the face of it, therefore, Abrahams fitted the bill. But a Blue alone didn't win you membership to the Hawks; you had to be nominated and accepted by the committee, you had to be socially acceptable, clubbable – even popular. And even by his admission, Harold wasn't popular.

Later he seemed to want to sweep what happened under the carpet. He said, 'I didn't belong to the Hawks Club, I belonged to another club called the Pitt Club, where the food was better.' Yet in the Dictionary of National Biography, Norris McWhirter was quite adamant about what had really happened. 'His election to the Hawks Club was opposed due to a contri-bution to *The Times*, which the committee regarded as immodest.'

Harold still didn't see any merit in false modesty. In fact he was positively full of himself. 'That's one of the problems of being prominent when one is too young in a limited sphere like athletics,' he admitted later. 'You get very easily a swelled head. Some people probably think I never recovered from it.' But he was in an awkward position, because he was one of the few athletes – perhaps the only one – who sometimes wrote about races in which he himself had taken part. Harold explained, 'I'd started journalism in 1920. I wrote for a journal called *All Sports* and for the *Evening News* in those days.'

So when did he write the offending article for *The Times*? He couldn't have penned that newspaper's description of his victory at the Queen's Club, because the article criticised his style. So the source of the controversy must have been something as innocuous as a brief description of his University Sports win a few weeks earlier, which had appeared without a by-line. The contests weren't important enough to warrant the presence of a staff reporter from *The Times*. So Abrahams appears to have volunteered to further his fledgling journalistic career by covering the occasion himself.

Under the headline: 'SPORTS AT CAMBRIDGE – SOME PROMISING PERFORMANCES' it read: 'H.M. Abrahams did well to win the Hundred Yards race in 10.2sec against this wind, and his winning leap in the Long Jump was a good effort . . . G.M. Butler did not extend himself fully in the heat of the Quarter-Mile Race and Abrahams, having won two events, ran only a little more than half way before retiring.'

The degree of 'immodesty' shown here was negligible. But Abrahams had committed a cardinal sin: he had dared to compliment himself in writing. It didn't seem to matter that he had gone on to praise R.S. Woods, who was 'in fine form in Putting the Weight', E.S. Burns, who 'did well' in the High Jump and H.B. Stallard, who 'won the Mile easily'. Three mentions of Abrahams in as many paragraphs amounted to a shameful piece of self-publicity. Why bother to refer to himself in the Quarter-Mile, for example, when he hadn't even finished the race? It simply wasn't on; and something had to be done.

There are no surviving records of any official Hawks decision to exclude Abrahams. Blackballed students were sometimes told discreetly that they needn't bother taking their application any further. That spared them further embarrassment. It is ironic, however, that even in the early twenty-first century, the Hawks Club was still trying to lay claim to Abrahams as one of its most distinguished members. In 2010, for example, Harold's name was being used on the Hawks Club website to emphasise its historical pedigree. The reality was that he had been cold-shouldered quite contemptuously.

Even if there was no anti-Semitic aspect to Harold's rejection, he might still have perceived there to have been one. He once acknowledged that perceived prejudice soon became magnified in his head:

> I think that being Jewish has played a very big part . . . There wasn't a lot of anti-Semitism when I was young and of course one imagines that a lot of things you don't get are not because you don't deserve to get them but because you are Jewish. You can distort it quite easily. And I was determined I was going to show myself superior in something where there could be no argument about it. And I WAS good at athletics. And this was a method of self-expression.

Later Harold confessed to journalist Neil Allen, 'There was some anti-Semitism at university, in my early days as a Cambridge athlete, but I think I had a bit of a chip on my shoulder about it.' Colin Welland, who wrote the film *Chariots of Fire*, claimed that 'Harold had a chip on his shoulder the size of a synagogue'. Less fortunate people might wonder what all the fuss was about. Even Harold's son Alan pointed out, 'it was a little strange that my father complained of discrimination because he went to Cambridge University and was not entirely downtrodden. He didn't exactly lead a tough life.' But once you are in any environment, even at a lofty and privileged level of English society, you want to be accepted by your peers and welcomed into every corner of that environment. So rejection by the Hawks must have hurt Abrahams all the same.

Just as well another club was about to be formed, one which would give Harold a lasting platform, first as a competitor and later as President. The Achilles Club combined the athletics forces of Oxford and Cambridge, and led to a renewal of contests against combined American colleges.

For the moment, however, Abrahams was finding the domestic athletics scene challenging enough. His early-season performances in Olympic year were indifferent – and he didn't seem to care. At various events he was accused by newspaper critics of being 'quite unable to keep his stride', of 'dawdling over the first paces' in both 100 and 220 yards races, of being a 'slovenly starter', and of 'fiddling about to strike the take-off board' in the long jump.

Another critic claimed on July 2, 1920, 'Abrahams is not yet fully matured, and moreover, he has a lot to learn about sprinting.' There wasn't much time to learn, even if he thought he needed to, because the

AAA Championships at Stamford Bridge were upon him. Harold explained, 'The AAA championships in 1920 were in the nature of trials for the Olympic Games.' Harold won his 100 yards heat but could only come third in round two. Almost as an excuse, Harold pointed to the small margin between success and failure. 'In my opinion the result was won by one foot and I certainly was less (if possible) than inches behind Harry Edward.'

It was a poor excuse, because the 100 would always be about small margins, and Abrahams knew that already. The truth was, he had gone down to London as a rising star and the pressure had proved too much. Later he admitted, 'I am convinced that a phenomenal success may hang like a millstone round a young man's neck. Modern publicity is responsible for a tremendous amount of failure on the athletic track. Could it be that this results in the athlete in question being over-anxious and failing to do himself justice?'

Harold had been full of himself at Cambridge; now he had been cut down to size in the wider world. It was Edward, a chartered secretary born in British Guiana, who stormed to victory in the 100-yard final that year in 10sec. He pulled off a double by taking the 220 yards in 21.6sec. And Abrahams must have noticed, somewhat enviously, that Edward was trained by Sam Mussabini, who had inspired Harold's hero, Willie Applegarth.

An admiring Abrahams said of Edward later, 'I think his 1920 wins were the best. He was a really lovely performer, with a perfectly controlled arm action working in faultless harmony with his legs.' Perhaps out of frustration, Abrahams experimented aimlessly in that 1920 AAA Championship. He tried the triple jump and finished fourth. In the long jump, he was ninth and last.

The England selectors knew that Abrahams was a work in progress. Understandably, they decided to make him no more than a reserve in the 100 yards for an international against Ireland and Scotland on July 10. But they gave Harold a chance to shine in other disciplines. The letter, dated July 3, explained:

AMATEUR ATHLETIC ASSOCIATION

Dear Sir,
    INTERNATIONAL AMATEUR ATHLETIC CONTEST
    I have the pleasure to inform you that you have been selected to

represent England in the Long Jump, 1st string, 220 yards, second string and 100 yards, reserve at Crewe on Saturday.

Harold knew that the selectors would be meeting again shortly to choose the GB team for the Olympic Games. Time was running out. He had to take his chance in England colours. He did.

One report described the rain-swept international at Crewe like this:

England won every race save the mile. The Furlong was a triumph for H.M. Abrahams, who showed again that this is his distance. The time, 21⅗ seconds, was splendid, seeing that for ten yards at the first, after starting out of a little pond, they had to run through very deep water. If the Cantab will now train over 200 metres and leave every other distance alone, he could perform with credit at Antwerp.

But would the selectors agree? They had one last chance to see Abrahams perform – for Polytechnic Harriers against The Rest at Stamford Bridge on Saturday, July 17. Again he was second to Edward in the 100 yards; but he won the long jump with an excellent jump of 22ft 1½in. And Abrahams impressed in the relays, teaming up with Edward and two others to beat The Rest in the 440. 'There was a remarkable finish in the Mile Relay race between Polytechnic Harriers and The Rest,' one reporter wrote, 'when Abrahams won a sensational victory for the promoting club by inches only in excellent time.'

Three days later, on July 20, 1920, Abrahams received the following letter from the Amateur Athletic Association:

Dear Sir,
RE OLYMPIC GAMES AT ANTWERP

I have the pleasure to advise you that at a meeting of the Special Olympic Committee of this Association you have been selected to represent Great Britain in the 100 and 200 metres and 400 metres [4 × 100m] relay at Antwerp at the VIIth Olympiad from the 15th to the 23rd of August next. I need hardly point out to you the desirability of continuing to train, so as to be thoroughly fit in order that Great Britain may be represented with credit.

I shall be glad to hear immediately whether you will be able to leave for Antwerp about the 9th, 10th or 11th of August, or if you

anticipate any difficulty in getting away from business, whether a
letter from this Association or any other source would be of assistance
to you.

For Harold, this letter was more than enough. He had done it; he had
achieved every athlete's dream, to represent his country at the Olympic
Games. He recalled, 'It was a Wednesday morning in July, 1920, when I
received a letter from the Amateur Athletic Association telling me that
I had been selected to represent my country at the Olympic Games at
Antwerp the following month. I can still remember the thrill.'

Even more than the honour of representing his country, Harold
thought about what it meant for lifelong rivalry with his brothers.

For my interest in Olympic matters went back to my early childhood.
My brother, S.S. Abrahams, had travelled to an Olympic celebration
in Athens in 1906, and competed for Great Britain at the Stockholm
Games in 1912. I knew, or thought I knew, all there was to know
about Olympic performances, and here I was going not only to see
the world's best athletes in action, but to compete against some of
them. I was a sufficient realist to appreciate that I had no earthly
chance of any success. I was a very, very long way behind the world
standard in these events.

Others had invested more faith in Harold's determination to rise to the
occasion and make an impact on the biggest stage of all. On August 8,
1920, the respected writer and athletics administrator F.A.M. Webster
wrote, 'Many critics, I know, have cried down the Olympic chances of
H.M. Abrahams: indeed, he himself told me just before the English
Championships that I was the only critic who seemed to retain any faith
in him. The reason I have faith is that he is essentially a fighter who
refuses to be beaten and because he has tradition behind him.'

Webster was referring to the achievements of Harold's brothers, and
also revisited the highlights of Harold's career before concluding:

The opening up of the Olympic Games is now less than a fortnight
away, and Abrahams has proved conclusively that he is reaching the
top of his form. At Histon last week he won the 100 yards in 9⅘ sec,
which equals the British record and is as fast a time as has been
shown by any sprinter who will be present at Antwerp, where it will

not surprise me to see the brilliant young Cantab credit us with a win in the 100 metres, for it must be remembered that the 9⅗ seconds [for the 100 yards] recorded by C.W. Paddock, USA, the favourite for the race, was returned on the Pacific Coast, where the atmospheric conditions make for fast times.

It was an optimistic assessment. Harold wasn't yet powerful enough to challenge the dominance enjoyed by the Americans. Photographs of Abrahams in Antwerp reveal arms devoid of muscle. His long legs are already built for speed; but the rest of him is unimpressive. Abrahams is still a boy, waiting to gain the strength of a man, knowing deep down that a momentous occasion has come too early. Still, as Abrahams pointed out, 'I had been selected to represent Great Britain, and that was all that mattered for the moment.'

The Antwerp Olympics were brave and groundbreaking. Baron De Coubertin, founder of the modern Olympic movement, saw these Games as a vehicle for a new world peace. So to be in Antwerp for that opening ceremony was to witness sporting history in the making. And it would have been difficult not to find inspiration from that gathering. Abrahams wrote:

> Saturday, August 14, 1920! The scene is the Olympic Stadium at Antwerp, all set for the opening ceremony. What an experience. The march past of athletes grouped according to their countries; the opening of the Games by King Albert of the Belgians; the fanfare of trumpets and the booming of cannon as hundreds of pigeons with the national colours of the nations round their necks were released!
>
> The appearance, for the first time in history, of the Olympic flag, five coloured circles entwined, linking the five continents of the world together in friendly rivalry. And finally, the Olympic oath: 'We swear that we are taking part in the Olympic Games as loyal competitors, observing the rules governing the Games, and anxious to show a spirit of chivalry, for the honour of our countries and for the glory of sport'.

Next day the competitions began. Harold started promisingly in Antwerp. He won the tenth heat of the 100 metres from Alexandre Penton, Canada, and Giorgio Croci, of Italy, in 11sec. 'That's about 10.2sec for 100 yards,' pointed out Abrahams somewhat guiltily. He failed by inches to reach the semi-final, so he was a spectator for that race and the final itself. For the most part, Harold masked the pain of mediocrity with customary humour. 'My own performances were not at all good. I had a very good back view of Charley Paddock in the second round of the 100 metres – in fact I needed a very powerful pair of field glasses to see him at all.'

Perhaps it was a sense of inferiority in such formidable company that also led Harold to take a verbal swipe at the way Paddock finished with such an extravagant flourish. He said, 'Paddock did a ridiculous jump at the finish, you've probably seen a picture of it at the 1920 Olympics. But you can't jump faster than you can run. He slowed up to make the jump. He had a terrible style. Our own champion, Harry Edward, one of the most perfect sprinters I have ever seen, was the only Britisher in the final of the 100 metres '

Paddock – 'The California Flash' – was aware of this sort of criticism and was quite happy to hear his jump described as 'the freak finish of a freak performer'. But he added, 'The "jump finish" has won so many more races than it has lost for me. You have to run high, "bounding" along, before the exaggerated final stride of 10–14 feet. It requires patience to learn it and courage to use it.'

Only 5ft 8in tall, Paddock's knee action was so high that he sometimes struck his own chin. As far as Abrahams was concerned, Edward's style was by far the most graceful, and it should have paid dividends in that final.

> He had beaten three of the Americans in the preliminary rounds and we had high hopes of a British victory. The start was appalling. Paddock had his hands over the starting line, and one of the marksmen called attention to this irregularity. Instead of the starter ordering all the competitors to stand up and thus start all the preliminaries again, he fired his pistol, and one American, Murchison, was left literally with one knee on the ground. Edward was badly into his running and never in the race. He finished third. Paddock was known as 'the world's fastest human' and won the final, which was a most unsatisfactory race.

At least Edward had a medal to show for his efforts. A 5ft 7in, cigar-smoking American called Jackson Scholz was also estimated at 10.9sec – but was relegated to fourth. At twenty-three, Scholz would have time to come again at the next Olympics. But he might have to go easy on those cigars.

Paddock, whose efforts were fuelled by a raw egg and a glass of sherry, ran 10.8 for his gold. No one could doubt his ability, but Harold disliked his gamesmanship and showmanship in equal measure. Abrahams would remember the unjust conclusion to the 1920 Olympic Games 100 metres four years later, when some of the same protagonists would be gathered in Paris. Back in 1920, there wasn't much he could do to right any wrongs. 'Well short of 20 feet,' as he only managed 6.05 metres in the long jump, he described it, which meant he failed to reach the final. 'My long-jumping was terrible.'

His Olympics didn't get much better. Having failed by inches to reach the semi-final in the 100 metres, he couldn't avoid the same fate in the 200 metres. He won his heat but then allowed himself to be edged out in the next round. 'I was tenth rate really. I got through a round of the 100 and 200 and that was it.'

Harry Edward reached the final of the 200 metres and finished third again. 'But by this time,' Abrahams explained, 'An old injury in his thigh had asserted itself; he ran with his muscles strapped up with plaster and never did himself anything like justice.'

Edward's bronze medals for Great Britain were still a magnificent achievement, and the 25-year-old's success further reinforced Sam Mussabini's reputation. Thanks to Old Sam, Edward had at least made an impact. He had come home with something to show for his hard work, whereas Harold looked back on those races with a frustrated feeling that he had failed to do himself justice. If only Harold had been able to develop what he had started with Old Sam down at Herne Hill, it might have been him.

All Harold could do was try to admire the sporting excellence all around him. Abrahams also recalled 'seeing an American [Frank Foss] clear what appeared to be an astonishing height of 13ft 5⅛in in the pole vault and the great Suzanne Lenglen winning the women's tennis singles and mixed doubles.' Most memorable was the great Finn, Paavo Nurmi, who reversed his 5,000 metres defeat at the hands of the Frenchman, Joseph Guillemot, by taking the 10,000 emphatically from the same rival.

But Antwerp had fallen flat for Abrahams. He always claimed, 'I represented Great Britain in four events at the 1920 Olympics, and in none with any distinction whatsoever.' This was typical Abrahams, his own harshest critic. If he felt he deserved it, he was more than willing to put himself down; just as he was quick to praise himself if he thought had done well. In this case his self-criticism was true of his first three Olympic disciplines, but not the fourth. He had a chance to redeem himself in the 4 × 100 metres relay and to an extent he took it. The trouble was, his three colleagues apparently failed to hit similar heights. One account suggested that 'in the 400 metres relay team Abrahams was the only man to run to form – and he ran exceedingly well.' They still missed out on a medal. 'We got fourth in the relay,' Harold recalled sadly. And if you couldn't win a medal at the Antwerp Olympics, Abrahams reckoned you would probably never win one. He explained, 'The Americans and Finns practically dominated those Games. The standard was low; it was lower than it was before the war.'

The poor state of the track had slowed everyone down; yet medals had been there for the taking if you were fully focused and expertly trained. Harold recalled, 'The Empire gained successes in the 400 [Bevil Rudd], 800 and 1500 metres and the 110 metres hurdles. Albert Hill gained a wonderful "double event" in the 800 and 1500 metres – the times were not fast judging by modern standards . Hill, like Edward, was trained by Sam Mussabini. What a great little man "Sam" was.'

Great Britain also won the 3000 metres steeplechase through Percy Hodge, and the 4 × 400 metres relay. Harold's Cambridge friend and rival, Guy Butler, anchored that final effort and therefore returned to university with a gold medal to his name. Abrahams returned with little more than envy and respect for those who had taken their big chance better.

Hill's achievement was all the more remarkable because, as Abrahams remembered:

> The semi final and finals of the 800 metres were held on the same afternoon and within half an hour of one another. This was an incredibly ignorant piece of organisation, but the whole organisation at Antwerp was rather primitive; races were actually run at half past nine in the morning, which meant that competitors either had to get up about six in order to have breakfast a sufficiently long time before the race to permit it to digest or go without breakfast altogether. In 1920, athletics were still suffering a little from the 1914–18 war.

Harold played down his first Olympic adventure later in life. 'As far as I was concerned in 1920, I attached far more importance to getting my

"Blue" at Cambridge, than being chosen to represent Great Britain at the Olympics. It was just a trip to Belgium and an athletic meeting – that was all.'

He wouldn't have said that if he had won a medal; but he had at least experienced the pressures of Olympic participation. And though he regarded himself as something of a failure at the time, he acknowledged later, 'I had an experience which served me well later on. I benefited enormously from that experience.'

CHAPTER SIX

CHRISTINA

They say love is blind; and Harold couldn't say he wasn't shown what blindness felt like, just before love struck.

Abrahams looked back later on what he called 'a bitter-sweet memory' down on the south coast later that summer. He was invited to compete against some soldiers who had been blinded in the First World War and were now living at a specialist centre called St Dunstan's, just outside Brighton. The athletics track there had been adapted to cater for their disability. Down the side of each lane ran a wire with a handkerchief attached at arm level, which competitors could hold on to in order to help them run straight. As he prepared to race the best blind sprinter, Abrahams was told to hold on to his handkerchief to even the contest up a little. But since he could still see and his opponent couldn't, he won an easy victory. 'My gallant opponent then asked if I would run against him on what he described as "level terms". With great trepidation I agreed, and was completely blindfolded. I knew that if I kept the handkerchief quite taut, all would be well, but when the pistol was fired I ended up about ten yards from the start, having run into the wire and badly cut my arm.'

Perhaps the years had softened the true extent of Harold's humiliation. A photograph shows him lasting no more than five yards as his blind rival prepares to pass, still perfectly balanced at the centre of his lane. It was the most emphatic defeat Harold had suffered to date. 'I had not realised how great a part sight plays in one's whole balance. If any reader likes to try running with his eyes shut in a large gymnasium, with nothing at all in his way, he will soon realise that it is almost impossible. How I admire these plucky blind men.'

Something else was beginning to affect his balance. He reflected later, 'Unfortunately, I did exceptionally well in my first year at the University, and while I do not think it did me any physical harm, it certainly upset my equilibrium for a year or two.' It had been hard to stay poised and focused on improvement when his already-inflated ego had been swelled to bursting point by the excessive adulation his sporting talent had received at Cambridge.

Beyond that Cambridge bubble, however, it hadn't been the best of summers for Harold. And running blinded into a wire was a fair indicator of how close his career was to coming off the rails completely. In contrast Jackson Scholz, the 'New York Thunderbolt' who had just missed out on a medal in Antwerp, stormed to victory in Stockholm that September by clocking 10.6 to tie the world record. Now he was in the big league with Paddock and Abrahams was still nowhere.

If Harold wanted to restore his confidence, he could always count on the familiar surroundings of Cambridge University, where he started the new academic year as Honorary Secretary of the Athletic Club. It was a prestigious position, given to Abrahams because he was expected to live and breathe athletics just like before. He didn't.

Harold's world turned upside down when he met Christina McLeod Innes early in his first term back at Cambridge. Christina was eighteen years old, petite and pretty, with blue-grey eyes and red-brown hair. 'Her brothers always called it "rusty", so that she shouldn't get conceited,' said Christina's daughter, Sue Smithson, many decades later. 'Typical older brothers.'

By the time Harold met Christina at Cambridge, her brothers were dead. From her expression in photographs of the period, you can almost feel her sadness. As Sue put it later, 'There was an abiding sorrow to her.' There was a quiet determination and strength about her too; the kind sometimes born of intense personal suffering. Life had hurt her horribly; and yet she was still only eighteen, and not ready to give up on that life so young. Harold saw all this in Christina, and learned of her connection to Donald, his tragic Repton school chum. He became captivated.

From Christina, Harold could hear what had happened to the young man who had written so movingly of his elder brother's death not long before he met his own. Donald had joined the Black Watch in the summer of 1918, was wounded in September and died in a French hospital in October, barely a month before hostilities ceased. To have lost one brother would have been devastating for Christina. To lose a second, the one to whom she was closest, must have been as much as she could bear.

Sue Smithson explained:

> Donald, the brother my mother was particularly fond of, was wounded in the leg, and got gangrene. The leg had to come off. This was in hospital at Amiens. And my grandmother, Margaret Innes, went over to nurse him until he died in that hospital aged just nineteen. It is just so awful that I can't bear to think about it even now. So you can imagine that my mother, possibly more serious than the average young woman, was so traumatised because she was so close to Donald.

Though Christina was desolate, she was determined to receive the education she thought she deserved – the one her brothers had been denied. There were only two women's colleges at Cambridge at that time – Girton and Newnham. Christina was at Girton where she was studying modern languages. The women's colleges were not considered part of the university fabric in quite the same way the male colleges were; women were not awarded degrees as such. Yet the Girton and Newnham students were still connected to the university; and they were allowed to join some of the university clubs.

Christina did so, and her younger daughter, Peregrine Morley, said later, 'I believe she met Harold through the Student Christian Movement at the University. I remember my mother explaining that Harold was a member of the SCM and was therefore not a practising Jew.' His adopted daughter, Sue Pottle, believed that Harold's decision to embrace Christianity was influenced by his need for acceptance beyond the Jewish community. She said, 'He always wanted to fit in. I don't think he was incompatible with being Jewish, more incompatible with the restrictions it put on him. He used to tell his brothers, "What's the point in not eating bacon or pork?" He ate them. I never remember him going to a synagogue, and we never celebrated Jewish festivals. He was up on Jewish things but not really immersed in them.'

At Cambridge his Christian links still centred on the Caius Mission for the disadvantaged in Battersea, London. A concert on behalf of the Mission took place in the College Hall on December 1, 1920. During the interval the Reverend R. Wimbush, Warden of the Mission, spoke of his work there.

But it was also the depth of Harold's feelings for Christina McLeod Innes which led him towards the Christian causes of post-war Cambridge. There was something about her brave spirit which brought out the best in him. And his philanthropic efforts during their first months as friends could have done nothing but impress the deep-thinking teenager. It wasn't long before Christina became Harold's first girlfriend. His nephew Tony was convinced that she contributed to Harold's religious fervour.

A Cambridge student after the Second World War, Tony heard all the stories about his uncle from staff who were still there and recounted, 'As an undergraduate at Cambridge in his second year, Harold formed a romantic attachment. The attraction became quite serious and this led for a short time to an interest in Christianity. There was some anecdotal evidence up at Cambridge of Harold "getting religion". Harold had a phase when he preached in public. That was Christianity. He was preaching – my recollection of the description given me is that he was out in the open; on the streets. I think Harold's enthusiasm for this girl conditioned the fact that he actively started giving public utterances in favour of Christianity.'

Sue Pottle also heard that her father became quite evangelical in his younger days. 'A long time ago a vicar wrote to me, saying that he had managed to get a lot of these Cambridge athletes converted. He said that he, my father and the others had gone round the East End of London "proselytising". That's the way he put it.'

Contrary to later claims that he converted to Catholicism in 1934, Abrahams made his greatest commitment to Christianity during his student days. And there is nothing in Catholic Church records to suggest that he ever converted to Catholicism, either while at University or later.

If Christina was also involved in street preaching, she didn't tell her daughters. Sue Smithson admitted, 'I never heard of it but certainly she did have a very strong faith. She had a very conventional Church of England upbringing. She was always a committed Anglican until the end of her days.'

Whatever the nature of their religious expression, that meeting in the Student Christian Movement sparked something increasingly powerful between Harold Abrahams, star university athlete, and Christina, broken-hearted intellectual. She knew life must go on, but she cherished the past. From her point of view, Harold was a living link to Donald, who had been the same age. It isn't hard to imagine how the bond between them rapidly grew strong. Christina's daughter Sue explained, 'I'm sure this is how

Harold came into the bosom of the family. I think it was this emotional bond, through having known her brothers.'

His Eastern European roots would also have been attractive to Christina. She had formed an attachment to that part of the world while getting to know Serbian refugees while at school in Cambridge and Rugby. Perry Morley explained, 'My mother wanted to learn Serbo-Croat. But she was advised by St. John Philby [father of the notorious spy, Kim Philby] that there was limited point in learning Serbo-Croat. But if she could speak Russian, French and English she could make herself understood anywhere in the world. So she decided to study Russian at Cambridge.'

Despite what Harold and Christina had in common, her father Hugh may have been taken aback by how quickly she fell for Abrahams. Hugh McLeod Innes was Bursar of Trinity College, a dour Scot whose father, General James John Mcleod Innes, had won a Victoria Cross during the Indian Mutiny. Hugh was not a man to be messed with either, despite his genteel surroundings.

His office was in the King's Hostel, just below the Big Clock in Trinity's famous Great Court. A few years later, Harold's friend Lord Burghley succeeded in running round the Great Court in less time than it took the college bells to strike twelve. McLeod Innes preferred to demonstrate the sharpness of his mind. Part of the Bursar's job was to buy and sell properties around Cambridge and beyond. He handled a huge budget with great skill. And Hugh was so shrewd and cautious that he drew up his accounts in such a way that only he could understand them.

If caution and reserve were her father's style, Christina had chosen as her boyfriend his perfect opposite. Abrahams was one of the most extrovert, conceited men in the university. Hugh McLeod Innes must have feared for Christina's emotional vulnerability after the family tragedies, because he was still getting over the shock himself. Trinity records indicate that 'he and his wife were hit hard by the 1914–18 war, in which they lost two sons'. The idea of losing his daughter to Harold might have been hard for Hugh to contemplate. What if the romance turned sour?

It certainly wasn't going to find much physical expression, because Hugh and his wife Margaret insisted that the courtship followed the conventions of the day. Sue Pottle said, 'I met Christina and she told me she always used to visit my father in the halls of residence at Cambridge with a chaperone. I don't think Christina and my father were having sex.' Christina's youngest daughter Perry suggested, 'It's unlikely that they got beyond hand-holding and the occasional kiss.'

Instead of seeking physical pleasure, the lovers put their combined energies into campaigning for various causes. Looking back on his university days with the benefit of a lifetime's hindsight, however, Harold gave the impression that he was being swept along at a pace with which he was not entirely comfortable. Christina, who had a great personal interest in the plight of Russia, is thought to have played a leading role in the way Cambridge Christians reacted to the Russian Famine of 1921–22.

Harold also played a prominent role in the Russian Famine Relief Campaign. His help appears to have been enlisted because he was a well-known sporting figure. Philip Noel-Baker, Harold's captain at the Antwerp Olympics, had been working hard to help create the League of Nations, forerunner to the United Nations. He had been principal assistant to Lord Robert Cecil on the committee which drafted the League of Nations Covenant. As an increasingly big hitter in post-war politics, he also became a trusted advisor to Norwegian explorer-turned-diplomat Fridtjof Nansen. Nansen was involved in organising the repatriation of prisoners-of-war and then refugee work. But in 1921 the Red Cross had asked Nansen to organise a relief programme for the millions who were starving in the Russian Famine.

Seeking support from the leading lights of Cambridge University, Nansen visited in person. As soon as Noel-Baker introduced Nansen to Abrahams, Harold felt obliged to help. How could he turn down his Olympic captain, or the girlfriend he loved, or a distinguished international figure like Nansen? It was inconceivable.

As images of the starving Russian millions reached Britain, it was impossible not to be moved by the suffering. Harold was no exception, yet part of him remained strangely detached from the unfolding tragedy. He knew he was doing the right thing by getting involved. But he didn't feel quite so passionately about the situation as many others did; and all the time there was the sneaking suspicion that he was being manipulated.

In a moment of typical brutal self-analysis, Harold said much later, 'I met Nansen and I was very susceptible. You see, I was all the time trying to find a means of self-expression. I did an awful lot of work helping to collect money for Russian relief. But I can't, if I'm honest with myself, say that I felt emotionally terribly sincere about it. I did the work, I helped to get the money, and I was appalled by the pictures of starving.'

But he wasn't so very deeply moved that he would have given all his spare time to the cause had he not been pressured by others to do so. At the time he loved Christina; and of course he would have done anything for her, even though he was conscious that he sometimes spread himself too thinly as he devoted his energies to the latest causes in a troubled world. Harold added, 'I once made a speech on "Parker's Piece" [a big open green in Cambridge] for Dr Barnardos. You see one was roped into a tremendous number of things, all of which one skated over the surface of.'

Yet he persevered. If Christina wanted to change the world for the better, in whatever way she could, so did Harold. On the face of it they seemed made for each other. Sue Smithson revealed:

> My mother was brought up on the Liberal party. She was always interested in sport, too. And she loved Swedish deep-breathing exercises. Stand at the window on a cold winter's day and breathe in and out. She loved athletics but it wasn't anything that she ever took up herself. Young ladies didn't, really. She probably went to see the Cambridge and Oxford athletics contests, though. I don't think she would have found Harold's athletics a bore at all.

Christina even helped Harold to train. 'She used to ride a bicycle beside Harold while he was running,' Perry revealed. You can imagine Christina cycling as fast as she could ahead of him, so that the greyhound had a rabbit to chase. Her eagerness to break the monotony of Harold's training might have given him new athletic impetus. Instead Harold's passion for athletics began to dwindle, at roughly the same rate as his passion for Christina grew.

Harold soon became unwell, the precise nature of his illness undisclosed. Whether this low-point was physical, mental or a combination of both is unknown. One report stated at the start of 1921, 'Harold Abrahams, the Cambridge Blue, is at present indisposed and will not be able to go into residence at Cambridge at the end of the month. Caius, favourites for the Inter-Collegiate Cup, will suffer seriously from his absence.'

On February 3, 1921, his low-key return to action was described like this: 'Abrahams, the Blue, who has been ill and only took up residence on Monday, turned out for Caius against St Johns and won the hundred and long jump without fully extending himself.' And why should he fully extend himself, when he had realised there was more to life than athletics? On February 16, 1921, he acted in a college legal drama called 'Bardell v Pickwick'. Two days later, there was a big athletics showdown between Trinity and Caius. Harold's great Cambridge University rival and Athletics Club President, Guy Butler of Trinity, beat him in the 100 yards in a time of 10.2sec. Abrahams came second in the high jump and 120 yards hurdles, which was no good because both events were also won by Trinity. It was something of a shock that Caius were defeated soundly; Abrahams and his great reputation had been well and truly dented.

At a misty Fenners in the University Sports of March 3 and 5, 1921, Harold was beaten yet again. Guy Butler defeated his CUAC Secretary with such ease in the 100 yards that Abrahams' style looked a mess. Harold was even beaten in the long jump. What was going on? 'I went back and back,' he acknowledged later, reflecting on this confusing period. 'Paying too much attention to my mother, yes. I can see it all!' joked Christina's daughter Sue later.

Harold's pushy brother Adolphe referred to this sporting crisis in his book, *Fitness for the Average Man*. Speaking of Harold, he wrote: 'As a freshman at the age of nineteen he was accepted as the fastest runner who had ever represented the Varsity. At the age of twenty-one he slumped badly enough to invite the "burnt out" explanation, which would (as is usual) have been accepted had he not been encouraged to continue.'

Abrahams later put it this way: 'Some people may argue that every human being possesses a certain amount of innate energy, and if he uses up an excessive amount of it in his early years, he will have to pay the bill later on. I doubt very much if the problem is as simple as that. I do think competition of a strenuous kind has a very subtle effect on the nervous system.'

Harold protested to an unimpressed Adolphe that he had reached his peak a year or two earlier, and had now hit a brick wall. He had enjoyed his moments of glory but just didn't feel he had any further improvement left in him. He admitted later that his slump 'made me wonder a good deal whether early success of a high character is not responsible for subsequent failures'.

You could almost hear Harold begging his dominant eldest brother to stop pressurising him; that he should now be allowed to enjoy his life as a young man and his burgeoning romance with Christina in peace. However, as Harold said of Adolphe later, 'He was much more of a father to me than a brother, at any rate for the first twenty years or so of my life.'

What Adolphe said, went. And it is easy to picture Adolphe refusing to accept Harold's apparent weakness. Besides, as a doctor, he would have insisted that a 21-year-old couldn't possibly know whether or not he had reached his peak. They would never know unless Harold stuck at it and kept making sacrifices. Adolphe didn't let Harold give up, and wrote later:

> One lesson learnt is that of bearing patiently with the deterioration which often occurs at a critical period and which I may submit may be temporary only. Of course, it may represent that the peak has been reached for that individual, a conclusion which only further trial can decide . . . And the young man as a free agent will have his own ideas; doubtless preferring the glory of early distinction to the more nebulous future, the promise of greater things provided he waits.

Harold's brother told him to carry on, at least for a while. If he really had nothing left to give, they would soon see as much and then draw an early veil over his career. In the mean time, why not try to enjoy what could be his last races?

Harold agreed to try, but it wasn't as easy as it sounded; not when attempts to iron out flaws in his technique were complicated by further illness in the middle of the month. When it previewed the all-important Oxford and Cambridge Athletic Sports, *The Times* of March 18, 1921 claimed, 'The Hundred lies on the knees of the gods. In this race, as also in the Long Jump, a good deal depends on Abrahams, of Cambridge. Last year he won both events. This year he is only second string in both. He is said not to have been quite fit, and to have developed a roll at the finish of the Hundred . . . With Abrahams having been hitherto disappointing, anything might happen.' Lateral movement as he neared the tape was a sign of a tension in the shoulders bordering on desperation. No wonder Abrahams was no longer regarded as a safe bet for the big one.

A few days later at the Queen's Club in London, Harold found himself locked in battle yet again with his greatest Varsity rival over the 100 yards. One report claimed that Bevil Rudd 'led to within yards of the tape', until he was hunted down once more, this time both Harold and his president, Guy Butler, sweeping past at the death. Another report explained that 'last year's winner made a great effort in the last twenty yards and beat his president by two feet'. Abrahams had triumphed over Butler in a Cambridge one-two. Harold's time of 10.2sec didn't set the world alight. But it wasn't the time that mattered when you were racing Oxford. Winning was everything. Harold raised his arms high in the air while the ever-popular Rudd shook his head in fresh disappointment.

For a second successive year Harold returned to Cambridge a hero, even though he had only managed third in the long jump with 21ft 3½in [6.51 metres]. The *Sporting Life* newspaper put that setback down to the fact that Abrahams 'had not recovered from his illness, and was not able to do himself justice in the broad-jump [long jump]'. He hadn't recovered from falling head-over-heels in love with Christina either.

That Varsity victory looked likely to be his swan song, especially when news arrived from America to crush any Englishman with the slightest Olympic sprint ambitions for 1924. In April 1921, on a cold and rainy day in Redlands, California, Charley Paddock did something almost incredible, with finishing tapes waiting for him at both 100 yards and 100 metres. Outstanding American reporter Maxwell Stiles wrote an eyewitness account of Paddock's progress, starting with his 9.6sec for 100 yards. 'Fifteen feet from the tape Paddock gave a mighty bound, and fairly flew over the finish line, coming down heavily. Recovering, he took two quick strides and leaped for the tape at 100m.' The time, 10.4sec, was a new world record. Stiles declared, 'Two such leaps as these made it appear that the boy must have wings or a kangaroo hoof.'

Later that day Paddock ran 21.2 sec for the 200 metres on his way to a world record 33.4sec for 300 metres. He had clocked 20.8sec for the 220 yards a few weeks earlier. Harold Abrahams could say what he liked about Charley Paddock, but the truth was he wasn't in the same league.

Harold recharged his batteries but wondered whether there was any point in persevering with athletics. As the weather became warmer, he decided to race for the hell of it. He starred in emphatic relay wins for the Achilles Club against the 'RMA/RMC' at Woolwich in early May. He and his Oxbridge colleagues won the 4 × 220 yards and 4 × 120 yards hurdles with ease. On June 11 Harold added to his momentum with an 'even time' 100 yards at Birmingham, winning by a comfortable two yards. He also took the 220 yards in 23.0sec, first to the tape by three feet. The times were tidy enough, but they didn't represent the sort of breakthrough he needed to make an impact on the world stage.

The university year was reaching the home straight. Though Harold's track and field form had been patchy, there seemed to be nothing inconsistent about his devotion to Christina. A romance born the previous autumn in Cambridge had flourished through the seasons. Soon the summer sun would rise a few short hours after it had set, offering even more warmth to the affair. First came the Caius May Ball, an occasion which seemed made for lovers, though it could test a relationship too. A party which began at 9.30 p.m. and lasted till after six the following morning, the May Ball tended to leave many of its revellers drunk or exhausted. Either way, the sensitivity some students showed towards their partners could become impaired. This seemed to happen in Harold's case, a story captured by the photographer when it was time to take the official 'survivors' picture. Frozen in time is Christina's faint annoyance as she realises that Harold is posing for the camera without paying her any attention whatsoever. Christina has no time to rectify this slight, because the picture is taken and she is left in limbo.

Perhaps the feisty Miss Innes let her feelings be known soon afterwards. We will never know. But if harsh words were spoken, they changed nothing. A decent sleep, an apology from Harold, and recriminations were forgotten. After all, Harold and Christina were *inseparable*.

The trouble was, the academic year was drawing to a close, and that meant they were about to be separated for a month or two. Harold hoped to run in the USA in late July; and Christina wouldn't be able to join him. For a vulnerable young woman deeply scarred by the loss of two brothers, the prospect of this separation may have created a disproportionate sense of anxiety.

Was this a key moment in their love story? One thing is certain: at around this time Harold asked Christina to marry him . . . and Christina said yes.

CHAPTER SEVEN

A Pivotal Decision

Aware that there might be strong opposition from their families, it appears that Harold and Christina decided to keep the news of their engagement to themselves for the time being. But there is no doubt they became engaged, albeit unofficially.

Sue Smithson explained, 'Harold wished to marry my mother. I think the word engagement probably was used. But I don't think they were ever formally engaged. Still, it is an important strand to his story.' Christina confirmed that she too wished to marry Harold. Later in life, she told his adopted daughter.

If Abrahams didn't feel any great urge to rush round to 6 St Eligius Street and ask Hugh McLeod Innes for his daughter's hand in marriage, there was a reason. The Bursar of Trinity College was tough enough, but Harold was even more intimidated by the Bursar's wife, Margaret. Perry revealed how, 'he had been scared of my grandmother. He told me that he had always thought my grandmother was "formidable" and that he was rather frightened of her.'

Could survivor's guilt have caused his fear? He hadn't fought in the war, while Donald, just six months older, had fought and died. Margaret McLeod Innes must have felt like a war veteran herself, having dashed to France to nurse her youngest son through his final weeks. She had seen the horror of war first-hand and yet he, a fine physical specimen, hadn't suffered at all. Now he was enjoying Cambridge, the reward that should have been waiting for Margaret's two sons. This gulf in human experience couldn't have created much common ground between them.

Then there were Harold's chauvinist tendencies; not uncommon for the day, but dangerous if they surfaced in any shape or form in front of Margaret, who was very keen on feminism. While he contemplated a lifetime with a mother-in-law he feared, Harold's focus on his racing wasn't what it might have been. However, he did enjoy one stunning success over a little-known distance, albeit in a very familiar arena. *The Times* of June 27, 1921, revealed, 'The London Athletic Club held their summer meeting at Stamford Bridge on Saturday. The feature of the afternoon was the running of H.M. Abrahams (Cambridge University) who won the 75 yards scratch race in 7⅗sec, which broke the world's "record" by ⅕sec.'

Unfortunately, it was subsequently discovered that the course had been eight inches too short; so Harold's place in history for that dash was denied him. And at the AAA Championships of 1921 he lacked the necessary edge to make such a big impact. Looking back, Abrahams recalled, 'I can remember vainly running behind Harry Edward in 1921. He won the 100 and 220, and also ran an amazing 440 yards in the one mile relay.'

Harry Edward, the black sprinter, twice defeated Harold Abrahams – in 10.2 and 22.2. It seemed that Sam Mussabini still had the measure of his former charge. At least Old Sam could have no influence over an entirely new athletic challenge that awaited Abrahams across the Atlantic. Harold explained, 'After the Championships I was selected to compete for Oxford and Cambridge against the American Universities of Harvard and Yale and Princeton and Cornell, and I made my one and only visit to the United States.' Though circumstances didn't allow Harold more than this single, memorable inter-collegiate trip to America, he certainly didn't underestimate their importance. While still a young man, he made an extraordinary claim. 'The value of these international contests is very great, much greater indeed than the Olympic Games.'

So the sense of anticipation felt among the men of Oxford and Cambridge must have been immense as they prepared for the six-day voyage across the Atlantic Ocean. The English team travelled on what Harold described as 'that luxurious liner, the *Olympic*'. The razzamatazz of the most energetic city on earth was waiting even before they reached dry land. 'About half an hour before we actually landed in New York a host of press photographers and "movie" men came alongside in a tender, and, having wormed their way on board, bombarded us with questions and shutters for quite a time,' Abrahams recalled. With prohibition in force, he added, 'This was our first experience of American methods; our first experience of America had taken place some few hours earlier when we entered American territorial waters, and the bar closed.'

They spent one night in New York, went to a Broadway theatre show and next day travelled by train to Swampscott, a seaside resort about fifteen miles from Boston, Massachusetts. That would provide their base for the first contest, which was due to take place on July 23. Harold confidently predicted how the match between Harvard and Yale and the Englishmen of Oxford and Cambridge would go. He wrote, 'We ourselves were certain that the Americans would win four of the five field events, and that we had a very real chance of winning all the track events. The quarter and mile were fairly certain for us.'

However, Harold's prediction fell apart in front of 7,700 spectators, and he was forced to report:

> Against Harvard and Yale the English Universities won only two events out of ten. I had heard a great deal about American hospitality and how considerate you were but I don't think you were very kind to me. I competed at the Harvard Stadium, when Harvard and Yale gave us an awful beating by 8 events to 2. I had to jump against Ed Gourdin at Cambridge in the Yale–Harvard meet. He was ungracious enough to jump 25ft 3in – a new world's record – at his first effort.
>
> Gourdin's leap marked a new epoch in long-jumping. Ever since P. O'Connor, the Irishman, had cleared 24ft 11¾in on August 5, 1901, men had strived to squeeze out that extra quarter inch. But it was twenty years before O'Connor's performance was eclipsed. As I had never at that time reached even 23ft my interest in the event after Gourdin's first effort was somewhat academic. You can imagine my feelings as I approached the take-off.

Harold did manage second place, but he only jumped 22ft 1in, more than a yard less than his rival. It was something of a humiliation. 'Still I forgave him, as I learned a tremendous amount from watching him in action,' Harold claimed.

Not enough, apparently. Harold never did drastically change his static, hanging position as he sailed through the air – even though Gourdin appeared to have gained extra distance with whirring leg movements. And the speed of those Gourdin legs was seen again that day. Abrahams recalled:

In the 100 yards my opponent was also Gourdin, who in 1920 won the Junior Championship in the States. We had a battle-royal from start to finish.

I felt the tape break as I reached the finish line. Gourdin was declared the winner, though I must confess that at the time I thought I had won, as did many spectators in the crowd. The judges decided otherwise, and of course that was the end of the matter as far as we were concerned. Not so the American press, which published photos taken from every conceivable angle explaining that really I had won. In fact photographs are pretty useless, because unless they are taken absolutely at right angles to the finish and at the very fraction of the second as the winner passes the tape, they are very deceptive.

Without knowing each other's choice, the three judges were unanimous in selecting Gourdin for first place.

Whoever really won, it was the start of the massacre. An American commentator described this 8–2 'licking' as 'the worst set-back for either team in the history of the rivalry' which went back to 1899. 'Only [Henry] Stallard and [Bevil] Rudd ran true to form and provided O-C victories.'

If the match against Princeton and Cornell was going to be so one-sided, the British risked disgrace. First they secured the chance of future revenge against Harvard and Yale. Bevil Rudd revealed:

Between the meetings we lived in the Princeton Clubs, the Cap and Gown, the Ivy and others . . . It was on this visit that we had a full meeting to discuss the prospects for a regular interchange of meetings. We formulated the four-year plan which I am glad to say has gone on to this day. By it, the Olympic year is left free; the year following the Olympic Games Oxford and Cambridge visit America and tackle Harvard and Yale, and then Princeton and Cornell, and vice-versa. The following year, Princeton and Cornell come to England, and the next year Harvard and Yale; then we have the Olympic Games again, and after that the same circle begins.

Back in 1921, a good performance in the forthcoming contest against Princeton and Cornell would salvage some pride. Harold was determined to play his part, even though there were those on his own side who thought him so conceited that they preferred to see him beaten by their American hosts. Abrahams explained:

At Travers Island [not far from New York] I competed in the first duel between Oxford and Cambridge and Princeton and Cornell. Anglo-American rivalry in athletics has produced Anglo-American friendship; that these friendships matter so much more than the result of the contest is, perhaps, best exemplified by an incident which occurred in the first Oxford and Cambridge against Princeton and Cornell meet in 1921. An Oxford man said to a Princeton man, 'I don't even care a damn who wins this sprint, so long as that blighter from Cambridge doesn't'.

But 'that blighter from Cambridge' did. And even the *New York Times* hailed Abrahams. It wrote:

The bright particular star in the visitors' demonstration was Harold M. Abrahams, wearer of the Cambridge Light Blue. He contributed two victories to the cause of his countrymen and paved the way for the unexpected recovery shown by the lads from across the sea. Abrahams started England off auspiciously by capturing the 100-yard dash, which opened the program. It was the work of this same athlete [Abrahams] in the broad jump which pulled the visitors within a single point of an even break in the honors of the day . . . The hero of the day was Abrahams, who was the only man to win two events.

Neither his sprint time nor the distance he jumped was anything to write home about; but this was a team event and allowed the drama of the day to reach a rousing climax. A spectacular run by Rudd in the half-mile gave the English universities a share of the spoils. The *New York Times* highlighted the 'remarkable recovery and surprising strength' of the English universities after their 'overwhelming setback of last Saturday'. Each side scored five wins and British honour had been restored.

As the summer drew to a close, however, it was time for Harold to face some harsh realities about his athletic standing at home and abroad. He had been defeated in the AAA Championships by veteran Harry Edward and completely outclassed in the long jump by Ed Gourdin. Charley Paddock looked unbeatable and had smashed world sprint records to smithereens. Perhaps it was time to admit that he would never be the best. His athletics career had brought him plenty of glorious moments but he had gone as far as he could go. What better time to tell Adolphe that his priorities had changed?

Imagine Adolphe's mounting horror as his little brother began to drop the bombshell; that he intended to announce his engagement to Christina. Perry recalled, 'My mother told us that Harold's brother was very strict with him and wouldn't hear of him becoming engaged while he was a student and had not established himself in some profession. I don't know whether the fact that my mother was not Jewish had anything to do with it.'

Sue Pottle revealed, 'Christina told me she thought the brothers had put an end to her relationship with my father because it was harming his athletics. She used the word "brothers" in the plural. That suggested "S.S." had backed Adolphe on this particular issue, though he was generally more kind-hearted.'

It was time for Harold to show his fiancée what he was made of. If he loved her enough, surely he would tell his brothers to respect his wishes or stay out of his business? Instead he wavered and even relented. Few women would be impressed if they saw their man's resolve buckle under pressure from his family. 'The sense I got was that Christina might have thought Harold was being a bit meek by accepting the decision of his brothers,' Sue Pottle added.

Adolphe was a lesser athlete and he wasn't about to watch his kid brother, who was blessed with so much more talent, throw away their Olympic dream. 'I think later in life he was competing, lived through me many of the dreams which he himself had not the prowess to achieve,' Harold reflected.

Later Adolphe claimed, 'The will to win telepathically influences others, even superior.' Therefore Adolphe used his own ambition to destroy Harold's romantic happiness.

Adolphe may also have used Isaac's will as leverage to scupper the engagement before it was formalised. There were financial implications to consider – consequences which seemed better suited to a Jane Austen novel. Yet Adolphe may have felt compelled to warn his little brother that, by getting engaged, he might throw away his inheritance as well as his athletics career. Harold's father, Isaac would have to be told; and that carried considerable risk. Sidney Abrahams, whose wife had converted to Christianity, had already been cut out of the family estate when a codicil was added to Isaac's will. And although Harold's father might not have taken such drastic action for non-religious reasons, Adolphe would have been alert to such danger, because he and Lionel were executors to their father's will.

Tony Abrahams, Sidney's son, suggested, 'It may have been significant that Adolphe didn't marry until after his father's death and then he soon married a Catholic. It is possible to speculate that, when Harold told Adolphe (or indeed Lionel) that he wanted to marry Christina, Adolphe advised against it, knowing what was in the will and codicil. Lionel might have expressed the same view.'

The legalities sounded complicated, but the threat was very simple. It would only require Harold's father to dislike Christina or her religion and the runner could lose his inheritance. Added to his brothers' disapproval, this was a serious setback for Harold and Christina's hopes of marriage. There could be no wedding if Harold had no means to support his prospective wife, because women of a certain social standing didn't usually work. Besides, they were both still students.

So Adolphe Abrahams seems to have undermined Harold's engagement on two fronts, using the inheritance issue and his younger brother's athletics career as twin sticks with which to beat him. Adolphe was a controlling character and often interfered in Harold's life. He admitted in one letter to Harold that he possessed 'a natural disposition to suspect everybody and everything' and advised his little brother to 'cut out ruthlessly the things that are too trivial and which won't advance you personally'. Though he probably didn't go so far as to call Christina trivial, Adolphe didn't see how the engagement could advance Harold personally – quite the reverse.

'To an extent Adolphe inherited some of his father's nastiness,' Tony Abrahams said. 'Isaac adored Harold but all the sons were fairly scared of him and, in the same way Adolphe didn't marry a Catholic until after his father died, I would not expect Harold to have broached the subject of marriage with Isaac. It seems Isaac continued to have a strong influence over the situation indirectly, even without being consulted.'

There is evidence that Harold's brother Solly adopted a gentler approach to his youngest brother's romance when he visited the McLeod Innes home. In a letter Christina later wrote to Harold about Solly, she described her 'personal recollection of his kindness and friendliness to me [when] you brought him and his wife, whom I also liked extremely, to 6 St Eligius Street'.

It shows that the families had recognised and accepted the relationship to a point. Solly might even have discussed Harold's situation with Christina's parents in their pretty walled garden at the back of their modest property. But his diplomacy could have changed little; Adolphe was never going to allow that engagement. And part of Harold may even have been relieved when the matter was taken out of his hands. He once said, 'I've got that sort of psychological temperament about things, I don't like getting too involved in something, I don't like caring too much about something.'

His love for Christina probably made him feel insecure. Even for one of the fastest men in England, things were moving too quickly. What if their love suddenly died just as quickly? For a young man like Harold, it was all a little frightening. Tony Abrahams concluded, 'He was serious about her but it was not a definitive relationship.'

Harold's inner confusion may have led to his poor performance at the Freshmen's Sports in early November. But soon there were signs that he was back in the groove, and leaping enthusiastically at a future free of responsibility. On November 28, he showed sparkling form in an inter-collegiate contest, winning no fewer than four events. He claimed the high jump with 5ft 2in, the 440 yards in 55 sec, and the 100 yards in 10.2 – all in Caius colours. He even came second in the shot put with 32ft 3½in [9.84 metres] and second in the 120 yards hurdles. But his extraordinary long jump of 23ft [7.02 metres] was by far the biggest achievement of the day, a personal best. He was well ahead of his age in feet again now.

Trotting off triumphant, Harold was saddened by the unexpected news that his father Isaac had died that very day. No matter how much trauma Isaac had caused during Harold's childhood, he had given his son the perfect platform to showcase his talents. Harold would always be grateful. In time, the numbness he felt at the loss of his father gave way to a greater sense of freedom. It could even have put Harold's engagement to Christina back on the agenda. It didn't.

Cracks may have begun to appear in their relationship much earlier, because as suggested by her daughter, they harboured different views on women's equality. An article in Harold's college magazine, *The Caian*, complained:

Women are taking a more practical view of life; they are trespassing in the domain that has hitherto been occupied by man alone; and the inevitable result is that the Female on the Pedestal is becoming rarer, and the Blue Stocking is coming into greater prominence . . . Woman belongs to the world of Art; her life is the love of the soul; and she has the leisure to cultivate that life uncontaminated by the

Mr Versatility: Harold Abrahams would have made a fine decathlete. His fiancée Christina Innes is the photographer capturing his high-jump prowess here, in an Inter-Collegiate competition at Cambridge University.

everyday struggle for existence, of which the industrial machine is
the expression.

Part of Harold was receptive to such chauvinism, something we know
from the psychological difficulties he experienced later in life. In time he
would admit that his view of women had been 'childish'. But at
Cambridge he merely regarded himself as romantically idealistic, just like
many young men of the day. It is difficult to see how the feminist in
Christina could have allowed her to remain soul mates with Harold
forever. Yet for the moment she remained close to him, and took a keen
interest in his sporting activities.

On Friday February 24, 1922, when Caius beat St Catharine's in what
Christina described as the 'Finals' of the 'Inter-collegiate Sports Div 1',
she was definitely present. We know this because Christina took
advantage of the clear blue skies to photograph her man in action. And
then she wrote on the back of her pictures, leaving a record of what she
had captured: 'H.M.A. winning the 100 yards at Fenners.' Although we
know from the records that Abrahams managed no more than 10.4sec for
the 100 yards, we also know – from Christina's picture – that he won by
such a huge margin that there was no one to test him properly on the day.
Christina was waiting beyond the finishing tape and took her photo as
Harold neared the line. She captioned another photo as 'H.M.A. High-
jumping at Fenners.' It was the same day and the same occasion – 'Caius
v Cats' as Christina put it. Harold appears to be jumping higher than the
head of a man watching. There was no 'Fosbury Flop' in those days and
Harold achieved his clearance using a simple 'scissors' style – making his
jump all the more remarkable.

His former fiancée kept those photographs for the rest of her life, a
visual record of an exceptional young man in his prime. Even as she
captured her boyfriend's magnificent athleticism in the cold sunshine,
she may have known deep down that their days together were numbered.
And yet, whatever the extent of their underlying problems, Harold
seemed untroubled in those pictures, as he casually put his opponents to
the sword.

Abrahams was a complex character, someone who could be buzzing
one moment and desolate the next. It was at around this time that a
Cambridge student called Walter Ashley was ushered into Harold's rooms
in Caius to meet the great sporting hero. Ashley wrote, 'I shall never forget
our first meeting. He was like a racehorse – highly trained, impulsive,

eager to be off. Exultant one minute; depressed the next (but usually the former). An artist in life, no less than in sport. An artist too, with real genius in both spheres.'

Though he had something of an artistic temperament – in sport as in life – he showed no genius for the arts. But that didn't stop him from taking centre stage on March 9 to pay homage to another of his lifetime loves – Gilbert and Sullivan. Christina, who was also a devoted fan, must have known what a fool Harold risked making of himself on Caius' College Hall stage. A musical genius he wasn't. As Harold told radio presenter Roy Plomley on *Desert Island Discs* later in life, 'I love music Roy. I love Gilbert and Sullivan. I'm not musical in the sense that I can't play a single instrument, and I sing out of tune. I change key, I do everything that's wrong.'

At least there was no danger of him forgetting his words on that Caius stage. As his friend Sir Arthur Gold said much later, 'He would produce apposite quotes from G & S as readily as any biblical scholar quoting from the Testaments.' Yet this was to be a duet; and his inability to hold his half of the tune threatened to sound almost tragically awful, especially when set against the skill of a good singer.

Despite the clear risk to the ears of Cambridge's music-lovers, Harold went ahead with his performance. Mercifully there is no recording of the result. The college magazine, *The Caian*, reviewed it:

> The Gilbert and Sullivan Concert was given on Thursday, March 9, in the College Hall, by kind permission of the Master and Fellows. The chief interest in the programme was due to the fact that many of the items were chosen from the less known operas, and many thus seemed quite new. It was a long programme, but it was, on the whole, quite successful. Much might be said, but there is no room for it here, and a detailed criticism would be as tedious as it would be out of place now that the concert is already buried in the past. H.K.P. Smith, in his solos and the duet with H.M. Abrahams, was enthusiastically received.

The review didn't say that H.M. Abrahams, in his duet with H.K.P. Smith, was enthusiastically received. But there must have been plenty in the audience who admired Harold's enthusiasm and pluck, if not his voice. And by the last week of March, Harold was back doing what he did best.

His next athletic experience was to go down as one of the most famous in Cambridge history. The Varsity Sports, held as usual at the Queen's Club in London, were so one-sided that it was almost embarrassing. Abrahams set the tone, with typical victories in the 100 yards and long jump. It was Harold's sprinting that caught the imagination of *The Times*, whose perceptive correspondent also noticed just how highly strung Abrahams was. On March 27, 1922 the newspaper wrote: 'Abrahams is undoubtedly a fine sprinter. He runs low with a big raking stride, and he has that touch of splendid frenzy which has been well described in the saying that "to be a sprinter a man must run like a madman".'

Mad or not, Abrahams was too much for Oxford. And by the time the mismatch was over, Cambridge had crushed their rivals completely. In his book *Cambridge Doctor*, Rex Salisbury Woods wrote: 'In 1922 Cambridge beat Oxford in the Sports by nine events to one, a record victory of which Harold Abrahams, already a sporting journalist, never failed to remind the "House of Lost Causes" for years afterwards, and, on the standard displayed, members of the Cambridge team and myself were invited to give demonstrations in Aldershot's newly-built stadium.'

Harold was now putting new energy into his work as Secretary of the CUAC. His commitment to university athletics increased as his commitment to Christina faded. She too stood to benefit from their loss of romantic intensity, because so far she had fallen short of fulfilling her academic potential. Although she had achieved a distinction in oral French, her Modern and Medieval Languages Tripos had only earned her a second in 1922. By her impeccable standards, this result was hardly covering herself in glory. She was Secretary of the Modern Languages Club by May 1922, and she would have hoped for a higher grade. By seeing less of Harold, she could at least improve her academic performance.

In their first university year together, Harold and Christina had been so in love. Their second university year had been full of problems and complications. Eventually there was nothing more to be done. Harold later referred to 'that hopeless feeling that you can't prevent love just vanishing'. It was a feeling that he never forgot. For more than a decade he was tormented by the dreadfulness of that feeling. He knew what Christina had been through, losing her brothers in the war, and felt terrible about the collapse of their romance. He also developed a morbid fear that he might one day suffer a repeat of love's 'vanishing act' with someone else. It meant he avoided serious involvement with women for many years to come.

Sue Smithson believes her mother accepted the break-up without lasting bitterness. 'I don't think my mother ever held it against him. In a way she was probably quite relieved herself. I don't know, that's speculation on my part. But I know she always spoke very warmly of Harold. I think they were serious about each other, but I think it was a first love thing which doesn't always last very long.'

Sue Pottle believed it was for the best that Harold and Christina didn't marry. She explained, 'I think she would have been unsuitable for Dad because she was so very intellectual. He was very intelligent but he wasn't a heavy intellectual like that. Christina and Dad were like chalk and cheese. She was a very strong-willed lady. I think she would have been happy to marry Harold when they were young. But I'm not sure it would ever have been a very good marriage.'

They were young and Harold in particular was still immature. Christina's daughters later agreed that it was best for the student sweethearts that they became lifelong friends instead. However, there were serious consequences for Abrahams in the long run, when we look at the way his life unfolded. As fate would have it, the failed engagement meant that Harold would never have children who were biologically his own. He couldn't know that yet, as he focused on his running again.

At the AAA Championships of 1922, he tried one last time to beat Sam Mussabini's protégé, Harry Edward. Even at the age of twenty-seven, the elegant Edward showed no signs of slowing down. Some regarded this final bow as Edward's most sensational performance in all his years at the Championships. Within an hour he won the 100, 220 and 440 yards in 10, 22, and 50.4sec respectively. No one had ever achieved that treble before. 'He was one of the most impressive sprinters I have ever seen,' wrote Harold Abrahams later. But the Edward era was drawing to a close; and 1923 would see Harold's resurgence.

CHAPTER EIGHT

RUNNING SCARED OF ERIC LIDDELL

With a new academic year just around the corner, Harold Abrahams was back giving all his love to the mistress he served for most of his life – athletics. Even before he went back up to Cambridge, he took an Achilles Club team to Prague and Budapest. Though his own results were nothing to write home about, his appetite was back.

Abrahams proudly took up office as President of the Cambridge University Athletic Club. It was a position which gave him the sort of power and prestige he was destined to enjoy for the rest of his days. Talent rather than popularity had earned him the presidency. Although Harold was well aware of that uncomfortable reality, he was more than ready to give his responsibilities the devotion they deserved. 'I was very good at organising things,' he pointed out unashamedly. But he wasn't just organising, he was inventing too. 'I was responsible for getting Professor Rottenburg to produce the first long-jump measurer on a slide-rule basis,' he added. It was called the 'Abrahams Long Jump Gauge', and a prototype was made by the London Instrument Company.

On the track, there was no instant rediscovery of his best form; and Harold must have been glad to see the back of 1922.

Yet when the University Sports arrived in the second week of March 1923, fate still seemed to be conspiring against him. The athletes had to contend with windy, cold, wet weather, and no one looked likely to shine. That didn't stop a very large crowd from turning out, and they expected heroics from the top student performers, whatever the conditions. And at

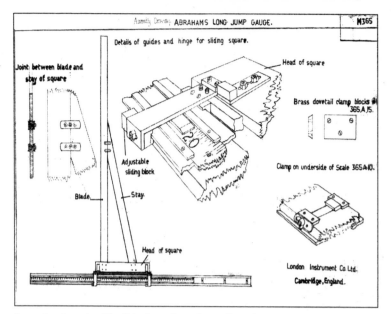

Innovator, inventor: The 'Abrahams Long-Jump Gauge'.

some point Harold must have realised that the strong wind was actually blowing from behind the sprinters, and would therefore assist them. Heartened, he simply sailed down the track in the 100 yards and finished two feet clear of his closest rival, easing up when he was sure of victory. His time of 10.2 suggested that he could easily have achieved 'evens' had he so desired.

In late March, Harold prepared for his last shot at Oxford in the Varsity athletics; but this time it felt different. As president, everything depended on Abrahams and the pressure was terrific. He even picked the team, and there was no room for sentiment. Harold left out S.E. Nelson of Fitzwilliam House, even though his father Alec Nelson was coach of CUAC. Dr Chris Thorne, a CUAC expert, believes the family connection might have worked against Nelson junior. 'Harold would have felt it awkward to put the coach's son in the team. He might have thought it would look like favouritism.'

Arthur Marshall, one of Harold's teammates at the time, didn't like the decision. As first choice for the 440 yards, Marshall expected to be consulted before his 'support act' for the Varsity race was selected. After all, the 'second string', as the second pick for any contest was known, traditionally danced to the tune of the better man. On the record, Marshall only admitted to 'surprise'. But privately he told friends about his dissatisfaction with Harold's unilateral approach.

It was particularly audacious of Abrahams to pick himself for the 440, because Cambridge were facing a vastly superior opponent – on paper at least – in Oxford's talented American, Bill Stevenson. The *Observer* newspaper of the time described Stevenson as 'the greatest American-Oxonian representative since Norman Taber. Two years earlier, Stevenson had won the amateur championship of the United States, and he seemed a class apart.' Stevenson had defeated Bevil Rudd on the East Coast earlier that year. He had broken 49 seconds in the USA and he had never been beaten in England, where he was a Rhodes scholar. The *Daily Mail* described him as 'a beautifully-built runner'. It was as though Harold, a comparative novice in quality races at this distance, had just challenged Superman. Stevenson was the AAA Champion, while Harold had only once previously run a quarter-mile in good class competition. Evelyn Montague admitted, 'We of Oxford roared with laughter at the idea of Harold's taking on Bill Stevenson.'

Later Abrahams tried to claim that he didn't have much more faith in the decision than Oxford. 'I was not only burdened with the responsibility of being Captain of the Cambridge Team, but much against my will I had been persuaded to compete in the quarter-mile as well as the 100 yards and long jump.' Who would have done the persuading? After all, ultimately it was Harold's decision. One can only guess that his brother Adolphe, an ex-Cambridge man, had come up with the idea, and then exerted the usual pressure as 'father figure'. Whoever was behind the decision, it nearly backfired even before race-day.

Just twenty-four hours before Cambridge faced Oxford, Harold came close to suffering a mental breakdown. The weight of responsibility on his own shoulders became almost unbearable; so many people were waiting to shoot him down if his plan failed. Abrahams revealed:

> The morning before my farewell performance at Cambridge, I woke up with a ghastly sore throat, felt feverish and ached in every part of my body. I was so bad that I called round on my brother Adolphe at his Brook Street practice for a complete check-up. He spent a good half-an-hour examining me and then he said, 'You bloody fool – it's nerves.' He informed me that I had never been fitter in my life. I had the 'wind up vertical'. The intense 'wind up'

had caused me to create all sorts of imaginary ailments. Of what was I afraid?

The answer, of course, was failure and humiliation. Harold explained, 'I had jumped 23ft in the Varsity trials and injured my heel, and I was down to represent Cambridge in three events: 100 yards, quarter mile and long jump. I was expected by many experts to win both the 100 and long jump.' But in that moment Harold didn't feel equipped to do so, mentally or physically. So there he was, in tatters and wondering what was happening to his mind and body. He knew that in some ways his many years at Cambridge would be defined by how he performed against Oxford on this final occasion. Big brother Adolphe helped Harold to pull himself together and recover his composure. Slowly a semblance of confidence returned to the younger man. Gradually, that confidence turned into a familiar, strutting arrogance.

Arthur Marshall revealed, 'In Kensington on the morning of the Varsity match, Harold suggested a walk to the Peter Pan statue. On the way he said, "Do you think you have any chance of beating Stevenson in the quarter-mile?" I said I didn't think I had a dog's chance. Harold said, "Will you give up any chance of winning and let me have a go then?"' Having already walked into Harold's trap by playing down his own chances, Marshall could hardly refuse. So Abrahams revealed what Marshall later described as 'cunning tactics, pre-agreed'. They may have sounded clever, but Arthur was the one being asked to sacrifice himself.

All the training the superior quarter-miler had done to prepare for the big race was going to count for nothing if Harold had his way. Chris Thorne said, 'I don't think Marshall liked being told what to do in that 440.' Though Marshall was disgruntled, he realised he would have little choice but to go along with the plan Abrahams had presented. So there was no argument between them, merely an unspoken tension as they headed to the Queen's Club. Soon they would put Harold's plan into action against the old enemy; and it would either be hailed as a masterstroke or ridiculed as lunacy.

Harold's team was already in pieces. A newspaper report explained:

> On Saturday he suffered really cruel luck as a President, for his team had to be reorganised at the last moment. All faith was being pinned on W.R. Seagrove, who by keen Cambridge partisans was confidently

expected to win both the mile and three miles, despite the strong opposition he was known to be up against. Everybody regretted that Seagrove was confined to his bed with influenza, but N. Durlosher was also unable to run owing to sprained ankles (he was second string in the three miles). These misfortunes put new life into Abrahams.

If the last-minute withdrawals meant that Cambridge couldn't accumulate enough points to defeat Oxford, then Harold would go all out to beat the 'enemy' personally. He would try to shine so brightly that the overall result would be almost incidental.

First he had to set the tone for the day in the most glamorous event of them all, the 100 yards. Abrahams revealed later, 'A study of past University records showed that no athlete had ever won the 100 yards outright four times. C.R. Thomas of Oxford had nearly done so with two victories and two dead-heats for first place. I wanted four clear wins, which was something which could never be beaten, though it might be equalled. No athlete can represent his University at athletics more than four times.'

The weather was described as 'exceptionally fine', as Abrahams carved out his starting holes. No one wanted to win more than he did. When he heard the gun, Harold exploded into action, whereas the Oxford pair were said to be 'very slow in starting'. There was no stopping Abrahams, who raced into a three-yard lead and won the sprint for the fourth successive year, equalling the Varsity record of 10sec. The *Daily Mail* even claimed he was 'easing up' at the end. His nearest opponent was Rex Alston, who later became famous as a BBC sports commentator. On this particular day, Alston wasn't good enough to bring out the best in Harold. According to the *Daily News*, 'Had Abrahams been pushed he could have got inside even time, a feat not yet recorded in Varsity Sports.' He was a record-breaker all the same. As Harold put it later, 'I was lucky enough to win my fourth inter-Varsity sprint, another youthful ambition achieved.'

But his day was only starting. Twenty minutes later, 'keyed up by his sprint victory', as the *Observer* put it:

[Abrahams] went all out for his second record of the day . . . Conscious of a damaged heel, he banked on his first long-jump effort as probably his last. A magnificent leap, a yell from the crowd, and a wave of the hand from the judge. The Cantab had cleared 24 feet but with his foot three inches over the board. Yet, after this heartbreaking misfortune, and with his heel 'gone', he tried again: 23ft 7¼in in a jump plumb off the board, and the Light Blue President confidently trotted back to the pavilion.

Abrahams had just beaten H.S.O. Ashington's 1914 record for the long jump of 23ft 6¼in. Even in 1959, Harold was able to say wryly, 'I am still lucky enough to hold the Oxford and Cambridge record, a miserable twenty-three feet seven-and-a-quarter.'

Now it was time for Harold to face his biggest challenge of all – the 440 race against Stevenson. Abrahams was drawn on the outside, usually a disadvantage for any runner. On this occasion, it rather fitted his plan. Lanes were quickly forgotten under the rules of the day, as competitors vied for the inside track. When Harold heard the crack of the pistol, he 'at once dashed for the lead'. Abrahams had told Marshall, 'I'll go off like a dingbat for the first hundred yards.' Though it looked like a foolish rush of blood to the head from Harold, the Americans still had to quicken their pace initially. But they seemed to be caught in two minds over whether or not to cover his move.

The Oxford men knew that Marshall was the chief Cambridge threat, so to an extent they judged their reaction by his. Marshall said of Harold, 'he started the race at a very fast speed for the first 50 yards, and I didn't follow, so Stevenson was watching me as first string and hanging back with me.' One report described how, 'When Abrahams had drawn the two Oxford men after him, he dropped back . . . but lengthened his stride.' Harold had already explained this phase to Marshall, 'I'll try to slow the race down until the open straight.' He did just that, acting like a whirlwind that had blown itself out too early. That was Marshall's cue to take over. An eyewitness account described how Harold 'went wide to allow Marshall to go through, and the public thought he was finished. Stevenson, the Princeton crack, no doubt thought he was too.'

Forgetting Abrahams, Stevenson stayed with Marshall, who seemed reluctant to take the race on with any great vigour. Arthur admitted, 'Abrahams slowed the race right down until we came round the final bend when he ran wide, with a view to letting me, his first string, through; but I didn't make any effort, and Stevenson didn't make any particular effort.' At this point the American must have known that he had the measure of his chief rival. Stevenson didn't need to kick hard for home to beat Marshall; so he went into cruise control, thinking the race was won. There was no reason to consider Abrahams, who was ten yards behind at that point. The American's overconfidence was, of course, exactly what

Harold had hoped for. Marshall explained his president's strategy. 'His idea was to run wide as if to let me through, then come up on the inside, staying behind Stevenson until the last few yards. "Then," said Harold, "I'll go for it." Which he did.'

Evelyn Montague described what happened next. 'I shall never forget my feeling of incredulous horror as I stood beside the straight and watched Harold, all arms and legs, rushing past Stevenson like an animated windmill.' He caught the American about fifteen yards from the post. Reports said that '[Stevenson] couldn't hold Abrahams down the all-important final straight', where Harold 'quickly overhauled the first strings'. With a mixture of admiration and envy, Marshall explained, 'Abrahams came up with a very fast finish in the last 30 yards and won the race. Harold came first, Stevenson second, and I was third.'

The time was astonishing, and one onlooker described how Abrahams 'wore [Stevenson] the Balliol man down in the straight and finished full of running in 50.8sec, probably a second faster than he has achieved in his life.' It wasn't just the impudence Harold had shown to run away with the quarter, as second string. The time was as good as any done in the next three or four years by 'proper' 440 runners. Harold's raking stride brought him home, though in reality brains had played as big a part as pace. Having won by about three yards, the Cambridge President received a tremendous ovation, which doubled when it was known he had broken yet another record. These were, as the *Sporting Life* put it, 'superhuman efforts'. As far as the Varsity was concerned, he had gone out in a blaze of glory.

Abrahams had established a new individual record of eight inter-Varsity firsts in total. No one seemed to care that Oxford had defeated Cambridge by seven events to four. Harold had stolen the show, just as he had planned. He was the hero of the hour, and even his enemies had to admit it.

Would he have been capable of such exploits at the height of his romance with Christina? Probably not, and now she could only watch with the rest as the Queen's Club went wild. Abrahams saw through the wild celebrations: 'We all like to jump on the bandwagon. I can remember when I was carried off in my last year at Oxford and Cambridge sports noticing the sort of people who were joining in that probably hated my guts really. I wasn't a popular person in a team. I knew that and that hurt a lot.' He wasn't a popular person in Oxford's team either. Montague wrote to his mother after the race and said, 'They chaired Harold Abrahams from the track, and I was just waiting for them to drop him on his arse.'

Harold had pulled off one of the most astonishing upsets in Varsity athletics history, and made himself a media darling in the process. The *Daily Mail* concluded, 'No finer all-round performance has ever been witnessed at the Varsity Sports than Abrahams gave on Saturday.' Joe Binks in the *News of the World* insisted, 'His efforts, however, did not surprise me, for my readers know how I have always expected something sensational from this erratic athlete.' But the *Observer* couldn't resist some point-scoring when its correspondent wrote:

> A certain athletic 'authority' of Saturday morning must now be reflecting upon the performance of that 'somewhat erratic athlete', H.M. Abrahams, who, having in his three previous years succeeded in winning five events for Cambridge out of the six in which he had competed, might well be amused at the criticism that, 'for some reason or another he frequently fails to give of his best in big events'. The Light Blue President is a big man, who is at his biggest on a big occasion.

He hadn't felt like a big man when he had asked Adolphe to examine him the day before the big occasion – more like a quivering wreck. The dismissive way in which Adolphe had chastised him had snapped Harold out of it. He would always remember that five-word diagnosis: 'You bloody fool – it's nerves.' 'And it was,' Harold accepted with hindsight, 'for next afternoon was one of the most successful athletically of my career.'

Could he take that success forward and finally strike gold at the AAA Championships that summer? Time would tell, but spring offered the prospect of a much-needed rest from track and field. Harold may even have studied a little, though not as much as his former fiancée. Christina McLeod Innes was busy proving that Abrahams had not destroyed her. By the summer of 1923, she had poured heart and soul into her Russian studies – and earned a First. No woman had been awarded a First in Russian, not in the long history of Cambridge University up to that point. It seemed that she and Harold really were better off apart.

Absurdly, Christina still wasn't given a degree for all her hard work; at least not one that equated to a man's degree. Despite annual campaigning by Girton and Newnham colleges, there was no breakthrough in the battle for academic equality for women. But Christina had survived and thrived, and she would continue to do so.

Harold was destined for no such academic distinction. And later he came up with a slightly baffling explanation for not attaining a better degree. 'I got Third Class honours on both parts of the Law Tripos. I ought to have got a Second but I was top of the Third Classes in the first part of the Tripos, then they changed it to alphabetical. Yes, it was alphabetical in the second part. The first part was merit; they changed it in 1922.' Was he really suggesting that he was denied a Second because his surname started with the wrong letter? He did at least accept that he could never have emulated Christina, if only because he was too busy. 'I wouldn't have got a First because I did everything else at Cambridge – Union, College Law Society and more.'

Above all there was athletics; and Harold's batteries were well and truly recharged. On 16 June, he completed an encouraging hat-trick to win the 100 yards, 220 yards and long jump in the Midland Counties.

A few days later a Jewish organisation called the Maccabeans held a dinner in honour of Abrahams in London's Holborn. Harold spoke about running on the Sabbath – which for Jews lasts from sunset on Friday to sunset on Saturday. Far from disowning his roots, Abrahams dared to claim that he was typical of young Jewry in his general outlook; yet he was unwilling to sacrifice his athletic ambitions for the observance of strict religious laws. In fact he went so far as to say that to follow Jewish religious law would rule out athletic distinction. He pointed out that he had gained all his inter-Varsity successes on a Saturday, and that it was necessary to travel to venues on the Sabbath. Furthermore, he claimed it was not possible to observe the Jewish dietary laws and still peak when it mattered.

Harold's remarks were not designed to outrage or create conflict, rather to encourage members of the Jewish community to relax their laws sufficiently to take the opportunities which came their way, now that they had finally gained equality in English social life. And in order to emphasise that equality, Abrahams told a little white lie. He told his audience that he had encountered 'very little anti-Semitism', even though the reality was that he had been hurt and even motivated by precisely such prejudice at Repton and to a lesser extent Cambridge. Despite the fact that he later felt so strongly about the anti-Semitism he had suffered that he wanted to speak and write about it several times, he chose to play down the problem for his Jewish audience. Perhaps he was conscious that many members of that audience had probably faced far worse anti-Semitism than anything he had known. So Harold simply explained that anti-Semitism was 'foreign to all sportsmen and thinking people'. Therefore he didn't see the need for Jewish public schools, as had been proposed, and gave the impression that life had been just fine for him at Repton. Abrahams took this conciliatory line, not just because he had embraced Christianity at university, something he wasn't anxious to share with the Maccabeans; more because he believed it to be in the best interests of the Jewish community to be flexible and open to the ways of others. That way Jews would not deny themselves the best opportunities in life.

Given the rigid Sabbatarian beliefs of a Christian called Eric Liddell, who was about to become Harold's sprint rival, the timing of Abrahams' speech to the Maccabeans was ironic. The first meeting between Harold and Liddell on an athletics track was less than a fortnight away. Before that, and just three days after his controversial remarks to his Jewish audience, Harold won three more events – 100 and 220 yards and long jump – in the first English Closed Championships.

These performances appeared to provide a perfect platform for success at the AAA championships at Stamford Bridge on July 6 and 7. By then, however, people had begun to talk of a new talent, a human whirlwind from Scotland. Eric Liddell came south with a great reputation, having won a number of big competitions in his home country. Versatile Liddell had even gained a Scottish cap as a rugby wing-three-quarter. But Harold didn't think this stocky newcomer could match his own class; and the Englishman felt that his own championships were going to plan when he won his 220 yards heat in 22.4.

Then he witnessed the Scottish storm, ugly and brutal in its force. Harold recalled:

> The first time I ever set eyes upon Liddell was when I watched him in a heat of the 220 yards at the AAA Championships in 1923. No runner of his superb ability ever possessed a worse style. Liddell had a style which was a complete model of everything that should not be done. It was unorthodox in the extreme. Head back, arms all over the place, and an exaggerated knee drive. There was hardly anything about his knee movements that would commend itself to the experienced onlooker. Indeed, my reaction on seeing him perform for the first time was that I was witnessing the most misplaced direction of energy I had ever imagined possible. But my goodness for energy and determination he was second to none.

Though it was strange to see a man throw his head back so far as he ran,

Abrahams may have been doing Liddell – the man he somewhat disparagingly called 'the human spider' – a slight disservice. The 21-year-old Scotsman was deceptively compact, and his balance remained unaffected by his idiosyncratic running style – otherwise he would have found it impossible to run so fast. One English reporter who witnessed the Scotsman's running at those Championships insisted:

> His style is splendid, for he is quick into his running, has a rare stride, and puts all his strength into the race. In the 220 yards he threw his head back in the last 60 yards, seemed to close his eyes, and yet ran as straight as a barrel, with unwavering resoluteness. There are those who thought that he wobbled, but he was in perfect alignment with his strings [lane].

Contrary to popular belief, the Scotsman had a coach, Tom McKerchar. Liddell's mentor, a printer from Edinburgh, was no fool; and Eric often paid tribute to the 46-year-old. In fact he put much of his success down to the training regime his coach had devised. Whatever the aesthetic imperfections of Liddell's style, it worked for him – and McKerchar already understood that.

Despite Liddell's brilliance, Abrahams remained confident that his more logical technique would carry the day against the Scottish upstart over any sprint distance. The semi-final of the 220 yards would give the Englishman the chance to establish his superiority, and expose Liddell's limitations. And when the race was done, one man's limitations were indeed exposed – though not Liddell's. Harold wrote, 'I realised his power to the full when I had a back view of him in the semi-final of that 220 later that same evening. I ran against him, was well and truly beaten up and did not reach the final.'

That simple account doesn't tell the full story of July 6, 1923. When Eric Liddell tore up the field and hit the tape in a record 21.6sec, Abrahams only clocked 22.0sec. The Englishman was a good four yards behind the 'Flying Scotsman'. But a report in *The Times* the following day stated that Abrahams dead-heated with William Nichol as fastest loser. The pair 'would have had to run it off in order to decide who should compete in the final'. Already 'beaten up' and facing another drubbing should he win through to be exposed to Liddell's searing pace again, 'Abrahams withdrew'.

Harold clearly didn't fancy his chances over 220 yards that day; but would the next 24 hours bring Abrahams revenge over the Scot in the 100 yards? In a radio interview much later, Harold explained what happened – and, more to the point, what didn't happen:

> I never ran against Eric Liddell in a 100. I think I was a better sprinter than him actually, although he did win the AAA Championship in 1923 in 9.7! But so far as one can compare people . . . I didn't get in the final actually. I had a bad throat and by the time I'd run two rounds of the 100 and one of the 220 I'd sort of shaken off my bad throat and I long-jumped 23ft 8¾in. Much to my sadness I failed to beat the Championship best performance by less than an inch.

Ah, the 'sore throat' again. Hadn't we heard that excuse a few months earlier, when Harold didn't feel as though he could face his responsibilities in the showdown against Oxford? He had complained of a 'ghastly sore throat', only to be told by his brother Adolphe that he had never been fitter in his life. Now Abrahams was effectively asking us to believe that his 'bad throat' caused him so much loss of form and speed that he failed to qualify for either sprint final, where Liddell would have been waiting. Then, miraculously, he shook off that sore throat so successfully that he suddenly found enough speed to make a British record-breaking leap into the long-jump pit.

A photograph shows Harold achieving an almost superhuman height as he flies through the air. The optical illusion sees his spikes hanging way above the sand-pit at the level of the judges' heads; and his head is up in the sky above the grandstand. You wonder how such athletic magnificence could have been achieved by a man who could barely swallow moments earlier. Mysterious indeed.

If he dared to watch the 100 yards final at 3.40 p.m., Harold probably did so with a blend of envy and relief. Had he been out on the track, he would surely have been burnt away by Liddell's pace in the hot sun. That winning time of 9.7sec gave Eric a new British record, which was to stand for thirty-five years. Abrahams never entirely believed what Eric had done.

Many years later, Harold wrote:

> I do not wish at this time to doubt the splendid ability of Eric as a sprinter, but quite frankly, I have always been a little sceptical about that British record. No reasonable criticism can be directed against the time-keeping, but both [his fellow finalists] Nichol and

Matthewman were within striking distance of Liddell and must have done 9.8 performances themselves. And they neither of them ever produced a performance really comparable before or after. Both these latter were good sprinters in their way, but they were never really in the front rank. Conditions that afternoon were exceptionally good and the record remains in the statute book. No one will begrudge Liddell his record, but I shall never believe he was a better sprinter than Willie Applegarth or Harry Edward.

Mel Watman, doyen of athletics statisticians and a man who learned his trade directly from Abrahams, admired Harold but didn't agree with him on this one controversial issue. Watman explained, 'He never accepted Liddell's 9.7 and I think that was less than generous from Harold. My view is that it may have been a case of sour grapes on Harold's part, with Liddell stealing his thunder at the distance "HMA" regarded as his territory.'

The three official watches registered Liddell's time at 9.67, 9.65 and 9.65 – and were therefore all rounded up to 9.7 under the rules of the day. A fourth, unofficial watch showed 9.62 – just two hundredths of a second outside the world record of 9.6. According to John W. Keddie, Liddell's biographer, 'Harold Abrahams afterwards cast doubt on the performance on the grounds that the starting line had been largely obliterated by distance runners.' Liddell explained his amazing breakthrough like this: 'The weather was perfect for short-distance running – very hot. Heat makes the muscles loose, so that there was no need for massage.'

The Scotsman's personal best for 100 yards before that day was 10.0sec – and he never broke ten seconds again. Then again, he didn't have many chances to do so, and British conditions were rarely if ever quite so inviting. Watman reflected, 'Progressing from 10 to 9.7 in one day is pretty remarkable, but then Liddell was running in good weather on a much better track than he was used to in Scotland.'

The conspiracy theory – that Abrahams had been running scared of Liddell at Stamford Bridge – was lightly aired in the *Daily Telegraph* just two weeks after the AAA meet. By then Abrahams had rediscovered his track form so convincingly that, 'one wonders how he came to fail in the AAA Championship. His own view may be that he met his master in the Scottish champion, E.H. Liddell, and that may be true, but on Saturday's running, he should have been fighting out the finish a fortnight earlier.'

When he looked back, Harold didn't think he had 'met his master', despite his confession that he had been 'well and truly beaten up' by Liddell in the 220. Indeed by missing the final showdowns with Liddell he was able to argue precisely the opposite over the years: that he was superior over the shorter sprint distances when it mattered. Much later, Abrahams claimed again, 'At this long distance [of time] from the actual event I can perhaps say, without seeming too self-centred, that I believe I was, in fact, better than Eric over 100 metres.'

It was an honest opinion, though controversial. The fans were denied the chance to find out for sure. We can accuse Harold of losing his nerve – or we can salute his tactical wisdom. By avoiding Liddell in the finals at the AAA Championship, Abrahams didn't lose face. He managed to steer clear of what would surely have constituted a psychologically damaging defeat. Fear may have motivated Harold on that English summer's day. But some would say there is nothing wrong with fear, if it helps common sense to prevail.

What times could Abrahams and Liddell have achieved, had they pushed each other in the 100 yards or 100 metres over two or three summers between 1923 and 1925? Could their rivalry have rewritten the record books further still? We will never know. After Eric's breakthrough summer south of the border their paths didn't cross again for another year. On July 14, there was a Triangular International at Stoke between England, Scotland and Ireland. Harold was rested so that he could be fully fit to run the following Saturday for Oxford and Cambridge against Harvard and Yale in London. In Stoke, Liddell won the 100, 220 yards and quarter mile. But it was the way in which he won the longer contest that became the stuff of legend. And what Eric did was arguably even more extraordinary than his 9.7 in London.

The *Scotsman* newspaper wrote:

> The circumstances in which he won the 440 event made it a performance bordering on the miraculous. Veterans, whose memories take them back thirty-five years, and in some cases even longer, in the history of athletics, were unanimous in the opinion that Liddell's win in the quarter mile was the greatest track performance they had ever seen. The runners were started on the bend, Liddell having the inside berth, but the Scot had only taken three strides when Gillis, England, crashed into him and knocked him off the track. He stumbled on the grass, and for a moment seemed half-inclined to give up. Then suddenly he sprang forward, and was after

his opponents in a flash. By this time the leaders were twenty yards ahead, but Liddell gradually drew up on them, and by the time the home straight was reached he was running fourth. He would be about ten yards behind Gillis then. It seemed out of the question he would win, but he achieved the apparently impossible. Forty yards from home he was third and seemed on the point of collapsing, but pulling himself together he put in a desperate finish to win two yards from Gillis.

He had won the 440 in 51.2sec after being knocked off the track. It was so remarkable that observers were convinced he had broken 49sec for the time he had actually spent running. The Flying Scotsman, who believed his talent and determination were God-given, seemed invincible.

CHAPTER NINE

GREAT BIRD AND OLD SAM

Eric Liddell's superhuman performances called for a swift reply from Harold Abrahams. His chance came the following weekend, by which time his batteries were fully recharged. The occasion would also provide an opportunity for revenge against Harvard and Yale, the American universities which had so outclassed their Oxbridge visitors two years earlier.

The venue in north-west London was new; it was called Wembley Stadium. The Duke of York – the future King George VI – was in an enthusiastic crowd of 10,000, which included many Americans. The stage was set and fit for a hero, though the English couldn't have felt excessively optimistic that he would emerge from their ranks. They hadn't won this contest since 1911.

Harold began his day by trying to win the 100 yards. His American opponents were 'the Yale crack', W.A. Comins, and E.J. Rusnak, almost as highly rated. In the opening phase of the race there was nothing to choose between the runners. But it was reported that a 'ghost of daylight' opened up between Harold and the rest of the field at 30 yards. His lead became more pronounced at 60 yards; and there was no way back for his rivals when he came 'whirling down the track like a human windmill', as the *Daily News* put it. According to the *Daily Telegraph*, Abrahams 'ran at such a tremendous pace for the last half of the journey that he made the Americans, both credited with "evens" over the water, look like "platers".' He won by three yards in even time to send out a clear message: the English did not intend to suffer fresh humiliation.

Later in the afternoon, Harold's problem was not so much the strength of his opponents as the impossibility of being in two places at the same time. His second event was the long jump; and the Americans seemed more than happy when the schedule was thrown into chaos. The allocated time for the 220 yards, the climax to the entire contest, was drawing near. An anxious Harold began to feel pulled in different directions. *The Times* reported, 'The long-jump was interrupted by various races, by photographs, by innocent bandsmen returning from a well-earned tea, by pole-jumpers who wanted to land almost on long-jumpers' toes. Abrahams looked restive and no wonder, with the 220 yards coming nearer and nearer. He deemed it wise to miss his last jump and have a little peace.' Harold had already jumped 22ft 9¾in, a couple of inches better than W.A. Comins.

However, as the *Daily Telegraph* pointed out, missing his last jump was easier said than done. 'When he was retiring, someone insisted that an agreement had been come to that each man should have six jumps, and after some delay, a further round commenced.' This was the last thing Harold needed – which was probably why the Americans insisted upon it. Harold used his anger positively on the runway to launch himself with a vengeance. He produced a winning jump, as the report noted: 'The Cambridge man cleared 23ft 2¼in and then withdrew to the dressing room to prepare for the 220 yards . . . The rest continued, but Comins did not beat his earlier jump . . . I think conditions were against jumping, which made Abrahams' effort all the more remarkable.'

The match was a tie going into the final event. Everything depended upon who would hold his nerve and find his speed when it really mattered in the 220 yards. This was to be a straight run, starting just outside the stadium. The athletes were to pass immediately into a tunnel under the stands. And after 100 yards of secret warfare, they would burst out on to the main track and conclude their battle in front of the fans. *The Times* set the scene nicely. Now came the tremendous moment when the four sprinters vanished into the tunnel for the start of the 220 yards. There was a dreadful pause, a muffled thud, and then – nothing. It was a false start.' With so much riding on the race and the crowd desperate to see the drama unfold, the tension only increased. 'Another pause and at last a loud bang,' after what 'seemed almost an eternity to the waiting spectators'.

The Times writer Bernard Darwin captured the moment memorably: 'A moment's agony, and then there was Abrahams scudding along like some great bird, with a four-yard lead. He went further and further in front, running superbly.'

The *Morning Post* described the reaction of the crowd to this surreal moment. 'Abrahams came out fast, having apparently lost or mislaid his rivals . . . winning so easily that the race had a ludicrous aspect, and caused as much laughter as cheering . . . Eric Liddell, the Flying Scotchman, would have found him a very difficult proposition in the longer sprint had the twain met on Saturday afternoon.'

When Harold hit the tape in 21.6, upright but perfectly relaxed, he was so far ahead that the next best sprinter was barely in sight.

Since 1919, Harold Abrahams had been the leading light in Oxbridge athletics. Now, as one newspaper put it, this 'was a fitting farewell to a distinguished university career'. He could hardly have chosen a more dramatic way to leave his Cambridge days behind. For Harold, it was a sweet moment. 'We got our revenge against Harvard and Yale for the awful hiding they had given us two years earlier. We won by 6½ events to 5½ at Wembley.'

Harold soon received a royal seal of approval. One account described how 'everybody was pleased when the Duke of York called him out of his prompt retirement among the spectators to receive a warm handclasp and words of hearty congratulation.' Even the Americans joined in the ovation for the Cambridge hero.

Harold had matched Liddell's Stamford Bridge time of 21.6 in his final appearance of the year, though the Englishman hadn't been required to negotiate a bend. The *Daily Telegraph* could already see what such scintillating form might mean for Harold and his country the following summer. 'His achievement assures us of the promise, all being well, of a superb athlete in the English [sic] Olympic team in Paris next year.' Abrahams, however, was a perfectionist. And he knew there was much work to be done before he could consider himself a true contender for the Olympics. 'I realised about nine months before the Games that some effort such as I had never made before would be necessary if I was to do at all well in Paris. Before I had trained reasonably hard – as hard as most people, I think, but now we were up against a really tough proposition, and no stone must be left unturned which could in any way contribute to a success.'

Cambridge runner Arthur Marshall recalled:

Liddell's achievement in winning the 1923 AAA 100 yards in the record time of 9.7 seconds was a devastating blow to Abrahams and shook him to the core. To date Abrahams had been a consistent ten seconds 100 yards winner but had only slightly broken 10 seconds on one or two occasions. He knew in the Olympics he would be up against overseas competition, particularly from the Americans, but this new and very serious opposition out of the blue and on his doorstep had come at a time when Harold had established his 100 yards supremacy in the UK.

Liddell was likely to be an even more devastating force of nature the following year, because he came to a difficult decision regarding his rugby career. Harold Abrahams explained, 'He wisely abstained from playing Rugby Football during the winter of 1923–24 for fear of sustaining an injury, a very real possibility in the case of such a speedy performer.'

With Eric's sporting focus now exclusively on the track, Harold was going to have to do something pretty dramatic in order to keep pace. He would do whatever it took. His adopted son Alan pointed out, 'When he was younger my father was extremely ambitious and focused. He was hard-working, and he wanted to win. At that time he was very driven.' And there was an older man who was equally driven – a man Abrahams had known about for a very long time. Ambition told Abrahams what to do next. Deep down, you suspect, he had always known.

The surprising thing was not that Harold Abrahams teamed up with Sam Mussabini, a man from a lower social class, in October 1923. It was more remarkable that they hadn't teamed up before. Cambridge University, and the way it frowned upon professionalism, had probably been a crucial factor. Given the way Harold's recruitment of Mussabini was portrayed in *Chariots of Fire*, this is a little ironic. In the film they team up during his student days to defy university traditionalists who still favour a more relaxed amateur ethos. In reality, Abrahams conformed slightly more to the Cambridge sporting philosophy than *Chariots* would have us believe. Though he had demonstrated an intensity of training that left many of his fellow students uncomfortable, he didn't go so far as to employ a professional coach. Now that his Cambridge career was over, Harold felt free to do just that, knowing full well that his obsession with self-discipline would be taken to a new and even more punishing place. If Mussabini could give him the edge over Liddell and an outside chance against the brilliant Americans, the pain would be worth it.

Mussabini had spent most of his fifty-six years searching for coaching perfection. Every aspect of athletics was given careful thought. But then attention to detail had always been important in his family. Mussabini's great-grandfather, a Syrian merchant from Damascus who traded with Trieste in Italy, had shown similar awareness. Assessing his situation in a cut-throat world, he had decided to take the Italian-sounding Mussabini surname for commercial reasons. When you are prepared to break from the past to succeed in a competitive environment, and even change your identity, it says something about your will to win in life.

Even so, the next generation of Mussabinis faced fresh challenges when they moved to London. Harold's future coach was the fourth of six children, born in 1867. His father, Neocles Gaspard Mussabini, was a member of the Diplomatic Service, a war correspondent, a journalist and an author. His mother was Aline, whose family traded in cattle in the Grenoble area of southern France. Born Scipio Arnaud Godolphin Mussabini, he decided at some point to drop his two middle names and replace them with 'Africanus'. Then he simply used his latest initials to form the name 'Sam'.

Most of his school years were spent in France. But he returned to England in the 1880s and became interested in the professional athletes of the London League. Tom McNab, an ex-athlete, coach and long-time historian of the sport, said of Mussabini, 'He came from the traditions of professional running, the lore and mystique of the old "pro" racers of the nineteenth century. He knew the likes of Harry Hutchens and much of what he had learned came from that era.'

He didn't just know the great Hutchens, he coached him. Harold Abrahams later described Hutchens as 'the Jesse Owens of his day', and with good reason. Hutchens, a professional sprinter from London, ran the 100 yards in 9.75 seconds and 300 yards in 30 seconds. These were extraordinary times given that Hutchens raced between the 1870s and early 1890s, using a standing start. He became known as the 'Fastest Man on Earth'.

Mussabini had also been a talented sprinter, footballer and cricketer. But his biggest talent lay in observing and improving upon the strengths and weaknesses in others. The mechanics of running fascinated Sam, and he began to develop training ideas based on the science of the body. Later he was almost apologetic about his brilliance and admitted, 'Quite possibly, I rely too much on what may be obtained by close observance and experimentation with the main motive parts of the human engine. This, no doubt, is my own personal kink.'

So was his hatred of the word 'trainer', which was often used to describe him at the time. 'I'm not a trainer,' he insisted. 'A trainer is a man who comes on with a bag and a little sponge. I'm a coach.' Whatever people called him, Mussabini's reputation began to build through the 1890s. But he was in demand with cyclists as much as runners. At the Herne Hill track he trained Bert Harris of the Polytechnic Cycling Club – and helped him win the national championships over one mile in 1894. Two years later Mussabini was appointed as trainer to the Dunlop cycling team, based at Crystal Palace. Athletics and cycling weren't his only passions, though. His love of sport stretched to billiards, which he played and wrote about with great enthusiasm. He penned a definitive book – *Billiard Player* – in 1897. By 1910 he was also editor of a magazine called *New World of Billiards* – and he went on to referee top matches.

Gradually, however, athletics began to take priority. And Mussabini's stock soared further still when he coached that young South African sprinter Reggie Walker to an Olympic gold medal in London in 1908. Walker, from Durban, remained the twentieth century's youngest winner of an Olympic 100 metres title. He achieved the feat at the tender age of nineteen. It was almost uncanny the way everyone Mussabini touched with his sporting philosophies turned to gold, silver or bronze. Mostly, it was gold.

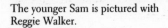

The younger Sam is pictured with Reggie Walker.

Mister Meticulous: the hats may have changed as the years passed, but the intensity in Sam's deep-set eyes didn't.

The following year Walker wrote, 'During my stay in England I have been trained by Sam Wisdom, who is famous as the trainer of the great Harry Hutchens – the greatest phenomenal sprinter of all time – from whom I have gleaned so much information concerning the methods of the professional sprinters.'

Sam Wisdom was a fitting alias for a man whose professional background meant it was sometimes safer for his athletes if he went by another name. After all, an athlete's disqualification from amateur events, as punishment for using a professional coach, must have remained a subconscious fear. At best a close association with a known professional could cause an athlete discomfort when they met with amateur officials. The 'Wisdom' alias provided the perfect smokescreen. If any single word summed up Mussabini, 'wisdom' was it.

His first book on athletics, *The Complete Trainer*, came out in 1913, though he was wise enough to realise that his knowledge would never be complete as such. He was learning all the time, and carefully studied scientific works on animal and human movement. He used the latest technology – moving pictures – to show his athletes what they were doing well and where their precious energy was being wasted. His achievements with Harry Edward, Abrahams' nemesis at the AAA Championships, were extraordinary.

No wonder Harold, whose previous allegiance had been towards the London Athletic Club, nailed his colours to the mast of the Polytechnic Harriers in order to secure Mussabini's services. As for Old Sam, he couldn't wait to work with the young man he had first come across when Harold was barely a teenager. Mussabini's moustache was much tidier these days, and his hair a little greyer; but his ambition had not been blunted by time.

Harold recalled, 'Mussabini was an absolute fanatic, a marvellous man. From the very first we plotted a plan of campaign. Sam told me that if I would put myself in his care and carry out his advice, he would make me an Olympic sprint champion. I laughed at the idea.'

Abrahams may have laughed, but Mussabini had his undivided attention from that very moment. In a sense Old Sam had replaced Christina McLeod Innes at the centre of Harold's world. There was no time for a personal life. Abrahams was ready to make all the necessary sacrifices, though he knew it wouldn't be easy. 'In the winter I went through some hard, conscientious training,' he remembered.

Norris McWhirter wrote later of how 'he could be seen with Mussabini working on his start and finish at Paddington Recreation Ground, or for a change of scene at Queen's Club or the old White City track.'

Mussabini didn't bawl at his athlete like a sergeant major. This was not the sort of motivation Harold needed or was looking for. Harold explained: 'He didn't motivate me, it was a very polite relationship. He always called me Mr Abrahams and seemed to have a great respect for me. He was a fanatic on arm action and I think he was right. We worked together a great deal.' When that work became tedious, Harold drove himself on. He decided, 'The really important factor is the will and determination to win – the power to stick to it when you are feeling like it and when you are not. This is the real essential for success.'

And on the rare occasions Harold didn't want to work, Mussabini didn't chastise him. Instead he adopted a milder approach. The older man wrote, 'If there is a falling away, a few words of calling attention to the importance of regularity, punctuality, etc., appeal to me as being better suited to bring about what is required than any unpleasant comments or strictures will ever do.'

There was room for the occasional compromise. By now Harold was living with his mother at 2 Hodford Road in Golders Green; and he revealed how his little back garden sometimes became his urban training ground. 'Occasionally, I would change and trot about my garden at home (which comprises a piece of grass about twelve yards square) simply because I was getting on edge and it was unwise to go to the track.'

Though Mussabini remained patient and polite, Abrahams couldn't always say the same. If he felt the need to challenge his coach's ideas, Harold did so:

I got a great deal of satisfaction from arguing with him, because I always believed and I say to people now: don't accept what a coach says because he is experienced. There is too much of this 'do it because I say so'. Argue with him because you'll do it much better if you are convinced it is right. Of course the fallacy of that argument is that there is no one road to success. I thought for myself. I argued with Sam if I differed with him. I said so. Every suggestion for improvement, every speculation as to what would be best, we argued out together, sometimes not without heat, but always with the best thought at our command. The part of a trainer should be to advise and correct. Any coach worthy of the name should be able to give reasons for everything he advises and suggests.

Tom McNab, a former national coach who worked as a consultant for *Chariots of Fire*, once said of the Abrahams–Mussabini dynamic, 'It was almost a master–servant relationship.' That sounds a little too simplistic, though Harold's nephew Tony Abrahams agreed that there was never the sort of intimacy you find in an equal partnership. 'What can you say about a trainer? Harold used Mussabini to professional good. He didn't worship him. He thought he was a first-class trainer and so it turned out.'

Old Sam knew how to stand his ground without antagonising his paymaster. When Mussabini suggested that the 220 yards be put to one side, it prompted a careful cross-examination from Abrahams, the trainee lawyer. But Harold soon saw sense in the strategy and wrote, 'We believed that it would be unwise to train for 220 yards as well as 100 yards, considering that longer distance is apt to take the edge, which is so important, off the performances over the shorter distance.'

Before he could sharpen his competitive edge, Abrahams had to get his basic action right. And through the winter Mussabini used thousands of feet of cine-film to study that action in slow motion and improve it. Abrahams spent about six months, from October until March, trying to perfect the various components of his style. Two or three of these were devoted to sharpening his reaction time to the starter's pistol and finding the right body-shape to make his first, vital strides.

Harold explained his routine:

> On a typical day's outing I made half a dozen starts from the holes, employing the 'slow cinematograph' method. By photographing movements at the rate of about 150 exposures per second, and throwing the film on to the screen at the normal rate of sixteen per second, we are enabled to see all movement analysed down to a series of primary actions. These actions as seen by the eye are not a series of jerks, but each action links up with the next, giving a harmonious, if uncanny whole.

Once Abrahams had studied his action carefully on screen, he applied the same slow-motion technique to his practical work. 'I tried to perform each movement of starting as slowly as possible. I moved not in a series of jerks, but performed the actions in the same way as I would when at full speed. I found that this enabled me to acquire the habit of good form, whereas if one always practises at full speed one is apt to acquire bad habits which are difficult to eradicate.'

It was, Harold admitted, 'a monotonous business', yet there were ways to fight the boredom and reduce lateral movement at the same time. He later talked of 'the importance in running of getting one's feet as near as possible one in front of the other – you can't do it actually, completely. I used to put bits of paper down on the track and pick them up with my spikes, but it was partly a gimmick to interest me.'

Abrahams had to put to one side the fact that Eric Liddell was almost a freak of physics. Harold knew he couldn't be wild-limbed and win like Liddell, though there was at least some scope for personal choice of style:

> One is driven to the belief that provided a style is not based on principles which are obviously contrary to the known laws of movement, it may well suit a particular individual, though it be recognised as unorthodox. I myself adopted a sprinting action which involved movement of the arms across the body. Most American coaches urge the cultivation of a piston-like arm movement. In the face of first-class exponents of both schools, it is absurd for anyone to protest that one is right and the other is wrong. Both styles possess very strong reasons for their adoption.

If anyone doubted how important arm action was to a sprinter, Harold had a simple challenge for them. He explained: 'Few people appreciate what an enormous part the arms play in sprinting. In fact they control the action of the legs. Try this experiment after your cold bath tomorrow morning. Walk along the road without using your arms at all. Suddenly bring the arms into play and increase the rapidity with which you move them. You will find it impossible to move the arms more rapidly without the legs following suit.'

Abrahams became a willing Mussabini disciple partly because so many of his own ideas matched those of his teacher. He had already realised the importance of indoor exercises, and Mussabini's routine merely complemented and extended Harold's. Looking back on that tough winter, he pointed out that the hard work didn't start or finish at the track, 'All this time I had been doing home exercises. Night and morning indoors.'

This was something he had done at Cambridge. According to Harold, any athlete could benefit from looking at his own reflection – a task Abrahams had never found too irksome. He later advised, 'Exercises in front of a mirror are designed to produce improvement in form and in control at slow speed.'

He would strip down to his pants and pick up a pair of running corks, which were circular pieces of cork, 'about as long as the hand is broad', as one writer put it. Sprinters gripped one in each hand 'for an exertion of will-power'. Harold explained, 'They tend to steady the arm action and enable one to keep the arms in the correct position . . . Where an extra effort becomes necessary, as it often does at the end of a desperately fought race, it is undoubtedly helpful to be able to grip something hard.' After warming up in front of his mirror, Harold would gradually move more quickly, until he felt ready to 'sprint' all out for ten seconds on the spot. Then he would pound the floor twenty-five times with each foot to signify fifty strides, before easing off again.

When Harold wasn't busy impressing himself in the mirror, he wasn't averse to showing off in more public surroundings, especially in London. He easily conveyed the boyish thrill of his athleticism when he wrote mischievously:

> A large part of training for sprinting consists of doing quickening exercises. One of the best is to run up a long flight of stairs a step at a time as fast as one can, being careful to keep good form. To race up a flight of stairs like this is highly stimulating. If the authorities in the Underground are not about, the pleasure of this exercise is considerably increased by running up the moving stairway which is descending. Nothing can be better than to ascend the moving stairway in this way, but you are particularly requested to avoid the rush-hours.

Such stunts were likely to impress women too, though they would have been less attracted to Harold's underwear had they glimpsed it. He revealed, 'Always go out for your training spins warmly clad. I have found long woollen pants an excellent garment for this purpose, even if not a becoming one.'

Running dominated Harold's thoughts, whether at home, on the underground or out on the track. At meal times he didn't eat excessively, but neither did he imagine for a moment that what he ate would in itself bring him victory. The key to success, he concluded, wasn't so much a punishing diet as sensible, regular eating, advice suggested to him by Adolphe who also stressed the importance of 'regular visits to the dentist and lavatory', simple habits which Harold credited with keeping him free from muscle tears.

Everything was geared to racing, and it was a wonder he had time for any legal studies at all. Somehow he managed to cope with those too, though he admitted the intellectual challenge wasn't what it might have been. He said later: 'I was reading for the Bar – and I was very anxious indeed to compete in the Olympics of 1924. In those days, quite frankly the [Bar] examination was not very, very difficult. It's much stiffer these days. If you had a Law degree at Cambridge, you ought to be able to get through, with very little extra work. I was also working in a solicitor's office to get some experience of the practical side of the Bar.'

Refusing to put all his eggs in one basket, he kept up his journalism too. And there was an exciting new area to explore in this fast-evolving field. Radio had begun to cover sport, though never live, and broadcasters weren't yet sure quite how to do it. So Abrahams wrote to the BBC and said he would like to talk about athletics on air. He soon received a reply, which asked him whether he was the same Mr Abrahams who had run so well for Oxford and Cambridge against Harvard and Yale. Able to confirm that he was indeed that Mr Abrahams, he was given his big chance in front of the studio microphone.

Harold's first broadcast for the BBC was on March 15, 1924, in the days when the corporation was based at Savoy Hill. The *Radio Times* scheduled fifteen minutes, between 9.45 and 10 p.m. under the title: 'Harold Abrahams, the famous runner, on Should sport be taken seriously?' His conclusion, of course, was that it should. These fifteen minutes heralded a BBC career which would last for an extraordinary fifty years.

Had Eric Liddell shared that broadcast time, he would have agreed with the verdict on sport, as long as he could add that other matters should be taken more seriously still. His priorities were about to become clear. On March 22, 1924, the Olympic schedule for the Paris Olympics was published. The heats for the 100 metres were to be run on a Sunday in the first week of July. From that moment, it was only a matter of time before Eric Liddell's religious faith would cause him to pull out of the blue-riband event.

He didn't desert the 100 just yet. In his book *Running the Race: Eric Liddell – Champion and Missionary*, John W. Keddie explained that Eric was invited to join Oxford and Cambridge athletes at the University of Pennsylvania Relay Festival – known simply as the Penn Relays. These took place on April 25 and April 26. Keddie claims that 'two individual sprint events had been specially arranged to accommodate the flying Scot'. If this is correct, they may have been arranged before Liddell realised that the Olympic sprints demanded Sunday racing. Eric would have been reluctant to pull out of races organised for his benefit. So he went on the trip anyway, and hoped to use the experience to his advantage.

Veteran athletics journalist Mel Watman claimed, 'The American races were sharpeners for Liddell. He knew he wouldn't be running 100 metres in Paris (nor either of the relays as the heats were also on a Sunday).' But perhaps he hadn't yet made a definitive decision; and if he hadn't, the American trip would help him to do so.

Seasickness hit Liddell hard on the outward voyage, though he was able to make a good recovery in the team's comfortable base at the Pennsylvania Cricket Club. Soon he was ready for the 100 yards, which proved a close-run affair. Only inches separated the first four men. Chester Bowman from Syracuse broke the tape in 10.0. Unfortunately Liddell was fourth in an estimated 10.1. He did better in the 220 yards, but was beaten again – this time even more narrowly – by Louis Clarke of Johns Hopkins University in a time of 21.6.

These were still good performances, given the stresses of the voyage. Harold Abrahams wrote generously about Liddell's defeats at the time. He argued, 'E.H. Liddell, the AAA sprint champion, was fourth in the 100 yards and second in the 220 yards at the Penn meeting. The time for the latter event was 21.6secs, and if one considers that Liddell cannot have been able to do much sharpening up so early on, this augurs well for his performances in June and July.' And Arthur Marshall pointed out, 'None of us won an event at the Pennsylvania Games.'

But Chester Bowman and Louis Clarke weren't the fastest Americans around. Charley Paddock and Jackson Scholz hadn't even been racing, yet Liddell had still only finished fourth. Despite the narrow margin of defeat, his chances of Olympic gold in the 100 metres suddenly seemed that little bit more remote. It wasn't hard for Eric to follow his conscience after the results in Pennsylvania.

Arthur Marshall, who would go on to become a Great Britain reserve at the 1924 Games, revealed:

> On the boat back, Eric and I became close friends. Eric was very strict about religion, but he was no prude and joined in all the fun

and games on board, including the fancy dress dance. We played cards and mah-jong with two American sisters who were 'doing Europe' and going to the Olympic Games in Paris. Eric and I said, 'If we get into the team, we'll see you there.' Actually Liddell had realised after the Pennsylvania Games that he couldn't win the 100 metres and this may have contributed to his famous withdrawal. The problem wasn't simply that the race fell on the Sabbath.

Doug Gillon, athletics correspondent of the *Herald* in Scotland, also claimed later, 'Eric might still have had designs on the 100 metres, but his fourth place in the 100 yards at the Penn Relays in spring 1924 surely put these prospects in perspective.' There is little doubt that Liddell would have sacrificed the Sunday races anyway. But the strength and depth shown by the Americans in Pennsylvania was almost frightening, and would hardly have left Abrahams feeling any more confident about his own chances. Perhaps those halcyon Cambridge days would represent the peak of his athletic achievement after all.

CHAPTER TEN

BRAINSTORM
AT THE BRIDGE

Looking back, Harold Abrahams hinted at a sense of relief when he realised that Eric Liddell's Sabbatarian beliefs had effectively removed a rival. Harold said:

> I was lucky in the sense that Eric Liddell, who had set up a British record the previous year, felt with his strong religious conviction that he oughtn't to run on a Sunday. The heats of the 100 metres in the Olympic Games were scheduled to take place on a Sunday and Liddell was always rigorously opposed to Sunday competition. The same considerations prevented his selection in the 400m [4 × 100m] relay and incidentally in the 1600 metres [4 × 400m] relay as well.

On a spiritual level, Abrahams was now closer to Christianity than Judaism. But he wasn't about to allow any 'strong religious conviction' to mess with his Olympic Games. Neither could career considerations cause him any further distraction.

Not a man who liked to be considered third rate at anything, Harold nevertheless had to face facts when, on April 30, 1924 he received news of his legal qualification. He passed the Examination for Call to the Bar, but was placed 'in the Third Class'. Had he been tested on the scientific theory behind sprinting and human locomotion, he would have earned first-class honours. But Harold knew the certificate didn't spell disaster. He already had the right contacts to make a career in law; and now he had the basic qualification too. Best of all, he could forget legal matters for a while, and focus all his energies on his true passion, athletics.

He was at the business end of his nine-month training schedule with Sam Mussabini. It would soon be time to find out whether all that hard work had been worth it. Harold explained, 'The months of April, May and June were the months in which serious training was embarked upon. From April 1924 onwards I was training three times each week and competition itself began in the first week of May.'

New Zealand sprinter Arthur Porritt, another Olympic contender that year, claimed:

> His training methods were way ahead of their time. They were absolutely unknown and I couldn't help admiring the way he trained, practised, dieted, did this, didn't do that, just to keep fit. This was entirely out of keeping with the spirit of the time. Harold was almost professional, though obviously not to the extent of receiving remuneration. For the rest of us, our training, by later standards, would make people laugh. A few hours on a Sunday morning, perhaps a few starts, a couple of hundred yards and some chatting. Harold was training long hours three or four times a week.

The pressure was on Abrahams. What an embarrassment it would be for an athlete to have worked so obsessively all winter, only for more casual rivals to beat him in the summer. He would soon find out if his underlying fears were founded. Meanwhile his fitness regime changed slightly to take in the imminence of competition. With a race beckoning every Saturday and training sessions on Tuesdays and Thursdays, Harold didn't want to risk burnout now. The hard work had been done.

Abrahams and Mussabini concentrated instead on perfecting a technique still used today by any sprinter hoping to steal a few inches at the tape. Harold claimed, 'I started the drop finish.' That was debatable, for the American Arthur Duffey had invented 'the lunge', which wasn't so different, at the start of the century. Harold's finish was arguably sharper, more clinical. He would dip down at the final stride, throwing his torso at the finishing line, his arms tucked straight behind him. To the uninitiated, it looked wholly unnatural. Surely a sprinter would lose speed by trying such a stunt? Abrahams and Mussabini begged to differ. They thought a properly executed dip finish could be worth eighteen inches to a foot.

With his start and finish looking so promising, repetition was the key. The middle section of Harold's race also came under fresh scrutiny. Pretty soon it would be a question of fitting all the sections together as seamlessly as possible. Abrahams remembered:

> Much time was spent in May and the earlier part of June in starting and finishing practice. In the first few days of May I ran a trial and measured every stride from start to finish. From a close study of the figures obtained, we decided to cut down my stride and, if possible, to get an additional stride into the 100 yards race, by increasing the rapidity with which strides were taken. I also aimed at increasing the length of the first few strides of the race.

You can just imagine Harold and Sam's excitement as they plotted their innovations using sound mathematical theory. Everything was designed to give Abrahams an extra edge. This carefully applied science began to pay off, too. He explained, 'The result of about six weeks' training was that I covered nearly eighteen inches more in the first half a dozen strides, without lessening the rapidity with which these strides were taken.'

It was all relative, because, as Abrahams pointed out, 'No runner attains his full stride until he has gone between thirty and forty yards.' Yet his adjusted pattern created something closer to the uniformity of stride he was looking for. Harold added:

> I have tried to take exactly the same length of stride and number of strides in every race I run. Loss of control inevitably leads to irregularity of action and consequent loss of speed. I find from experiment that a crack sprinter covers between 35 and 36 feet per second when travelling at full speed. How soon after the start does a man attain to this speed? From my own personal experiment I find that I go on accelerating till the end of the seventh second.

There was so much precision involved in using various data to get his race just right, that many gave Harold credit for introducing scientific training to world athletics. Abrahams replied, 'I wouldn't claim as far as that. I think that in my day I probably trained harder than anybody. I was always interested in the scientific side of it, you know. I had to study it as a science and I did study it very closely.'

'I was probably the first person who said that length of stride isn't speed, speed is length of stride multiplied by the rapidity with which you take them. It's an obvious truism but nobody had ever said it.' Given that the greatest sprinter of that era, Charley Paddock of the USA, had actually worked hard to lengthen his stride by six inches instead of shortening it, Abrahams seemed to have a point.

He added:

Let me say right away that it isn't necessarily the long stride that counts. Speed is so obviously the combination of rapidity of action and length of stride that each man must find the length of stride that enables him to move fastest. For example it is better to take five strides of 6½ feet than four strides of 8 feet. In my own case I found, after experiment, that my best running came from a stride 7ft 3½in long. The advantage of the shorter stride is that the runner has more control and that his body is well over his advanced leg. You should avoid a high knee action and any kick up behind. The feet should always be as near the ground as possible . . . If you cut down your stride by an inch, and this enables you to get another stride into your running for the same number of seconds, you will increase your speed by perhaps as much as a yard. Thus I take forty-five strides in, say, ten seconds. If I take an inch less at each stride I shall lose 3ft 9in. But if this enables me to put another stride into the same number of seconds of running, I gain 7ft 3½in, or a net gain of 3ft 6½in.

And that's what Harold did. This theory differed from the sort thinking that had been all the rage before the First World War, and still lingered after it. Bevil Rudd, Harold's old Oxford rival and Achilles Club team mate, certainly hadn't tried to shorten his stride in the old days – far from it. He explained, 'Elongated striding was cultivated in the belief that the fewer strides taken in a race the less energy was expended.' So the Mussabini–Abrahams approach, simple as it may sound today, was revolutionary at the time.

Previously, as Evelyn Montague put it, Harold's 'general style was more ferocious than elegant'. Now Mussabini described Abrahams as 'crack-a-Jack and twinkle-footed'. He was also machine-like. Harold admitted, 'A sprinter has to become an automaton. He must not worry about his opponents in a race. All he is concerned with is to listen for the gun and when he hears it run like hell until he reaches the tape. In fact, if sprinters could run in blinkers they might be able to keep their form better. Form is everything in sprinting.'

Harold Abrahams was robotic, fine-tuned and driven by time, by now almost inhuman. This computer-like condition was one from which he would never fully recover. Later in life he remained obsessed by time, carrying at least two stopwatches everywhere he went. He would time everything, from flights around the world to going to the toilet. Such intensive training with Mussabini may have scarred Harold for life, though the seeds of his obsession with figures were already there.

Tony Abrahams was once asked whether his uncle's obsession with time as an older man was born partly of the pressure he put himself under as a young man. He replied, 'Yes, I think so. I think it came in part from his relationship with Mussabini.' Harold didn't seem to care about the price he had paid for his athletic excellence; and, looking back, he reflected simply, 'By 1924 I had learnt to be very good at sprinting.' Nothing else mattered except the race against the clock. And at last he began to put theory into practice under genuine race conditions. He recalled, 'From 3 May, I had races every Saturday with two exceptions, up to the Olympic Games themselves. My first race in 1924 was on May 3, at Wembley, where I beat Nichol by two yards in the 100 yards.'

For his next race, at the RAF Stadium in Uxbridge, Harold had to show extraordinary dedication just to get there. It took a fifty-minute train journey from Paddington, then a one-mile walk in atrocious weather to arrive at the required location. For the pleasure of participation, Harold was expected to pay a full train fare out of his own pocket. The AAA refused his request for a reimbursement of expenses, and a subsequent headline explained Harold's reaction: 'Abrahams calls for cheap fares on railway for athletes travelling to training.'

As usual, Harold also channelled his anger into his running. 'On 10 May I won the Middlesex 100 yards and long jump,' he pointed out. But he never did win that discount on train tickets. At least he seemed to be winning everything else. 'On 17 May I ran for Achilles against the Services and also long-jumped. On 24 May I won three events in the Midland Counties. A week later I won the 100 yards and long jump with 23ft 9¾in (7.26m) at the Kinnaird Trophy.'

Meanwhile Liddell had begun to focus on the 400 metres and 440 yards. Still relatively new to the longer distance, Liddell opened up with 51.5sec on May 28, and improved on that time on May 31 with 51.2. Without the unnerving experience of Liddell at his shoulder, Abrahams was far more spectacular. And on June 7, 1924 at Woolwich, London, he did something which seemed even more extraordinary than Liddell's AAAs heroics the previous year. Harold was timed at a world record equalling 9.6sec for the 100 yards. But he knew instantly that he couldn't claim to be in the same league as Charley Paddock, the fastest man on earth.

Abrahams was brutally honest when he told the story of what happened in the moments after he hit the tape:

> At Woolwich on 7 June I won the 100 yards 'with a slight following wind' in 9.6sec. There were no wind gauges. When the timekeepers told me of the time, I asked how far Nichol was behind and was told 'one yard'. In that moment I knew I had not done a genuine 9.6. Therefore I queried the time and no application was ever made for a 'record'. As far as I remember in those days a sprinter was expected to ask for his record to be accepted.

That didn't stop the *Morning Post* from describing Harold as 'an athlete evolved out of granite by the genius of Rodin – no stylist but with tremendous stride and grim determination.' And *Country Life* pointed out that 'nobody is ever recorded to have run faster. We seem this year to have a chance of making a fight of it even against the highly trained and "specialised" Americans.'

There can be no doubt that Abrahams generated some astonishing speed that day at Woolwich. For he broke another record – and this one counted for a very long time indeed. Harold leaped 24ft 2½in (7.38m) in the long jump, and no one questioned the validity of that performance. Abrahams recalled proudly, 'It was my best jump ever, which was an English native record for over thirty years.'

Harold always called it as he saw it, seeking to be fair in his self-analysis. While he admitted to being boastful on occasion, he was often just as dismissive of his own efforts. And his recollection of that day at Woolwich seemed to sum up his even-handedness perfectly. One record he had consigned to the trash can, the other he had gone to some pains to highlight. Of his long-jump feat he later confessed, 'Actually there had been no English native record before then, so I created them because I fancied a bit of recognition.'

If he had been forced to play second fiddle in British athletics the previous summer, he was now very much the star of the show. Not even the great Eric Liddell was making such seismic waves in the run-up to the Olympics. But Harold's stunning new results set tongues wagging. Jealous traditionalists claimed privately that Harold had broken unspoken rules during the winter and spring by taking his training too seriously. Tony Abrahams acknowledged, 'It is perfectly true that Harold was criticised by the "Corinthians" of the day for employing a professional to train him. But he didn't care about that.'

At least his 'local' paper was appreciative of his dedication. That June, the *Cambridge Daily News* wrote, 'There is no keener athlete in England than H.M. Abrahams and I think that most of the credit is due to the man himself. He has made athletics a religion – and a man who works at a pastime as he has done deserves all the success which comes his way.'

A feisty Harold mocked 'the argument so often advanced to defend our beaten athletes. "We are sportsmen – we don't take as much trouble as the other nations – and (implied) if we did we should wipe them off the earth." The sooner it is understood that to win an Olympic contest requires a good many months, nay, years of training, the better. This training is as much part of the game as the natural ability. The British public seem to regard this concentrated training as rather despicable.'

And so, in all probability, did the purists of Oxbridge, who could speak more freely among themselves now that Harold had left that particular stage. Yet everyone had to train to some extent, and many did so under supervision. Eric Liddell was still using his own trusted coach, Tom McKerchar. Their partnership was paying off, too. On Saturday June 14, at Hampden Park, Glasgow, Liddell showed that he hadn't deserted the sprints just yet. He won the Scottish 100 yards title in 10.0sec This he did for fun or as another sharpener, since he had pulled out of the Olympic 100 metres weeks earlier.

Liddell didn't stop at winning the 100 yards on that memorable, mid-June Saturday at Hampden Park. He took the 220 in 22.6 and the 440 in 51.2, to become triple Scottish title-holder. It was a phenomenal display of running, and perfect preparation for the AAA championships in London the following weekend. Harold would also compete there, without having to dodge his former rival. The end to track hostilities could have led to friendship. Yet Harold and Eric were such different characters that no strong friendship ever developed. Tony Abrahams explained, 'I don't think Harold had a relationship with Liddell as such. He knew Liddell of course, and he very much admired the way he ran, but he wasn't a particular friend.' And Alan Abrahams echoed, 'I don't think my father and Liddell were friends or unfriendly. He never said he hated the man and I'm sure he didn't. They were polite to each other, I believe.'

As the biggest domestic event of the summer loomed, Harold didn't feel like being much more than polite to anyone. He tried to recharge his batteries, fearing burnout. Later he explained:

> I did not race between 7 June and 21 June – the second day of the AAA Championships. I was – in fact – very stale. The week before the AAA Championships was spent at Brighton with other athletes, and here we were out in the open air all day and actually on the track every morning and afternoon. A hot salt-water bath and a massage at the beginning of the week and an indoor sea-bathe every morning helped me to obtain looseness of muscle and limb.

After lunch he went to bed for an hour every day. It was the calm before the storm.

Abrahams couldn't get away from the sense of anticipation created by his extraordinary performances at Woolwich. He imagined that the public would turn up at Stamford Bridge expecting even greater heroics. He would have to oblige, or else lose face. Some people already thought he was cheating by training so hard with a professional coach. How they would laugh if he still didn't win! He had to come first. He just had to, or it would mean total humiliation.

Such thoughts kept returning at night. They put more and more pressure on him, until he was almost ready to crack. Harold explained later:

> Public opinion, however unjust, has great weight with us all. If we fail we are condemned unheard . . . In 1924 the emotional state from which I suffered before the AAA Championships was appalling. The championships were on the 20th June. I was at the top of my form, and with a week at Brighton intervening, ought not to have had a care in the world. Yet three days before the race I suffered from 'wind up' almost amounting to panic; couldn't sleep or get running out of my head. I was terrified of disappointing a crowd of twenty thousand people whom, I imagined, were all expecting me to win, terrified of being a failure.

The atmosphere at the Championships in London was enough to test the nerves of even the steeliest campaigner. Harold explained, 'There was a record crowd at Stamford Bridge . . . Many supporters came from Scotland to see Eric Liddell . . . I saw several Scotch enthusiasts outside who had walked all the way from Edinburgh, and were too tired to climb over to see the sports.' If they had come to see Liddell take on Abrahams in the 100 yards, they would have been disappointed anyhow. Eric's absence from the big race left Harold clear favourite in front of a huge crowd. The obligation he felt to please each of the many thousands of gathering spectators only intensified as the race drew near. And Liddell, the younger man who had dominated the 1923 Championships, would be still there, watching him.

When ten seconds suddenly become a man's life, nothing can take the edge off the tension he feels. In Harold's case, there was no romance with Christina any more. There was no balance, no perspective or sense of proportion, just the driving imperative of victory. The very thought of defeat was terrifying; so much so that Harold almost had a breakdown on the spot. He thought seriously about pulling out of the race completely. Abrahams revealed later, 'I'd been very keyed up for the British Championships, so tense I was almost having a brain storm.' And as he stiffened with the tension, he knew that his chances of success were diminishing further. Harold explained: 'The truth is that perfection in any sport is the result of a perfect co-operation of mind and body and a beautiful synchronisation of the nervous system and the muscles.'

Harold's nervous system was shot to pieces, so how were his muscles supposed to perform adequately? There was no Sam Mussabini to hold his hand now. This was an amateur championship, and professional trainers had to keep their distance. Luckily Harold's brother Adolphe, a doctor with experience of psychiatric patients, was on hand – not for the first time – to bring some much-needed perspective to the moment. Harold recalled, 'On this occasion, as in 1923 [at Queen's Club], I was so ill with excitement that I consulted a doctor, who informed me that I had never been fitter in my life.' Adolphe probably added one word to his 1923 diagnosis: 'You bloody fool, it's nerves – again!' Just as before, Adolphe's harshness helped his kid brother to snap out of it.

Slowly, the nervous energy he was losing to sheer panic began to stay, and flow around his body instead. Soon he felt a little more like himself again. He decided to face the sporting challenge and try to be brave. He had always loved running fast. That was all he had to do now, wasn't it?

Tap into that love, which was almost innate? 'If the spirit moves you, all will be well,' Harold told himself. He began to focus, wishing he was blinkered from the many thousands of spectators banked high on terracing to his left, all the way down the straight.

Abrahams went into his pre-race routine, taking comfort from his trowel. Simple actions would help to banish wild thought. Yet he was still scared. He crouched, waiting for the starter's pistol to put him out of his misery. Would his training then kick in, or would he be left rooted to the spot? As soon as he heard the pistol, Harold sprang from his starting holes, staying low on the first stride. Adrenalin electrified him. Now the fear of failure could be used positively, his speed sharpened by the enormity of the occasion. He ran like the wind. The fans roared him on – a blurred, heaving mass which stretched from track to sky. It was Abrahams from start to finish. No one else stood a chance. His soaring spirit did not prevent Harold from staging the calculated finish he had learned from his coach. Not that Abrahams really needed to find a few extra inches on this particular day. For all his anxiety, he remained in a British league of his own when there was no Eric Liddell to race. On another day, it might be different.

There is a marvellous picture of Harold breaking the tape with that famous drop finish, an expression of sheer joy on his face. 'It was the glorious thrill of winning,' he explained later. He looks almost maniacally elated, his expression captured on the cover of this book. From that dramatic face, one can barely guess what a mess he had been just a few minutes earlier. Perhaps the intensity of the elation hints at the severity of his pre-race jitters. 'The terror did not leave me until after I had won the 100 yards,' he explained.

The time – 9.9sec – was still a fifth of a second outside the AAA championship record set the previous year by Liddell. It was also ⁳⁄₁₀ of a second outside the 'world record' time he had notched at Woolwich on that slope a fortnight earlier. But it was also a tenth of a second faster than the time Liddell had clocked north of the border the previous week. Abrahams had recaptured the limelight. In truth, the time didn't matter. Victory at such a big event would give him confidence for the weeks ahead, and that was what he really needed. Somehow Harold had come through his personal crisis. But after the battle against himself, he felt totally drained.

'Then the reaction set in and I couldn't long-jump to save my life,' he admitted. 'On this occasion I performed none too well. I had become too excited.' The *Yorkshire Herald* concluded rather uncharitably, 'H.M. Abrahams had an "off day". He was a little stale and far from well. His sprinting lacked the usual fire whilst his final coordination, so vital to accurate long-jumping, was wanting. But such is the penalty of setting such a superlative standard.' He still did the double. 'I managed to win the 100 yards in 9.9sec and the long jump with a miserable 22ft 6½in (6.87m),' Harold concluded.

He felt shattered though; and the Olympic Games were just around the corner. Liddell, in stark contrast, still seemed fresh. But then Eric's positive, almost selfless approach to running was so much easier to handle than Harold's burdensome ego. The terror Abrahams felt at the mere prospect of losing face didn't exist for his Scottish counterpart. For Liddell, the race was a celebration of the ability God had given him. Why should there be any fear of failure? He felt a fierce determination to serve his Maker by running as fast as he could on any given day. That would honour Him. When Liddell's inner fire resulted in him winning races, he was naturally pleased. When it didn't, that was God's will and Liddell would try to do better next time.

The difference between the two men was as marked as the difference between their respective environments. When Colin Welland visited Edinburgh many years later, in order to research for his screenplay for *Chariots of Fire*, he wrote to producer David Puttnam about Liddell's background. 'There is a Calvinistic simplicity about the man and his world that makes Abrahams' set-up look positively Baroque.' Liddell took that valuable simplicity into all his races, wherever they were. And he was also successful at Stamford Bridge, winning the 440 yards final in 49.6sec. The time would not have struck fear into his Olympic rivals. Even so, when compared to those of the previous month, it represented considerable progress. So when he only came second to a South African called Howard Kinsman in the 220 yards, it wasn't the end of Eric's world. In fact the result guaranteed Liddell's Olympic selection at that distance too.

Though Liddell wasn't the sort of man to look for excuses, the schedule at the AAA Championship had worked against him. The man who was generous enough to point this out in print was none other than Harold Abrahams, in the *Sunday Express* of June 29, 1924. Harold wrote:

> Howard Kinsman, who has put up some fine performances in the Cape, beat Liddell, the holder of the furlong championship, in 21.7sec. In all fairness to Liddell it must be said that he had run two

220s and two 440s on Friday evening, and was obviously suffering from the effort on Saturday. He managed to win the 440 in 49.6secs, and in this race he ran with great determination from start to finish. This time speaks volumes for his greatness as an athlete. People may shout their heads off about his appalling style. Well, let them. He gets there.

Harold could afford to be generous. He and Liddell might yet meet in the 200 metres at the Olympics; but it was the 100 that really captured the imagination. It was the 100 that Harold had trained for above all other disciplines. Liddell no longer represented a threat to his self-esteem; and the better part of the Englishman's nature had come to the fore. For all that, there was still an element of competition between them, beyond their anticipated clash over 200 metres. It was unspoken, and Harold probably felt it more than Eric. Who would hold centre stage and command the most limelight in Paris? It might be Abrahams, if only he could recover from the stresses of Stamford Bridge in time. Or it could be Liddell, if he adapted fully to the physical rigours of the 400 metres.

Two outstanding British athletes, each man destined to hang up their spikes long before their time. They had one sporting chance remaining. The big day was fast approaching, to be seized or squandered.

CHAPTER ELEVEN

PARIS

The passing years didn't entirely remove the sense of alarm in Harold's words, as he revealed just how much the trauma of his triumph at the Bridge had taken out of him. 'I was dead stale. After the Championships I took five days of complete rest. Another weekend by the sea; a game of tennis or two and a couple of light outings on the track just to convince myself that I had not forgotten how to run.'

He spent part of his time trying to work out why he had come so close to a breakdown, so that he could avoid a similar scenario at the Olympic Games. In a *Sunday Express* article about 'Getting the Wind Up', Harold asked himself why any athlete would suffer so badly from nerves:

> There are two kinds. One form consists of a perfectly natural excitement – a suppressed tension to get at the foe. This is undoubtedly necessary and useful – it is nature's way of producing the best in an animal. But sometimes, coupled with this, is a kind of morbid anxiety – a feeling of defeat, of disgrace, and of not doing one's best; often almost a moral certainty that one will not be able to move a muscle, and then, when the pistol goes, one will be glued to the ground unable to run. This morbid anxiety becomes less with experience, but it is always there.

He read *An Introduction to Social Psychology*, William McDougall's ground-breaking book on such matters, first published in 1908. Before long he was able to write, 'Analysis shows – if we are honest with ourselves – that we are afraid of doing badly before a crowd . . . It is the fear of shame which to my mind is such a strong factor in getting the "wind up". In his world-famous book, *Social Psychology*, Professor McDougall analyses in detail the emotion of shame . . . We are afraid of not living up to our own ideas of ourselves, and also of lowering ourselves in the eyes of others.'

Later he added, 'Before a race every athlete experiences (in varying degrees) that sinking feeling – just as if one's stomach were taking a walk up to one's mouth and leaving a vacuum behind it.' When faced with the prospect of 'black failure', as he put it, Harold knew that he experienced that feeling far more acutely than most, and likened the rising tension to 'steam pressure in a boiler with no safety valve'. By now Abrahams had realised that the amount of pressure was proportionate to the size of an athlete's ego.

> If the person concerned has a very great opinion of himself, his qualms, when contemplating his failure and his anticipation of making a fool of himself, will be considerably greater than those of a man who realises after all that he is a very unimportant factor in the world . . .
>
> How should this problem be tackled? First a man should try to realise that what really is of paramount importance is not the winning or losing of a race, but the amount of energy and effort that he has put into training.

In short, it was about doing your very best, not making excuses if you lost or blowing your own trumpet if you won.

Harold observed, 'Most boasting is caused by the individual feeling that in some way he is really rather inferior and is only another way of trying to force your own opinion of your worth (and even you yourself quite often don't really believe in it) on others.'

By the time he began to focus on the forthcoming Olympics, Harold had certainly learned how to play down his chances in order to reduce the pressure he felt. 'I am being completely honest when I write that I never seriously thought I had a chance of an Olympic medal,' he insisted later. It was a strange claim from a man who had trained all winter to give himself the best possible chance. But Harold made this claim consistently for the rest of his life. 'This wasn't mock modesty,' he insisted, 'for I always (according to my friends) had far too high an opinion of my ability. But the Americans appeared to me to be in a different class from myself.'

Such a belief suited him, for it helped him to recover mentally from the strains of Stamford Bridge.

If Abrahams really thought he had little chance of success in Paris, he believed many of his seventy-odd team mates had even less of a chance; and there were 'several whose chances appear to be as remote as the proverbial blue moon'. What's more, he said so in print. The article appeared in the *Daily Express* on June 25, 1924, written 'By a Famous International Athlete'. Abrahams argued, 'The team is much larger than that sent to Antwerp four years ago, and it is to be hoped that the British Olympic Association have sufficient funds at their disposal to justify the inclusion of a good many athletes who must of necessity, from the point of view of Olympic achievement, be ranked as "also rans".'

Many fellow squad members must have known the author was Abrahams, since in April he had presented a similar argument under his own name:

> To send men hopelessly below [top six] standard is a waste of public money, and of time to the individual. Moreover, the inclusion of such men may well not only lower the tone, but also the morale and spirit of the team. Such members of the team as have a chance of gaining premier honours should be given every opportunity to enable them to produce their best form. Since funds are not unlimited, to take people who are not up to standard is to spend money on them which could be spent on others. Thus you are not giving your best performers all the attention that might be given.

The British Olympic Committee had completely ignored his advice, and now Harold braced himself for the backlash when he met up with the squad. He could expect many a cold stare from less talented teammates, only too aware of what he thought about their inclusion. At least Abrahams had also argued against his own inclusion in one particular event. After the squad was announced, the unnamed 'Famous International Athlete' wrote, 'H.M. Abrahams is chosen for four events, which is unfortunate. From the point of view of the Olympic Games, this athlete should leave the long jump severely alone. The authorities surely do not imagine that he can perform at long jumping at two o'clock and running 200 metres at 2.30 on the same afternoon. Let us hope that Abrahams has been told by the authorities to concentrate his efforts on the 100 metres.'

This was a high-risk strategy; but it worked. The selectors duly approached Abrahams and offered to withdraw him from the long jump. For a man who didn't believe he was a serious medal prospect, Harold was making plenty of sacrifices to give himself the best possible chance. He began training again, too. Harold confirmed, 'I had rediscovered my form by the time we left for Paris on the Wednesday before the Games.'

In comparison to the domestic championship, Harold felt under no great pressure to succeed in Paris. He later explained, 'Fortunately in those days no one in England thought an awful lot about the Olympics, and few writers ever bothered to predict Olympic winners. In my view there is nothing worse than to be picked as the "favourite" for an Olympic title. Much much better to be an outsider as I surely was. I wasn't nervous for the very simple reason that I wasn't really bothered by what happened.'

That last remark might have been stretching credibility a little too far. But there was precious little star treatment for the athletes. Harold recalled, 'The British Olympic Team departed for France in their ill-fitting blazers made of shoddy material, almost without comment. For Paris we had ghastly team gear of white trousers, blazers and straw hats, we had a small union jack on our left breasts.'

Abrahams wasn't exaggerating about the uniforms. A photo from this time survives, with Harold wearing a jacket and a pair of trousers that look as though they have shrunk in the wash. Yet the careless approach of the Olympic officials didn't do Abrahams any harm. With his ego ignored, his nerves remained steady. Only once was Harold given the sort of attention an Olympian expects nowadays. And even then, the brief media interest was enjoyed by the entire group and not just the best athletes.

Harold's Caius colleague Henry Stallard, who was chosen to compete in the 800 and 1500 metres, recalled a commotion as the team received their send-off at Victoria railway station. 'On 2 July at 10 a.m. the Continental Departure Platform at Victoria witnessed a scene of hilarity. Some twenty-five staid and elderly gentlemen (officials of the AAA) were endeavouring to extricate seventy undisciplined youths from a melee of luggage and press photographers.' Abrahams claimed this media scrum was unusual because, 'The newspapers were interested only in Wimbledon and golf.'

There was no outcry when the Olympic team was sent from Victoria to Paris by the least comfortable route. Abrahams added, 'I tell you in those days we went from Newhaven to Dieppe as a British team because it was the cheapest sea route even though it was the longest.' The official reason given was somewhat more fanciful; that the train from Dieppe came in at the right Paris station. Abrahams explained: 'allegedly because the Gare St Lazare in Paris was the nearest station to the "Hotel Moderne", where we were billeted. We had a ghastly crossing: "Sea rough and a risk of thunderstorms." I spent the entire journey keeping my lunch down and my spirits up by singing Gilbert and Sullivan with Malcolm Nokes [Hammer thrower] entirely disregarding the possible effect on my fellow athletes. I still have a very clear picture of Douglas Lowe, immaculately dressed (as ever), lying prostrate on the deck. Less than a week later he was 800-metre Olympic champion.'

They arrived at the Gare du Nord after all, despite their suffering on the long crossing. At least there was a welcoming party, which consisted of Earl Cadogan and General Kentish from the British Olympic Committee, the British Ambassador, and several other dignitaries. But the Olympic team's afternoon soon took another turn for the worse when they were sent on to the Hotel Moderne in the Place de la Republique, where the Hungarian team was also housed. The state of the hotel quickly removed any sense of importance the athletes might have gained from their welcome at the station. Harold remembered, 'It was a miserable little hotel in one of the busiest centres of Paris. My room was on a corner and the high-pitched motor horns were not exactly conducive to sleep before the competitions. The Americans were in their own kind of village.'

The USA team had endured a far longer sea route from New York; but they had done so in some luxury. The promenade deck on the chartered liner, the SS *America*, had even been fitted out with a 220-yard cork track so that the athletes could train during the week-long trip. These preparations befitted a group of men hailed by their chief coach Lawson Robertson as the greatest athletic force ever to leave the country. Writer and television producer Neil Duncanson's description of the Americans' arrival in Paris made the British experience sound woeful by comparison. 'When they arrived in Paris they were greeted by thousands of cheering fans and boarded a convoy of seventy cars taking them to their own Olympic village, an estate outside the capital, once used as a stately home by one of Napoleon's marshals.'

The atmosphere in the French capital was beginning to build. Over three thousand competitors gathered in Paris. It was crowded and each man wanted to familiarise himself with the most important place of all. Harold noted, 'On Thursday and Friday a visit to the stadium – a couple of starts and one or two bursts. Incidentally a long jump (could not clear 21 feet).'

It is incredible to think that, after all his meticulous training, Harold did something as risky as attempt a long jump at full throttle, when there was no logical reason for doing so. Perhaps there was some truth in his claim that 'I got to Paris in 1924 at the top of my form, but not bothering about the race too much,' after all. Luckily he emerged unscathed from that moment of foolishness in the long-jump pit; though not entirely unscathed from his preparations in the crowded arena. Abrahams revealed, 'I bumped into another athlete while I was training and bruised a thigh.'

Fortunately there was time to recover; and on Saturday he took a complete rest. There was no chance to benefit from a last get-together with Sam Mussabini. Harold's coach didn't even try to stay in the British Olympic team's hotel, because, as a professional, he knew that he would not have been welcome. Abrahams explained, 'Old Sam wasn't allowed to mix with the British team. He was not persona grata with the AAA.'

Nevertheless, Mussabini still found a way to take the tension out of the build-up, and instil belief into his athlete at the same time. He penned a simple note, and made sure the tone was almost matter-of-fact. Sam sent it on the morning of 5 July 1924, from the Hotel Franklin, his frugal base on the Rue Bouffault. Handwritten in a barely legible scrawl, it read:

Dear Mr Abrahams,
You must please pardon my not coming to see you, much as I would like to do so.

However – I believe and hope you will win the 100 metres.

Go out determined to do your best and don't forget to go down at the first stride.

A sponge and some cold or preferably iced water used around the nape of the neck, under the ears and at the wrists and elbows will brace you up.

Get nicely warmed up and then react to the gun.

I should use the springy old 6-spiked shoes.

All the best of luck from

Yours Truly

S.A. Mussabini

P.S.

Please wish Fred Gaby [an ex-sprinter converted by Mussabini into Britain's best 120 yards hurdler] good luck from me.

Looking back at this note, Abrahams said:

A few words of explanation. 'Go down at the first stride.' I had practised for many months so that my first stride was as regular as clockwork, and I was not too upright. Many sprinters take too long a first stride and are in too upright a position. The reference to spikes was advising me not to use a new pair I'd had made some weeks before the Games, but an old pair I had been using for a year or two.

Mussabini's message was wonderfully familiar, as if sent from a kindly uncle just before a village sports day in some picturesque corner of England. But this wasn't England; and his rivals came from the most prolific 100 metre breeding ground in the world – the USA.

It wasn't just the presence of the mighty Americans that added to the sense of occasion, as the teams prepared to march in full regalia despite sweltering heat. Harold's team mate, Henry Stallard, gave a marvellous description of the Colombes Stadium and the pageantry as it unfolded on the opening day of those 1924 Games, the same day Mussabini wrote that memorable letter. It appeared in the *St Bartholomew's Hospital Journal* the following month. Stallard wrote:

The Arena is oval in shape, the green grass in the centre contrasting vividly with the red track and the white concrete stands, with their blue and gold-coloured iron framework . . .

At 10am on July 5th a most impressive service was given to the athletes of all nations in Notre Dame. At 3pm the Stadium was packed and ready to witness the march-past of the athletes. The day was perfect – a blazing sun in an azure sky.

An overture was sung by choirs of male voices. Then followed a deathly silence, broken a few minutes later by the sound of massed bands, the Marathon Gate was opened, and to the crashing of cymbals and the rolling of drums the South African team entered the Stadium, heading the parade. 'Those of us who had the good fortune to watch this spectacle will never again see anything to equal it in its splendour. Not even the most phlegmatic of us could fail to be thrilled at the sight of the wiriest and lithest bodies of the athletes of forty-five nations, clad each in their respective national uniforms, and marching with heads erect behind their flag-bearers.

Cheer after cheer went up as each column entered the Stadium, and, marching round the track, dipped its flag and saluted at the President's box. The Americans formed the largest detachment, being some 350 strong. Haiti and China were the smallest, and were represented by one standard bearer, one flag bearer and one rank and file. The national uniforms were splendid. The French deserve special mention for their smartness, and next to them the Turks, with uniforms of green sweater coats, white flannel trousers and crimson fezes.

The British, with their 'ghastly team gear of white trousers, blazers and straw hats', took their turn but won no prizes for style. Ignoring this handicap, Stallard continued patriotically, 'The demeanour of each nation was interesting to watch – the French with their characteristic alertness and vivacity; the Americans with their air of self-assurance; the Italians always demonstrative and emotional; and the stolid Britisher, displaying a calmness and a resoluteness of purpose in the face of odds.'

In Harold's case, those odds were still remote, as he continued to insist:

The prospect of meeting the great Americans, Paddock, Scholz, Murchison and Bowman, put any ideas of supreme success out of my head. I didn't think about winning because one was so impressed about the Americans in those days. I used to say, 'Britain is ahead of America in only one thing . . . five and a half hours.' They had four of the world's best sprinters. So I was helped by a lack of intolerable pressure.

In June, Charley Paddock, Jackson Scholz and Chester Bowman had all run 10.6sec at the US Olympic trials. There was no reason to suppose they wouldn't go even faster in Paris, once the adrenalin really started pumping. Loren Murchison had clocked a less impressive 10.8sec in that US trial; but he had been an Olympic finalist four years earlier, and knew how to raise his game when it mattered. Just as well for Harold that the US selectors had left black sprinter DeHart Hubbard out of their 100 metres squad, so that he could concentrate on the long jump – which he won. A few weeks after the Games, Hubbard clocked 9.6sec for the 100 yards. 'I always wondered how I would do against those boys [sic] from England,' he said later wistfully.

Even against the chosen American quartet, Harold was up against it. His Olympic experience in Antwerp, though limited, might help him. It wasn't much, but at least the magnitude of the Olympic stage wasn't quite so daunting this time around. His Cambridge friend Stallard, on the other hand, still seemed in awe of the opening ceremony in Paris as he described its conclusion:

> When each nation had marched past and taken up its post in the centre of the ground facing the Presidential box, the flag-bearers advanced and formed a semi-circle around Andre (France), the chosen athlete, who, with his right forearm extended forwards and upwards, took the Olympic oath in these words: *Nous Jurons, que nous nous presentons aux Jeux Olympiques en concurrents loyaux, respectueux des reglements qui les regissent et desireux d'y participer dans un esprit chevaleresque pour l'honneur de nos pays et la gloire du sport.* This oration was followed by a salvo of artillery and forty-five baskets full of pigeons were released. The massed bands struck up 'La Marche Heroique' and the teams marched out of the stadium.

Though Harold may also have found this scene stimulating, he did something else to prepare for the challenge ahead: he took a little strychnine to help him on his way. People thought of it as a murderous poison, and used in larger doses it could be. But in the right amounts, strychnine was an effective stimulant. There was nothing illegal about it. Every athlete had his own little way of coaxing the best out of himself. Half a century later, Harold explained, 'I concentrated on looking after my diet and my bowels. I took some tonic called Easton's Syrup which had some strychnine in it, so perhaps I would have been disqualified for taking "drugs" today.'

His last remark was meant to be flippant. Though strychnine became a banned substance later, it certainly wasn't banned in 1924. Had it been outlawed, Harold wouldn't have taken it. He was no cheat. Sam Mussabini is believed to have favoured strychnine for athletes covering short distances, and may well have been the man behind this controversial habit. It is inconceivable that Abrahams would have done anything so drastic without his coach Mussabini's approval; and Harold must have kept the tonic close to hand in case he felt the need to take it.

The 'Easton's Syrup' certainly wouldn't have been the brainchild of Adolphe. As medical advisor to the British Olympic team, he wrote a few months later:

> The healthy sprinter needs no drugs of any description, and, unless he is actually ill, medicines of every kind should be avoided as poisons. Just as certain foodstuffs are invested with peculiar virtues, so we hear of 'nerve tonics' and 'strengthening medicines' to produce or increase athletic efficiency, extravagant claims which any reasonable person must dismiss as nonsense, but the keen athlete is only too prone to believe a lot of nonsense which he would like to believe.

Later still Adolphe admitted that he had once reluctantly given strychnine to an athlete who had been seeking the swiftest possible nervous reaction to the starter's pistol. That athlete had promptly performed abysmally and had subsequently blamed the doctor. No wonder Adolphe became less impressed by drug use and more outspoken against it the older he became.

By then Harold agreed with his brother about the limited benefit of drugs, and was advocating something far less extreme. 'A healthy man should need no drugs whatsoever and should avoid them. I have found that hypophosphites in moderation have a beneficial effect, say, for two or three days in the mid-week when one is racing on consecutive Saturdays. Taken as a tonic, good very often results.' The term 'hypophosphites' included substances such as calcium and iron salts, which were incorporated in patent medicine tonics in the belief they could help to repair damaged nervous tissue. But the Olympic schedule was far more demanding than racing on consecutive Saturdays. Back in Paris, Harold seemed to think that something more than calcium and iron salts was called for. So he took his 'Easton's Syrup' and waited for the effects of the strychnine.

Harold's Games started steadily enough, though he was less than satisfied with his running when his turn finally came. There were no fewer than seventeen heats to accommodate eighty-two competitors in the 100 metres. Abrahams was in heat 14, along with 'Slip' Carr from Australia. By the time Harold tried to focus, his four American rivals had already qualified, two of them clocking 10.8. Abrahams won his heat in 11.0sec, a time he described as 'slowish and not very encouraging'. He was even harder on himself when he added, 'I seemed to be moving like a dilapidated cab-horse.'

Fortunately there were two hours before the second round, and Harold had a chance to talk to Philip Noel-Baker, a Cambridge man he respected for having reached two Olympic middle-distance finals at his peak. 'He suggested that I had not limbered up enough before the event, and I certainly remedied this,' Harold explained.

The second round of the heats involved six races for a semi-final spot. Harold was in the fourth of six heats in that round, with the first two in each to go through to the semi-finals. The first three heats, won by Murchison and Bowman (both USA) and Coaffee (Canada), were run in 10.8sec.

With Hester of Canada among the field in his heat, Abrahams couldn't afford to run like a dilapidated cab-horse again. Mercifully, he felt more fluent this time around, but was still astonished to hear that he had broken the tape in 10.6sec, which equalled the Olympic record. Further delight lay in the fact that none of his American rivals matched that time.

The Games record had been set by the great American, Donald Lippincott, in a 1912 heat back in Stockholm. Now, when he least expected it, Harold's name was also carved in Olympic history. And in that moment he knew it was time to take his chances seriously. 'I didn't think I had any chance whatsoever of winning a gold medal (in fact one never thought of winning gold medals in those days as such) until 24 hours before the final. And that was the first time that I realised, "My Goodness! I'm not going to be outclassed, after all." I realised I had a chance of victory.'

Though Abrahams had hope, he quickly reminded himself that races were not won on paper, and times could be deceptive:

> While happy with my effort, I was far too experienced to take too much notice of the fact that I was, on paper, $\frac{1}{5}$ of a second faster than the other runners. I was sufficiently knowledgeable to appreciate that sprint times are completely fallacious. Timing at that date was by hand to $\frac{1}{5}$ sec so that two runners given the same time could in fact be nearly two yards apart, whereas two runners given times on the watch a fifth of a second different could be only inches apart. You see a stopwatch moves in a series of jerks, that is to say it is stationary at $10\frac{3}{5}$ for the best part of a fifth of a second and then moves on to $10\frac{4}{5}$sec. So one runner may finish just before the watch moves on to $10\frac{4}{5}$sec and another just after it has moved on to $10\frac{3}{5}$sec. They will be given the same time, though more than a yard apart on actual performance.

In addition to the unreliable nature of the stopwatch, there was another factor to take into consideration – the personal memories he had of the American sprinters and their previous, ruthless brilliance on the Olympic stage. Harold explained, 'We hardly had any information about foreign athletes in the 1920s. Scholz, Paddock, and Murchison I had seen run in 1920 – all had reached the final, so I knew all about them and I had the greatest respect for their abilities.'

Now they were all through to the semi-finals. Could Harold really hold his own against the giants of his sport? The next day would bring all the answers. In the meantime he showed more composure than he had managed prior to his recent big race at Stamford Bridge. Amazingly, despite enormity of the task ahead, and those persistent Parisian car horns, he slept well.

CHAPTER TWELVE

LAZARUS AND THE TOWER

If Harold had been given the chance to read some of the US newspaper reports on the morning of the semi-final and final, they would have fired him up in no time.

One read like this:

SCHOLZ THE FAVORITE IN 100

Jackson Scholz is the favorite among the majority of French news-papermen to win the final in the 100 metres dash today. Murchison, Bowman and Paddock, the other three members of America's famous quartet of sprinters, each turned in the time of 10⅖sec. It appeared from their races yesterday that any one of the four could have clipped off another fifth had he been pushed a bit harder. In the semi-finals and final Abrahams, the great English sprinter who made the only 10⅗ time yesterday, will furnish them with the necessary opposition.

So now we knew. Abrahams was just there to make the Americans go faster – a pacemaker in the fastest discipline of all. And you could understand the American point of view, because no European had ever taken the 100 metres Olympic title. The French had their own man in the first semi-final, an outsider who – judging by the American report quoted below – was rather too anxious to even up the odds:

Colombes Stadium, Monday – Thirty thousand spectators turned out to the second day's competition in the track and field athletics of the Olympic Games at the Colombes Stadium this afternoon . . . The runners were manifestly nervous when they lined up for the first heat of the 100 metres semi-finals. The strain in the audience was great as the men got off to three false starts, Degrelle, of France, being the offender in each case. Scholz of America took the lead when the dash started and pulled away from the field, finishing in 10⅘sec, just ⅕sec above the Olympic record and ⅖sec above the world mark. Porritt, of New Zealand was second, and Murchison, of America, third.

Harold had every reason to feel confident as he prepared for his own semi-final. The previous day's 100 metres times told him so. But it was what happened now that mattered. His Olympic record wouldn't mean much if he was rushed out of it on the most important day of all.

There would be no strychnine-based 'Easton's Syrup' on this day. Harold decided that adrenalin alone would suffice on such a big occasion. The mere thought of facing Charley Paddock, 'the world's fastest human', was enough to sharpen anyone. Harold was also up against the Canadian captain Cyril Coaffee, who had clocked 9.6 for the 100 yards to become joint world record-holder alongside Paddock. Chester Bowman was there, buoyed by his 100 yards victory over 'The Flying Scotsman' Eric Liddell in America that spring. The crack Australian, Edwin 'Slip' Carr and Giovanni Frangipane of Italy completed the line-up.

Paddock and Coaffee were the most fearsome foe. Even with a perfect start, their speed promised to test Harold to the limit and determine just how good he was under pressure. In the space of a few frantic seconds, nine months of intensive training would either find their reward or be rendered futile. The start meant so much, and Abrahams was counting on Dr Moir to do his job well.

But the man with the pistol didn't see Australia's 'Slip' Carr move before the gun, and Harold was left for dead. Charley Paddock was already racing Chester Bowman, his fellow American. Carr and Coaffee were off to flyers too, and even Frangipane was briskly out of his starting holes. Harold only sprang into action after he had given all his rivals a couple of yards' start. Faced with that sight, not even the most fervent optimist could believe the Englishman still had a chance of qualifying for the final.

'Go!!' Abrahams told himself and exploded off the back wall of his rear starting hole. The wall held firm and did its job. With near-horizontal thrust, Harold executed a controlled 'fall' out of his holes, and he was into his first stride. He hit his mark, bringing his arms into play immediately. Under the circumstances, with his entire inner being in turmoil, this was a remarkable demonstration of self-control. It is the first step that decides the whole poise of a sprinter. The body position at the end of the first stride was the foundation on which Harold had to build if he was to achieve perfect poise. If he had been forced to correct his balance, he would have lost forward momentum. Already facing an uphill battle, he might as well have pulled up right there. Instead his body, low at first, began its steady journey towards a more upright position, just as Mussabini had demanded. His 11st 10lb frame would soon be pumping at full force. Yet his rivals were well on their way to completing this tricky, transitional first phase of the race. Harold always remembered how close he was to panic at the realisation:

> I got a shocking start and I was more than a yard behind in the first ten. My first inclination was to get into a panic and make a superhuman effort to catch up with the others as quickly as possible. Had I done this the result would have been a complete loss of form and bad running. Here I was in a desperate situation, and if I panicked I would not even reach the final. I almost shouted aloud, 'For goodness sake keep your form.' The only hope now is that by doing so you may qualify. Here I was in an Olympic semi-final, slow off the mark with five sprinters ahead of me in the first twenty-five yards. I was furious for three seconds.

Negative thoughts were trying to take over his head. Why hadn't he just ignored Carr and gone like the rest? All that training, with Mussabini firing the starting pistol. All that work to shave precious fractions of a second off Harold's reaction time. All that personal sacrifice. How could he be so stupid, just when it mattered? Somehow he had allowed himself to be caught in two minds at the crucial moment. Insanely, he had tried to do the starter's job for him. It had never happened like this before. Why now?

Harold dismissed these thoughts and held himself together. He recalled:

> The whole of my training came to my assistance and I realised the only way I could win was by not throwing all I'd learned in training myself to the winds. If a performer has done enough training he can keep his head in a crisis. 'Don't panic,' said a small voice inside me.

'Keep those arms well down.' Now was the time to rely on my faith, to keep my form. 'Don't hurry too much.' By the mercy of heaven, my trainer and a little voice inside me, I did not panic.

Harold could control his own emotions to an extent. But he couldn't control the rest of the field. And the calibre of that field didn't suggest that Harold would be given a second chance. Why should rivals let him back into the fray? It is kill-or-be-killed on the track, where only the ruthless belong.

Abrahams knew he had to be patient. Acceleration towards top speed has to be a smooth curve. No sudden jerking, jabbing or straining would help him to find top gear more quickly. He had to let the familiar process run its course. The good news was that Harold had already found his seven foot, three-and-a-half inch long racing stride. That stride length had been chosen because it gave him more control than any other. With his torso angled over the advanced leg, he achieved supreme balance, and with it came speed. Harold knew he would move fastest by taking forty-five strides in ten seconds. He still hoped that would happen naturally.

He also knew that his arms, bent at the elbows, were as important as his legs. The propulsion of his arms was coming from his shoulders, so he kept those shoulders loose and relaxed his back too. However bad the crisis, he would only stand a chance through relaxation. Sure enough, there was rhythm in those arms as he moved them instinctively across his body in what he described as a 'criss-cross' action. His hands were tightly clenched and little more than waist-high. The sets of knuckles were six inches, sometimes only four inches apart as they flashed past each other.

Everything was working in perfect harmony. 'Gradually I found myself closing that ghastly gap,' Harold recalled. But at fifty metres, he was still one stride down. Abrahams stayed positive and kept pounding away as the clock ticked and his opponents neared safety. He tried not to look at them, though the temptation was great. He resisted that temptation because even a glance to the left or right might have upset his balance. By now Harold was moving at his maximum speed of thirty-six feet per second. But had he reached top gear too late to catch the rest? It seemed so.

He could either be negative about this nightmare and tighten because his rivals were just seconds from the tape and still ahead; or he could take heart from the fact that he felt speed in those twinkle-feet like never before – a searing pace that was eating up track and bringing him to men who should by now have left him for dead.

The clock ticked some more. Four seconds, three . . . Harold would always remember these moments. 'Twenty yards from the tape I was almost on level terms.'

Two seconds, one . . . The roar of the crowd increased as the field raced for the tape. Harold's momentum was extraordinary, and almost brought him level with his rivals. He was flying, and then he swooped like a bird of prey. 'I thrust myself forward,' he recalled. He dropped down for that tape, hoping not to lose power and rhythm. His arms slung slightly behind him, he executed the dip-finish he had practised on hundreds of occasions with Mussabini. Time it right and you can steal a victory. Go too early and you lose speed at the vital moment.

Would he feel that precious tape? Or would his rivals burst through first and take the prospect of an Olympic final out of his reach? Harold lunged with his torso, the crowd screamed, but he heard nothing because his senses were focused on the tape alone.

I felt a slight pressure against my chest. But I was too experienced not to know that to feel the tape does not necessarily mean that one has broken it. Often the tape is broken by another competitor, and as it breaks at its weakest part it does not necessarily break opposite to the winner. The second man may feel it on his chest when it has snapped elsewhere. I thought I felt it break. But experience told me that very often you can feel the tape and yet not have won.

Half the field probably experienced the same sensation. Paddock was jumping at the tape and Bowman had already raised his hands as if to welcome it. Others were storming through in a blur. An American newspaper report described the finish. 'The audience waited breathless as the three first men dashed across the tape shoulder to shoulder. From the stands it was impossible to tell the winner.'

The race was over in an instant – and Harold's fate was sealed one way or another. It had all happened in roughly the time it takes to read the following stream of consciousness out loud.

'Bang! False start! No! Go! Don't panic, keep your form, arms low. Ghastly gap, halfway, getting closer, level, the tape! Have I won? Don't know.'

Optimism gave way to total confusion as the sprinters finally slowed to a standstill then turned. For some the quest to become the fastest man on earth was over. But whose dreams had been shattered? The outcome hung in the warm Parisian air. Harold waited . . . Still nothing. In his own words:

> I walked disconsolately and almost despairingly back to the start. Had I won? Had I even qualified? An agonising few minutes which seemed like hours. At last, the French loud-speaker. '*Allo! Allo! Le cent metres, deuxieme demi-finale. Premier. Quatre cents dix neuf.*' Four hundred and nineteen! My number! What a relief! '*Temps Dix, trois-cinquiemes. Record Olympique egalise!*' I had qualified and equalled the Olympic record for the second time. The relief was tremendous. Fortunately I had just got home.

He had done more than that. Officially Abrahams had equalled the record and that is what the history books still say. But in real terms he had smashed it because he had started so late, well after the gun had set the clock ticking. As Norris McWhirter said later, 'This indicated that Abrahams was capable of covering 100 metres in 10.4 seconds.' Philip Noel-Baker, Abrahams' roommate in Paris, explained, 'The time was 10.6sec. But if you want his real time, you must deduct that yard and a half – or perhaps two yards – and that brings him to the Olympic records of [later Games].'

Harold gently rejected these theories, though perhaps he was being excessively modest. 'I still managed to win and many people think that was the best effort I ever made and they all tend to say, "Well, what would have happened if you hadn't been left at the start, wouldn't you have done a better time?" My answer is no, because I produced something that I never would have produced if I hadn't been left behind.'

His seemingly hopeless situation undoubtedly brought something special out in Harold. But the suspicion remains that, if someone had been able to time Harold Abrahams from the moment he finally sprang from his starting holes to the moment he hit the tape, he might have equalled the 100 metres world record. Incredibly, he had given the legendary Charley Paddock – the world record holder with 10.4 – a clear head start and still triumphed. Lazarus had nothing on the Englishman from Bedford. Paddock came in second and Bowman third.

Looking back on that near-disastrous start, Abrahams reflected:

> I did a very stupid thing which nearly lost me the race. When the starter had told us to 'Get set' I saw the runner on my right move. The

gun went. I thought the runner had beaten the pistol. But there was no recall. I had been left. I took my mind right off the work in hand, and started badly as a result, nearly two yards behind the others. I had nearly lost that very important race by allowing my attention and gaze to wander in the direction of my right-hand opponent. It is impossible properly to do two things at once. Keep your mind on the job in hand.

He was angry with himself, yet proud like never before: 'That semi-final, when I was still a yard down at 50 metres, was my finest piece of sprinting,' he reflected later. 'The semi-final was really the most crucial race of my life, where I got left at the start and showed, if I may put it so, that the training I'd done and the determination which I believed I possessed came out at the critical moment. The semi-final of the 100 metres was the climax of my career. I broke the tape inches ahead of the Americans, Paddock and Bowman. That semi-final was the best piece of running I ever did.'

When Harold returned to the British dressing room, however, Eric Liddell was there to take the wind out of his sails. Liddell recalled, 'When he came in, I said, "You were badly away." He said, "Don't talk of it; I saw five in front of me. But I won't be left a second time."'

Another mistake might prove fatal in the sheer adrenalin rush of the race for medals. The final was due to take place three hours later; and although Harold appeared to have tamed Paddock, the latter had qualified and would be out for revenge.

For the *New York Times*, the obvious differences between the two men only added to the fascination. 'Their styles and build completely contrast, Paddock leaping forward with chest out, elbows in and knees up, while the Englishman, a lean figure, uses a tremendous stride and moves over the ground with arms flaying the air, his long legs stretched like a greyhound.' Paddock loved the big occasion, and might produce his very best in the final. Then there was the dynamic energy of Jackson Scholz – the 'New York Thunderbolt'. Add Bowman and Murchison, and you had an American quartet ready to overwhelm the upstart Englishman.

Harold didn't know it at the time, but some of the Americans would soon be plotting against him. In a locker-room exchange which later caused huge controversy, Paddock allegedly wondered whether they might be able to use the false-start system to drive Abrahams half crazy before the final; take it in turns to jump the gun, tear the Englishman's nerves to shreds. If the Americans could mess with his mind, Harold's body would be powerless to perform at the level he had just shown.

Even without a Machiavellian plot to undermine him, it was asking a lot of Abrahams to repeat his heroics again so soon. To expect him to find more speed than he had summoned in the semi-final was probably unrealistic. With the right game plan, the Americans might just push Abrahams over the edge. 'For the glory of sport,' the Olympic oath said. But sportsmanship wasn't what the Americans had in mind.

The long wait for the final began, and Harold tried to prepare body and mind for the supreme test. In truth, he had been preparing all his life. It didn't make the wait any easier. Harold described it as 'the worst of my life. I felt like a condemned man feels before going to the scaffold.' There were hours of thinking time, even longer than the organisers had planned. Harold explained, 'The final was scheduled for 6.00 p.m. In fact it was eventually to be run at five minutes past seven.'

Three and three-quarter hours; more than enough time for someone as highly strung as Harold to be troubled by the realisation that he was now a serious contender. The weight of expectation could strike at any second, the moment he began to put pressure on himself; the recent memory of his near breakdown before the 100 yards final at Stamford Bridge never far away.

Thankfully, Sam Mussabini came to the rescue. He knew his mission; to ensure that Harold's demons didn't take over. Old Sam hadn't been allowed near the British team hotel, but Abrahams was too intelligent and determined to be foiled for long. He had taken the trouble to rent a small hut just outside the stadium, away from the officials who frowned upon Mussabini's existence. There he could benefit from Sam's wisdom when it really mattered. This was to be their rendezvous point before the final; the first time they had come face to face since arriving independently in the French capital. Harold confirmed, 'I only saw Mussabini once in Paris before the 100m, for he kept well clear of the officials.' In the sanctuary of that hut, Sam could help Abrahams keep things in perspective. To help defuse the tension, Harold made a smart move; he asked the other British Empire finalist, Arthur Porritt of New Zealand, to join them.

Mussabini later described his task, though he was careful not to name Harold or the Olympics. Perhaps even then he feared there might be reprisals from the authorities, for the indirect involvement of a professional coach in a strictly amateur event. He wrote, 'I can recall a hot summer's afternoon and a three-hours wait between the semi-final and final heats of a World's Championship sprint. It was my job to do the best I could for two of the leading candidates. As a believer in and a practical exponent of the many virtues derived from variety in this life of ours, my task really amounted to whiling the time away usefully yet pleasantly.'

Porritt explained:

> I thought this was a superb gesture, because here was a man who had devoted his whole life for a year to winning this race and it had now reached its most crucial stage, yet he was willing to take in somebody he only knew vaguely to let him share the peace and quiet of his hut at this very last stage. We mostly just lay on our backs, chatted a little, listened to Mussabini and had a rub down. It was very quiet and restful. I don't know what the Americans were doing but Harold and I were now in a totally different state of mind.

Though they undoubtedly spent part of their time in the hut, Porritt's account isn't complete. Mussabini might have given each man a brisk rub-down with a towel after they had taken a cold, cooling shower. But Sam summed up one of his golden rules in two words: 'No massage.' He considered all that pummelling of the muscles to be quite unnecessary, and wouldn't have wasted a minute on it. So Harold had no reason to spend the best part of four hours in one confined space, risking cabin fever. Instead he found a surprising antidote to his claustrophobia. He revealed, 'You can imagine, we had four hours to wait for the final. I took a ride in a taxi. I went away from the ground, I spent all the time with old Sam Mussabini and Arthur Porritt, who'd also got to the final.'

Norris McWhirter didn't mention Porritt in his own account of those intervening hours. But his friend Harold had clearly told him about his magical mystery tour. 'To kill time Abrahams and his coach, Sam Mussabini, were reduced to long drives round the neighbouring suburbs. A car ride is not an ideal preparation for an Olympic final, but in this case keeping Harold's mind occupied took priority over keeping his legs from stiffening up.'

Harold's legs weren't at risk of stiffening up, because they didn't spend all their time in the taxi. A BBC commentary colleague of Harold, Norman Cuddeford, made a startling claim: 'Harold explained to me that he had four hours to kill. This is what he told me: "I thought, what am I going to do? I wanted to fill in the time so I took a taxi and went up the Eiffel Tower." He didn't mention Mussabini or Porritt when he talked about this.'

A mad dash to the Eiffel Tower between the semi-final and final? It couldn't have been in Mussabini's game plan; but he would have preferred that stunt to the thought of Harold hanging around the stadium. Old Sam once advised, 'Spend as little time as possible in the dressing-room as is reasonably necessary both before and after your training sprints and races.' A trip to the Eiffel Tower might just have taken Harold's mind off the enormity of the race ahead. Lord Puttnam later confessed to having no knowledge of this twist to the sprinter's tale. 'I don't even remember that being in early script,' he said. 'It is a lovely story. Personally, I would not let it get away.'

Had Harold so much as dared to suggest climbing the hundreds of steps to the top of the Eiffel Tower, Mussabini would have put his foot down. By taking the lift, however, the athlete could have been there in no time, while the others waited below. The fresher air in the sky above Paris would have given him a bracing boost. What better way to gain an overview on the biggest day of his life, some much-needed perspective on the ten seconds waiting for him far below?

Whether or not Harold actually went up the Eiffel Tower, the impromptu sightseeing seems to have been an essential component of his preparation for the final. The remainder of the time between races was spent back at the stadium. And it was during the last hour that Sam Mussabini really earned his money. For the moment Abrahams reached the Stade Colombes again, his dreaded nerves began to attack. Harold admitted, 'At six o'clock I was almost at breaking point, still with an hour to go.'

Mussabini explained his own dilemma. What could he do to keep his man from panic?

It is not by doing a spot of 'backwash', talking or indulging in buffoonery that you take the minds of those due shortly to take part in contests where a World's Championship is at stake. Nor is there much consolation to be found in minutely detailing the essential racing points, as these should long before have been well digested and assimilated.

The coach's business in these somewhat nervy conditions is to be no less at his ease, with his thoughts intent upon the well-being of his charges, than on any ordinary day. He may exercise a trifle more care than during ordinary everyday associations with the track. Now, however, is not for watching or checking the poses and carriage of a sprinter, nor any deficiencies of style that one has to guard against. You just rivet your attention upon personal and practical details. First comes the comfort, well-being and cool, calm state of the runner.

But Harold wasn't calm, and he intimated later that his mind had started to play numerical tricks, so desperate was he for reassurance:

It is curious how superstition creeps into one's mind before a race, however one may try to ridicule the possibility of good luck and bad luck. I was told some time ago by a palmist that my lucky number was 4. Well, this is the year 1924, which ends in 4 and is divisible by 4, and adds up to 16, which is the square of 4. That seemed a pretty good start. My number in the Games was 419, which adds up to 14. Our dressing room was number 4. The race was run on the seventh day of the seventh month – 14 again.

At least these were positive thoughts; but they were becoming too fanciful and far-fetched. Mussabini knew this overuse of the mind was Abrahams' Achilles heel. Old Sam also knew that it was his job to find a solution. Lt. Colonel F.A.M. Webster, the great British athletics authority of the day, wrote this of Mussabini: 'He had an analytical brain, the coaching eye and the genius of a scientist or psychiatrist for analysing what was going on in the body or brain of an athlete.'

Mussabini later explained how a lifetime in the game had taught him to keep things simple:

One has to undergo the experience of being with Championship competitors right up to the last moment of their going into the arena for their contests to appreciate how a coach has to sink his own personality and try to infuse it with that of the athlete. His sole aim should be to take every precaution that will assist in bringing the very best out of the runner or hurdler. At the very last moment any particular failing – and there are few runners who have not a weak spot somewhere in their technique – may be recalled and be given as the final instruction.

Harold's weak spot was that he thought too much. He was too intelligent for his own good sometimes. He complicated things. He anticipated actions in others that didn't always come. That's why he had been left on the blocks in the semi-final. Now he was trying to think too much again, finding the figure four in every number he spotted. This was neurosis at work. If Harold's only hope of reassuring himself came through mathematical permutations, he was in trouble. Now was the time for Mussabini to cut through all that rubbish and take Abrahams right back to basics. With the near-disaster of the semi-final in mind, Old Sam came up with something so ridiculously simple that it was brilliant.

Harold revealed, 'Before the final, my trainer said: "Only think of two things – the report of the pistol and the tape. When you hear the one, just run like hell until you reach the other."' After nine months of scientific analysis and heated debate, this was what it all boiled down to. This was what Harold needed to hear. The purity of sprinting, distilled in a message that wiped away intellect and made the challenge Pavlovian. Mussabini's basic instruction stayed in Harold's mind as he and Porritt descended into the bowels of the stadium. Sam wasn't allowed down there. It was a private underworld, where Abrahams and Arthur would soon endure the rituals the occasion demanded.

Henry Stallard described what it was like for 1924 Olympic athletes who gave themselves up too early to the tortuous stadium routine, and were lost to the long concrete corridor which connected some thirty dressing rooms, showers and bathrooms. To listen to Stallard was to understand why Mussabini had been wise to keep his highly-strung sprinter out of the dressing rooms for as long as possible:

> It would need an Edgar Allan Poe to do justice to the description of those specific sensations experienced . . . There is an atmosphere of tension in the changing room; the manager and captain are whispering into your ear those last few words of advice while a burly masseur is kneading your biceps femoris. The air is richly perfumed with the aroma of rubbing oils, and some cheery fellow remarks that it will all be over in half an hour.
>
> One lapses into a reverie, only to be awakened rudely by the sharp crack of a pistol shot fired from outside. It is only the start of another race, and you express a desire to be one of those poor devils who have already got it over.

Harold Abrahams didn't have to feel like a 'poor devil' awaiting his fate. There was only time for a swift, morale-boosting visit from royalty. Just before the race he and Porritt were taken to a holding room where the

Prince of Wales, the future King Edward VIII, came down to see the two British athletes. Porritt recalled, 'He wished us well. It was quite a kick.'

In the American dressing room, meanwhile, there was no royalty; only an ambition which went way beyond the normal confines of sport. Harold later complained that Paddock had made an astonishing confession on American radio. He had apparently admitted to what Abrahams described as 'a dastardly plot by which I could be defeated in the 100 metres in Paris. He was declared to have said that a plan was discussed in the American dressing room by which the four Americans in the final should each arrange to get two false starts. Then it was figured I would be worn out by the time the fair start was obtained.'

Would the Americans put their plan into action? The time for combat had come. Soon after the Prince of Wales had left the Empire men in peace, they heard the shrill cries of the French official, whose job it was to summon athletes to their fate outside. Stallard later described this process of being:

> painfully disturbed by a maniac dashing down the corridor outside and bawling [your event details]. How one loathed that man! Somebody, kindly intentioned, thrusts a wet sponge into your face. Feverishly you collect your gear, and inserting your upper incisors into your lower lip, you advance to the fray. From the corridor a subterranean tunnel labelled *Entree de la Piste* leads into the centre of the arena. The journey affords one a strange mingling of weird sensations. The earthy smell of this haunt is so comforting as one ponders on what is to be seen on ascending that last flight of stone steps leading up to the arena. Suddenly you emerge into a blaze of sunlight and, if you are a favourite, a roar of applause goes up, making you feel more unsteady than before.

By now Harold Abrahams was indeed one of the 100 metre race favourites, thanks to his amazing recovery in the semi-final. He could feel the pressure to satisfy the British elements in the crowd. He could hear their roars of recognition. But the British supporters were often drowned out by the more organised and vociferous yells of the American contingent. Perhaps that was a good thing.

Harold recalled, 'Just before the final I didn't really think much about the Americans. The crowd was about 10,000. I remember there was a kind of college yell from the Americans. "Rah, rah, rah, USA, America,

A.M.E.R.I.C.A. Paddock, Scholz, Murchison, Bowman." But it didn't worry me.'

It didn't worry him, it merely strengthened his resolve. Somewhere in his subconscious, the persecution complex he had developed as a youngster went to work yet again. He used it to his advantage. We know what was going on inside his head, because when he reflected further on these vital pre-race moments he added: 'One of the reasons why I felt so determined and so alone was that there was some anti-Semitism in those days. At Repton it was there and at Cambridge. I may have exaggerated those things. Perhaps I found it when it wasn't really there. I didn't run for all the Jews. I ran for myself.'

He ran for himself, and he had always thrived on the sense of isolation and injustice that anti-Semitism – imagined or otherwise – had given him at school and university. That was the anger he knew like a friend, that was what had always made him want to get even. So rather than feed off the British support in the crowd, he fed off American yells in support of his rivals. They may have been chanting the names of others; but it was almost as though they were calling him names. At best they were ignoring him; they were against him. And that was good, because Harold had a talent; and he had always used it to ensure that he could not be ignored. Rejection was the source of the fire in his belly. In those final pre-race moments, Harold felt rejected again by the majority. That's what he wanted. That's how the fire was lit again that evening in Paris.

The American quartet – Charley Paddock, Loren Murchison, Chester Bowman and Jackson Scholz – were doing their best to psyche out their opponents. Arthur Porritt recalled later that Scholz was more amiable than the others. But that wasn't saying much. 'Those four Americans were pretty aggressive,' Porritt explained. 'Jackson Scholz was a charming fellow. The other three had the idea they were the best in the world, and to hell with anyone else. The Americans were very over-keen on winning.'

So was Harold, though. And he was ready. The lane draw meant something to him, though he knew it shouldn't. Think only of the pistol and the tape, Old Sam had said. But Harold's lucky number was four. Rosemary Warne, who was friends with Harold in his final years, remembered what he told her. 'They had a little leather pouch full of ivory markers with numbers on.' The numbers corresponded to the lanes and he drew out a number. And Harold recalled, 'Strangest of all, I drew number 4.'

CHAPTER THIRTEEN

NOW OR NEVER

Harold Abrahams had reached the sanctuary of the pre-race rituals without suffering meltdown. Considering what had happened at Stamford Bridge a few weeks earlier, that was no mean achievement.

He limbered up, discarded his 'warm-up suit', and set about digging holes in the cinders, just as he had for the semi-final. First Harold made sure his toes were touching the starting line. Then, staring at his feet, he took his trowel and sketched two grooves into the track at right angles to the start-line. If they continued on that same line towards him, they would pass through both his little toes. These lines gave Harold the correct alignment for his starting holes. Harold knew the importance of working out all the angles and measurements. 'If the holes are not dug square and the right leg is immediately behind the left, in the effort to swing the leg clear at the first stride, the body will become unbalanced and the first stride will be a crooked one. The result of digging the holes too closely to one another will be that the body will be too cramped and too uncertain in the "get set" position.'

The English journalist, F.A.M. Webster admitted that 'up in the press box little Freddie Dartnell of the *Daily News* was chattering with excitement and offering the wildest odds on Abrahams.' Harold later claimed, 'I think one British journalist said I was going to win it.' But in those final minutes before the race, it was what Harold thought and did that mattered.

Continuing his routine, he placed his left foot eight or nine inches behind the starting line. That was where the front hole would be created. He knelt down on his right knee, so it was in line with the ball of his left foot. He moved his front foot an inch or two backward and forward until he was in a comfortable position. He adjusted his right knee accordingly, keeping it in line with his left foot. Now that he knew exactly where he would dig a home for his left, he checked to see where his back foot had come to rest. It always settled along the line of the original notch, the one he carved with the trowel by the little toe of his right foot.

Having marked the two spots, the serious excavation began. A steady hand was required as Harold started to use his trowel like a scalpel. His springy old spikes would find snug homes during the pressurised seconds before the pistol was fired. Within those spikes, his 'twinkle' feet had been made equally welcome. For further comfort, Harold had had loops of broad elastic sewn into each shoe. When his feet passed through the loops and he felt the elastic caress the arches, he was buoyed by a happy sensation. His feet and his shoes effectively became one. Even his laces gave him an added sense of security, because he had followed Mussabini's pre-race instruction: 'Test the laces of both shoes so they will not burst at the critical moment.'

Harold could breathe easily until he heard the gun. Then breathing would become a mystery. He had never known nor cared to what extent he took in air as he flew down the track. 'Anyone who thinks about breathing in a sprint race is not concentrating properly on his running,' Harold had always said. Habit would take care of it. Besides, there would be time for calmer breathing at the end of the ordeal; and perhaps for a fuller life.

A French newspaper described how, 'At exactly 7 p.m., a great silence descended on the stadium. Perhaps the best collection of sprinters ever seen together was ready to race the 100 metres.' Taking their marks at 7.05 p.m. were Paddock, nearest the inner field in lane one; then Scholz in lane two, Murchison in three and Abrahams in his lucky lane four; Bowman was in five and finally, nearest the huge crowd and the press box, was Porritt in six, wearing the famous all-black of New Zealand.

One report observed, 'There were no signs of nerves among them, only a perfect calm, shared by the starter, a doctor who is used to delicate operations.' In an old film of the race, Dr Moir can be seen ushering the racers to the starting line in no-nonsense style. Had Moir found a way to relax better before the final too? He certainly seemed to be handling the competitors with more authority. Could the Manchester University man get it right this time? Surely lightning couldn't strike twice in the same place, and leave Abrahams for dead again?

Perhaps the behaviour of the crowd was helping Dr Moir to focus better this time around as well. While the loudspeaker had been forced to appeal for silence before each semi-final, no such plea was necessary before the biggest race of all. Everyone understood the importance of the occasion. Webster, noted, 'The silence seemed electrical.'

Harold felt the back of his starting holes. Those launch-pads had served him well in the semi-final, even though lift-off had come dangerously late. This time there could be no distractions, whatever the rest of the field had planned. Harold knew how big this moment was, potentially life-changing. Unusually he felt no fear. He knew what he had to do differently. 'I was determined that I would get a good start this time, and I felt that if I could give two Americans a start and still win, I was jolly well set to win without a handicap.' It was one thing to feel confident, and quite another to convert that feeling into explosive action. The first fraction of the first second would be key, and Harold knew it. 'Ten seconds out of a lifetime! The smallest error – less than one per cent – and all would be lost!' He longed for those ten seconds to begin.

Meanwhile Webster had just enough time to take his seat in the stand – a privileged one at that. He didn't want journalists for company at the moment of truth. So he sat with the one man who might have shaken Harold's confidence during the build-up, had his religious convictions allowed him to race – Eric Liddell. Webster confirmed, 'Liddell was already in training as a missionary to China. He had given way in the matter of playing as an international in the 1923–24 rugger season, but nothing could shake his religious convictions. We sat together in the stadium stand and saw Abrahams.'

When he heard the word '*prêt*', Harold raised his body slightly but menacingly, his spikes nestling against the back of his starting holes. He composed himself among those whom had agreed to do battle on a Sunday. All Liddell could share was the thick silence. Down on the track, the silence was broken by the crack of the pistol being fired behind the row of runners. Had one of the Americans executed a deliberate false start, as previously planned? No. The first report of that pistol was the only one. What had happened in that American dressing room, once their darkest thoughts had been aired? Where were their carefully coordinated plans to break the Englishman's will, even before he was out of his holes? Harold explained later, 'For some reason – Paddock said "American sportsmanship" – the plans never matured.'

Webster told how Moir 'got his field away to a perfect start at the first attempt. There was a great roar at that, followed by an even greater hush as the men sprang from their starting holes.' Harold heard neither roar nor hush. The pistol and the tape; they were all that mattered. 'The start was a perfect one,' he remembered, even if the film footage shows him moving up into the vertical position just a fraction earlier than Mussabini might have liked. Under the circumstances, Harold was more than happy. 'No false start this time. I made a very good start.'

A French reporter marvelled at the blanket reaction of six supremely focused men. 'The start was magnificent, the six men getting under way as one. They were quickly into action and already into their stride.' For the first quarter of the race, nothing could separate their talent or desire. Webster observed, 'They seemed to hang together in a dead straight line until five and twenty of the 100 metres course had been covered. One could hardly breathe.' And even at the halfway point, nothing could spoil that sweeping beauty, except that Porritt was half a yard behind. That was when Abrahams felt himself change gear. And he would never forget the moment for as long as he lived, though he didn't make a conscious effort to break free. Harold put it like this: 'I had the supreme feeling of running just a tiny bit faster than the others, and, gradually, centimetre by centimetre, drawing away. I just found myself, a glorious feeling, just going a little bit faster.'

That sparked pandemonium in the crowd as each faction, previously struck dumb by the sheer speed, suddenly found its voice. Webster explained, 'One could have heard a pin drop until Abrahams broke clear and seemed about to forge right ahead. The Americans and English were roaring out encouragement but Scholz and Bowman came again and Porritt, although he looked beaten, was still to prove a danger.'

It was the moment of truth for Harold, as he sensed his rivals coming back at him. Many sprinters struggle to stay relaxed and keep their rhythm under such pressure. They try too hard and the magic deserts them in an instant. The temptation in Harold to strain those sinews just a little more was irresistible. Film footage shows those broad Abrahams shoulders tightening slightly, momentarily. Had he given in to that temptation for a split second longer, he might have dealt his hopes a fatal blow. He emphasised, 'The smallest error and all would be lost. What is the good of being second in an Olympic final? Forever one's name appears on the roll of Olympic champions, while the second man is soon forgotten. The winner gets all the flowers; it may not be justice, but it is life.'

Harold pushed such thoughts to the back of his mind. The report of the pistol, the tape; Mussabini was right. And now he was nearer the tape than the pistol. He relaxed back into the sheer simplicity of his mission. He did not want to be second. If there was anonymity to be inflicted, he would inflict it. He had not worked obsessively all winter, just to falter at the death. He had not spent his life trying to better his brothers just to invite their sympathetic smiles when the race was done. With controlled passion, Harold's hands stabbed ever more quickly at the humid Parisian air. Yet there was no sense of frenzy, only the power of an engine going into overdrive. A Parisian reporter described how 'Abrahams pumped his arms low in a brisk movement some thirty metres from the tape. He started doing it as sharply as it is possible to do.' He suffered no loss of form or balance. His reward was speed.

When asked what he remembered of Abrahams during these defining moments in the race, Jackson Scholz later replied wryly, 'I remember his ass.' Harold never forgot the feeling of satisfaction as he put daylight between his own body and those of Charley Paddock and Jackson Scholz. 'The best part of it was that I showed them the best part of my anatomy,' Abrahams echoed mischievously.

But pride often comes before a fall. And in those frantic fractions of a second, when victory seemed certain, it suddenly became clear that the race still wasn't over. Porritt, the unfancied New Zealander who had prepared for the race with Harold, found something special in the final metres. Where he had been struggling earlier in the race, now he was flying as fast as anyone – including Abrahams. Porritt struggled to explain it, but he did try. 'Then something, which I've never understood to this day, hit me and I just started getting into high gear and I could feel myself going through the whole crowd, passing one after the other. Had there been another five yards I'd have been second, I was catching up so fast.' Webster, watching alongside Liddell, confirmed: 'Porritt passed Bowman in an astounding burst of speed.'

Still ahead, Harold held his form. Someone built on Bernard Darwin's unforgettable description of Abrahams from the previous year, and wrote that he was now 'scudding like some vast bird with outstretched wings, a spectacle positively appalling in its grandeur'. At Wembley against the Americans of Harvard and Yale he had ruled supreme. This time the Americans were the best in the business, and yet Harold's flight looked even smoother.

As mere men jostled for position just behind him, the 'vast bird' refused to be drawn into a premature swoop for the tape. Porritt still felt ready to take Scholz with his late charge, but he was running out of race. 'They could not catch the Englishman, strive as they would,' Webster reported. A respectful Porritt admitted later, 'I'd never have caught Harold. He was a clear yard ahead.'

All that remained was for Abrahams to end it. Strange as it sounds, he took his time. 'I did not "dive" for the tape until I was within a couple of strides,' he said. The French called it the '*Fleche*' – the 'Arrow'. Harold's finish was suitably lethal. Like Liddell, Webster was sitting close enough to the finishing line to see the expression on Harold's face. 'I shall never forget his gritted teeth and the look of desperate determination on his set features as he staged his sensational streamline finish,' the journalist said. The 'Arrow' had found its mark, and Abrahams recalled his relief. 'And through to the tape . . . The tape! It is over.' A photograph captured the split second in which Harold's grimace began to turn to joy, his 'thrusting chin and gritted teeth, a record of concentrated, dynamic energy', as the writer A.J. Wallis described it.

There was an angular magnificence about his body-shape as he stretched the tape. His left knee pointed the way to glory, while his sinuous left thigh rose at a perfect right-angle to his leaning torso. His strained face jutted almost as far as his leading leg, while both arms were tucked neatly behind him, like the folded wings of a hawk reaching prey.

There is something almost mockingly logical about the winner's technique, for no one else in the picture is applying that logic. Harold's entire being is moving in one direction only at the vital moment – forward. Meanwhile Scholz looks right and flails, torn between the tape and his English conqueror. Porritt is bolt upright as he speeds towards the tape, the tension in his back betraying the realisation that first is impossible. And then there are the non-medal winners, the also-rans. Their faces are frozen in horror as their dreams are exposed. They slacken, knowing that all is lost. They are mere spectators to the drama exploding in front of them. Abrahams' face, where effort turns to ecstasy, is the focal point. 'This was the most exciting moment of my athletic career,' Harold explained. 'In just over ten seconds I had achieved the ambition of a lifetime. What luck! Top of the world. And then it's fun.'

As Porritt observed later, 'Harold had to win that race – and win it he did.' The margin of victory was put at two feet by Webster or, as a French reporter preferred it, 'By 50 centimetres, Abrahams won the most beautiful race I have ever seen, and one that will go down as one of the best in history.' Harold had left legends behind him. Scholz clocked

10.8sec and Porritt 10.9. Chester Bowman, who had beaten Eric Liddell in Pennsylvania that spring, didn't even get a medal. Paddock, reigning champion, and Murchison, another former record-holder, were fifth and sixth. Charley's famous jump finish looked like a badly-timed joke that day.

Abrahams didn't smash Paddock's world record. Given the effort required to stage his comeback in the semi-final just a few hours earlier, that was hardly surprising. However, Norris McWhirter explained how Harold's actual time was faster than many record books might indicate. 'A one-hundredth-second timer showed 10.52sec (worth faster than 9.7sec for 100 yards.)' If that was the case, Abrahams had generated enough speed to have beaten Liddell the previous year. Unfortunately the rules stated that anything over 10.5sec should be moved up to 10.6sec. So he had to make do with equalling the Olympic record yet again.

Much later Harold confided to his friend Rosemary Warne, 'I was a bit better than that.'

Other factors had to be taken into account: the lack of proper starting blocks, the primitive track shoes and the crushed cinder-dirt tracks. Considering those disadvantages, he had clocked a wonderful time – one that stands proudly against the quicker times of the twenty-first century, generated as they are with the help of all the modern aids to sprinting technology. Harold's consistency was historic – he had succeeded in equalling the Olympic record for the third time in the space of twenty-six hours.

L.L. Owen – the latest correspondent from *The Times* of London to watch Abrahams in action, seemed less than impressed, though Harold wasn't bitter. 'He was not exactly one of my *fans*.' – the champion suggested, remembering his critic's precise words. 'Abrahams again ran a fine race and was first to reach the tape – but could do no more than equal for the third time the Olympic record of 10⅗sec.' This was a line Harold quoted for the rest of his life. He could do so and appear self-deprecating, while reminding his audience of his achievement.

Back in Paris, that achievement was appreciated instantly by those who were waiting at the finishing line. A.J. Wallis described the commotion. 'The finish is greeted with indescribable enthusiasm, and the British contingent goes mad with joy. The cheering is renewed when the Union Jack is hoisted on a flagstaff of honour for the first time in the Games.' Meanwhile another journalist, G. Ward Price, wrote, 'The crowd burst into loud cheers, which were renewed again and again, while Abrahams was kinematographed, photographed and shaken by the hand and clapped on the back by scores of fellow athletes.'

Eric Liddell, who shared in the joy, paid tribute to Harold's killer instinct when it really mattered, the grit he displayed despite a privileged upbringing. 'It is an inspiring thing in these days, when we hear so much about the decadence of England, to realise that post-war England has produced a runner, indigenous to its soil, who at the zenith of his career has no equal in the world as a match-winner.'

Even the Parisian crowd was delighted that a European athlete had won the 100 metres title at last. More than that, they were thrilled that the Americans had lost. The Americans had saved the French during World War One, but that left an inferiority complex, aggravated by the USA's determination to meddle in post-war European politics. So in these glorious moments Harold Abrahams was France's hero too. He had put the Americans back in their place.

Harold recalled, 'I remember being surrounded by cameras, I remember clearly Paddock coming up to congratulate me.' Paddock, who minutes earlier had been plotting to drive Abrahams to distraction with a series of deliberate false starts. When Paddock later let slip what he had contemplated, Harold initially refused to believe that the story was true in any shape or form. But not long afterwards, he had an opportunity to challenge Paddock on what he had said. Abrahams revealed:

> He said that the story as printed in America and other papers was garbled. He still maintains, much to my amazement, that it would be quite legitimate according to the rules, for a runner deliberately to try to beat the pistol. That is not the British idea of sportsmanship, nor does it represent the true American view.

Harold could scarcely disguise his disgust at Paddock's apparent lack of sporting ethics. No longer did the Englishman dismiss the plot claim as absurd. However, in the immediate aftermath of the race, Abrahams didn't know about the 'dastardly plan'. All sweetness and light, Paddock felt he had earned the right to embrace the sporting purity of Harold's triumph.

As Abrahams passed wearing a dressing-gown, a beaming Paddock shook his hand warmly. Words were exchanged, and Paddock couldn't resist a provocative little joke. 'What a pity you're not American,' he is reported to have said. 'With our training you would certainly have broken the record.' Abrahams could afford to let that remark go, even if he didn't agree with it. He simply asked Paddock where he finished. 'Waal, I guess I was so far behind the judges couldn't see me,' Charley replied.

For four years the 'California Flash' had retained the right to call himself the fastest man in the world. With a toothy grin, he now passed that title to Harold Abrahams. On behalf of the Americans, Paddock said soon afterwards, 'We think your Harold Abrahams is one of the most wonderful sprinters in history – in fact we have never seen a better man in action.' The better part of Paddock's nature had prevailed. And in a fair race, without a succession of deliberate false starts, Abrahams had come out the clear winner.

He didn't celebrate wildly for the cameras, as so many of the modern-day Olympic champions do. But he did give off a glow of satisfaction. Arthur Porrit recalled, 'Harold was obviously delighted, you could feel it. There was no arm-waving or great joy, he just smiled. On the other hand I could sense that all his tension had gone. He'd achieved what he'd set out to do. Harold did a lot after that race, but I think it was an apex in his life. The whole of his subsequent life depended on the fact that he'd won the Olympic 100 metres.'

And his performance in that final depended largely on the fact that he had taken so much confidence from the semi. He explained:

> It wasn't until the semi-final when I was left a yard-and-a-half down that I knew, absolutely knew, I could win. When I won my semi-final in 10⅗ seconds and Scholz won the other semi-final in 10⅘ seconds, I knew that I would certainly win the final. I knew at that moment I would win the Olympic final, and four hours later I was lucky enough to do so. I got much more satisfaction in retrospect from my running in the semi-final than I ever did in the final.

It was easy to say afterwards that he knew he would win. But, as he had already pointed out, there were no certainties in the Olympic Games – not until victory was secured. And even then, Harold wasn't about to do a lap of honour with a Union Jack draped around his shoulders. 'I didn't have any feeling of patriotism though I was pleased for Britain,' Harold admitted before adding strangely, 'There wasn't any Union Jack. There was no victory ceremony, no prize-giving; no national anthem. Olympic champions of those days were not rated as highly as they were later. If they had been, perhaps I should have worried and not been one! There was no fuss. When I say fuss, I think some of these victory ceremonies are rather nice. I a bit regret that I didn't have one.'

It was a curious recollection, since some accounts of Paris '24 tell a different story. They certainly played anthems and raised flags for the rugby tournament which started the Games back in May. And Harold's account also seems to conflict with that of his friend Stallard, who wrote of the post-race procedure at the 1924 Games just a month later:

> The loud-speaker proclaims that the Olympic ceremony for that event is about to take place, and the massed bands play the national anthem of the victorious country. At the north end of the Stadium the flags of the nations who have gained first, second and third places are slowly hoisted and float languidly in the breeze. It is an impressive sight to see thousands of men and women of various nationalities bare-headed and standing to attention, paying solemn respect to the victorious nation.

Perhaps Harold was too busy accepting the congratulations of those around him, though he insisted later, 'You know I don't think I was interviewed at all after I won.' He certainly didn't receive his medal as part of any ceremony – that arrived weeks later. But Harold didn't need a medal to appreciate the value of his victory on a personal level. Not only had he justified the sacrifices he had made; he had outshone his elder brothers. 'It gave Harold the final confidence over them,' Tony Abrahams explained. That mattered more than anything else. They could only dream about what it felt like to win an Olympic title; yet they were also part of his triumph.

His staunch supporter among the press corps, F.A.M. Webster, revealed:

> After his victory I met him on the way to cable his brothers, Sir Adolphe in England and Sir Sidney in East Africa. At Cambridge the former was a good half-miler, and the latter a 100-yards and long-jump Blue who represented Great Britain in the intercalated series of Games at Athens in 1906 and in the accepted cycle of the Olympiads at Stockholm in 1912. By their example and sound advice both the older brothers did much to inspire the younger to his Olympic and other triumphs.

Harold always seconded that sentiment. 'I had enormous help from my brothers, particularly Sidney and Adolphe with his medical knowledge. In his prime, Adolphe was one of the best Medical Officers British athletics has ever had. Yes, British athletics owes Adolphe a great deal, and I would only add from my personal point of view that he contributed very largely to my success.'

Without Adolphe's pushiness, Harold probably wouldn't have been competing at all, because he would have been married to Christina McLeod Innes instead. But Webster was wrong about one thing: Adolphe didn't require a telegram. His nephew Tony explained, 'Adolphe was in Paris! My father was in Africa; in '24 he was in Uganda I think.' It was probably the third brother, Lionel who was waiting for a telegram back in England. And Harold couldn't wait to contact his family, so that he could tell them what he had achieved. Not that he or anyone else could do justice to that achievement in the few words allowed on a telegram.

Abrahams had climbed as high as any athlete can. On the way, he had beaten the bigots, using their mixed-up heads as stepping stones. 'There was much more anti-Semitic feeling in those days and it provided me with the driving force to succeed in athletics,' he told David Emery of the *Daily Express* much later. Now he had the last laugh over the Repton public school house which had refused him entry as a boy, because his father was a moneylender. 'I just hope they were a bit peeved when I won my gold medal,' reflected Harold, looking his interviewer squarely in the eye as if to stress the seriousness of the point.

As it turned out, that medal would take weeks to arrive at Hodford Road. Harold explained, 'Everything was so low-key that I had to wait before they mailed the medal to me. It got to me a month later and I tell people I even had to pay the postage.' But news of Harold's victory reached Golders Green far more quickly. Even before Abrahams had left the Stade Colombes, his mother Esther probably knew. Harold always claimed, 'My mother had to wait for the nine o'clock news to know whether I'd won or not.' But a British newspaper insisted, 'Immediately the result was known, the *Daily Express* telephoned the news to Mr Abrahams' home in Golders Green. "It's fine, we are overjoyed!" was the response.'

Had he still been alive, Isaac Abrahams would have been overjoyed too – and proud of the way Harold, the 3lb baby, had taken his chance in life. Isaac's youngest son explained:

I think luck can play an important part in athletic success, though to be frank my definition of luck is a personal one. I believe that we all have opportunities, and it is the fortunate man who recognises the opportunity when it arises and has prepared himself to take advantage of it. Luck is no good if you don't see it; luck is no good if you see it but have not trained to take advantage of the fact.

Harold Abrahams did both. And now he had his reward – sporting immortality.

CHAPTER FOURTEEN

LIDDELL'S REPLY

Although there was no chance to celebrate with Sam Mussabini in the immediate aftermath of victory, Harold Abrahams was fully aware of the debt he owed the older man. 'Please make it clear that the credit of my win is due to the coaching and genius of Mr Mussabini, the greatest trainer of sprinters in England,' he told reporters. The amateur athlete must have been fully aware that his tribute to a 'professional coach was controversial. He carried on regardless. 'Without our combined effort, the result accomplished would never have been achieved. He has encouraged me very much during the last six months, and made me stick to it when I sometimes felt inclined to neglect serious efforts.'

Despite Mussabini's slick work, Harold's style still wasn't good enough to win universal approval among the so-called experts. If he expected unqualified praise as Olympic champion, he didn't get it. One critic began positively enough when he claimed, 'Abrahams owes much of his improvement to the more forward carriage of his body and head, and to keeping his arms in front of the body, so getting a forward balance. It is merely observing Sir Isaac Newton's teaching regarding the laws of gravity, and if other athletes will take note, they will profit.' But then he added, 'Abrahams can still be greatly improved, as at present his lurching movement inwards with the shoulders is overdone, marring the rhythm and smooth carriage of his body, which is so desirable.' Another critic, Hugh H. Baxter, of America, admitted, 'I felt sure his lurching style would lead to his defeat. He won in spite of it, which is a tribute to his great strength.'

Norris McWhirter said later, 'Abrahams' drop finish was much disliked by some critics, who said it broke rhythm.' Even Eric Liddell, whose running style Harold had dismissed as 'the most misplaced direction of energy I had ever imagined possible', was scathing about Abrahams' own basic running action.

Comparing Harold's style with that of Scholz and Paddock, Liddell said, 'If you watch the trio in action you will probably think that Abrahams is the more laboured of the three; he seems to expend more energy to get the desired result, yet this very fact only serves to confirm his real greatness ... Scholz may have been a sweeter mover, with more rhythm and balance, and Paddock may have been more machine-like in his stride, but, when it came to a fight, Abrahams was supreme.'

It isn't known what Sam Mussabini thought about the pseudotechnical nature of the criticism, when he had used science so carefully in his illustrious coaching career. With another gold medal winner on his C.V., he was more than entitled to blow the critics a great big raspberry.

Besides, Harold wasn't short of admirers, particularly among his hosts. One observer remarked, 'Abrahams is beyond question the outstanding figure among the athletes of all nations. His performance of equalling the Olympic record three successive times has struck the French public imagination, and the press is generous in its admiration of him.'

It didn't take long for some of the most powerful spectators in Paris to raise a glass to the big hero of the hour. The British Olympic Association basked in the reflected glory of Harold's victory by holding a celebration dinner in Paris, with the Prince of Wales in the Chair. General Charles Sherrill, who was the US representative on the International Olympic Committee, was invited. He made a witty speech in recognition of the English sprinter's achievement. Sherrill said, 'America has every modern thing to help them win the 100 metres, but you in England went back to Abraham's day and you won.'

The *New York Times* was preparing its report for the following day's paper, under the headline, 'Sprint Upset Startles Americans'. They had 'suffered an unexpected setback when Harold Abrahams, the Cambridge University star, outraced the four fleetest American sprinters and captured the 100 metres championship for Great Britain.' Later, the same paper described the hero as 'Harold Abrahams, the nemesis of American sprinters', and then as 'The English Wonder'.

Unfortunately Harold had few close friends on the British team with whom he could share his supreme moment. 'I wasn't very popular with the Cambridge crowd and the others in the British team didn't have much to do with Oxford and Cambridge athletes,' he added. 'I remember there was some clapping when I came into the dining room that night and I made a little speech and said I hoped they'd all do the same.' No pressure there, then. 'Perhaps that wasn't very tactful,' acknowledged Harold later.

Many of the team knew they didn't have what it took to strike gold – because Harold had told them in print. Though it wasn't intended as such, the 'hope' Harold expressed may have sounded like a taunt. But one man at least was good enough to take his best wishes at face value – Eric Liddell. The 'Flying Scotsman' would have his chance to compete with Abrahams soon enough. Abrahams emphasised, 'I didn't celebrate because I had to go out and run the 200 metres the next day. In my heat I beat Paddock in 22.2sec and in the second round another American B.M. [Bayes] Norton in 22.0.'

It begged one delicious question: could Abrahams pull off an impossible double? One journalist wrote, 'His victory by two feet over Paddock, the American champion, in the first heat of this same race on Tuesday encouraged British spectators to hope that Abrahams might add the 200 metres to the list of the triumphs of himself and of Britain.'

Liddell was showing slightly less promise in the same event. He won his first race in 22.2 but came in second to Australia's 'Slip' Carr in the next round. Abrahams still looked the best British bet, though the opposition was flying. Harold recalled, 'On the following day in the semi-final, I just managed to reach the final behind Scholz and George Hill (USA).' He did so in a personal best time of 21.9. Meanwhile Liddell was beaten in the other semi-final by Paddock, the man Abrahams had defeated in his first heat. If Harold could find something special again in the final, the gold medal was still there for the taking.

Controversially, he joined forces with Mussabini once more – to discuss what had happened in the semi-final and plan for his shot at the sprint double'. Harold revealed, 'I had felt very tired and my trainer Sam Mussabini suggested that I had gone off a little too fast. Consequently I decided to start rather more slowly in the final, with the result that I lost whatever chance I had in the first 50 yards.'

This revelation is extraordinary, because it amounts to a confession that Abrahams and Mussabini, for all their combined experience and intelligence, got their calculations totally wrong for the 200 metres final. Without actually saying as much, Harold seemed to blame Mussabini's analysis of his semi-final start; either that or he blamed his own interpretation of Mussabini's observations. Whatever the reason for the error of judgement, Paddock compounded it by setting off at a frightening pace. As they straightened after 100 metres, the American was well ahead, while Abrahams lagged a good two feet behind the chasing group. One British writer observed, 'Abrahams left his dash and speed behind him on the 100 metres track, and, coming into the straight, he completely bogged down.' There was astonishment in the press box as he fell further behind with each stale stride.

Liddell could have suffered no such hangover, and another British scribe conveyed the excitement as the Scotsman:

> made a great fight with the USA contingent, Charley Paddock, Jackson Scholz and Bayes Norton. As the runners approached the finish of the 200 metres it looked as though Paddock still had the issue well in hand; but like Lot's wife he looked back, and like Lot's wife he paid the price. No doubt he succumbed to the temptation to see by how much he was beating his opponents. He staged his usual sensational jump finish but Jackson Scholz, USA, had gone past him like a flash in that last fraction of a split second to win by inches in 21.6sec. That equalled the Olympic record set up by Archie Hahn when he won the event in St Louis, 1904. Liddell, head and shoulders thrown right back, did excellently to finish third.

Jackson Scholz had triumphed at the age of twenty-seven, and it was Harold's turn to view the American's backside from a distance. Later Scholz revealed that he had beaten Paddock, timed at 21.7sec on this occasion, in twelve of their fifteen career races. 'I was fast,' he said with quiet satisfaction. And what added to that satisfaction was the fact that Jackson wasn't very fond of Charley anyway. 'He never missed an opportunity to plug himself,' Scholz said of Paddock later.

Liddell clocked a creditable 21.9sec for his bronze – but that was no faster than Harold had gone in his semi-final. Yet when it mattered Abrahams had been a spectator; and he remembered sadly:

> When we entered the straight I was well down and I finished a very bad sixth. I have always regretted that I did not run better in that 200 metres. Naturally the reaction after the 100 metres was to be expected. I still believe that I was better over 200 than 100. If only I could run that 200 metres again! I have never ceased to blame myself

for my indifferent running. I had a theory that I would reserve some of my speed for the last 100 yards, and I reserved so much that I finished up far down the course, with more than half my money to spend and the bar closed.

Liddell thought Harold was deluded if he believed he was better over 200 than 100. The man from Edinburgh explained:

Abrahams finished last, quite run out, and his defeat rather confirms my suspicion that his style takes a heavy toll on his physical attributes, especially over a distance greater than 100 yards. Scholz, on the other hand, seems to take less out of himself and keeps his balance better. This was not enough when he just went under to Abrahams in the 'hundred' because Abrahams had the will to win, and was able to maintain it until the finish; over longer distances, however, the stylist prevailed.

Paddock has had a marvellous career and he, too, is a 'made' runner rather than a natural runner – I mean that he always gives you the impression that it is costing him much effort to win, like Abrahams, whereas Scholz just moves easily on. The trio, however, have probably never been excelled in the history of athletics for speed – as a trio.

But Harold's speed had deserted him, and one reporter reflected, 'It must be seldom that H.M. Abrahams, the brilliant winner of the 100 metres on Monday, finishes last in a race, but that was his position in the 200 metres yesterday . . . But he was clearly stale yesterday after his tremendous efforts of the previous three days.' By the time F.A.M. Webster came to write a book called *Great Moments in Athletics*, he was quite brutal in his choice of words. 'The reaction upon a highly strung athlete, which Abrahams was, of a major victory, is, I think, noteworthy. Virtue seemed to go out of him.'

It was the last time Abrahams and Liddell ever met in track competition. Many years later, Harold Abrahams looked back on his rivalry with the 'Flying Scotsman'. This time here is his full assessment: 'I never ran against him in a 100. I ran against him in a 200 and he beat me. He beat me but I think I was a better sprinter than him, actually. At this long distance from the actual event I can perhaps say, without seeming self-centred, that I believe I was, in fact, better than Eric over 100 metres – though it is equally fair to say that on the only two occasions on which I ran against him (over 220 yards and 200 metres), he defeated me. In the final he finished third behind Scholz and Paddock, beating two other Americans, G.L. Hill and

B.M. Norton, in the process. Liddell was a pretty fair way ahead of me. I was last.'

Despite acknowledging the margin of Liddell's 200 metres victory over him, Harold was pointing to the Scotsman's indifferent progress through the competition. Abrahams, on the other hand, had remained undefeated on the way to 100 metres Olympic gold. In the king of all sprint events he had felt invincible. Therefore he had the superior Olympic sprint record and could claim to be the better sprinter.

Yet even someone as confident – some would say arrogant – as Harold harboured doubts. And he finally gave voice to those doubts many years later. 'I have often wondered whether I owe my Olympic success, at least in part, to Eric's religious beliefs. Had he run in that event, would he have defeated me and won that Olympic title?' The thought nagged away at him, and may have tarnished his description of Eric's early progress in the Olympic 400 metres. Again Abrahams seemed keen to put Liddell's success in perspective, and pointed out:

> Next day he ran in the preliminaries of the 400 metres. He won his heat in 50.2sec and easily got through the next round, running second to Paulen (the Dutchman). But the sensation of the second round was the Swiss, J. Imbach, who returned 48sec for a new Olympic and world record. (Incidentally at that date a world record for 440 yards – 2½ yards further than 400 metres – was not recognised as a record for the shorter distance, even though it was better than the previous best. In 1916 the untouchable J.E. Meredith had run 440 yards in 47.4sec, but the world record for 400 metres still stood at 48.2sec.

By mentioning Meredith's 47.4, Harold made sure he took some of the shine off Liddell's subsequent world record in the final. It was a shame, because Harold's boyish enthusiasm, as he recalled his own keen anticipation of Liddell's big race, was so much more endearing.

> When we went back to the hotel on the Thursday evening of July 10, 1924, we had hopes that Liddell might win the final on the morrow. But we had to confess that he had not to date done anything like 48.0sec for the distance. Indeed, his best was over a second slower.
>
> At three o'clock the following day (July 11) the two semi-finals took place. In the first the American champion, H.M. Fitch, set up a

new Olympic and world record of 47.8sec, with Guy Butler second
and D.M. Johnson (of Canada) third. In the second semi-final Eric
won comfortably in 48.2sec, with Imbach second and the American,
Taylor third.

The final was run nearly three hours later. I remember that as the
seats allotted to Olympic competitors were in a very unfavourable
position – at the start of the 100 metres – I paid my ten shillings to
have a seat near the finish.

Just as Liddell had watched Harold's 100 metres, so Abrahams returned
the compliment. He went on:

Liddell was drawn in the outside lane, the worst position since he was
compelled to set his own pace the whole way and could not see any
of his opponents. The 400 metres in Paris was run round two bends
only, that is to say there was a starting straight of, I should think, very
nearly 200 yards.

From the crack of the pistol Liddell ran like a man inspired. He
dashed off with all the frenzy of a sprinter. Indeed, the thought in my
mind as he started off as if he were running 100 metres instead of 400
was 'He can't possibly keep this up'. He set off at a pace which looked
so ludicrously fast that we expected him to crack when the home
straight was reached. At half distance he was yards and yards ahead of
all his rivals, and it seemed impossible that he should last the
distance. But he seemed to maintain it right to the finish. Every
muscle in his body seemed to be working overtime in this wild rush
to supreme victory. Eric never seemed to slacken in his pace, though
of course he must have slowed appreciably, and he won that glorious
Olympic final by a good six yards in the new Olympic and world
record time of 47.6sec. Fitch (USA) was second in 48.4sec and Guy
Butler third in 48.6sec. Eric's brilliant victory at the Paris Olympiad
will always remain an epic.

And it would always leave Harold in awe, because he could never quite
understand it. Looking back he wrote, 'The outstanding memory is of
somebody who was really regarding winning a race as a tremendous
experience and putting the whole of his being into his running. He
probably had the worst style of any great athlete that's ever been seen.'
The brilliant athletics writer, Peter Lovesey, described that style most

memorably. 'Liddell, head towards Heaven, body almost in a backward lean.'

But even Abrahams argued that it was far too late to make Liddell a smoother runner. Looking back he explained:

Liddell's style was quite the most unorthodox ever, with arms revolving like the sails of a windmill, head thrust back and an exaggerated knee lift. People are apt to ask whether he would not have been an even greater runner if he had possessed a more polished style. In theory the answer is 'yes', but often in trying to impose a style on a runner you ruin his individuality and spoil his performance. If you can teach a very young boy good style, it is well worthwhile, but you must study an athlete as an individual and not be too keen on 'orthodoxy'. I do not mean to suggest that good style is not a tremendous asset and if one had started when Liddell was very young something advantageous might have resulted.

One question begs itself: would Eric Liddell have been able to achieve even more, had he teamed up with Sam Mussabini? Maybe the wily old coach would have appealed to Liddell's burning desire to serve God on the track; he might have told Eric that he could serve God with even greater distinction, if only Liddell would listen. 'Never alter a man's style, always try to improve upon it,' Sam had told Reggie Walker back in 1909. Mussabini had improved upon Harold's style; and it is hard to believe he wouldn't have been able to improve upon the brilliant Liddell's too – without ruining him.

As it was, Harold never could fully comprehend Liddell's success; and that sometimes gave rise to a more grudging analysis of Eric's 400 metres record. On another occasion Harold pondered, 'I often wonder how Liddell would have fared against the great ones of 1936 – Brown, Roberts and Rampling – all of whom beat his times handsomely.'

Such comparisons pointed to Harold's underlying insecurity in relation to Liddell. He seemed to have a complex about his Scottish rival, which was ridiculous because Abrahams was a sporting god himself, from the moment he hit the tape in the 100 metres. The hosts of the Games even printed a postcard of that moment, to reflect Harold's superstar status. Tony Abrahams revealed, 'Harold sent one to Derek, his brother, Lionel's son. He was proud of the fact that he had won, after all that work.'

He remained proud; and there would always be one fellow competitor to help him relive that race annually. On July 7 at 7.00 p.m. for the rest of his life, Harold Abrahams met Arthur Porritt for dinner, in Paris if they could make it. For Porritt, who became Surgeon to the British Royal Family and Governor-General of his native New Zealand, it wasn't always easy to respect the arrangement. He did so in spite of his responsibilities; and they never tired of savouring those thrilling seconds when they both fulfilled their dreams.

Back in the Paris of 1924, there was one more dream left for Abrahams to chase. Having let his 100 metres success spoil his 200 metres chances, Harold was determined not to let his relay teammates down. 'By the end of the week my form had returned and I think I ran well in the relay,' he said with some understatement. He and his colleagues actually achieved a world record in the first heat of the 4 × 100 metres. Harold recalled, 'I ran the first leg. The others were Walter Rangeley, George (W.P.) Nichol and Lance Royle . . . Sir Lancelot Royle as he became. We did 42 dead in the heat.' That beat the existing world record by one fifth of a second. The British were jubilant, knowing they had made history. Ten minutes later the Dutch equalled that new world record. No matter, it still felt sweet to be a joint world-record holder. Twenty minutes later the joint record was smashed. The American quartet of Francis Hussey, Louis Clarke, Loren Murchison and Alfred Leconey set up a new record of 41.2sec.

Abrahams and his relay teammates equalled that time the following day. But the USA quartet ran even faster. They broke the world record again by clocking 41 dead. Harold remembered, 'In the final we ran the relay in the remarkable time of 41.2 but we were beaten by the Americans. We were second. Nobody remembers that I got a silver medal.'

It might even have been another gold. The British team ran their rivals desperately close, hampered only by the changeovers. One British writer observed, 'The event provided plenty of thrills, and whilst the British team is to be heartily congratulated on the effort it made to win the race, we feel compelled to point out that lack of practice handing over and receiving the baton may possibly have lost us the race.' How they could have benefited collectively from some expert coaching from Sam Mussabini in the art of relay racing. Even so, Abrahams and his friends had achieved a time so stunning that it remained a British record for 28 years. And it was typical Harold to ensure that his world record, however fleeting, was recognised forever. 'I've still got a world record plaque,' he pointed out many years later. 'I insisted on having it!'

A world record and Olympic silver to go with his gold; it was a wonderful way to conclude his French adventure. Unsurprisingly, Abrahams and Liddell were the great heroes of the hour. The crowds which pressed against the British team's train when it came to a halt at London's Victoria station carried Liddell shoulder high to a waiting taxi. But they didn't so much as catch a glimpse of Harold; because he wasn't there. His new friend Porritt, who travelled with the British as a Rhodes Scholar and member of the Empire, recalled: 'He didn't come home with us. I think he was just terribly emotional. He was just overcome by having achieved his objective, and also he was completely deflated mentally, worn out.'

Since there was no wife or fiancée waiting to hug Harold, there was no need to rush home. He had sacrificed marriage and the early chance to have a family in pursuit of sporting glory. Now that the glory was his, he didn't know what to feel, and euphoria gradually gave way to an anticlimactic emptiness. Harold knew that public adoration couldn't fill the void. So he took a few days' vacation in Paris. Did he take the opportunity to have that famous drinking session with Sam Mussabini, the one depicted in *Chariots of Fire*, which allegedly left the pair so legless that they could hardly leave their restaurant? There is no evidence of such a session, and Harold wasn't a great drinker. Yet the chance was there to indulge freely without fear of discovery. Harold, like Mussabini, was able to slip back over the English Channel quietly on his own – with or without a hangover.

When he did finally reach London, Abrahams found that he was still the toast of Britain. He and Eric were both guests at a celebratory dinner in the House of Commons towards the end of July. A menu has survived down the ages, and carries the signatures of the many British Olympic athletes present, including the autographs of 'H.M. Abrahams' and 'E. Liddell'.

Maybe, just maybe they talked that night about who would have won the 100 metres final had the heats not fallen on a Sunday. Liddell was too modest and principled a man to have staked any claim to Harold's crown, even in jest. But that modesty wouldn't have made Abrahams wonder any less. Still, the crown belonged to Harold; and he decided that Mussabini deserved something more than payment for his work. 'When I got back to England I bought Old Sam a pair of starting pistols as a present and he was delighted,' Abrahams remembered.

The stars of Paris were the main attraction when an adoring British public flocked to see their heroes perform back home. Unfortunately, Abrahams' relay display in a post-Olympic showdown with the Americans at Stamford Bridge caused only embarrassment. Perhaps he suffered from the jitters again in front of a vast, expectant London crowd, which was estimated at between 30,000 and 40,000. At any rate, Harold felt obliged to explain the calamitous error he had made. He wrote:

> There have been many different descriptions about the 400 [4 × 100] yards relay which the Americans won in the world's record time of 37⅘ secs. The true facts are these: I ran the last stage, and owing to a big error of judgement on my part, did not start to run at the proper time, so that W.P. Nichol, who was handing over to me, had to slow down for fear of passing me. As he did not seem to be catching me I hesitated, and a man in two minds in a race of less than 100 yards is no good to anyone. When I did get the baton I was well behind Leconey. The error of judgement was due to lack of practice. The British Empire team had never once been together before. In a short relay like 4 × 100 yards the changeover is everything. And it takes a good deal of hard work to perfect this branch of athletics.

In stark contrast, Eric Liddell's breathtaking relay display at 'The Bridge' that day would go down in history. To hit yet another peak, less than a fortnight after his Paris heroics, was truly remarkable. This time Harold had nothing but praise for the passion Liddell showed in the 4 × 440 yards relay, so soon after his Olympic win. Abrahams recalled:

> Ten days later, before a record crowd at Stamford Bridge, he again showed an astonishing resolution when, as 'anchor-man' and against Fitch, one of America's finest quarter-milers, he turned an appreciable deficiency into a three-yard victory. There is no man in the world other than Liddell who could give six yards to a crack American quarter-miler, who has recorded 48⅒, and beat him. The thunders of applause from a crowd of over 30,000 at Stamford Bridge as Liddell, his arms and legs working like some great helicopter, caught his man still sound in my ears whenever I hear the race. The excitement of the crowd as Liddell, with his arms radiating like an animated windmill and his head thrust right back, overhauled his American opponent at the last bend to win was tremendous. The applause they gave him was a combined acknowledgement for his

magnificent win for Britain in Paris, his phenomenal victory that afternoon, and his popularity as a great sportsman. The relay meeting showed the British public first, how exciting relay racing can be, and second, how real is the friendship between the athletes of the British Empire and the United States. Liddell's quarter must have been something in the region of 48 seconds. It was his last race in England (though he did win three Scottish titles in 1925). It was the last time I ever saw him run. The following year he left for China to carry out his life-work as a missionary. No words can describe Liddell's running, and the passing years did not dim the picture of that indomitable courage.

In that summer of 1924 there was no further chance to find out which sprinter was best, Abrahams or Liddell, because the post-Olympic road-show lost Eric before it moved a mile or two across west London to the Queen's Club. There, the Achilles Club faced the British Dominions. Since Liddell was allied to neither, he headed home.

Harold's Paris sidekick, Arthur Porritt was at Queen's, though. Many expected the New Zealander to be the support act in this show too, just as he had been in the French capital. This was Abrahams' territory. The Queen's Club had played host to Harold's first important triumph, the narrow victory over Bevil Rudd in the Inter-Varsity sports four years earlier. It had been a happy hunting ground ever since. Abrahams had every reason to feel confident. But he also felt the mounting pressure of living up to his new billing as Olympic champion. And as Harold explained on numerous occasions, he never did like the feeling of being the favourite for any race.

Porritt confirmed later, 'I beat him on that occasion, within a fortnight of him getting a gold medal at the Olympics. It shows that he was tired out. I was on top of the world achieving what I did.' A.J. Wallis explained what happened. 'The New Zealander, Porritt sprang a surprise by beating Abrahams in the 100 yards flat. Abrahams ran so poorly for him that he could do no better than finish third. The British runner was probably jaded after his exertions in the Paris Olympiad. His brother Dr A.A. Abrahams (as he then was) advised him not to run for a year.'

Coming from Adolphe, who had so often placed pressure on Harold to run at all costs, that advice seemed extraordinary. In fact there were rumours that Harold had suffered a complete mental breakdown, a full-blown manifestation of the anxieties that had plagued him for some time.

The speculation prompted Adolphe to speak publicly about his brother's predicament. He said, 'There has been a lot of rubbish talked about Harold's breakdown. There is no question of such a thing. He is simply acting on my advice that he has been tired out by his crowded programme of late and needs a rest.'

It was something of an understatement to describe that proposed break from racing 'a rest'. Harold revealed later, 'After the 1924 Games at Paris I had resolved to give up sprinting, at any rate for a year or two, and to concentrate on long-jumping.'

Just a few weeks later, with the entire future of the Olympic Games under threat, Harold felt well enough to come out fighting, in print at least. And in that critical moment, he did as much to protect the future of the Olympic Games as any man alive at the time. The prognosis was not good. The 1924 Olympic rugby final had ended in a riot when the USA defeated favourites France. American players and fans were assaulted. An Italian fencer called Oreste Pulitti had wounded a Hungarian judge named George de Kovacs in a duel, after Kovacs had disqualified the Italians for collusion. And a French middle-weight boxer called Roger Brousse was only belatedly disqualified for biting his British opponent Harry Mallin, when every English-speaking boxing nation threatened to withdraw from the Games in protest at Brousse's 'victory'.

As Great Britain's star man in the blue riband event in Paris, it fell upon Abrahams to defend the Olympic movement. He did so in some style, in the *Sunday Express* of August 3, 1924:

> A great deal has been written the past few days on 'Whether the Olympic Games are a good or bad thing'. Certainly no good can come of whitewashing the unpleasant incidents which undoubtedly did take place, but only harm can result from the attempt which has been made to suggest that these incidents are typical of the animosity which permeates the whole games.
>
> Now, because 'unpleasant incidents' have occurred in three of the eighteen Olympic sports, it is suggested: 'The events have shown the world is not ripe for such a brotherhood' as Baron Pierre De Coubertin, who was responsible for the revival of the Olympic Games, anticipated.
>
> Because the French nation, or a section of it, forgot themselves at a Rugby football match, because one or two fencers displayed lack of character and indulged in petulant and childish outbursts of anger,

because a Frenchman confused boxing with biting, we are asked to endorse the suggestion that the Olympic Games are a bad thing, and that we should cease to take part in them.

I cannot speak with experience of any section of the Games but the purely athletic one, and here a whole week's programme was carried out with hardly a single minute of unpleasantness. There was stupidity over a walking race, but otherwise the spirit of true sportsmanship was wonderful. It would be a calamity if the athletic section of the Games – the pure Olympic Games – did not take place.

The fate of the Olympics was very much in the balance. And it is hard to underestimate just how influential the opinion of Harold Abrahams was in the summer of 1924. His defence of the Games proved to be as successful as his 100 metres. As was so often the case, Abrahams led the way . . . and others followed.

PART II

LOVE, HITLER AND LONDON

CHAPTER ONE

FALLING FLAT ON HIS FACE

Being Olympic champion opened doors for Harold Abrahams in that late summer of 1924. Whether he should have walked through all of them is another matter. But then Harold had no way of knowing that time was running out on his athletics career, and he would barely get the chance to fulfil fresh dreams in track and field. So he took on extra challenges, as though burn-out had never been an issue.

Despite having been mentally and physically exhausted by the ups and downs of athletics, he still had the nerve to address large crowds before that summer was out. It takes a certain self-assurance for a top sportsman to try to speak with authority about a subject which confounds so many great brains – politics. Abrahams gave it a go.

When he made a major political speech at Spen Valley on August 21, 1924, the political situation was every bit as intriguing as it became in 2010. The first Labour government had been formed in December of the previous year, by virtue of a hung parliament. The Liberal Party – which Harold supported – had effectively put Labour leader Ramsay MacDonald into power, even though Stanley Baldwin's Conservatives had won the most seats. The minority government was not popular, and the Liberals seemed to be on their last legs.

Responding to claims by the Conservative and Labour Parties that the Liberal Party was dead, Harold quipped that it must be extremely aggravating for the Labour Party to have to rely for their very existence on a corpse. If the Liberal Party were dead then they still had 4,000,000 very active ghosts who intended to do a good deal of ghost-walking during the next ten, fifteen, twenty or thirty years. The listening crowd laughed heartily, so Abrahams warmed to his theme and added that if the Liberal party was dead, death was a very pleasant thing, and he had no fear of it. The difference between life and death seemed to be somewhere about 200,000 votes, he concluded, promising that the Liberals, having secured a budget to suit them, would continue to support their Labour friends until the next election as long as their proposed measures benefited all classes.

It was a strong speech which went down well, to cries of 'hear, hear' from the mostly-Liberal gathering. But he was wrong on a number of points. First, the election came sooner than Harold thought – just two months later, in October 1924. 'I was 'adopted' actually as a Liberal candidate for Walthamstow,' Harold recalled later.

This was all getting a little too serious. Harold liked making speeches and he enjoyed making people laugh, but was he really passionate enough about politics to want to make a career out of it, to the exclusion of law and anything else? The ego trip which came with candidature was something different to anything he had previously experienced. But should he really allow himself to be seduced by the hope of power, when politics didn't burn in his soul like athletics did? Harold was intelligent enough to pull back before it was too late, though his withdrawal was embarrassing enough. 'I very quickly realised that it [my political conviction] wasn't genuine, that I was flattered. And I was adopted as a Liberal candidate. But I decided very quickly that I ought to go back [to law].'

As it turned out, the General Election was a disaster for the Liberals, both in the long-term and the short-term. Under Herbert Henry Asquith, they lost 118 of their 158 seats. Even Labour lost 40 seats, and Stanley Baldwin's Conservatives won by a landslide. It was the start of the two-party dynamic which arguably lasted until 2010.

By the winter of 1924–25, therefore, Harold had reason to feel relieved that he had chosen law instead of politics; but he didn't feel all that passionate about law either. If he thrived in a legal arena, he felt he did so because the job required quick yet superficial thinking. Later he explained, 'I do work quickly, I can pick up a thing superficially very quickly indeed. I can pick up the thread of something while people are talking.' Even so, a part of him felt uncomfortable – particularly in the early days about some of the legal games he had to play:

It is all a little superficial, you see, that would be my criticism of it. But it was most entertaining. I was doing quite a lot of good work at the College Mission as a poor man's lawyer. My first experience at the Old Bailey was when some boy belonging to the Caius Mission had tried to commit suicide. He'd pinched all the money from the gas meter and I went to plead for him.

While I was waiting they put a most venomous-looking man into the dock, who was asked if he wanted legal aid, and the judge said, 'you can choose any man in court'. And I must have had a very white wig because he said, 'I'll have that young man there.' Of course I got very, very red, and my stomach turned over like before a race, and then you go down into the cells to get your £1 3s 6d, that's a guinea for you and 2s 6d for the Clerk. [The defendant] told me his story and, in my sweet innocence, I said, 'Don't think much of that,' whereupon he replied, 'What do you advise me to say?' That rather non-plussed me.

I would like to be able to say that I got him off, but I didn't. He had a terrific list of previous convictions.

Harold's work for the Caius Mission still received grateful recognition from the new Warden, H.R.H. Coney, who had taken over from Reverend Wimbush by 1924–25. He wrote, 'The Poor Man's Lawyer in the person of an old Caian, Mr H.M. Abrahams, gives free legal advice at the Mission House.' This was humble work at the height of Harold's fame.

Though Abrahams was clearly doing something useful, he considered his chances of becoming a legal high-flyer to be remote. He explained, 'To be quite frank, I never would have got a great way at the Bar. I worked very hard on the individual cases, but I hadn't got a profound legal knowledge because I had never been able to study a subject at random.'

Neil Allen, *The Times* journalist who knew Harold well later in life, explained what made Abrahams tick. 'This was a boy who never grew up and he was happiest in the world of sport. He wanted an easy job, not the cut-and-thrust of the court as a barrister.'

Whatever gaps may have existed in his legal knowledge, Harold's status as a national sporting hero saw him through. He explained, 'Of course it made a vast difference to my life. I remember, when I was a barrister appearing in a case after the Olympics, Lord Justice Burke remarking "Mr Abrahams, as one would have expected, covered a great deal of ground in a short space of time." People knew about you.' It was with Harold's athletics career in mind that a courtroom rival also once acknowledged,

'My friend goes in for swift settlements.' But Abrahams didn't just rely on the respect his Olympic success had generated. He had a network of allies for another reason; he had just entered the secretive world of freemasonry.

Harold was initiated into Oxford and Cambridge University Lodge Number 1118 on January 16, 1925. On March 20 he was Passed; and he was Raised on November 20. He went on to join the Athlon Lodge Number 4674 two years later. Being a Freemason helped Harold as he started out in the wider world; but it could only assist him up to a point as he pursued his ambitions. Networking was all very well, but it couldn't help you to jump further.

And in the spring of 1925, Harold's burning ambition was driven by what might now be described as a form of obsessive/compulsive disorder. Every year since his adolescence at Repton, he had improved his long jump personal best to stay ahead of his age. Most recently he had managed to jump over 24 feet in 1924, aged 24. And with the arrival of 1925, there was only one target in his mind. Still engrossed by the numbers game, he confirmed, 'I badly wanted to clear 25 feet, and believed that with hard work and specialised training I might do so. In those days that was getting on for world record form. Long-jumping doesn't combine all that well with sprinting, so I didn't do much in 1924, but I determined that next year in 1925 I was going to concentrate on it.'

Harold didn't feel the need to make any radical changes to his action – even though he had seen the likes of Ed Gourdin achieve stunning success by kicking in mid-air. Abrahams insisted that any conscious attempt to try to copy this action would be counter-productive. 'Imagine the burden imposed on a brain (already fully occupied with the anxiety of the take-off) by the labour of carrying out elaborate reasoning,' he argued.

This seemed to fly in the face of what Abrahams had proved in sprinting; that one could teach oneself to execute seemingly elaborate moves without thinking, if one practised hard enough. And it left Harold with a dilemma: 'How can a body in mid air attain any additional impetus?' With Mussabini, he embarked on one final mission: to find a way to jump further without resorting to the 'kick' used by some of his rivals at the time.

It didn't take long to come up with a solution, which was 'decided with Old Sam during the winter of '24. I did a lot of experimenting indoors at the Poly Gymnasium in Regent Street, chiefly with seeing how one could, with one's stomach muscles hold the legs up during flight, so they didn't drop. But I wasn't doing any of those comic kicks in the air, I used to do a straightforward sail-tuck.'

A season or two of long-jumping and then back to sprinting; that was the plan. His brother Adolphe saw no reason why Harold could not hit new heights on the track in good time for the Amsterdam Games of 1928. The British Olympic doctor said: 'Although with increasing age elasticity diminishes, there is the added advantage of increased strength and stability, so that a critical point is reached when the curves representing speed and strength intersect at a maximum for each individual. And I am sure that twenty-four is much too young. I should place it at three or four years later . . . the optimum sprinting age is distinctively later than that popularly supposed.'

By the sound of it, Adolphe intended to keep Harold's athletics career going right through to Amsterdam, 1928. By steering his little brother away from Christina Innes, he had cunningly guided him through a period of staleness back in 1921–22. Why shouldn't he exert the same sort of influence indefinitely? It was just a question of ensuring that women didn't matter as much as athletics.

He knew that Christina could no longer be regarded as a threat to Harold's athletic excellence, because she had fallen in love all over again – and this time she was formally engaged. 'We are going to be married probably in May so time is shortish, and there is such a lot to do,' Christina wrote to a friend in early 1925. 'But it is all very pleasant. I should like you to meet Francis some time.'

It so happened that Francis was a relative. Sue Smithson explained:

My father, Frank Vigor Morley, was my mother's first cousin. He was always around. They had known each other since childhood. He was American, brought up in America, but his parents used to bring their sons over every summer on vacation to England, more or less to show the three boys off. My father went up to Oxford as a Rhodes Scholar in about 1920; and obviously at that time, he and my mother would have known each other as cousins. My father knew Harold.

One can only imagine Harold's feelings when his former fiancée suddenly announced her engagement to her first cousin, a young man he had undoubtedly met on many occasions.

Francis and Christina? It was hard to take in. Their mothers were sisters, whose maiden name was Bird. One sister, Lilly, had married a mathematician called Frank Morley and gone to the United States. The other, Margaret Bird (known as 'Daisy'), married Hugh Mcleod Innes. They had never lost touch – and there was no chance of that now.

The fact that their mothers were siblings didn't deter Christina and Francis, whatever doubts others expressed about their relationship. And once the romance had begun, it wasn't very long before they knew they wanted to spend their lives together.

While Christina focused for a second time on the prospect of marriage, Harold focused on the 25-foot barrier. Since adolescence, he had never been older in years than the feet he had jumped. By spring, he had endured more than four months of it. Now he was sure those nagging numbers could be balanced to his satisfaction. The first day of the 1925 season offered him the opportunity he had been waiting for. Yet Harold soon found himself having to record the moment like this. 'On May 6, 1925 – strangely enough the anniversary of the King's accession – I retired from active competition. I had been performing in a long-jump pit at the old Stamford Bridge track – as it developed, for the last time.'

In a match between Bedford County and the London Athletic Club, Harold finished in second place with a distance of 22 feet or 6.7 metres. That stark statistic masked a disaster which was caused by a combination of factors. In addition to his obsessive desire to jump 25 feet, there was the boyish impulse to nail a really big jump in front of a posse of photographers. Sue Pottle explained, 'Harold told me he damaged his leg by showing off for photographers doing the long jump.' Rosemary Warne, who knew Harold so well in the final years of his life, agreed. 'It was probably true. A young man like Harold would want to show off if all those cameras were there. I can't imagine him otherwise.'

Then there was the prospect of Christina's wedding in Cambridge, to which her children believe he was invited. Perhaps he wanted to arrive at the church a hero once more, fresh from new, ground-breaking exploits in British track and field. A boost to his self-esteem would help him to handle an emotionally challenging day.

There can be no doubt that Harold was fully focused on the task in hand as he sprinted towards take-off at Stamford Bridge. But he may already have sensed, from his opening jump, that there was a problem with the board. Harold revealed, 'The long-jump run-up at Stamford Bridge had been used a great deal of the day before by a lot of schoolboys, and the take-off was very badly worn. I ran up to the take-off board, I took off, and my take-off leg trailed instead of coming up to meet the other one. I think I must have twisted it.'

Harold would never forget the agony of these moments:

> Anyway I went straight into the ground at about 15, 16 or 17 miles per hour with a straight leg. I heard a noise, rather like Smee tearing a bit of sail cloth in *Peter Pan*. I heard this, didn't realise that it belonged to me, and I passed out. The pain was so acute that I just passed out. I broke my leg, tore badly through a lot of muscles. My leg was nearly doubled up. When I got up my leg was all bent and I had to be carried. I think I was actually carried off the track to the dressing room on a hurdle.

According to Rosemary Warne, the take-off board wasn't just worn – it was wobbly. She recalled, 'He was very upset about it because he said the take-off board was not fixed down properly. The board put him off balance. He didn't blame anybody, though at the time it was absolutely ghastly.'

Had he not realised the danger after his first jump? Only the previous year he had advised athletes to examine carefully the pit sand, the board and surrounding area before committing themselves in a full-blown jump, emphasising the danger of 'the run-up immediately behind the take-off board being worn away, and the jumper, when taking off accurately with his toe well on the board, catching his heel on the sharp edge of the wood'.

In his early-season exuberance, Abrahams had thrown caution to the wind – and his injury was far more devastating than a bruised heel. Rex Alston, a fellow sprinter who later became Harold's co-commentator on athletics for the BBC, recalled:

> I had already run that afternoon and was getting changed in the dressing room when there was a great shout outside. A few minutes later the door opened and Harold was carried in by three ambulance men. He looked absolutely ghastly, as white as a sheet and and only barely conscious from the pain. I had never seen a man look so ill or in such terrible pain. As he fell into the pit the momentum of his body tore all the muscles and the nerves of his leg.

Despite his agony, Harold wouldn't let anyone touch him until his eldest brother arrived. Adolphe finally took him away, as carefully as he could, to what was described as a 'nursing home'. The next morning Adolphe returned to Harold's bedside, bringing with him one of London's leading surgeons. As he inspected the damage, even the surgeon looked mildly horrified. Then he looked Harold in the eye and said, 'I can operate. But if I do there's a risk you'll lose your leg.'

That was not a risk Harold was prepared to take. If only the break had been clean and simple. But there had been so much collateral damage before the impact of his fall reached the bone. The initial reluctance of the bone to snap had caused devastation around it. 'I'd torn through everything without breaking the leg. If I'd broken my leg it would have been simpler. I'd taken all the strain on the muscles and nerves, torn everything I'd got.'

Harold remembered the surgeon's words for the rest of his life:

> He, and many others, commiserated with me – 'Such bad luck at the height of your career.' It was really a magnificent sight; it was purple from the ankle to the hip bone. That was the end, so far as athletics was concerned. I'll be absolutely truthful, I laid back there and I said, 'This is marvellous.' I was very uncertain about what to do in athletics, and here I had no option, my mind had been made up for me. What did I think of it? Strangely, my first reaction was of relief, outweighing any disappointment. I was faced no more with any problem of when to retire.
>
> The athlete's farewell to his speed is as embarrassing as the 'positively last appearance' of an actor past his prime. Would I have gone downhill and tried to go on? That was the decision I never had to make. It was made for me. Rather painfully, but it was made. Now I could not be accused of retiring because I was afraid of being beaten – indeed, all sympathy was with me on my enforced departure. I wonder, in a sense, if it was not another piece of good bad luck. It is difficult to climb to the top of the ladder in any sport, but so much more difficult to stay there. Of course one shouldn't mind being beaten; many people, perhaps, do not. I did; which is why my retirement was such a relief. But I still feel sad that I never jumped 25 feet.

Above all, perhaps it was that fixation with numbers which had finally done for him. He admitted later, 'My age runs conveniently with the years, and I resolved that I would set my ambition as a long jumper to keep for as long as possible ahead in feet of the date. At 18, I jumped 20ft 5½in; at 19, 21ft 8in; and in 1920 I cleared 22ft 7in. By the end of 1921 I had reached 23ft 0½ in. In 1923 my best was 23ft 8¾in, and on one most fortunate occasion in 1924 I cleared 24ft 2½ in. Alas, with 1925 I had to abandon the task.'

Part of his relief may have lain in the mathematical inevitability of eventual defeat in this neurotic battle with time anyway. How could he ever have been expected to jump 30 feet at the age of thirty, for example? Now the pressure was off. But his long-term sprinting career had also been destroyed in an instant.

Evelyn Montague believed there would have been so much more still to come.

> It was cruel luck that in 1925, with the new [running] style mastered and endless vistas opening up before him, his career should be brought to a sudden end. He tore clean through the nerves and muscles behind his right knee . . . If it had not happened, he would have gone on for many years, for his is the devouring keenness which never dreams of retiring discreetly in the moment of success . . . It would have been particularly interesting to see how his jumping developed, for he was the last great jumper who did not use the hitchkick. He gained his distance by the old-fashioned virtues of speed, spring and float, and to this day he will not wholeheartedly accept the hitchkick, though he admits that, to judge by results, there must be something in it.

But Montague knew that Harold's loss to sprinting was the greater sporting tragedy. 'In actual fact, he had only begun to realise his full capabilities. I firmly believe that, if he had not broken down, he would have won both the 100 and 200 metres at the 1928 Olympic Games, and would have proved himself one of the three or four greatest sprinters of all time.'

We will never know, and Harold liked it that way. 'I got every sympathy, with everyone saying "Marvellous, what would he only have done if he had gone on?" No question, I had to stop dead, more or less go out at the top. I was very relieved that it had happened.' Relieved, and a little frightened. Rex Alston pointed out, 'For a while it was feared he would never walk again.' Harold remembered the uncomfortable months of uncertainty. 'I didn't like the pain very much, and it was months before I got my leg to the ground.' He gradually found that he could walk, but the limp made it painfully obvious that, as Montague put it, Harold's leg was 'permanently useless for strenuous athletics.'

'And that put an end to my career as an active athlete,' Harold concluded. He couldn't take part, but he would never desert athletics. He simply had to find a different role. 'It enabled me to do much more in athletic administration and I did quite a lot of lecturing in the early days, it was quite well paid.'

There wasn't always much of an audience waiting for the Olympic champion, though. An amused Abrahams recalled:

> I went down to give a lecture and there were five people in the room with a fee of ten guineas. I said to the secretary, 'Look, I can't really take ten guineas. It works out at about £2 per head!' And he looked at me and said, 'That's all right, some old lady has left the money in trust and we have to give the lectures.' So I took the money and I thought 'I wonder why the Dickens they selected me?' And I think the explanation is very simple. 'AB' is the beginning [of the alphabet], and the first name on his list of lecturers was Abrahams – so he took me. I don't know who the lady was who gave me the money, but I took it with a clear conscience.

Whether he was dabbling in law, lecturing or working in administration, Harold soon had the sense that his gold medal would continue to work strongly in his favour. And he had always been interested in journalism. Harold confirmed, 'I determined in the early days that I was going to write, because I didn't want to have all my financial eggs in one basket. That's why I wrote and broadcast, to have a second string all the way. If I'd been more courageous, naturally I'd have gone out for one thing. [But] I don't think I'd have been any happier.'

A new life as a famous ex-athlete was waiting – a life defined by ten seconds in Paris. Later he was able to say:

> I think my own good luck in winning has made a tremendous difference to my whole life. I like to feel that if I had been second by six inches I would still have managed to achieve a number of things I've been happy to achieve, but they don't say how much you're second by . . . The winner is outstanding in people's minds; far more

His brutish father, Isaac had a soft spot for baby Harold.

Harold with his doting mother Esther.

The perfect escape: Harold (circled centre) on his brother Lionel's back in an early race against his siblings. The simple thrill of moving fast helped Abrahams to deal with family trauma.

Child star: Harold was just ten years old when he beat all the other young relatives of London Athletic Club members to take the Lotinga Cup in his first big race, a handicap at Stamford Bridge.

Role model: His brother Sidney, pictured on the right in the portrait, was an Olympian and Cambridge Blue, who inspired Harold's early success.

As a schoolboy at Repton, Abrahams experienced anti-Semitism and homosexual advances.

Once at Cambridge University, he was admired for his many victories against Oxford. This Varsity win at London's Queen's Club shows how the sprint lanes were separated by short poles and string.

Crashing back down to earth: Harold Abrahams went to the 1920 Antwerp Olympics as a Cambridge hero, but his limbs lacked the strength to trouble the world's very best.

Later that summer he was further humbled when he injured an arm racing a blind man on equal terms near Brighton.

Feeling neglected? First love Christina Innes, who soon became Harold's fiancée, looks annoyed as the 'Survivors' photo is taken at the 1921 Caius College May Ball, with Harold apparently oblivious to her presence. (Reproduced by permission of the Masters and Fellows of Gonville and Caius College, Cambridge University)

Running scared: Complaining of a sore throat, Harold Abrahams avoids the embarrassment of defeat to Eric Liddell in the sprint finals at the AAA Championships, where the Scotsman takes the 100 yards title in a blistering 9.7 sec.

Lift-off! Yet on the same day Harold feels well enough to leap into the stratosphere to register a winning 23 feet, 8 ¾ inches in the long jump.

The King's reach: The Duke of York, the future King George VI, extends an arm to congratulate Harold Abrahams on his victories for Oxford and Cambridge over Harvard and Yale at the new Wembley Stadium in 1923. Like Harold, the royal had an award-winning movie made about him – *The King's Speech*.

One way to motivate an athlete! Fortunately for Harold Abrahams, this is an optical illusion; and what he once described as 'the best part of my anatomy' was spared by Sam Mussabini and his starter's pistol.

Harold travelled to the 1924 Olympics in what he described as 'ghastly, ill-fitting team gear of white trousers, blazers made of shoddy material and straw hats'.

Pure magic: But he looked the part when he broke the tape in the 100 metres final, and his manic intensity turned to joyous relief.

First and last: Harold won the 1924 Olympic 100 metres because everything about his body is pointing forwards, while others flail aimlessly.

But in the 200 metres final, shoulders are tense and he (second from the right) starts to roll as he realises that Eric Liddell (second from left) and the other medal-winners are beyond his reach.

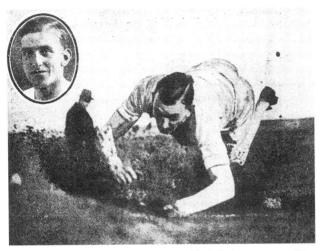

Biting the dust, counting the cost: Abrahams falls foul of a worn-out, wobbly take-off board at Stamford Bridge in May 1925 – and the injuries sustained end his career.

He feels a strange relief, though there is also visible pain as an irritable Harold recovers at home.

Love of his life: A glamorous opera singer called Sybil Evers helped change Harold's attitude to women before their marriage in 1936.

They couldn't have children, so they adopted – starting with son Alan as they dodged bombs during World War Two.

Champions: Harold first met Jesse Owens in the Olympic village in Berlin, 1936 – just before the Games began, and Owens destroyed Hitler's theory of Aryan supremacy.

Friends for life: Abrahams considered Owens to be the finest sprinter in the history of athletics, and continued to tell him so whenever they met in the Caribbean or USA.

Easy rider: Harold knew that Roger Bannister was just as highly strung as he had been as an athlete. So Abrahams invited his young friend for weekends in the country, where Bannister could really relax.

Out of place: This picture clearly shows that Harold Abrahams (arrowed) is in a poor position to gauge the precise split second when Roger Bannister's torso hits the tape for his historic sub-four-minute mile at Iffley Road, Oxford. Harold assumed official timekeeper status, even though the appointed timekeepers were gathered in line with the tape on the other side of the track.

The daughter and the spy: Sue Abrahams (right) married Pat Pottle, who helped spring the infamous double agent George Blake from Brixton jail. Here Sue relaxes in Russia with a still-grateful Blake (left), whose wife's face has been obscured at Sue's request.

Harold with Rosemary Warne and some friends' children in Germany. Harold's platonic relationship with Rosemary gave him great joy and he spent his last Christmas with her.

importance is attached to winning than I believe ought to be attached, but that's human nature.

He was a winner in his sporting and professional life, but not as yet in his personal life. As if to remind him of his emotional isolation, just eight days after tragedy struck Harold in the long-jump pit, his former fiancée was married.

The wedding took place on May 14, 1925 in St Michael's Church, Cambridge. The certificate comfirms that Frank Vigor Morley, 'writer', married Christina McLeod Innes in the presence of her father Hugh, mother Margaret, and other relatives. Christina's husband went on to become a distinguished publisher with Faber and Faber. Frank edited the work of T.S. Eliot; and Harold was pleased to see Christina immersed in an intellectual world she adored.

Harold Abrahams wasn't in with the literary crowd; but when in 1928 he wrote a book with his brother Adolphe, *Training for Athletes*, the publisher was the London-based G. Bell and Sons – the same company for which his old flame Christina had worked as secretary after leaving university.

He and Christina would never forget their Cambridge days and a mutual affection lasted a lifetime. But Christina loved Frank now, and they soon had two sons, Donald and Oliver. The boys were followed by two daughters, Sue and Peregrine. T.S. Eliot became godfather to Sue and even wrote a poem called 'Cows' for the children.

Harold never had children of his own; but he didn't begrudge Christina her happiness. Though she had been his first love, she wasn't destined to become the great love of his life. Harold had to wait a good few years before he met the woman who could justifiably lay claim to that title.

It was a love story that was to prove even more dramatic than his first.

CHAPTER TWO

A Pioneer's Path To Sybil

Anyone who loved Harold Abrahams had to share him with athletics. He spent his entire life devoted to the sport.

Yet Abrahams didn't consciously set out on some sort of lifelong mission to make millions of people love track and field as much as he did. It just turned out that way, and his energy seemed endless. Norris McWhirter, who later created the *Guinness Book of Records*, was able to declare, 'Harold Abrahams raised athletics from a minor to a major national sport.' That process had started with his 100 metres triumph in Paris. And Harold's career-ending injury would not diminish his ability to infect others with his own enthusiasm.

His first contribution to the *Sunday Times* newspaper came on June 28, 1925. Abrahams became a permanent fixture, bringing more and more new supporters to his chosen sport. Looking back a quarter of a century later, he wrote, 'I can still feel the sense of astonished pleasure with which I read, on page 15, that I was to contribute articles on athletics.' Readers shared that pleasure, and his following grew.

To have any real influence over the direction of his sport, however, he had to join the administrators. Therefore, ten weeks after he left the Stamford Bridge stage in agony, he returned with a clip-board to officiate as a field judge at the AAA Championships.

Peter Lovesey, respected writer and athletics historian, plotted Harold's early rise through the administrative ranks. 'He became Hon. Treasurer of the Middlesex AAA; served on the Southern Committee and, from 1926, the General Committee of the AAA. Not one of these enterprises was skimped. He worked at them as he had worked at winning a gold medal.' The irony was that, by his own admission, Harold's motives weren't purely altruistic. He said much later:

> I wish I could feel honestly that one's inclination to take part in athletic administration was a sort of virtuous response to all one owed to athletics. I would be dishonest if I said that. I have always liked administration. I have liked more than anything else using my knowledge in negotiation in getting things straightened out, untangling problems. And of course there is a certain amount of power complex involved because I like helping to direct things. But my biggest urge is that I hate more than anything else quarrelling. I've done my share of it.

The reason Harold hated quarrelling was that deep down he thought of himself as a team player. Abrahams was once asked if he got as much satisfaction out of being a journalist and administrator as he did out of being an athlete. Harold replied, 'I think to be absolutely frank, more. And while I would be a fool to say I am not proud of having been successful – I am – I believe I really get more out of team effort. I think one wants recognition in a way for subduing one's own personality in a team job.'

But Harold didn't have to subdue his own personality too much as he experimented in a brand new journalistic field – live radio sports commentary. He was like a test pilot, making the airwaves safe for the 24/7 live outside broadcasts of the twenty-first century. The newspapers were terrified that their reports would be rendered pointless; and there was much negotiation behind the scenes before anything was actually broadcast.

Harold remembered those pioneering times and explained, 'I think I must have given the first athletics commentary. We did some trials. Originally they weren't allowed to do running commentaries, because of the press. So there was a lot of practising. I did the first in 1926.' But it was on March 26, 1927 that Harold Abrahams broadcast live to the nation from the Varsity sports between Oxford and Cambridge at the Queen's Club. It was the first outside broadcast of a sports event and blazed the trail for so much of what we take for granted today. It also came close to recreating the adrenalin of competing, though nothing could quite do that.

Meanwhile he continued to establish himself as part of the British athletics administrative team, in a variety of roles. Abrahams was Press Steward at the AAA Championships in 1926 and Official Recorder in 1927. Unspectacular titles, but his influence was growing all the time.

Harold may have joined the athletics establishment, but that didn't stop him from launching a withering attack on the International Olympic Committee in 1927. 'The composition of this autocratic body, the IOC, has always been veiled in obscurity. Membership seems to consist of those who are invited by the body itself to join,' he complained controversially. Harold had spent enough time in the company of that formidable outcast, Sam Mussabini, to know that 'the establishment' had left plenty of room for improvement in athletics administration at home and abroad.

Sadly, however, Mussabini's opinions could no longer be sought. On June 27, 1927 he died in London, aged 64. He still held the post of coach to the Polytechnic Harriers. Among his possessions, they found a photo of Abrahams breaking the tape in the Olympic 100 metres, with the inscription 'To S.A.M., in memory of nine months together.' How lucky Harold had been to work with Mussabini, just a few short years before the master passed away. A host of successful athletes had already confirmed Old Sam's place in history as one of the great coaches of all time.

For Harold, life went on, and he always had an eye for innovation. Norris McWhirter later said of Harold, 'His drafting ability enabled him to transform the rules of competition – making sensible changes which are today taken for granted but which were revolutionary in the mid-1920s.' This process had actually started during that Olympic summer of 1924, when Abrahams complained that the unlimited numbers of entrants at the AAA Championships that year had made a mockery of serious competition. He had drawn attention to the plight of his great rival for public affection, Eric Liddell, as the most scandalous example of administration gone mad. 'The whole programme is full of absurdities on account of this unlimited entry. E.H. Liddell had to run three 220s and three 440s in less than 24 hours . . . And the long and high jumpers could have almost gone to sleep between the times they were called upon to perform . . . The running of three quarter-miles in the space of under twenty-four hours is no light task for any man.'

Abrahams wanted seeding – and byes to the second round for those of known AAA standard. He wanted harmony between track and field, all the things that ensure the smooth running of major championships these days. That we have continuity today is partly down to Harold Abrahams' belligerence the best part of a century ago.

Meanwhile, as technology developed, Abrahams was often the first to take advantage. Harold became the first announcer at the AAA Championships to use a loudspeaker instead of a megaphone. That happened in 1928. But it was on the radio that his rich voice was starting to become familiar to a wider public.

Prior to an England v. France international at Stamford Bridge, he explained to listeners, 'The running commentary is given from a hut which is situated in the South-East corner of the ground. The position (if we imagine an oblong with an oval representing the track inside it) is in the right-hand bottom corner. The track is 440 yards round, and we are at the first corner in most races. The runners run with the grass on the left-hand side.' It was simple, informative and effective, preparing the listener for the image he would try to paint with words during the race itself. This was pioneering work, uncharted territory, and Harold was becoming an important figurehead for the sport; a popular link between the casually

Pioneer broadcaster: Harold (right) peers out of a mobile commentary box, which looks suspiciously like a converted garden shed, and is one of the first to be used by the BBC for outside broadcasting. The microphone is suspended by wire between Harold and his co-commentator, leaving them free to make and consult their race notes. The producers down on the left are clearly very proud of their rudimentary creation.

interested listener back home, and the intense world of the athletes themselves.

As McWhirter put it half a century later, 'Harold possessed one of the finest speaking voices in the country. Those wonderful articulated and modulated words of his and his meticulous statistical preparation set a standard and comprised a whole technique of live commentary and summary on which the BBC reputation as the world's premier sports service can justly be said to have been founded.'

That year of 1928 brought Harold an even higher honour, because in April he was made captain of the GB athletics team for the forthcoming Amsterdam Olympics. The BOA wanted to salute Abrahams for his achievement at the previous Olympics; and also to recognise how he had remained a national hero despite his injury, and was still a symbol of conscientious excellence in athletics and beyond. His friend Walter Ashley wrote that year, 'Through it all, Harold has maintained his eagerness to help the underdog. He has lectured regularly to working boys and working men. I have never known him refuse a request to help a good cause. It is these qualities of character and leadership, even more than his own athletic record, which so well qualify him for his important task in Amsterdam.'

Abrahams wasn't so sure that he met the requirements of the job. 'I went as Captain of the Athletic Team in 1928. A sort of non-playing captain. Not a very successful one, I think because I was doing a lot of writing at the time.' Some of it prior to the Games wasn't very complimentary about members of his own team. 'Our ten representatives in the field events have no possible winners and only a couple of possible finalists,' he stated somewhat brutally. He wasn't wrong, but his team members couldn't have wanted to hear such bleak realism just before they embarked on their Olympic adventure.

Harold seemed unconcerned as he recalled, 'I left London with the British team on Wednesday, July 25, and sailed from Harwich to Flushing. The competitions began on Sunday, July 29, and Lord Burghley was the first athlete to break a tape at the ninth Olympiad, for he easily won the 400 metres hurdles, and the next day we yelled ourselves hoarse when he ran magnificently to win the final in record time. He had enormous courage when he wasn't 100 per cent fit.'

Another British hurdler caught the eye. Fred Gaby, mentioned in Mussabini's simple note to Harold back in Paris, was representing Great Britain again. In 1924 he had performed with credit by reaching the semi-final of the 110m hurdles. This time he did even better. Abrahams admitted, 'The performance of Fred Gaby in reaching the final at the age of thirty-three was deserving of the highest praise.' Though a medal remained just out of reach, Harold admired him just the same. 'Gaby's career is a model for athletes to follow. I remember him as a very ordinary sprinter before he took to hurdling. Like many others he came under the care of Sam Mussabini; and by years of hard work made himself into a first-rank performer.'

The news from Amsterdam wasn't all positive, though. Abrahams found himself at the centre of a huge controversy, which dated back to the previous Olympics in Paris. The row almost resulted in his former rival Charley Paddock from being banned from running in Amsterdam. Significantly, the British were the ones pushing for that ban – though Abrahams let his superiors do the talking. The *New York Times* of July 26 explained that, 'The Executive Committee of the International Olympic Committee was engaged in stormy secret sessions last night.' They were deciding the American's fate, after 'the question was first raised in the Executive Committee by Brigadier-General R.J. Kentish of Great Britain over an alleged radio talk by Paddock, in which the runner is said to have declared that in the 100 metres final at Paris in the Olympics of 1924 four Americans had decided to make false starts in order to wear out the British star, Harold Abrahams, who eventually won the event.'

Several American officials threatened to throw Paddock out of the US team if the allegations turned out to be true. It was left to Paddock to defend himself in a make-or-break meeting with General McArthur, the US Olympic chief. Ever the smooth talker, Paddock insisted that his words had been distorted, and he had only been speculating that the Americans might have made false starts had they been professionals. Since they were pure amateurs, the idea had never entered their heads.

Jackson Scholz quickly denied having discussed false-starting in that 1924 changing room. Since Scholz was also running in Amsterdam, he could hardly have said anything else. To admit to even a half-hearted conversation along those Machiavellian lines back in Paris might have jeopardised his own involvement in the latest Olympics, in addition to Paddock's. And despite the collective denials, the most likely scenario is that Paddock did raise the possibility of systematic false-starting prior to the Paris final. After careful consideration the scheme was dismissed, perhaps even before it reached the ears of the more sporting Scholz.

Whatever the truth, Paddock escaped a ban, and was allowed to run in the Amsterdam 200 metres after all. But he failed to reach the final, probably distracted by the scandal which had engulfed him. Like Scholz, Abrahams would never entirely warm to Paddock – and neither man could have been too upset to see the great showman flop at his third Olympics.

Harold soon had something more positive to shout about. 'The other victory which fell to Great Britain was in the 800 metres, which Douglas Lowe won for the second time by nearly 10 yards in 1 min 51.8sec – a new Olympic record. He dominated the entire field.'

But the Brits were still preparing the amateur way. No one had followed Harold's lead by trying to adopt his intense training methods. And Abrahams didn't seem quite so anxious these days to advocate that intensity. He wrote, 'One American trainer asked me how many coaches we had got for our gallant little team. I replied, "Oh, we have two – motor-coaches".'

It was all a bit of fun for Harold by now, and he admitted, 'I am afraid too that on more than one occasion I allowed my pro-British exuberance to overcome my judgement and lost bets. But betting is not allowed on athletic events, so do not let this get any further will you?'

The Olympics had felt like a matter of life and death to Harold four years earlier. Afterwards he had needed a few days alone just to get over the ordeal. This time the test for Abrahams came from the debates which took place away from the track. There was one very tricky question to field from his fellow journalists. As British captain, he was asked to comment on an IAAF resolution in Amsterdam which recognised the existence of doping, and provided for 'the exclusions of persons who knowingly dope from places where IAAF rules prevail'. Abrahams clearly didn't consider his own use of the strychnine-based 'Easton's Syrup' at the previous Olympics to constitute a case of doping; rather the casual use of a legitimate tonic. However, he wasn't about to reveal what he had done when he gave the following reply:

> I myself have never come across a case of doping, and, further, from conversations I have had with medical men on the subject I have been unable to discover that there is any drug that would be of assistance. The first thing that has to be decided is: 'What is doping?' Most of us use sugar between the heats and the finals. Would that be considered doping? Also, what about any tonic taken for health purposes? To imply that people would inject a drug with a

hypodermic syringe would be nonsense. Supposing it were discovered that the taking of cocaine or opium would assist runners, how could this question be tackled if athletes consumed foods containing those things? Altogether, I think the problem much too fantastic to tackle.

Time would show that doping was a problem that would have to be tackled before it ruined Harold's beloved sport completely. Having made his point in Amsterdam, however, and having left the authorities to decide what constituted doping and what didn't, Harold returned to the Olympic party. He basked in the reflected glory of what he described as Douglas Lowe's 'unforgettably brilliant effort', and that of his friend Lord Burghley too. Unlike his delayed, low-key return from Paris four years earlier, this time he enjoyed the full fanfare of the British team's welcome back to London.

Athletics writer Tony Ward later described the British team's homecoming. 'A great crowd assembled at Liverpool Street on the team's return to England, and, in scenes reminiscent of four years earlier, rushed the train as it arrived. Their cries of "Burghley!" and "Abrahams!" were followed by cheers. He [Harold] was still a celebrity.'

In 1931 Abrahams teamed up with Paris and Amsterdam gold medallist Douglas Lowe to restore order to British athletics, when some of its national associations were pushing for individual representation on the International Amateur Athletic Federation. Peter Lovesey said of Abrahams, 'His ability to present a case persuasively came to the rescue of British athletics. With another able lawyer, Douglas Lowe, he resolved the crisis over the United Kingdom representation on the IAAF by negotiating the formation of the International Board, known later as the BAAB [British Amateur Athletic Board].'

Despite that notable piece of fire-fighting, no one saw fit to send Abrahams to the Los Angeles Olympics in 1932. And he couldn't justify going under his own steam because of the cost. He explained a few years later, 'I hadn't the money to get to Los Angeles in 1932. I had no means to get there. I stayed up till two o'clock every morning eagerly watching the tape machine as it ticked out the results.'

Harold couldn't help but spare a thought for his old GB colleague, Eric Liddell. 'Eight years after Liddell's triumph in Paris, an American [Bill Carr] was to win the title at Los Angeles in 46.2. I wish Liddell could have been present on that Californian path!' And Harold wished he could have been there watching. He vowed never to miss another Olympics in his lifetime.

But just as he was starting to set his journalistic sights on the next Games in Berlin, he was distracted by an opera singer called Sybil Evers. When she invited Abrahams over to her table at the Grosvenor hotel early in 1934, it marked the start of a great love affair – and the end of a decade or more without a serious relationship.

The simple truth was that Harold had a fear of commitment – except to athletics. But now there would be two loves in Harold's life. Athletics would never have to give way; but it would often have to share the top step. To those who knew Harold Abrahams, such a change was scarcely imaginable; yet it happened.

Like Harold, Sybil had grown up at a boy's public school – her father Claude was a housemaster at Rugby. Asked once by a radio interviewer whether she was an athletics expert, she replied, 'No I'm afraid I'm not. I was born and brought up at Rugby with boys and used to watch the sport there. But I'm very far from being an expert. I can't manage to keep the times in my head.'

Music was her absolute passion. Sybil's artistic leanings came from her mother, Jessie, who was a talented water-colourist. In a book called *Butterflies in Camphor*, a relative called Elliot Evers confirmed:

> Sybil's great interest was in the stage, and particularly in musical comedy. As a child she had produced playlets and composed tunes. She sang well and was pretty, though petite. She was extremely attractive, full of gaiety and able to take things as they came with a smile. She studied at the college of music and then achieved her ambition of a stage career. She acted in *The Beggar's Opera*, was the Lily Maid in the opera of that name, and was in the D'Oyly Carte Opera Company which suited her perfectly as she loved the operas and relished every moment of them. Her charm as one of the three pretty maids from school in *The Mikado* is still remembered. She had many other singing parts on the stage and on the radio.

The book also revealed that 'Sybil had a youthful serious illness and operation, [which meant she] could have no children.' Her adopted daughter Sue Pottle confirmed, 'She had suffered from TB of the uterus.' Sybil still married Noel Brack, an Old Haileyburian, but the marriage quickly fell apart and they were divorced.

When Sybil was asked to look back on her life before she met Harold, she airbrushed Brack right out of it. 'Well, I was a singer. I trained at the Royal College of Music. I used to sing in light opera. In fact I was employed by the BBC for some time, second soprano of the Wireless Singers before the war; that was in the old Savoy Hill days. And then after that I used to work fairly often for their music production department, which gave performances of light operas.'

She had played a number of supporting roles while performing in the D'Oyly Carte Opera Company from March 1930 to September 1931. In January 1934, Sybil appeared in a children's play called *Ever So Long Ago* at the Cambridge Theatre in London. It was reportedly the first play attended by Princess Elizabeth, the future Queen.

At around this time fate took a hand, and put Sybil in the same room as Harold. 'I met him at an old school dance,' Sybil explained simply. It was the first time they had talked together, though not the first time Abrahams had laid eyes on the alluring Miss Evers. By then she had finished a two-year spell with the D'Oyly Carte and was alternating between the Webber-Douglas and the Chanticleer opera companies. 'I think he had actually seen her performing,' his nephew Tony explained. And a singer friend called Julia once wrote later to remind Sybil, 'Do you remember telling me about your [first] meeting with Harold, when we were doing *Figaro?*'

In *The Marriage of Figaro*, Sybil usually played the part of Susanna (Maid to the Countess). The *Figaro* plot saw Sybil spurning the advances of the Count who, tired of his wife, pursues her maid Susanna. Sybil's character is about to marry Figaro, which explains her unwillingness to do the Count's bidding. It is an alluring role; and one critic described what Sybil brought to the part: '*Figaro* being what it is, a combination of "opera buffa" and sophisticated comedy of manners, those who perform it must be able not only to sing well but also to act well . . . For Susanna we have Miss Sybil Evers and she is entrancing. She also knows a thing or two about acting and oh, the difference to us!'

We can picture Harold gazing at the stage, similarly entranced. On stage, Sybil was playing hard to get in scenes alongside the Count Almaviva. Off stage, Harold would soon see whether she still played so hard to get. The daughter they later adopted, Sue Pottle, set the scene for that first meeting. 'It was a party for old girls from Wycombe Abbey [a top public school]. It was held at the Grosvenor and each group of old girls had their own guests sitting at their respective tables. As far as I understand it, Dad was at one table and my mother was at another. And I have been told that it was my mother, or at least those on her table, who invited my father to come over and join them at some point in the evening.'

Even in the mid-1930s, Harold remained something of a celebrity. Most people knew about his Olympic win in Paris back in 1924. Sybil might even have been able to tell Harold where she had been on his big day; because July 7, 1924 had been unforgettable for her too. At 3 p.m., just as Harold was preparing to run his epic semi-final in Paris, Sybil had begun to perform over in London – 'In the presence of Her Majesty the Queen', as the theatre programme put it. The occasion was a private dress rehearsal of *Hugh the Drover*, a romantic ballad opera in two acts, at the Parry Opera Theatre. Queen Mary was invited to attend. Sybil played Susan, hardly the leading role; but it wasn't every day you performed for the Queen. It wasn't every day you won gold at the Olympic Games either.

Since Harold and Sybil were both accustomed to being the centre of attention, onlookers must have been fascinated to see how their egos would interact at the Grosvenor. Instead of clashing, they fed off each other very comfortably indeed. What started as a daring, fun flirtation in front of Sybil's friends became something more. It isn't hard to imagine Harold plucking up the courage to ask Sybil to dance, even though by his own admission he was a hopeless dancer at the time. Sybil clearly didn't hold that against him, because they agreed to meet again. Perhaps Harold was invited to see *Figaro* a second time. And there would be more opportunities to hypnotise her suitor.

When Sybil performed in Milton's *Comus*, at the Open Air Theatre in London's Regent's Park that summer, a reviewer in *The Times* purred, 'The appeal for indulgence on behalf of Miss Sybil Evers, who had taken up at short notice the part of the Lady, was quite unnecessary; she was the very incarnation of Milton's idea of the queen-hood of innocence, and her first entrance onto an empty stage was pure beauty.'

If hardened critics were so touched, it is easy enough to picture Harold completely captivated. Sybil, with her background in light opera, seemed almost made for him. She had made a career of bringing passion to the kind of music that already left Harold spellbound.

That she was equally enchanting in real life touched Harold more deeply than he had thought possible. And although she had suffered an unhappy marriage, she couldn't prevent herself from falling in love with him either. 'It was a whirlwind affair,' Sybil admitted a few years later. Yet it was the sheer depth of Harold's feelings that sparked moments of extreme crisis in the early years of their relationship, as we shall see.

Harold once said, 'I am much too terrified of putting all my eggs in one basket and doing one thing, getting involved in one thing, then it being lost. I dare say a Freudian analysis would suggest that someone took something away from me as a kid that I liked very much; it could be as simple as that. But certainly the pattern is there.'

By September 1935, Harold had seen fit to put some distance between Sybil and himself. This was a move that seems to have caused her some anxiety. On September 1 she wrote a mock-formal letter to him, her own little protest against the lack of contact between them, and put an unspecified little present in the envelope:

> Miss Evers presents her compliments to Mr Abrahams, and trusts he is in good health and has enjoyed a pleasant week out of Town. She begs to inform him that to her the week has seemed endless – and hopes he will take an early opportunity of acquainting her of his safe return. She further begs that he will accept the enclosed as a very small token of her affection and esteem, and desires to remain only ever his faithfully.

On September 3, Sybil showered Harold with love in the form of a poem called *Gifts*, which talked of a permanence which Harold didn't feel he could promise.

> I would give you Beauty
> Were Beauty mine to give,
> And all the happy things of Life
> As long as you may live.
>
> The glory of the sunlight,
> The laughing summer hours –
> The wonder lying 'neath the scent
> Of hay, and sun-warmed flowers.
>
> And you should hear the music
> Of softly-falling rain,
> And watch the ever-changing light
> And shadow on the plain.

> And I would give you starlight,
> With the pale moon above,
> And gentle peace, and quietness –
> And love.

This created anything but a sense of peace in Harold. It wasn't that he didn't feel any love for Sybil; but he was afraid of deep feelings, and more likely to reject them. He wondered whether any two people could love each other for ever. His parents hadn't. Sybil and her first husband hadn't. Harold and his first fiancée hadn't either.

Abrahams wrote from personal experience when he later voiced his concerns to Sybil, 'God, suppose our love, my love just peters out like that? You know that hopeless feeling that you can't prevent love just vanishing.' Harold felt ill-equipped to deal with romantic intensity. Memories of the impermanence of his love for Christina came flooding back. Harold and Sybil had also begun to talk about marriage; but deep down the idea terrified Harold.

Meanwhile his determination to reach the 1936 Olympics in Nazi-run Berlin was never far away. Professional and personal pressures were about to collide.

CHAPTER THREE

BREAKDOWN ON THE ROAD TO BERLIN

In May 1935 William Temple, the then Archbishop of York who had been the departing Repton headmaster just as Harold had arrived at the school, tried to send a letter to Adolf Hitler through the British Olympic Association. Part of it read as follows:

> International sport may either conduce to friendly relations or exasperate unfriendly relations. If the Olympic Games in Germany are to fulfil their historic mission, they must, as Your Excellency will agree, open in an atmosphere of friendship and reconciliation.

Despite his natural hatred for any kind of political interference in sport, Harold Abrahams found himself agreeing wholeheartedly with those sentiments, and in the late summer of 1935 he pushed for a similar request to be sent to Herr Hitler from the British Olympic Association or International Committee.

> I would like to say that if either the B.O.A. or the I.O.C. could see their way to sending Herr Hitler a dignified request in the terms that the Archbishop of York suggests, it might do a tremendous amount of good. I fully appreciate the very natural reluctance which athletic bodies feel in 'meddling with politics' as it is sometime put. But I believe that the more liberal elements in Germany would greatly welcome an opportunity of reversing the present policy of

oppression, and I think it would provide an attractive weapon for the present regime to be able to mitigate the present extremity without the appearance of climbing down. To be able to give as a reason for generosity the upholding of the Olympic ideal, would provide a world-wide gesture which might very well appeal to those in authority. And of course if Herr Hitler was able to make some concession, the effect in Europe would be tremendous. I don't want to exaggerate, but such a gesture as the Archbishop visualises might literally result in more genuine co-operation with Germany in disarmament and allied problems.

I know full well that it is said that the Olympic Games should keep clear of politics, but if I rightly understand the fundamental principles which underlie our enthusiasm for international sport, it is that we have here a means of emphasising the similarities between nations, and we are, I think, shutting our eyes to reality, if we believe that the mere organisation and support of such institutions as the Olympic Games, constitutes the end of our duty in this matter. Quite legitimately the common bond of sport can be used to ameliorate international relationships, and unless all our profession that the Olympic Games are a good thing is so much eyewash, a body such as the British Olympic Association can legitimately regard it as within its provinces to point out that racial and religious prejudices such as exist in Germany to-day tends [sic] to undermine the good which sport hopes to achieve.

I naturally feel very strongly that the total negation of all liberty in Germany is a deplorable thing, and I believe that a dignified appeal to Herr Hitler, taking the form of a request and not a protest, would tend to do much more good than many people imagine or even hope.

If such a request could come from the I.O.C. representing all nations, it would of course be far better than one from the B.O.A., but I hope that the Council will feel it right and desirable to do something.

With the benefit of hindsight it seems absurd that Abrahams could have believed that a maniac such as Hitler might have been swayed by some gentle persuasion from Britain. Harold's belief that there was a fundamentally kinder Hitler just waiting for an excuse to come out was hopelessly naive. Yet in 1935 many people still thought the monster could be tamed with the right kind of persuasion. Beside, when there were so many moral complications associated with going to the Berlin Olympics, particularly for a man of Jewish origin, it was desirable to be attempting something – anything – to make the situation in Germany more bearable.

The BBC knew that it would be no simple task, ethically or logistically, to mount their first ever outside broadcast of an Olympic Games from Nazi Germany. That is why they had started planning almost a year early, with Abrahams soon prominent in their considerations. The question was this: who would be the main British voice of the Games, the man with the microphone for the showpiece track and field events? In early September 1935, it was clear that Harold Abrahams was the favourite, though even he had expressed the fear that his Jewish heritage might complicate matters in Nazi Germany.

Already by then, Adolf Hitler had been in power for two-and-a-half years, and the Dachau concentration camp was open. Jews and any other groups who disagreed with the Nazi regime were being hit hard. And even though the Holocaust was still a few years away, the climate in Germany was disturbing.

Looking ahead to the following year's Olympics, Seymour Joly de Lotbiniere, the BBC's Outside Broadcast Director, advised the organisation's Foreign Director:

> We shall probably want a number of afternoon running com-
> mentaries, beginning on Monday, August 3, and ending on Friday,
> August 7. They would be quite short, and we should want Harold
> Abrahams to do them. In any event he will almost certainly be going
> over for the Games, but he feels that for racial reasons he might be
> able to get better facilities if he were recognised as our representative
> and not as a mere private spectator. I gather that I can reassure him
> as to any possible victimisation, although perhaps you would explore
> a little in the meantime to make certain as to this.

Beneath this typed memo was a note, handwritten after a meeting of the BBC's Programme Board. It read rather more ominously, 'Prog. Board decided better to leave the Abrahams question until we were justified in predicting what the situation would be next August.'

If Harold picked up on the delaying tactics at Broadcasting House, it couldn't have helped his already fragile state of mind. For his relationship with Sybil was built on an unrealistic view of the opposite sex. Sue Pottle revealed that Harold's attitude to women was so seriously awry that he sought psychiatric help for his condition. 'My understanding is that he went into therapy because he put women on a pedestal and thought they were just pretty sweet things who needed flowers, rather than seeing them as equal human beings.'

'Harold thought that education was wasted on women. He was a chauvinist, not a misogynist. Sybil wasn't having it; and she knew she wanted to carry on singing, whether she and Harold married or not. Sybil probably persuaded Harold to see a psychiatrist – to help him to see that women didn't just need flowers.'

Abrahams family letters show that Sybil called in a 'Dr Rees'. She agreed to see the therapist too, so that she could try to understand Harold better. The doctor in question was probably John Rawlings Rees, who in 1934 had become director of the Tavistock Clinic, the leading force for the new Freudian school of psychology. If Harold was still too attached to his mother, perhaps that led to putting other women on a pedestal which was always going to lead to disappointment. How could Sybil or any other woman live up to that sort of ideal? She could hardly project an image of virginal perfection when she had been married before. She was what she was; and there should have been plenty for Harold to admire.

Increasingly, however, Sybil bore witness to Harold's inner conflict. Though she still didn't fully understand that battle and the extent of her lover's marriage phobia, Sybil felt that she was the cause of the angst. She also knew deep down what was best for both of them. Dr Rees recommended a long separation, which might even become permanent. Trying to be objective, despite the strength of her own feelings for Harold, Sybil agreed.

On September 10, 1935, she wrote:

Harold, my dear, this is going to be a difficult letter to write – and I must ask you to be very patient with me, and to read it over carefully several times before passing judgement. I have just seen Dr Rees, and his advice – which perhaps he has already outlined to you? – is that we should drop all idea of marriage for the present. It may sound a dreadful thing to say, but I am entirely in agreement with him – for it seems to me that in the present circumstances we can do each other no good. He suggests that we call a complete truce for the space of a year – so, my dear, I think that is what we must do.

I wonder if you understand how sad I feel that it should be

necessary, and how very hard I find it to say? I do feel, though, that this is right. The most important thing of all is that you should be free and able to work to get things right with yourself and rid your mind once and for all of the things that are torturing you. A man with your intellect will never be happy while these things remain unconquered – and how, while still going in fear of them, can you hope to make anybody else truly happy?

Bless you – always Sybil.

This letter caused Harold to take such a good hard look at himself. He went into intensive therapy at once – with a female psychologist. Perhaps that would sort out his problem once and for all. On September 20, 1935, Harold wrote to discourage even friendship between the troubled lovers.

Sybil, my dear.

I have been wanting to ring you up for some days, but have refrained from doing so. I have started treatment with Dr Jane Suttie (a very experienced psychologist of between 50 and 60) and it is plain after only three visits that there is a good deal to get straight.

My dear, I should dearly like to see you again and do so many things we enjoy doing together, but before I do this I would so much like you to know what is in my mind. There has been so much wrong in the childish attitude which I have towards women in general and which has been an ingredient of my affection for you, that I wonder very much when in six or nine months I have got things straight all my ideas about marriage will not have so fundamentally changed that I may not want to get married at all, or may want to marry someone very different from you!!

What I am so anxious about is that you in the generosity of your affection, should not be called upon to give me friendship and perhaps then find it even more difficult later on to break (if the eventuality arises) than it would be now.

I am much calmer in my mind – impatient still to get to the bottom of things in a desperate hurry, but really trying to cooperate with Dr Suttie in disentangling very tangled emotions.

Please, my dear, think only of yourself in this connection – I know you find this somewhat difficult – almost as difficult as I do to think of you instead of myself.

Dr Jane Suttie was one of the pre-eminent psychologists of the day, who had suddenly been left alone to pursue the theories that she had helped her husband to develop and put into practice. Dr Ian Suttie had recently died, just as his ground-breaking book, *The Origins of Love and Hate*, was about to roll off the press. So it was left to Jane Suttie to continue their work, which had begun while they both worked at the Glasgow Royal Asylum.

In 1928, they had moved to London and established a practice in Bloomsbury, where they rented two adjacent flats. Ian had found a place at the pioneering Tavistock centre, where new psychoanalytical work had begun. Broadly, the theories of Sigmund Freud were used. But increasingly the Sutties came to believe that Freud may have been mistaken in one fundamental area. They claimed that the mother, not the father, was key to releasing a child from the threat of Oedipal neuroses. This could be achieved by a positive repression of Oedipal feelings in her child, since repression didn't always need to have negative connotations associated with fear.

As Ian Suttie put it, 'I reached the conclusion that repression was a function of love, not of fear, and that the repressor of the Oedipus complex . . . was the mother, not the father.'

How this impacted on Harold's treatment is impossible to say with any precision. But in broad terms, Abrahams was encouraged to ask himself where the extreme anxiety he felt in his relationship with Sybil might have originated. Jane Suttie would have explored a possible connection with the anxiety he had felt in his relationship with his mother.

The Origins of Love and Hate, to which Jane Suttie contributed, claimed that such problems arose when a domineering father – and Harold certainly had one of those – dented a mother's self-esteem. Put in the simplest layman's terms, the knock-on effect left the mother subconsciously needy, and therefore unable to create an appropriate emotional and sexual distance from her son sufficiently early. This kind of childhood made it harder for someone like Harold to develop mature feelings for a woman, distinct from the idealistic, protective feelings he had harboured for his mother.

Beyond the psychobabble, however, Harold had every reason to be afraid of marriage. He had seen his parents' marriage disintegrate and he didn't want to go through the same hell with a wife of his own. It was frightening to think that his partner might leave him; and it was almost as frightening to think that he might let someone down by leaving them. He had let Christina down that way, even if he'd had the excuse that his eldest brother demanded it.

Whatever the reasons for his inner demons, it had been so much easier for Harold to cope with superficial relationships since Cambridge. That way, murky waters were left undisturbed. Here he was, aged thirty-five, and he hadn't enjoyed a really significant relationship with a member of the opposite sex since he was twenty-three. You didn't need to be a top psychiatrist to know that he might be suffering from an aversion to commitment.

Then there was the problem that Sybil didn't sit very comfortably with the Sutties' idea of matriarchal utopia. A family's mental health was supposed to depend upon the mother being given great respect for staying at home and doing the nurturing. This was at odds with Sybil's situation. She hadn't stayed at home, she couldn't have children and she still valued her career as a singer. She wasn't, on the face of it, someone who could help realise the Sutties' vision of a healthier society. So was she right for Harold?

Abrahams knew he had to tackle his problems without Sybil, at least for now. She had seen that even before he did. But there was a complication: Harold Abrahams and Sybil Evers loved each other. And even when Harold, Sybil and the doctors knew that a trial separation would help bring clarity to a tricky situation, it wasn't easy to follow the prescribed medical advice. Every so often, therefore, they would see each other on the quiet, and then fret about what they had done.

For Harold there was no escape from insecurity, because he couldn't feel any more certain about his professional life than he did about his personal life. The coveted BBC commentary spot for the Berlin Olympics had still not been confirmed as his. At least in November 1935 he seemed to be winning the BBC executives over. 'By the way we have a record of Abrahams doing a commentary at the White City. He is very good,' one told Lotbiniere in a memo – as if Harold's boss didn't know it already.

The word 'very' was underlined. So there was no doubt about Abrahams' broadcasting ability, or indeed his suitability for the Olympic role. The BBC was still worried by the idea of being represented by a Jew in Nazi Germany. Harold was having similar concerns about the prospect of reporting from Berlin. Though he desperately wanted to go, he also wanted to make sure he would be made welcome and allowed to work unhindered. So he decided to ask the Foreign Office if they could arrange a discreet meeting, perhaps an informal dinner, with German diplomats in London. That way he could seek the assurances he was looking for.

However, others in the free world already felt that collaboration with the Nazi regime would do far more harm than good. Across the Atlantic, such feelings were running particularly high. On December 3, 1935, Madison Square Garden played host to strong protest against American participation in the Berlin Games. Hitting back at those who insisted the Olympic ideal was noble, and therefore had to be respected at all costs, the American Federation of Labor had stated, 'There is nothing noble in the persecution by sixty million Germans of six hundred thousand Jews.'

Back in London the BBC continued to assume that a British team would go to Berlin, in which case they still had to select their broadcasting team accordingly. On December 5, 1935, Lotbiniere wrote to his bosses again on this issue, supporting Abrahams as much as possible:

You will remember that at a Programme Board meeting in the late autumn we discussed the advisability of using Mr Harold Abrahams as our commentator at the Olympic Games. It was then felt that, while we were not prejudiced against him for racial reasons, it might be advisable to postpone a final decision as to his employment by us until nearer the time, when we should be able to see the state of feeling in Germany, and the consequent probability of their differentiating against him in the matter of facilities.

Mr Abrahams came to see me a few days ago, and while he had no wish to force us into a decision that we did not wish to make, he said that it would be a great help to him to know whether he was likely to be our official commentator. His point is that he does not feel justified in provoking a possible unpleasantness by going as a private individual, but he would not have any scruples about going in some official capacity. He thinks he might be able to 'arrange' that he should go as a team official, but he does not want to do this if he could go as our commentator. I asked him whether a present decision of ours to use him as commentator, which might be reversed nearer the time, was of any use to him. He said that it was.

In these circumstances, and recollecting F.D.'s [Foreign Director's] expressed conviction that they would never dare to interfere in any way with our commentator, I should now like to know if we could give him the use of our name.

S.J. de Lotbiniere

That 'possible unpleasantness' didn't bear thinking about. But with the

BBC's full support, Harold seemed confident that all would be well. Abrahams knew he could count on the support of Lotbiniere. He was flattered, and he wanted to repay that faith by going to Berlin. 'I wanted to go because I thought it was a tremendous compliment. It was the first time the BBC had ever done an Olympics. I very desperately wanted to go and I knew it would be very much criticised, and I didn't know whether I might do more good by going or not going.'

With subtle pressure and persuasion, Lotbiniere seemed to be tipping the balance in favour of Harold's involvement in Berlin. Then on December 6, 1935, Cecil Graves, the BBC Programme Controller, wrote the following extraordinary memo:

> The point about this is, of course, that Abrahams is a Jew. He is our best commentator on athletics. Apparently if we are prepared to come out into the open and label him the BBC commentator for the Olympic Games, he is quite ready to go to Germany. The question arises as to whether we should do this. We all regard the German action against the Jews as quite irrational and intolerable and on that score we ought not to hesitate, but should we, as between one broadcaster and another, put aside all views of this kind and take the line that however irrational we regard another country's attitude to be, it would be discourteous to send a Jewish commentator to a country where Jews are taboo?
>
> My own reaction is that we should write to the German broadcasting people and tell them that our expert man, whom we are proposing to send for the Olympic Games, is Mr Abrahams and leave them to raise any objections if they want to. I made some enquiries about the reception accorded to a member of a recent delegation to Germany who was a Jew and I was told that he was very well received and there was no question of any discourtesy or unpleasantness.
>
> C.G. Graves December 6, 1935

And so, with a breathtaking nonchalance, a British television executive offered to hand over the entire question of Harold Abrahams' presence at the Berlin Olympics to the Nazis. If Hitler's regime said that Abrahams the Jew was welcome as the BBC's official man, then all would be well. If the Germans didn't approve, then the BBC were not going to cause a controversy. After all, Cecil Graves clearly reasoned, it simply wouldn't do to offend the hosts on a point of principle.

Six days later, on December 12, a seemingly jubilant Harold wrote to his BBC boss to make it perfectly clear that no such offence would be caused, and there was no element of risk in sending him officially. The way Abrahams had secured this confirmation seems truly extraordinary even today.

> My dear de Lotbiniere,
>
> It will interest you to know that last week I had an interview of nearly half an hour with Herr von Tschammer und Osten, and among other things he gave me his personal assurance that I would be *welcome* in Berlin next year at the Olympic Games.
>
> I gave him my personal undertaking that I would not disclose to the Press the fact of our interview, so that you will appreciate that the information given to you is confidential !!!!!!
>
> Yours ever,
>
> Harold M. Abrahams.

Hans von Tschammer und Osten was Hitler's Reich Sports Führer, whose organisation of gymnastic displays at Nazi rallies promoted Aryan superiority. This was the man who went on record saying, 'Sport is a way to weed out the weak, the Jewish and any other undesirables.' He also played a major role in excluding non-Aryan competitors from the German team for Olympic Games. It seems amazing that Harold could be so blinkered, so focused on his own ambition to get to the Games, that he would see fit to associate with such a man. Though the Holocaust hadn't begun, the writing was already on the wall – quite literally – for German Jews, whose shops were already being boycotted and vandalised. It was no secret in England that the Jewish community in Germany was already being persecuted. The idea that Abrahams wished to appease such an individual and give him any kind of 'personal undertaking', seems distasteful in hindsight. And it was a measure of the Nazi desire to project a positive image abroad that von Tschammer und Osten was prepared to give a Jew so much time.

But before we condemn Harold outright, it should be remembered that he did not act independently when he sounded out Hitler's Sports Minister. Later Abrahams revealed that he had also sought advice at the highest level of the British Government. 'I had met Sir Robert Vansittart, who was head of the Foreign Office, at Sir John Simon's house, and I asked if I could go and see him and talk about it at the Foreign Office and he advised me that the right thing to do was go [to Berlin].'

Sir John Simon had been Foreign Secretary until June 1935. Vansittart was actually Permanent Under-Secretary at the Foreign Office, where he supervised the work of the diplomatic service. He was suspicious of Hitler from the start. He did not favour the broad and naive brand of appeasement that was adopted in time by Sir Neville Chamberlain and his supporters – including Sir John Simon. So it may seem strange on one level that Vansittart advised Abrahams to go to Berlin. However, Vansittart agreed with Harold that there was little to be gained from a boycott of the Olympic Games. Such a blatant insult was no way to tame the beast. Rather, Vansittart believed, Britain should maintain diplomatic relations to better understand what was coming. Only that way could the British Government act in their country's best interests in the long run.

As for Abrahams, here was an opportunity for him to make a point about the abilities of people of his racial origin. Harold revealed, 'I went to see Sir Robert Vansittart who was head of the Foreign Office. He said that I should go to Berlin to show them that the BBC had picked a Jew for their first Olympic broadcast.' The irony, of course, was that Vansittart had read the BBC's position incorrectly; for they were still terrified of offending Hitler's lieutenants by sending a Jew to Berlin. But a decision had to be made soon, and it was. On December 16, Stephen Tallents, the BBC's first Director of Public Relations came out strongly against sending Abrahams to the Games:

> I am inclined to think it would be wise not to send Abrahams to the Olympic Games. I noticed the other day that the American Games authorities had only by a small margin agreed to participate in the Games at all – as a result, I imagine, of the restrictions alleged to be imposed in Germany upon the training and entry of German athletes, a question which was dealt with a week or two ago in two long articles in the *Manchester Guardian*.

The paper argued that, since Jewish athletes were being denied the same opportunities as their Aryan counterparts, participation 'means endorsement of all the injustices, discrimination and tyranny under which German sport now suffers and which is directly opposed to the Olympic ideal.' By sending Harold, a man of Jewish origin, the BBC was going to cause itself trouble. Either he would fall foul of anti-Semitism, or be manipulated for the purposes of Nazi propaganda. Tallents added,

'There are so many possibilities of friction in the situation that I feel it would be wiser to avoid the risk. There is even the minor danger that if Abrahams went, and were courteously received, Germans would make capital out of their courtesy, as showing that their ways with the Jews were misrepresented.'

Programme Controller Graves, who had sat on the fence so stubbornly that he had wanted the Germans to decide on Abrahams, promptly sat on the fence some more. He asked Lotbiniere what he thought. Two days later, Lotbiniere replied by openly disagreeing with Tallent's assessment, 'since by all accounts there will be no discrimination (and *Abrahams* is a good commentator). I think the first argument might be used to show that we should leave the games alone – not so as to rule out Abrahams. His second argument is, with great *respect*, a shade far-fetched.'

However, by New Year's Eve, Harold's hopes had been all but dashed. Graves wrote: 'I brought this up at Control Board this morning and it was very generally felt that we should not send Abrahams out as our commentator to the Olympic Games. The name of Rudd was suggested instead.'

Nearly sixteen years after they had first met on the track for Oxford and Cambridge at the Queen's Club, it seemed that Bevil Rudd and Harold Abrahams were still competing for the big prize. Not for the first time, Rudd had taken a commanding lead.

CHAPTER FOUR

FEAR AND ACCUSATION

Lotbiniere bristled with irritation at the apparent injustice of Harold's fate. He gathered evidence from those who knew Germany best, including Miss Isa Benzie, Director of the BBC's Foreign and Overseas Department. Then, on January 2, 1936, Lotbiniere openly challenged his superiors:

> In view of Miss Benzie's evidence that there would be no backlash against Abrahams and the importance of having someone at Berlin whom we know to be a first-class broadcaster, I am not satisfied that Control Board have made a wise decision. Since I feel this, I conceive it to be my duty not to let the matter rest until I am satisfied that their reasons are sound or until I am told exactly where to get off.

Just when Lotbiniere seemed to be about to launch a defiant campaign on Harold's behalf, he did a U-turn. Had he been threatened with the sack, or 'got at' by higher government, as Britain sought to maintain the best possible diplomatic relations with Germany?

On February 10, 1936, Lotbiniere wrote a letter to Graves and marked it 'Confidential'.

> I have had the opportunity of talking unofficially with someone closely connected with the German Embassy. He was reluctant for me to pass on anything that he said, but I think you should know that his opinion about Abrahams and the Olympic Games was that it would be definitely impolitic for us to send Abrahams as our official

commentator, but that there would be nothing unwise in using him if he was out there.

As a matter of fact I have been getting a bit worried about the idea of sending out as a BBC representative any special commentator, such as Abrahams, and I am inclined to think that in the end we shall find it best to send out a member of staff, whose duty it will be to organise the OB's [Outside Broadcasts] from Berlin, both for the general programme and for news, picking up expert commentators from people on the spot.

We are inclined to think of athletics as the major part of the Olympic Games, but in fact there are lots of other events which will be important – boxing, hockey, football, swimming, rowing, to say nothing of polo, fencing, riding and yachting. The games are being held during the first fortnight in August, which is normally rather a 'dead' period for broadcasting. So we may find nearer the time that we shall want more from Berlin than at present appears likely.

I would suggest, therefore, that we stick to Control Board's ruling against sending Abrahams as our special commentator, and feel free to use him discreetly for some of the athletics.

If you approve of this I will explain the position to him and there the matter can rest.

So athletics had mysteriously lost some of its importance all of a sudden, and Harold was to be 'used discreetly' if he turned up in Berlin independently. It was almost as though he were a source of shame to both the British and Germans. The assurance from von Tschammer und Osten – that Harold would be welcome to work at the Games – suddenly carried less weight than the opinion of an unnamed German Embassy official that it would be 'impolitic' to send him. Even those who had argued long and hard for Abrahams were finally cowed into making lame excuses to justify sidelining him, their principles tucked back in the desk drawer.

There is a case for arguing that the BBC made the right decision for the wrong reasons. Some will say that Abrahams should never have considered putting himself up for Berlin; that he should have taken a stand on behalf of his fellow Jews instead. The fact was, however, that Harold didn't consider himself to be a Jew any more; he hadn't done so for a long time. Abrahams had become Christian; and even if he didn't consider himself to be a devout Christian either, people were missing the point. He didn't want to be restricted by his roots, or by any kind of racial or religious stereotyping. He was Harold Abrahams; unique and irrepressible. So he quickly approached the British Olympic Association, to ensure that he could travel to Berlin as an assistant manager to the team. That kind of guarantee would provide some kind of consolation and keep alive his hopes of broadcasting from Berlin as a 'guest expert'.

The problem remained that Harold was also quite troubled emotionally and vulnerable on a number of levels. Everywhere he looked, in his personal life and career, there was confusion and frustration. Whether the discouraging news from the BBC laid him low, or whether he was affected by the anxieties of his on-off relationship with Sybil, Harold was admitted to hospital. And it seems that Harold's health problems brought matters to a head in his personal life.

In a make-or-break moment, Harold and Sybil realised they faced a straight choice: either they would have to put their faith in each other or go their separate ways. Living in limbo wasn't doing either of them any good. Harold would have to overcome his aversion to commitment, grasp the nettle and pop the question; or else risk living the life of a bachelor forever, with the risk that he would die a lonely old man.

For the second time in his life, Harold proposed to the woman he loved. For the second time, that woman accepted. This time it was going to be different, or at least Harold hoped so. As for Sybil, she was happy from the moment she left the hospital, engaged to be married. In fact she was hardly home before she sent him a note, to 'Harold Abrahams Esq'.

7.30.
Feeling energetic I walked here from Hampstead Hospital. Hope you've had a good afternoon, darling, and will sleep well. *I'm* feeling *grand*!
S.

Harold would sleep better after he had found the words to ask Sybil's father for her hand in marriage. This time he intended to make his engagement formal before anyone could change his mind.

On February 19, 1936, mindful that Harold's doctors had advised the couple to play down their romance, Sybil wrote the following amusing note to Abrahams from her West London base. Harold was out of hospital by now because the letter was addressed to 'Harold Abrahams Esq, 29

Abercom Place, N.W.8'. Sybil had clearly broken the news of their engagement to her parents a few days earlier.

> Wednesday. 19.2.36
> Watcher, Mate.
> Hope you're feeling better? I heard from my Mamma this morning – a bit cold and cautious, but otherwise all right. She expanded rather more in a letter to Mary! [Sybil's sister]
> Hope this finds you as it leaves me – in the pink.
> Just off to Pinner
> Bless You. S

On the very same day, Sybil's father wrote to Harold with more warmth than her mother was initially willing to show, giving the engagement his blessing. Now it was official.

Under these new and seemingly definitive circumstances, it was time for Harold to try to put his psychological problems behind him. There was a future with Sybil to fight for; and there was an Olympic Games to prepare for. He still had to satisfy himself that he would be doing the right thing by going to Nazi Germany. But he had a point to prove, a last laugh to enjoy over anyone who treated Jews shabbily. It had been that way since Repton. And even though he didn't consider himself to be a Jew any more, he had never forgotten his family roots. How could he, when he had never quite shaken off the inferiority complex that anti-Semitism had given him as a youngster? But he wasn't ashamed of his Jewish origins, far from it. By doing things well – better than anyone else – he usually found the perfect answer to the bigots.

It had worked until now, so why should the Berlin Olympics be different? The problem was that the anti-Semitism of Nazi Germany in 1936 was far crueller than anything Harold had experienced or could even imagine. Organisations with links to the political left were the first to condemn Hitler's Fascists. Pretty soon the entire free world condemned the Führer's persecution of the Jews. The arguments centred on what the free world could do about it.

There was organised opposition to the idea of sending a British team to the Berlin Games. G.H. Elvin of the National Workers' Sports Association moved the following resolution: 'The AGM of the AAA is of the opinion that the spirit which prompted the organisation of the Olympic Games cannot be forwarded by participation in the 1936

Olympic Games in Berlin, and instructs the Association to withdraw its support, and withhold the necessary permission for a permit to participate.'

Harold argued against this, though he acknowledged that the matter had given him no little concern. He approached it, he said, as an Englishman who had been fortunate enough to represent his country at two Olympic Games, as a man who had enjoyed working with his athletic colleagues for over ten years on the AAA, and 'as a man of Jewish origin'. It was interesting that Harold now fell short of calling himself a Jew. He argued the case for Olympic participation like this:

> I know there is not a single person in this room who does not deplore the conditions in Germany today: but in spite of these conditions, I ask myself whether it is ultimately in the best interests of world sport and better world relationships that the AAA should pass the resolution and withdraw from the Games.
>
> We must remember that the International Olympic Committee, the body solely responsible for the Games, has, rightly or wrongly, decided that it is still the right thing to hold the Games in Germany. This body is entrusted with the observance of the Olympic Charter. We must remember that the British Olympic Association, the body responsible for Olympic matters in this country, has decided to support the Games. I have no delusions about the situation in Germany today; and if I had been born in Germany, knowing myself as I do, I doubt if I should be alive today.

With these words, Harold was admitting that he was so opinionated and outspoken that he would have found it impossible to stay silent as a persecuted German Jew. Instead his objection to the Nazi regime would probably have resulted in his death. However, this dramatic assumption didn't change his position on the Berlin Games:

> I still think the right thing is for us to show the German people what Great Britain believes to be real sport. After all, in my opinion, to isolate an individual because his behaviour does not meet with your approval never ultimately achieves anything. Countries are only collections of individuals and to isolate Germany will never achieve what we ultimately want, namely, the furtherance of these ideals in sport – absolute freedom for all to participate – in which we all believe.

With most of the facts which Mr Elvin has put forward in support of his proposition we must all agree, but I nevertheless do not believe that any real good will come if this resolution is adopted; on the contrary, I believe that it will do harm.

Seeking to leave Mr Elvin an honourable way out, Abrahams proposed an amended motion:

This General Meeting of the Amateur Athletic Association, while deploring the existence of certain conditions in Germany, which are inconsistent with the highest ideals of amateur sport for which the Olympic Games stand, nevertheless is of the opinion that since the International Olympic Committee, the body solely responsible, has decided to hold the Games in Berlin next August, the best interest of world sport will be served by Great Britain's participation therein.

Lord Desborough, the retiring AAA President, urged the meeting not to pass any resolution at all. Mr Elvin withdrew his on tactical grounds, having received assurances that he had the right to call the General Committee to a Special General Meeting within two months, should he wish to discuss the matter further. But he didn't give up there, and held a meeting at Shoreditch Town Hall in the East End of London under the auspices of the Workers' Circle Friendly Society. Over 2,000 people turned up, and the meeting 'unanimously adopted a resolution declaring that no time was to be lost for the cause of peace and progress if the entire annihilation of the Jews in Germany was to be prevented'.

History, of course, lends more weight to Mr Elvin's argument than that of Harold Abrahams. And the idea that the health of world sport was more important than the health of millions of Jews under Nazi rule seems ridiculous now. Yet Abrahams was adamant that he was doing the right thing, even when he was asked to defend allegations – levelled at him by *The Jewish Chronicle* – that he had fraternised with Hitler's Minister of Sport.

The newspaper recounted how, 'Interviewed by *The Jewish Chronicle*, Mr Abrahams said he had always been opposed to boycotts of all sorts; he did not think they ever did any good. He had shaken hands with Herr Von Tschammer-Osten, the Nazi Sports Commissioner, and he was not ashamed of it.'

The Jewish Chronicle further reported that Abrahams 'did not realise, however, that his action in publicly opposing the boycott might cause hurt to the Jews of this country, and be taken by them as an act of treachery. Nothing was further from his desires, and if he had realised what the psychological effect of his action might be, he would probably have remained silent.

'He had been invited to accompany the British team to Berlin and he had accepted the invitation. If, however, he could be convinced that such action would do more harm than good to German Jewry, he would definitely not go. "I want you to understand," said Mr Abrahams, "that this offer is made in all seriousness."'

Yet no one could persuade him he would in fact be harming the cause of German Jews by going to Berlin. He remained determined to go, even when it emerged that he would not be the BBC's official commentator. His private misgivings were not enough to change his mind. He admitted later that he had viewed the prospect of Berlin 'with a good deal of misapprehension, unhappy about it really, because that was the height of anti-Semitism in Germany; when I say "the height", that's not a very good description because it became much worse. And although I hadn't been a practising Jew for years, I was very uneasy about going at all.' Not uneasy enough to pull out, though.

It was just as well for Harold that Sybil saw beauty in the strange blend of stubbornness, arrogance, confusion and vulnerability that defined Harold Abrahams. Sybil was prepared to be patient while he worked through his inner turmoil. With Sybil on his side, Harold felt ready to tackle anything, even a few weeks as a nervous guest of Adolf Hitler. When she wrote to Harold from Rugby on April 9, 1936, Sybil was clearly still basking in the joy of their engagement:

> I'm writing at Mummy's desk in the drawing room, with the sun blazing in – particularly nice of it, as I'm only wearing squash clothes! . . . You may not believe it, but you'll make a *splendid* husband . . . Take care of yourself, and enjoy yourself, and *rest* and *relax* please, as much as you can . . . Hope you are feeling as much at peace as I am. It is wonderful to be so happy.
>
> With my love and blessings. If you can see me as you read this, you'll see the smile on the face of your Tuppenny.

Letters like that should have made Harold happier than he had ever been, and probably did on one level. Yet he was still being hounded about Berlin. *The Jewish Chronicle* became a thorn in his side. Harold knew their criticisms failed to take into account the private advice he had been given by the Foreign Office: that it would be right to go to Berlin. But he also knew that most people prefer to take the advice that they want to hear in the first place. He reflected, 'I took that advice and was subjected to a lot of criticism, which I absolutely understand. Whether anybody could have had any effect on the Nazis, one doesn't know. I mean, if the world had been courageous enough to say "no Olympics" would it have had any effect on the political situation?'

Harold was also a human being with a conscience. And the compromise Abrahams made with his conscience was this: he promised himself that, while in Berlin, he would make some kind of personal protest against Hitler's Nazi regime. He didn't know precisely what he was going to do; it might be something quite small or more widely noticeable. But in some way or other, he planned to make a stand, however superficial or futile.

He told his fiancée Sybil of his intentions, and this worried her greatly. Sybil soon wrote to him about a confidential chat she had just had with a friend who had just been to Berlin and felt that she understood the psyche of the average German. 'She gave it as her opinion that a protest such as you have considered would make no impression at all. The answer would simply be "You cannot possibly appreciate our difficulties". She also said that the people themselves were not inimical, and could not be held responsible for what their leaders did.'

Knowing Harold's mental fragility, Sybil wanted him to focus on their wedding rather than worry about how to protest effectively against Hitler. She hoped to marry Harold quietly somewhere, perhaps even before the Berlin Olympics. 'My lovely "wedding dress" has at last arrived from Rugby, so now I really am complete, and can be ready to come off at a moment's notice! If possible I should prefer the "moment" to be 48 hours – or 24 would do! – as I should like to get my hair done.'

Harold was torn between a desire to please Sybil and an urge to displease Hitler. Then there was the Jewish community of Britain to consider. He had taken on board *The Jewish Chronicle*'s criticism of him that a man of Jewish origin had made a public stand in favour of British participation in the Hitler Games. For that reason, when a Special General Meeting of the Amateur Athletic Association was called to discuss further the possibility of pulling Britain out of the Olympics,

Abrahams made himself absent. That didn't take him out of the firing line, though. And someone who sounded very close to the debate wrote into *The Jewish Chronicle* to try to shame both Harold and the British Government into action. The letter read:

A Special General Meeting of the Amateur Athletic Association last week threw out, by an overwhelming majority, a resolution against participation in the Olympic Games in Berlin. Mr Harold Abrahams was not present at the meeting, but, after his speech on a similar occasion in March, in which he asked 'whether it is ultimately in the best interests of world sport and better world relationships that the Association should withdraw from the Games', and left no doubt as to his answer, the action of the Special Meeting could not have been in question. After all, a gathering of Gentiles could not have expected to be more Jewish than the Jew.

So we read, in the report of the Special Meeting, that while every speaker stressed his sympathy for the oppressed in Germany, the general view was that the sufferers would be better helped by England's participation, and the Nazis can now throw their hats into the air in jubilation. English sportsmen will be proclaimed – after the Games are over – to have given their cachet to the rotten Nazi regime. We might leave the matter to Mr Abrahams' own reflections.

Harold's torment over the Olympic controversy was not the sole source of his anguish. Both he and Sybil were suffering pre-wedding nerves – even though they hadn't set a date. Harold promptly sought fresh help from his therapist, Dr Jane Suttie. She advised a three-month cooling-off period for Harold and Sybil, because they both seemed on the verge of hysteria. The lovers now agonised about any form of contact between them.

On May 30, 1936, Sybil wrote the following to Harold:

I cannot decide whether we ought to be writing now or not. Will you ask Dr Suttie about this? . . . I am coming back on Monday night – Marylebone 9.55 . . . *Don't* come to see me unless Dr S. agrees. We *must* be sensible and I wouldn't have told you the time had I not feared you might meet all sorts of trains! . . . Be wise and happy about it – as I am . . . Please give my love to your mother and Dorothy. I shall hope to see them soon – perhaps at *Thistledown* [her latest musical project].

With all my love and confidence in you.

Sybil.

Sybil cracked a few days later and wrote to Harold, 'Can you and will you dine with the Darwins on Sunday 14? It is Bill's birthday and they'd like us to go – but you must decide, dearest. I cannot, and will not mortgage the future for the sake of any present pleasure – and you alone know if it will be doing so.'

Harold thought it better not to meet, but he was suffering from a fresh bout of depression. All his old fears about the impermanence of love had surfaced again. What if they refrained from seeing each other for three months, and then Sybil realised that she didn't want him any more? She was left to encourage him from afar, and to try to allay his fears.

On June 6, 1936, Sybil expressed complete faith that Harold was on the verge of defeating his demons. 'Darling, I *know* – with my mind and heart – that you *will* win in the end. My confidence in you is boundless – more so alas than my patience!! – but I will be patient too, knowing that the end is in sight.'

She knew what was eating away at Harold, and added calmly:

Dearest, you spoke of a fear lest I should no longer love you in two months' time or three, or whenever the time comes. Examine that fear. It is a very ordinary and reasonable one – but root it out nevertheless.

And then, remember this: I have loved you for longer than you realise, perhaps, with a love that has been growing steadily, and I can see *no* reason why it should fade in two months or three, or a thousand and three.

Passion might wear out with frustration – but that we are now conserving, by being wise and self-denying. Only, I think, if I felt you were letting me down by not *trying* to get right would love then turn to hate. So, my love, 'do you amend it then. It lies in you.' You have nothing in the world to fear, since you have the means and the determination to get right. Please God the reward at the end may be worthy of you. Your own Sybil.

It all sounded so careful and considered; but the very next day Sybil wrote again, as if there had suddenly been a frenzied liaison. 'My darling, I don't know whether you'll go back to the flat before going to Chambers so there'll be a note in each place for you! . . . Hope you are all right. No nasty reactions? Scuse scrawl – just off to BBC. In haste. Bless you. S.'

What a strange courtship this was. It seemed that Harold and Sybil couldn't be happy together or apart. It was enough to send anyone to the edge of madness. Yet Harold would soon have to cope with Nazi Germany too. He was to travel as a freelance journalist, with a vague managerial role with the British Olympic team when time allowed. He was confident that HE would be accredited by the Germans; but there was no guarantee he would be respected or left alone by the Jew-haters.

On July 2, 1936, the servile BBC gave their German hosts the names of the men they had chosen for staff duty in Berlin. They were Mr Alan Wells, a member of the News Department, and Tommy Woodroofe of Outside Broadcasts. Woodroofe was to be in charge of the pioneering 'live' Olympic commentaries and pick commentators as he saw fit. Having grown up in South Africa and seen much of the world while in the navy, he had been chosen because the BBC felt that he retained 'no confirmed belief that the Englishman is worth two of anyone else – not that such a belief could survive the first day or two of the Games. Mr Woodrooffe has tried his hand, too, at most outdoor games and he is sufficiently fond of them all not to try and take them more seriously than they deserve.'

So the BBC had picked someone with a casual interest in sport, who could commentate with neutrality. As it turned out, BBC coverage in Berlin would be defined for all time by Abrahams, someone with an obsessive interest in sport, whose partiality would go down in commentating history.

As the Games neared, Harold and Sybil continued to steal secret moments together, even though they knew they weren't supposed to. In a letter to her father, dated Sunday July 26, 1936, Sybil made no attempt to hide the fact that they were together:

> This is a poor letter. Harold is here hammering away at newspaper articles on his typewriter. He goes to Berlin on Tuesday with E.A. Montague and will be there about a fortnight. We had thought it possible that we might have married first and gone there together, but it is really better not. For one thing the three months prescribed by Dr Suttie are not yet ended, and for another I find that I should really

be an extra anxiety to him at a time when he will be unusually busy and don't feel it would be a good way in which to embark on married life. He will have to be at the Stadium – 10 miles outside Berlin – at 10 every morning, and will be there all day long. Then at 6 o'clock every evening he has a half-hour telephone conversation with London newspapers, after which he has to broadcast and get all his writing done. So I feel sure we are being wise.

Ironically Sybil accepted a late invitation to travel to neighbouring Austria with opera friends. They would stay at a lakeside hotel just outside Salzburg, and go into town for the music festival. Hitler's shadow stretched to Austria too, as Sybil would soon find out.

CHAPTER FIVE

HITLER, OWENS AND LOVELOCK

It was a heavy-hearted Harold Abrahams who boarded a train bound for Berlin with his good friend Evelyn Montague, former Oxford rival and GB teammate from the 1924 Olympics. Harold wouldn't see his beloved Sybil for weeks and he didn't know what awaited him at the end of his journey. Still aware of his mental fragility, he was pleasantly surprised by the way he adapted. He wrote to Sybil, 'After a good dinner and a lot of athletic chat with Monty practically all signs of gloom dispelled and the expected reaction from the excitement and such of yesterday did not materialise.'

Sybil had bought him a ring, as though he were now her property. You can almost feel his anxiety as he wrote, 'My love, I do like the ring. Honest. I never thought I should. Of course for a day or two it will feel unfamiliar.'

When he reached the German border, Harold had a surprising reaction to what he saw, probably brought on by underlying tension:

> The train rolled into Germany and there are literally hundreds of Swastika flags about. I was particularly amused at the railway engines and their tenders. The tender has five Olympic circles painted – the engine a huge Swastika. I don't expect the Germans would appreciate the humour. Many people have suggested that the Olympic Games are being exploited by Germany to political ends, and the idea of Nazism dragging the Olympics after itself rather tickled me.

It may have looked absurd, but the significance of the sinister symbolism couldn't have escaped Harold. Perhaps he and Montague preferred to poke fun at Hitler's regime, because they didn't want to consider the more serious implications of what they were seeing. These Olympics were to be nationalistic like no other. But as they reached Berlin, Abrahams couldn't deny that the German talent for organisation already pointed to a spectacular event.

Abrahams added, 'We saw the Stadium from the train – most impressive – surrounded by trees. Gosh, we shan't be able to do the Games as magnificently in London, if we get them in 1940 – a matter which is most wisely not to be announced until these Games are over . . . Darling I'm going to make this job one of the best I have ever done. Curious all the mental conflict about coming at all – I mean apart from our own problems – and once the decision is made all is relatively peaceful.'

At least there could be no confusion now. He was in Nazi Germany, there was no turning back. For her part, Sybil kept her correspondence supportive and light-hearted, knowing the pressures her partner would face. 'I am so glad you really like the ring,' she wrote merrily. And, reacting to his account of his journey, she wrote, 'Your descriptions of bits of it are excellent . . . Am so very glad that you will be seeing much that is new and interesting.'

Some of Harold's observations would prove portentous. On July 30, soon after arriving in the German capital, he wrote, 'We eventually got our press passes and Monty's seat is next to mine. From [the Press Bureau] we were taken by coach to the Olympic village where our team and the 5,000-odd other competitors are housed. It is incredibly well done and will doubtless serve easily for quarters for troops hereafter.' He added, 'Berlin is a fever of excitement about the Games and the place is extremely gaily adorned.'

Harold was soon very busy and that made him feel strong, independent and happy. 'We've been hard at it all day and it completely puts London and even you right out of my mind. Six months ago the ability to live my own existence would have profoundly disturbed me. Now, thank heaven, it doesn't.'

He had already extended his journalistic repertoire in Berlin. Of his first newspaper assignment for the *Daily Sketch*, Harold wrote:

When I had finished my athletic story I was told the News Editor wanted to speak to me. Did I know anything about a big fire at the Opera House in Berlin? I didn't, but would he like me to find out and call him up? 'Yes.' Monty roared with glee at the idea of my acting as a news reporter. Anyway out I went with my LARGE German vocabulary to find the streets heaving with *Politzei* and people. Judicious enquiries elicited the fact that the Opera House was not on fire, but that a building nearby in which scenery for operas was stored had been blazing. You would have laughed at my token pigeon German. However I got a bit of a story over which apparently caused much amusement in the Sketch office.

As a former Olympic champion, Harold could spot a man with even greater ability. And he already suspected that no member of the Aryan race had as much athletic talent as Jesse Owens. He made a point of meeting Owens and being photographed alongside him in Berlin's Olympic village. And Harold explained why he already considered Jesse to be extra-special: 'In the year previously, the incomparable Jesse Owens had, in the course of an hour, set up world records for 100 yards, 220 yards, 220 yards hurdles and long jump – the latter went with a leap of 26ft 8¼in which remained for 25 years.' But it was Jesse's sprinting prowess that astounded Harold. 'Owens was lovely to watch,' he added. 'Jesse just seemed to float down the track.' Having met Owens and seen him to be in perfect mental and physical shape for the challenge ahead, Abrahams must have sensed what would unfold when the Games got under way. He could also have predicted how Hitler would react and probably couldn't wait; especially once he was inside the arena itself.

Harold wrote to Sybil, 'Our seats are in the 69th row together with a perfect view of the finish, though it is a long way off. But I've never seen such super arrangements. Of course the place was built completely regardless of cost.'

Later on there was a fleeting opportunity for the lovers to speak by telephone, when a newspaper colleague back in England thoughtfully arranged for them to be connected. Harold wrote a few hours later, 'It was a surprise to talk to you tonight . . . Imagine my unalterable joy when at the end of dictating my *Daily Sketch* story, he said, "Hold on a minute I've got Miss Evers." Dearest, I came over all funny as I expect you did too. I couldn't hear you too well, but it was lovely in the extreme to hear you at all. It was nice of him to arrange the switching through. I know you understood my closing down so quickly, but the D.S. [*Daily Sketch*] were

paying and my conscience rather took me.' Then Harold added that he
had gone to the 'Opening Ceremony, which was quite indescribable. I
shall have to tell you about it when we meet. I am awfully glad I didn't
miss it.'

Harold was mindful of the fact that journalists' letters were being
opened and read, and therefore he was reluctant to describe the
disturbing nationalistic fervour that dominated the ceremony. But later
he was able to reveal:

> The atmosphere at the Berlin Olympic Games was something new
> and unpleasant. It was the determination to win, the determination
> that Germany should come out of the Games as the conqueror,
> which spoilt the fun in Berlin in 1936. It was quite obvious from the
> moment one arrived in Germany, that Germany considered 1936 an
> occasion to advertise herself. In Antwerp, in Amsterdam, in Los
> Angeles, in Paris, there was no sense of national arrogance but only
> of honour being paid to the Olympic Games themselves. Germany
> seemed to leave this honour on one side and claim the Games as a
> national occasion.

All of a sudden it was no laughing matter that the Nazis had hijacked
the Olympics with their swastikas. But Harold was effectively under
censorship, and therefore couldn't raise his concerns in writing.
Correspondence with Sybil continued. It was probably with a touch of
irony that she made reference to Hitler's growing political stature. She
would surely have chosen her words differently had she known what the
near future would bring:

> Well, my beloved, by now the Games will have been opened, and
> you will have seen the great Hitler . . . Cannot tell you how glad I am
> that all so far has gone well. I know that feeling of being in another
> world very well – the same will be true of me in Austria and I do think
> it a most excellent thing for you at the moment – bless you. Your
> letter sounds so happy – it makes me happy too . . . Glad to hear you
> and Monty can be together in the stadium. Have you quarrelled
> yet?!! Please give him my love and all good wishes to [British athlete]
> Godfrey Rampling. You will let me know too about Jack, won't you?

Harold was soon to tell the world about Jack Lovelock, the New

Zealand 1500 metres runner and a close personal friend. His fellow New Zealander Arthur Porritt, Harold's sprint rival in the 1924 100 metres, recalled that 'Jack Lovelock was a very temperamental runner – he was very highly strung.' Abrahams had first seen Lovelock as a freshman when he came up to Oxford in the autumn of 1931 as a Rhodes scholar. 'I can remember a slight, but perfectly relaxed figure with curly hair, playing a big part in the victory of the Oxford four-mile Relay Team.' Lovelock's running may have been relaxed, but his mind wasn't. Abrahams sensed that he could help Jack, and showed him how to channel his nervous energy positively, by maintaining a healthy perspective on his talent. In return Lovelock gave Abrahams his trust and friendship. When Lovelock travelled to Los Angeles for the 1932 Olympics, Harold supported his new confidant from afar, and shared his disappointment when Jack returned empty-handed. But here was another chance to try for Olympic gold – perhaps Lovelock's last. Harold had seized the day back in 1924, after messing up his first Olympics. Now it was Lovelock's turn to show his worth in Berlin in front of the Führer.

Jack would have to show great strength of purpose if he was going to focus on his goal and shut out the oppressive nationalism of 'the great' Hitler's Berlin. Athletes couldn't fail to hear the din or sense the blind adoration every time the Führer made his appearance. You had to be bloody-minded to put your personal aims before the will of such a powerful man.

Later, from the safety of England, Abrahams was able to write, 'Hitler attended the Games several times and made it obvious to everyone that he was only interested in Germans winning.' At the time, under scrutiny in Berlin on the first day of competition, Harold described the German wins like this: 'The German crowd were roused to the height of enthusiasm when in the presence of Herr Hitler they gained two Olympic victories . . . And for quite three minutes thousands of Germans present yelled with unrestrained enthusiasm . . . The Stadium was packed; the track is obviously in wonderful condition, and the presentation of the events was carried out with great showmanship.'

Had Abrahams unwittingly become part of Hitler's monstrous propaganda machine, or was he simply reporting the facts? Any criticism of the Nazi regime could have rebounded upon him while he was still in Germany, and he knew it. That was enough to keep his tone positive, though there is also a suspicion that part of him – the boyish sports fan – really was swept up in the sheer drama of it all.

Yet something was pricking his conscience, even while he acknowledged the great theatrical aspect to the Games. He would later express his regret at not confronting Hitler. And from what he told his nephew Tony, he certainly had the chance. 'Harold used to say to me that he was as close to Hitler as from here to there,' Tony said, marking out a distance of just a few yards.' He regretted not killing him. He used to say, "What a difference it would have made if I had." In reality though, he wouldn't have been allowed to do it even if he had tried.'

Sue Pottle confirmed that the idea had crossed her father's mind. 'He told me, "I wish I had shot Hitler." Judging by the number of times he used to say he could have shot him, I think he really felt he could or should have done something.' Alan Abrahams said that his father had discussed a different method of assassination, 'He told me that he wished he had a bomb in Berlin, to chuck over the railings at Hitler.' Tony Abrahams, who did become a war hero, took it all with a pinch of salt. He observed, 'I can't see Harold shooting anybody really. Harold couldn't have killed Hitler anyway.'

Maybe Harold couldn't have killed Hitler but there were still opportunities to undermine the Führer's belief in Aryan superiority. Several of those opportunities fell to Jesse Owens. And fortunately he wasn't intimidated by Hitler or the fanatical German spectators. If only his sprints could have lasted longer, to make Hitler's humiliation slower and more painful. At the time, his graceful glide through the preliminary heats came and went in the blink of an eye.

Harold wrote, 'The only trouble is to watch so many magnificent achievements at the same time, which is rather exhausting. Indeed, when Jesse Owens is in action, if one looks away for a few seconds he's gone. It's a case of "That's Owens – that was".'

To the connoisseur, however, Owens was already standing head and shoulders above everyone else. And there was no greater connoisseur of sprinting than Abrahams. If we remind ourselves not to be offended by the language of a bygone era, we can appreciate the quality of the following newspaper dispatch from the Olympic Stadium. Abrahams sometimes wondered whether Eric Liddell would have beaten him in the 1924 Olympic final; but he had no such doubts when it came to Jesse Owens:

> I thanked my lucky stars this morning, and again this afternoon, that
> I was not born twelve years later. If I had been I certainly would never
> have had the proud distinction of winning an Olympic event.

Jesse Owens, the 21-year-old negro from Ohio, is certainly the most beautiful moving human being I have ever seen tearing down a sprint track. But 'tearing' is really the wrong word. He seems to float along in effortless precision, and it is only the fact that he makes his opponents, who themselves are first-class sprinters, look like selling-platers that indicates the glorious speed with which this modest whirlwind traverses the cinder path.

In his heat this morning he equalled the world and Olympic record for the 100 metres of 10.3sec. This afternoon he beat Haenni, of Switzerland, reckoned to be the fastest sprinter in Europe, by quite four yards and set up a new Olympic and world's record of 10.2sec, equivalent to about 9.4sec for 100 yards.

The record couldn't be ratified because the following wind was too strong at 2.3 metres per second. By now, however, the long-anticipated coronation of Owens was inevitable. To Hitler's frustration, there was nothing he could do about it. And Harold Abrahams had to overcome some frustration of his own. For Woodroofe, the BBC staff man, had over-looked him for the prized slot to commentate on his new friend Jesse and that showpiece 100 metres final. Despite the fact that neither Woodroofe, nor his staff colleague Wells were prepared to do the job themselves, Harold was deemed unsuitable. Apparently the fact that he was a former 100 metres Olympic champion, and was also the most experienced athletics commentator in the business, was not enough. An American commentator from CBS was brought in to do the job instead.

Woodroofe's patronising account of how his colleagues performed, and how the 100 metres commentary selection was made, is priceless. He wrote later, 'Abrahams was very good, keen and always ready to learn. Husing and Henry of C.B.S. were only too ready to help (not unnaturally) and they were useful for filling in on occasions . . . I chose Husing for the 100 metres because I considered that he would be able to follow the race better than Abrahams. Abrahams agreed that he might have been inadequate on this occasion.'

It is hard to believe that Harold would have thought himself anything but equal to the task – unless of course his recent mental problems had caused him to doubt his ability to put what he was seeing into words in double-quick time. That seems so unlikely that Woodroofe's claim simply fails to ring true. Harold had been born for such moments and he was in his element. His beautiful description of Jesse Owens for the readers of his newspaper would not have been so very hard to reproduce on air. Such was Owens' dominance of the event – from start to finish – that the race wouldn't have provided the greatest observational challenge for a commentator. And Harold's description of Owens in full flight would probably have become just as legendary for its frenzied excitement as his commentary on Lovelock a few days later. In a way, the BBC's decision to silence Abrahams for his own specialist event represented the ultimate humiliation; a hideous conclusion to the discrimination they had exercised in the first place by not making him their official man.

Abrahams kept a recording of the 100 metres commentary from the 1936 Games. His American replacement's attempt to capture the moment was less than impressive. At one point, the commentator's voice fades into crowd noise completely. It sounds as if he has forgotten to direct his words into the microphone. When a commentary is barely ten seconds long, there is no time for such an oversight. Of course, it should be remembered that these were pioneering days, and any audible commentary was something to appreciate. But would Harold have done better? Almost certainly.

As it was, he captured the moment on camera. Harold's nephew Tony explained later, 'He showed me a photograph he had taken of Jesse Owens winning the 100 metres and he pointed out how extraordinarily relaxed Jesse was when he ran. Some runners throw themselves about or move their head all over the place; and they seem to be straining. But Jesse Owens didn't seem to be straining at all in Harold's photograph.'

On Jesse's effortless style, and his peerless beauty as an athlete in flight, Harold had already said what he wanted to say in print. He sounded almost deflated when he wrote about his new hero's success in the final. By then he knew the time was slower, and the medal-winning performance technically inferior. 'As expected, Jesse Owens won the 100 metres, beating his fellow negro, Ralph Metcalfe, by a couple of yards in 10.3 seconds, which equalled the Olympic and world record . . . Today Owens was not very quick off the mark, but after thirty yards he was clearly in front, and he won decisively.'

With a following wind of 2.7 metres, that record of 10.3sec couldn't stand either. But the record didn't matter to history as much as the offence Owens' victory caused Hitler. Albert Speer, Hitler's architect and future Armaments Minister, said his boss was 'highly annoyed', blaming Owens' 'primitive jungle antecedents' for his superior strength over 'civilised white men'.

And the Führer was further infuriated by what he saw at the long-jump pit the following day. A German jumper called Luz Long showed friendship towards Jesse Owens, even advising him on technique during competition. A grateful Owens promptly beat his rival into second place, though later praised his sportsmanship. Owens ended up with four gold medals in Berlin – he added the 200 metres and 4 × 100 metres relay to his collection. It was one more than Abrahams had predicted.

Denied his right to make a mark with the microphone as Owens stunned the world, Harold probably thought his chance had gone. But then he was handed the opportunity to commentate on his friend Jack Lovelock. Immediately, Harold was aware that he might let his emotions run away with him. On a postcard to Sybil, by now in Salzburg, he wrote, 'Jack Lovelock got through to the final all right [and] I have every hope that he will win. If he does I think I'll burst the microphone.'

If Lovelock failed it wouldn't be for lack of preparation. Whereas Abrahams had trained almost obsessively for nine months prior to his Olympic challenge, Lovelock had been stalking his opponents for years by going to the same athletics meetings around the world.

He had met Glenn Cunningham of America in the 'Mile of the Century' in 1935. Cunningham had broken the world mile record in 1934 with a time of 4min 6.8sec. Lovelock had already met the top Italian, Luigi Beccali, too. Beccali was the reigning Olympic champion from 1932 in Los Angeles, where Lovelock had flopped in the final.

Adolf Hitler came to the stadium especially to see the race. And among the finalists was a Nazi favourite called Fritz Schaumburg, one of the Reich's big hopes on the track. Another German called Werner Bottcher would also compete, and hope to spur Schaumberg along. The scene was set as 100,000 packed the arena: it was Harold's friend against the Aryan supermen and the best milers of recent years. Abrahams wouldn't have missed this for the world. In another letter to Sybil, he described the build-up to the big race that Thursday. 'I went to my broadcast pitch about 5 and at 5.10 started to give information about the 12 runners. I wonder if you heard the effort?'

She didn't, but millions of others did. One newspaper went on to describe it as 'the most human and dramatic broadcast ever sent out by the B.B.C.' The report added, 'For the first three laps he gave a clear description of the race, but on the fourth lap excitement got the better of him and all he could do was to cheer on Lovelock against his American rival, Cunningham.'

Abrahams seemed to have completely forgotten that there was a British runner out there too – Jerry Cornes. Lovelock had started slowly, and it was Cornes who led the field around the second bend. Then there was a huge cheer as Bottcher came through, setting up an inviting platform for Schaumburg. Cornes raised British hopes once more when he regained the lead after 400 metres.

A lap later, Cunningham had surged into the lead, but then the American stumbled and almost fell. He recovered and did battle with the Swede, Eric Ny. To Harold's private delight, the Germans soon began to go backwards, destroyed by the early pace. Cunningham looked the chief threat to the steadily advancing Lovelock. He was a formidable opponent, yet Jack seemed focused and fearless. As the duel developed, the excitement up in the broadcasting position reached fever pitch. A transcript of Harold's commentary hardly does it justice, because it was the wild emotion behind the words that made them so unique. This is what Abrahams said as battle was joined during that final, frenetic lap.

'Lovelock's running beautifully, in perfect position . . . Lovelock's running perfectly now . . . come on Jack! Lovelock's up to second position . . . Lovelock leads, 300 metres to go . . . Lovelock, come on Jack! . . . Cunningham's leading . . . no, no, Lovelock leads by three yards . . . Lovelock leads by four yards . . . Cunningham's fighting hard, Lovelock leads, Lovelock!'

By now Harold was shouting hysterically and he didn't seem to care. Back in Britain, where suppression of emotion was still regarded as a virtue, listeners to the broadcast could hardly believe their ears. But people became caught up in the excitement, hanging on Harold's every word. Abrahams brought his commentary to a glorious climax like this:

'Lovelock! Come on Jack, only 100 yards to go! Come on Jack, my God, he's done it! Jack, come on! Lovelock wins! Five yards to go, he wins, he's won! Hooray!'

It wasn't complicated or poetic; but it was liberating. Back in London, the BBC didn't know quite what had hit it. Where had the British runner finished? No one seemed to care any more, but the answer was sixth. The Germans had flopped horribly in front of Hitler, Schaumburg tenth and Bottcher last. It only added to the joy. Lovelock had broken the world record to win gold in 3:47.8. That was a full second faster than the previous world record set by Bill Bonthron of America. Cunningham had come in second but a good five yards behind his Kiwi conqueror. Beccali had to settle for bronze. Harold only cared about Lovelock, and even then he was too overcome to put across all the relevant information. Again, no one cared about the others because Harold didn't. Jack had won, the commentator's favourite, and that was all that mattered. The broadcast was over.

A few moments later a dry, formal BBC voice said, 'We are now back in the studio . . . the next part of our programme is a selection of gramophone records.' It was the perfect anticlimax.

Not for Harold, who had made broadcasting history with his unbridled enthusiasm. Many years later, when he was able to put something more measured into words, he said of Lovelock's race, 'He was always where he wanted to be, and when, just before the others were expecting it, he made his final effort, it was the most perfect climax to a race I've ever been privileged to witness . . . a runner whose action was the nearest thing to perfection I've ever seen, typifying controlled relaxation . . . the complete harmony of mind and body in action.'

Harold's commentary had hardly reflected that controlled relaxation. Not even his mind and mouth had achieved harmony; words had tumbled out at random. Somehow the commentary had worked anyway, and Abrahams had emerged a winner like his younger friend. He rushed down to trackside to congratulate Jack personally. He wrote to Sybil, 'I saw him immediately after the race, gave him your love and said I knew you would be as delighted as I was.'

If Hitler had been as close to Abrahams during the commentary as he usually was – 'close enough to kill' – he might just have heard the joy in the British Jew's voice as the Nazi favourites were humiliated. In his book *The Olympians*, Lord [Seb] Coe described Harold's extraordinary moment on air as, 'the least objective athletics commentary by an Englishman that can ever have been recorded for posterity'. If there was the slightest chance that Harold's voice had carried across to Hitler, the bias was worth it. What did objectivity matter in this context? Though Harold Abrahams was too old to win more medals, he had achieved something as great as his gold in Paris. He had allowed his soul to dance, in an era when it was still unusual to show much emotion in public. He had celebrated his humanity, and his individuality, in a stadium built for mass-produced Aryan super-humans. That was his own little slap in the face for the Nazis. And it felt good.

When Harold was asked to pick the most exciting moment of his broadcasting career, it was no surprise when he picked 'Jack Lovelock winning the 1500 metres in that Berlin Stadium, where I disgraced myself as a commentator. I was doing a commentary. I spent most of the last lap shouting, "Come on Jack, come on, come on, by golly he's done it." . . . And of course, the thing one really enjoys is where one's got a particularly personal interest, and my wife and I knew Jack frightfully well, and all he'd done towards training. And of course, one really almost shares in him winning.'

It was no accident that he changed 'My God' to 'by golly' in his recollection on air. At the time of the original commentary, some complained to the BBC that he had blasphemed in his excitement. On another occasion Harold admitted, 'I got into awful trouble with that broadcast because people wrote in and said how profane it was, because I said, "My God, he's done it."'

When he was a guest on the iconic radio show, *Desert Island Discs* later in life, Harold revealed to the presenter, Roy Plomley, why he hated the idea of being shipwrecked alone. 'I think it's ghastly. It fills me with horror, because I essentially love people. I don't like my own company very much.'

But Britain had loved Harold's company in those immortal seconds from Berlin. And for Abrahams the euphoria didn't just go away straight after Jack Lovelock's race. In the early hours – at 1.50 a.m. to be precise – Harold wrote:

> Darling, it is quite impossible to go to bed. Monty and I are so excited over Jack's win that although it happened nearly nine hours ago we have not yet recovered and the best and happiest thing is to write to my love.
>
> What a day! After Jack's running yesterday we felt confident he would win. I think we have been the only two who have backed him all along . . . Jack's run was unbelievable, I forgot everything and everybody in a delirium of joy.

Sadly Sybil had missed the iconic broadcast. 'You can imagine my frantic efforts to get you – turning of knobs, and making awful noises!' she wrote. But when the news of Lovelock's victory reached her in Austria, she shared Harold's elation. 'I sent Jack a wire, and hope he got it in time. We nearly went mad here – with excitement and delight on hearing that he had won! Please give him my very heartiest congratulations. You must be simply delighted. I *am* so glad.'

CHAPTER SIX

UNDERMINING ADOLF

The Berlin relay races evoked some strange and powerful emotions in Harold. Another close friend was involved; someone Abrahams had helped in times of trouble, by drawing on his own experience of burnout.

Godfrey Rampling was a handsome, 6ft 1in, 400 metres runner, who became father to the famous actress, Charlotte. His path to Berlin hadn't been smooth, as Abrahams explained. 'I had had a lot to do with him when he was in one of his slumps, which all athletes get, in helping him back to success.'

A blood disorder had compounded Rampling's problems; but in 1934 he was back with a bang at the Empire Games. Harold recalled, 'One of the things I enjoyed most in the whole of my athletic career was announcing in the White City that Rampling had done a British record [48.0sec] in the 440 yards, and realising that he knew, and one or two people knew, but not the public at large, that I played a part in that, for which he was grateful.'

Rampling had a good chance of gold in the 400 metres in Berlin. 'If by chance Godfrey should win today you will probably get a telegram from Monty to say I have passed away peacefully,' warned Harold, still ecstatic after Lovelock's triumph, in a letter to Sybil.

Unfortunately Rampling wasn't able to hit Lovelock's heights in his individual event. But he had one more chance of a medal – in the 4 × 400 metres relay. The British public was not treated to a live commentary because the race took place on a Sunday, and in those days sports broadcasts weren't allowed on the Sabbath. Had Harold been allowed to take the microphone again, he would probably have 'disgraced' himself just as gloriously as he had over Lovelock.

Rampling's performance certainly warranted that sort of hysteria. Running second, he took the baton fully eight yards behind the Americans, and ran the second lap with such effortless speed that he handed over five yards ahead. His personal time of 46.7 was out of this world, and set up Britain's gold medal. Abrahams described Rampling's run that day as 'the most gloriously heaven-sent quarter-mile I had ever seen'. For someone who had watched Eric Liddell, it was a remarkable tribute. Harold told Sybil jauntily, 'His effort in the relay was marvellous. He won it for England [sic] and he is quite happy I think.'

But there was another relay at the Berlin Olympics which caused a much stranger elation in Abrahams. Something had been building up inside him; a disgust for the Nazi philosophy that had polluted the Games. Harold recalled, 'The atmosphere was extraordinary and very uncomfortable. It had a queer effect on me. I remember myself cheering when a German girl in a relay race, which the German team were winning next up, dropped the baton. I cheered loudly, though I felt ashamed of myself and frightened too.' With that one defiant cheer, Abrahams the Jew had made a blatant personal protest against Hitler's murderous regime.

The young woman whose error caused the commotion was 24-year-old Ilse Dorffeldt; and ordinarily Harold would have felt sorry for her. But he explained later, 'Of course one gets to the stage where there is hatred. One longed to see the Nazi athletes beaten in Berlin. Which is human but not very healthy.'

And it was also human for Harold to be high on the adrenalin of his personal success. He told Sybil, 'Well, this Olympic Games is nearly over. I don't remember ever such a hectic time though I've really enjoyed it . . . The *Daily Sketch* say my articles have been good and the broadcast about Jack's race seems to have created no little excitement. I was told today that John Snagge who runs part of the broadcasting of running commentaries . . . said it was the best thing he had ever heard.'

Harold's sister Dorothy had also written to tell Harold that their mother had heard the broadcast and 'was thrilled almost to tears'. And Abrahams had made good money as a freelance in Berlin. 'Please feel that you can spend a bit more than you otherwise would,' he told Sybil.

Some of the journalists at *The Jewish Chronicle* would probably have called it blood money, though Harold added, 'I really would have done it for no pay at all. It is a compliment dearest to have the job of all jobs – and certainly that running commentary on Jack will be remembered always, simply because it expressed all that personal emotion.' Harold wasn't modest in his self-appraisal, but he was absolutely right about his own impact.

He had enjoyed the Games, just as much as he had abhorred the distasteful undercurrent in Berlin. He couldn't wait to express some of his deeper concerns, and finally felt able to do that by writing to Sybil while taking the train out of Germany:

> We are now about 1½ hours from the frontier and I shall breathe a sigh of satisfaction when we get over it. Dearest, I suppose I am biased and I'll tell you lots when we meet that will take too long to write and which in any event I deliberately refrained from writing in Germany, as most letters are opened if not all. One of the most priceless examples of this occurred when a British journalist, who, telephoning his copy on a Friday evening said something complimentary about the German organisation. His remarks were quoted on *Saturday* morning.

Harold had looked further into Nazi Germany than most journalists in Berlin that summer. He did so just before leaving, and told Sybil:

> This morning I went on a two hours' tour of Berlin with that Jewish lawyer I met in London and whose flat I was at one time anxious to rent for the fortnight. He is of course unable to earn a living and lives with his mother aged 65 – Heaven knows on what . . . Darling, such a refined, cultured and gentle woman, who could not be capable of any unkindness I'm sure. Lived in Berlin all her life and so proud of all it really should stand for. Talked halting English with a very pleasant accent. She told me how lucky I was to be born in England where everyone is free to say and think what we like. The iniquity of persecuting any human being like that!! Did you know the shops in Berlin had got out the flags of every nation except Deutschland? Jews not being Nationals are not allowed to fly the German flag.
>
> Well dearest, I'm glad to be out of it. I've not felt really depressed because I have in the most part had so much to do – but every time people said '*auf wiedersehen*' I felt 'you won't see me again while this regime lasts'.

Sybil replied from Salzburg, 'I can understand what you must have been feeling.' Then she offered a warning that served as a further reminder of the constraints that the Nazi regime placed on people. Sybil added, 'Letters to (I don't know about from) Austria are opened too, so be discreet, darling. One from my mother arrived opened the other day.' Hitler's paranoia had already spread back to his native land.

The persecution of Jews disgusted Harold, but did not make him feel any more fervently Jewish. In reply to a letter from a man writing a book about Jewish runners, Abrahams was quite firm in his refusal to be categorised exclusively in this way. He explained, 'With regard to Jewish National Sport, that is the "Maccabi", I am not a supporter thereof, believing that people of Jewish origin who are British subjects should play their part in British National Athletics, and not encourage a separatist movement.'

Harold had played his part in British athletics more passionately than most; and having been to Nazi Germany, there was only one thing about his sprinting career that he would have changed if he could. 'I would do it all again except that I would love to have won gold at the Berlin Olympics in 1936.' As his train took him back to freedom, how Harold envied Jesse Owens, for his ability to show the German people that the Aryan race was not superior after all. Abrahams would dearly have loved to illustrate that truth himself.

But could he really have challenged Jesse for gold, had they raced each other? Philip Noel-Baker, Britain's 1920 and 1924 Olympic captain, thought so:

> I have always believed that Harold Abrahams was the only European sprinter who could have run with Jesse Owens, Ralph Metcalfe, and the other great sprinters from the US. He was in their class, not only because of natural gifts – his magnificent physique, his splendid racing temperament, his flair for the big occasion; but because he understood athletics, and had given more brainpower and more will power to the subject than any other runner of his day.

As honest as ever in his self-appraisal, Harold couldn't go along with that. Even in the 1970s he reflected, 'Many are the arguments as to who is the greatest sprinter of all time . . . If I had to plump for one man, it would be Jesse Owens . . . If it were possible to line up those who could claim to be the world's greatest, Jesse Owens should win. No sprinter I have ever seen was such a delight to watch.'

The task of shattering Hitler's delusions – temporarily at least – had fallen to Owens; and he had exposed German limitations beautifully. Harold observed later:

> In the field events the Germans were successful, on the track no. They didn't get a higher place than third in any single one of the running events. I think because the track events required much more individual initiative. The training of the Germans seemed to me to have been mass training and much too mechanical. You can't sprint straight with the weight of the Swastika on your shoulders. The importance of winning had been too much stressed.

Jesse Owens had made a mockery of the Nazi philosophy and Harold loved him for it. They struck up a friendship that stood the test of time, as Tony Abrahams recalled. 'Harold was fond of Jesse Owens and they kept up the relationship even after the ['36] Games.' Abrahams would sometimes see Owens in the States, or the Caribbean, when the former Olympic champions were working at track and field meetings there. The two men enjoyed an easy rapport. 'He told me he liked Jesse Owens,' Tony added. 'He just liked him, nothing particular in that.'

However, despite the magic of Owens, the birth of their friendship and Harold's own iconic success in the Berlin commentary box, Abrahams declared in his old age, 'I'm inclined to think that if I could put the clock back and decide that again, I wouldn't go.'

He went because he couldn't see past the glory of international sport. For example, when Harold produced the BOA Official Report of the 1936 Olympics, he focused so much on sport that his document was later criticised for 'its utter lack of political discussion'. But Richard D. Mandell, who made that point in his 1971 book, *The Nazi Olympics*, didn't seem to understand the motivations of the report's author. Abrahams had excluded political debate from his account precisely because he wished the Olympic movement to remain free from political interference. As for Harold's belated expression of regret for having gone to Berlin, it is hard to imagine a 36-year-old Abrahams, so ambitious and passionate about athletics, ever refusing to go. And here was a man who never did boycott an Olympic Games, or indeed favour any boycott, for the rest of his life – no matter how compelling the case. He never stopped believing in the power of sport to provide common ground for very different people.

So Harold had braved Berlin and returned to contemplate one burning question: did he have the courage to get married? Just when it seemed he did, Harold's phobia of marriage returned. He was hit by a new crisis of confidence, sparked by the separation of close married friends. 'They were so much in love – so *sure*,' he told Sybil, admitting that 'such a thing is apt to frighten me if I let it'.

In turmoil, Abrahams sought fresh psychiatric help. 'I am writing by this mail to Dr Suttie to resume treatment on Tuesday.' But he remained in a state of despair about the collapse of his friends' marriage, partly because he had been best man at their wedding and was godfather to their children. He wrote to Sybil from Loughborough, where he was lecturing on the Berlin Games, and poured out his fear and confusion. 'What did disturb me was that the attraction which undoubtedly *did* exist has entirely gone and the thought crossed my mind, "Heavens can that attraction absolutely go so that physical contact would be repulsive? Could it ever happen that I shouldn't be thrilled at having my little tuppence in my arms? And what then?"'

Harold's wild mood swings were perfectly illustrated by the way he signed off this deeply serious letter with the following postscript: 'Darling, I've lost my heart to a lovely golden-haired . . . RETRIEVER – aged ten weeks.'

In a thoughtful reply from Austria, Sybil wrote:

I do know and understand how very upsetting it must be for you. I *long* to be with you, to talk about things sanely and sensibly, and feel most horribly far away out here. It is wretched that it should have happened when you were feeling tired and low – but I do believe that when you are less tired you will reason it out fairly, and not take so much to heart.

As to 'being so sure' and 'so much in love' at first, I have lately come to the conclusion that those who are *not* sure, and not too blinded by love in the beginning are 100% more likely to be successful in married life. Looking round among my friends, too, I really believe that this *is* so.

There is everything, darling, in being prepared to give, to work, and to wait for happiness – and in having real friendship and understanding for one's patience.

One thing, to me, is a never-ending source of wonder and joy – and that is the way in which we seem to bring out the best in each other, even in the most trying circumstances! This alone fills me with confidence – so, beloved, here's hoping!

Bless you, my dear, dear love. May you feel better – with each succeeding day, and come back feeling really fit and happy to

Your own loving

Sybil

It was a wonderful letter to a troubled man, and exactly what Harold needed to hear. All the psychotherapy in the world wasn't worth a few home truths from Sybil Evers, opera singer, beauty and, it seems, dream partner for a man she brought back from the brink.

'What a perfectly precious darling you are!' wrote Harold by way of reply. 'Your complete understanding – and our knowledge that each of us wants always to give of our best and to try and work with the other – is so comforting.'

It was time for the fretting to stop and the loving to be rewarded. Harold could only achieve this if things were done spontaneously, and almost secretly – which was exactly what Sybil wanted too.

She revealed what happened next to a *Daily Mirror* reporter a few weeks later when it was too late for the press to spoil the big day. 'It was so quiet that nobody knew about it. I came back from Glasgow, where I had been singing, and Mr Abrahams met me with, "What about getting married in two days' time?"

'I replied, "What about it?" – and we arranged it. Not a single member of either family was told. We had been engaged for some ten months.'

Harold Maurice Abrahams and Sybil Marjorie Evers were married on December 22, 1936 at Hammersmith Registry Office. Sybil was living in nearby Brook Green; so Hammersmith Registry Office was the logical place for a divorced woman to marry. Perhaps it wasn't the most romantic wedding London has ever seen, because Harold's new wife had to be recorded on the marriage certificate as 'Sybil Marjorie Brack, formerly Evers'. While Harold could happily record that he was a 'Bachelor', Sybil had to explain that she was 'Formerly the wife of Noel Douglas John Brack, from whom she obtained a divorce'.

But there was still a strangely romantic strand to the wedding, revealed by the daughter Harold and Sybil later adopted. Sue Pottle explained, 'My mother always told me that her wedding ring was made of gold clippings taken from my father's Olympic winner's medal.' That might not have been every woman's idea of a romantic gesture; but Sybil knew what the gesture meant, how Harold was still trying to give her the very best of himself.

No one could spoil the wedding day, the simple climax to a very complicated courtship. Only the fridge in their new home tried. Sybil explained, 'The only celebration we fixed was a bottle of champagne at lunch, alone together, at our flat. When we got there, after our wedding, we found the wine had frozen solid. It had been put in the refrigerator the night before. So we thawed it – and celebrated.'

The story broke in the *Daily Mirror* of Tuesday, January 12, 1937, under the headline, 'Olympic Runner Wed Secretly to Opera Singer'. There had been no honeymoon at that stage because, as the paper pointed out, 'Miss Evers is playing the leading part in *The Lily Maid*, the new opera by Rutland Boughton which opens at the Winter Garden Theatre tonight.'

Later they honeymooned in Finland – around one of Harold's athletics meetings. That's when the long-suffering Sybil must have realised that she would always have to share Harold Abrahams. But there was never a dull moment in their life together. The irrational fears of one very highly strung former Olympic athlete proved groundless. Their love did not die. Harold and Sybil remained happily married – until death did them part.

CHAPTER SEVEN

WAR

In September 1939 Britain went to war with Germany, putting on hold an important breakthrough for British sprinting. Just when starting blocks had been officially approved by the Amateur Athletic Association, meaningful competition stopped. It meant that Harold's recent appointment as Assistant Honorary Secretary to the British Amateur Athletic Board was also rendered temporarily irrelevant.

For a man as addicted to athletics as Harold Abrahams, the war was going to cause some severe withdrawal symptoms. Only a year earlier, he had managed to convey his love for athletic achievement almost as memorably in print as he had done with the microphone in Berlin. When a skinny, bespectacled British runner called Sydney Wooderson broke the world half-mile record in a stunning time of 1min 49.2sec, he had written the following:

'So Wooderson did it. There's only one word – amazing. I feel rather like the small boy who was taken to the Zoological Gardens for the first time and shown a giraffe – and he didn't believe it. I'm not at all sure that I believe it!'

Now the thrills and spills were over for the foreseeable future. And Abrahams wasn't the only one struggling to come to terms with the shocking truth. Just as war broke out, he received a newsletter from the Organising Committee for the Twelfth Olympic Games, which were due to be held not in London, as Abrahams had foreseen four years earlier, but in Helsinki, Finland between July 20 and 4 August 4, 1940.

The newsletter stated confidently: 'During the Olympic Games, sixteen special cables will be reserved at the stadium for the use of foreign commentators.' On September 8, 1939, Harold wrote a dark but amusing letter to his BBC boss, S.J. Lotbiniere, known by now as 'Lobbie'. With the Helsinki newsletter attached, it read as follows:

My dear Lobbie,

I received the enclosed from Finland this morning, and I am sending it to you, not that I anticipate that it is of any use at all – the chances of an Olympic meeting next year are a little remote (!!!), but I thought it might go into the archives of the BBC for use in 1944 – if any of us are alive by then.

I am at present awaiting some indication from the Central Register people as to my War Work, and biding my time with the A.R.P. [Air Raid Precautions].

I have to use my stopwatch, and you will be glad to hear that my time from bed on hearing the siren to the Post, including dressing and 1¼ miles by car is 5min. 20.4sec. I expect to knock a lot off this as I had to return for my false teeth, seeing that I cannot blow the whistle without them.

All the best,

Yours ever,

Harold M. Abrahams

Knowing that his permanent limp ruled him out of combat, Harold thought he could best contribute to the British war effort at the Ministry of Information. His political contact was well placed. Sir John Simon was Chancellor of the Exchequer by now, and wrote from 11 Downing Street on September 22 to tell Harold the situation as he saw it. Unfortunately, the Ministry of Information was fully staffed and Sir John feared there was little he could do for Abrahams.

Instead of moping, Harold tried to think of some other way to help undermine Hitler. He and Sybil had already fostered a German Jewish boy, Kurt Katzenstein. The lad's parents had laid hands on three visas for South America – enough for them and only one of their children. Harold had stepped in to ensure that at least one young life wouldn't be ruined by the Nazis. Kurt Katzenstein had become Ken Gardner, and soon began to thrive in England under the guidance of Mr and Mrs Abrahams. Now Harold wanted to do something for the British war machine; and if he couldn't join the Ministry of Information, he was more than willing to join another ministry:

I eventually got into the Ministry of Economic Warfare, where I started a thing called the Enemy Exports Committee, which is the opposite of contraband. With contraband you automatically stop things going into a country but with this you captured things coming out from a country. I remember how excited I was on my very first day in the Ministry of Economic Warfare, which was in the London School of Economics. A red box arrived marked to me. I had to get a very special key to open it from the director of the whole thing. Inside were two sealed envelopes – Secret and Top Secret. I thought, 'My Dear, I'm really beginning to win the war,' and when I got inside it was from someone to tell me he couldn't attend a meeting.

Before long an idea came to Abrahams; a way in which he could get out of London and play a role in rallying the troops. He would use his experience of Berlin 1936 to belittle Hitler in lectures he could give to British Armed Forces abroad. The aim was to highlight the sporting victories that undermined the Fuhrer at his own Games, thus boosting British morale. And so, in January 1940, having used his political contacts to secure authorisation, Harold headed for Hendon, ready to be flown over to France to give a series of lectures, illustrated by lantern slides, to Royal Air Force units still stationed there:

We left in a six-seater plane at 11.15 a.m. . . . We flew into thick fog about five miles from the French coast . . . Eventually the pilot got his bearings though we had to fly very low indeed, we were on occasions actually lower than the cliffs . . . I set off for Amiens with an RAF padre driving a Renault car . . . Being driven at between 80 and 90 kilometres an hour by a very indifferent performer on what seemed all the while to be the wrong side of the road, was far more frightening than flying . . . I eventually arrived at my destination . . . The audience was composed of officers and men from squadrons stationed in the vicinity . . . A picture of Hitler in the Olympic Stadium met with the kind of catcalls to be heard when the villain comes on to the stage in a pantomime.

Next afternoon we motored north . . . My lecture this time was given in an air hangar belonging to a Fighter Squadron . . . The lantern and cinema arrangements were naturally somewhat primitive . . . it was impossible to get all my picture on the sheet at the same moment. This caused a good deal of amusement, as I had to ask the lanternist first to show me Jesse Owens' legs and then, since the arms were at the same moment projected on the door of the canteen, to shift the lantern so as to produce the arms on the screen, while the legs were wandering round the temporary refreshment bar.

No matter, the light relief did the pilots some good; and the overall message to the British Expeditionary Forces was not lost; the Germans were far from invincible, as Jesse Owens had shown to devastating effect in Berlin four years earlier.

Abrahams added, 'The spirit of the troops was extremely good, the only bugbear being a little boredom that nothing was happening. I frequently heard the expression "when the war begins I shall do so and so".' Unfortunately within months the B.E.F. would be longing for normality, as they were forced to retreat in desperation to Dunkirk in the face of a huge German onslaught. It would be a good many years before Harold Abrahams could venture onto the Continent again. At least he had done what he could, while he could. And from England he continued the propaganda war.

On March 10, 1940, Harold and Stanley Rous, the football administrator, broadcast a Home Service programme called 'Sport Under Nazi Rule'. With the help of selected guests, they belittled Germany's lack of track achievements at the Olympics of Los Angeles and Berlin. Meanwhile on the suggestion of BBC man Ronald Turnbull, who was soon to join the Special Operations Executive, Harold was given the chance to broadcast to the sportsmen of Finland:

At this very moment, if only the dictators were not making such nuisances of themselves, I should have been in Helsinki. Instead of sending a short message to you, I might have been sending to England an account of [The Finn, Taisto] Maeki's brilliant victory in the 10,000 metres. The Helsinki Olympics are not abandoned. They are postponed. When Great Britain has played her part in restoring liberty to Europe, and removed from the Swastika those barbaric growths so that the Cross of Peace remains, British athletes will hasten again to your country to renew those friendships which we all value so highly.

Harold meant it. Although Helsinki would end up hosting the second Games after the war rather than the first, the pre-war friendships Harold forged among the Finnish athletes held firm until their Olympics finally came to fruition.

In the meantime Harold and Sybil continued to stay strong in the face of the growing threat from Nazi Germany, and did what they could to make a difference at home. The outbreak of war had caused chaos in many a family. Having fostered 'Ken', they also took in an Austrian Jewish refugee called 'Minka'. Harold, Sybil and their fledgling family were living in Rickmansworth in a house called 'Whiteladies', situated near the local golf course. Unfortunately, an important building belonging to the Admiralty was also close by, and the Germans were apparently trying to flatten it. In September Sybil wrote to her father describing what life was like:

We've been having nightly air raids for a week now, and two or three each day as well. During the day we are able to carry on much as usual, though it does mean I have to bicycle to the Warden's Post – a mile and up-hill pretty much all the way! – whenever the warning goes . . . At night . . . the trouble is that Harold is often on duty from 6–12 or midnight to 6 a.m., and it has been difficult for him to get enough sleep. The regularity with which the German planes come over is quite astonishing. The warning now goes about 9.30 p.m. and after half an hour we have them coming over, usually one at a time, and flying very high and out of reach of the searchlights. One night they came over exactly sixteen minutes apart . . . Then at 3.30, approximately, they finish and at 4 o'clock punctually the 'All Clear' goes.

You can just imagine Harold sitting there with his stopwatch, a part of him grudgingly admiring the discipline of the German Luftwaffe's time-management. But this was a cruel kind of sport, a game that could easily end in death for those below. Sybil and Harold suffered some early near misses, as she explained:

We've had some excitements, the worst being when a salvo of bombs was dropped on the golf course, exactly opposite our house, five hundred yards away! Luckily they were small ones – 110 pounds – and fell on soft ground, so all we heard was the rattling of doors and windows, and the sound of eight rather large fireworks, and we saw a blinding yellow flash like sheet-lightning!

The nearest air raid shelter still didn't tempt them, unless duty called. 'Harold says nothing will induce him to leave his bed and seems to sleep very well. I couldn't sleep at first when these wretched planes came over, and found the sound even penetrated cotton wool in the ears, so that, try as I would, I lay tense, listening for them. However, since Wednesday night we've been getting used to them and their astonishing regularity seems to make sleep easier!

Inevitably there were moments of light relief. In early November 1940, Sybil wrote, 'We had a good laugh on Tuesday. Harold came in on Sunday evening from feeding the hens saying that he had been having a heart-to-heart talk with Selina the chief hen and Selina had informed him that she would lay her first egg on Guy Fawkes Day! Well, the joke was that she actually did, and Harold couldn't believe that we hadn't planted the egg there for fun. You can imagine how the children enjoyed it all.'

Sadly local life soon took a tragic turn. Sybil told her father, 'We had a drum roll during dinner the other night, the sound of which caused Harold and me to duck beneath the table!' Landing at the bottom of the hill, a bomb burst a gas-main and killed four people. But other bombs had landed without detonating, and Sybil was charged with a task that would have tested the mettle of many a man. 'Next morning I was sent out to look for an unexploded bomb which was thought to have fallen on the golf course between us and the road to the Club House. I didn't feel very brave but managed to search pretty thoroughly and found nothing, so presumably it was a mistake.'

Poor Sybil. Back in 1936, she had admitted to feeling unnerved by cockroaches in Austria. Now she was steeling herself to seek out bombs on her doorstep. But Rickmansworth was still safer than central London, where Harold had worked. Sybil added:

You have probably heard that there have been a number of bombs on the Temple? Harold's Chambers in Elm Court have been completely demolished by a land-mine, and all his books, law notes, and some athletic records, furniture and other possessions including a stop-watch are lost. The only remaining possession is his name, still clearly visible on the door! How lucky that it happened at night, when nobody was there . . . but the law notes and records are, alas, irreplaceable.

First Harold's precious possessions, then perhaps Harold. By 5 February, 1941, the big picture looked bleak. Despite victory in the Battle of Britain the previous autumn, Harold had warned his family to prepare for the worst again. Sybil wrote to her father with a casually disturbing question. 'What do you think about the impending invasion of this country? I gather from Harold that it is thought officially to be imminent any time this month, in fact. Then, presumably, we shall be under martial law, and have to "stay put" for an indefinite and unpleasant period. It won't be nice but we shall have to try not to worry about one another, shan't we?'

Either Sybil was trying to block out the obvious implications of invasion for a man called Abrahams, or she really didn't comprehend the inevitable consequences. Her husband was already on a list of prominent British Jews, who would be swiftly rounded up in the event of a Nazi invasion. Rosemary Warne, Harold's friend later in life, revealed, 'He told me on more than one occasion that the Nazis had put him on a list of British Jews to be dealt with if they invaded. He was under no illusions about what would have happened had they invaded, because he always said he wouldn't be here now if it had happened.'

Tony Abrahams, Harold's nephew, believes the original information about the death list may have come from Solly after the war. Tony said, 'My father showed me lists of British people who had been identified by the Germans. The Nazis had cobbled together a series of lists, not just one, and Harold's name was there.' The famous 'Black Book' or *Sonderfahndungsliste* also contains one entry for the name 'Abrahams'. Since there is no first name or initial, we cannot say for sure whether it refers to Harold or not. The entry reads: 'Abrahams, brit. ND-Offizier, vermutl. England, RSHA IV E4'. Experts believe this could refer to an Intelligence officer, and it is doubtful whether Harold's work with the Enemy Exports Committee at the Ministry of Economic Warfare would have put him in this category in the eyes of the Gestapo.

However, surviving family and close friends of Harold Abrahams have no doubt that the Gestapo were ready to target him if Britain was successfully invaded. For Harold, 'staying put' for any 'indefinite and unpleasant period', as Sybil put it, would have involved a grim term in a concentration camp before extermination.

Between 1941 and 1942 the threat of invasion eased. And Harold was able to go on the offensive to ensure that athletics wasn't tarnished by a Nazi takeover. He had first attended the International Amateur Athletic

Federation Congress in 1934. Before the war he had begun to make a name for himself within the IAAF, joining the Rules and Records Committee which shaped the very nature of competition. Now that Hitler's Third Reich was trying to seize control of athletics, Abrahams became even more prominent, as the leading voice of the resistance.

The IAAF President, J. Sigfried Edstrom, had appointed pro-Nazis to positions of power in the IAAF European Commission. Dr Karl Ritter von Halt became its president, without reference to the IAAF Council. Abrahams complained to a colleague in supposedly neutral Sweden about these 'autocratic actions'. He added:

> We can only conclude that President Edstrom made his 'appointment' at the 'request' of Dr von Halt. If such a request was made, then in my judgement the reply should have been 'I see no necessity after the situation has been vacant for three years, suddenly to fill it, and even if I thought there was such necessity I have no power to make such an appointment'.
>
> The position of President of the European Commission must remain a sinecure until the war is over . . . but if the rules of the IAAF are to be ignored and Germany is to use the appointments and the European Commission for her 'New Order' ideas in athletics, then one can understand the enthusiasm of Dr von Halt, and only deplore further that President Edstrom has perhaps unwittingly assisted German designs.

In what was fast turning into a diplomatic incident, Vilgot Hammarling of the Swedish Legation in London wrote directly to Abrahams to protest that the Swedes had not gone Nazi, but had been forced to appease the Germans with a gesture.

Harold issued a defiant warning by way of response:

> We shall, of course, see in due course whether Germany makes any capital out of the appointment of von Halt – but to my mind any move by Germany during the war to dominate European athletics should be met by a strong statement by the IAAF President. I need hardly add that when the United Nations have won the war, it won't matter very much what athletic organisation the Nazis have tried to foist on a conquered Europe.

At a stroke, Abrahams had entirely discredited the hair-brained attempt by the Germans, assisted by certain Swedes, to run roughshod over IAAF rules. That would teach Hermann Goering's Luftwaffe to destroy Harold's beloved athletics records. Now he could return to his work at the Ministry of Economic Warfare. And one can only assume that his love of statistics helped enormously within that particular Ministry.

At home, meanwhile, Harold and Sybil made a decision which took them way beyond their early successes as foster parents. In December 1942, they formally adopted a baby boy called Alan. He later explained, 'I was adopted when I was only eight weeks old, so effectively there was no period of time in my early life when I wasn't with them.'

Life was kind, considering the restrictions and dangers of war. Mercifully Harold, Sybil, Alan and the children they fostered, all survived that war. Unfortunately, a key figure from Harold's hey-day didn't. It was with some sadness that he penned a personal tribute to a fearsome rival. 'Eric Liddell gave his life during the war,' Abrahams wrote. 'He so tragically lost his life in the Far East.' It was Liddell's work as a missionary in China that had 'led to his untimely end', Harold explained. The tough Scot had passed away from a brain tumour in a Japanese prisoner-of-war camp. Abrahams realised the news would 'cause deep feelings of regret to his many admirers and friends', not least because Liddell 'was a man whose intense spiritual convictions contributed largely to his athletic triumphs'.

So Liddell was gone, though *Chariots of Fire* would ensure he was remembered forever. But what of the Olympic movement, violated by Hitler back in 1936? As peace broke out, there were those on both sides of the Atlantic who were determined to see the Games snuffed out, or at least suspended for a further decade. They wanted to ensure that no monstrous leader could ever again use the Olympics as a platform to proclaim his might. It was a powerful argument, and the very future of the Games hung in the balance.

CHAPTER EIGHT

LONDON '48 – THE FUTURE

In order to protect his beloved Olympic Games from extinction, Harold Abrahams went on air in Britain to make one of the most important broadcasts of his entire life. It was 1945, and the war in the Far East was not even over.

> There has been considerable discussion lately in America and at home about the future of the Olympic Games; and the opinion has been expressed that they are not wanted for at least ten years after the termination of hostilities. It has also been said that the Olympic spirit is dead. As I have been a Member of the Executive Committee of the International Olympic Committee for a number of years, and it is that committee which is responsible for Olympic festivals, I felt it might be of value if I put forward a few facts for the consideration of all those who are anxious to form an accurate and unbiased opinion on the value of Olympic meetings in the post-war period.

Abrahams then went on to make it abundantly clear that it was the IOC and no one else who would decide when and where the next Olympic Games would be held. He added:

> The Olympic Games of 1944 were actually awarded to London, and therefore it is not too much to hope that if London should request the celebration of the first post-war meeting, the International Olympic Committee would accede to such a request.
> My colleagues on the International Olympic Committee and I

are satisfied that the Games could be staged in London with even greater efficiency, and with far wider facilities, than would have been possible before the war. We are confident that the Games could be celebrated in the true spirit of sportsmanship – avoiding the nationalistic twist which the Nazi government gave to the 1936 festival. And may I emphasise that the Games had been accepted by the city of Berlin in 1931, that is to say, before the Nazis assumed complete power in Germany.

In a few confident sentences, Abrahams had countered those who were conspiring to bring down the Olympic movement completely, and had restored the authority of the IOC. More importantly from a British point of view, he had prepared the ground for London 1948. In order to eliminate any lingering fear that the Olympic stage might be hijacked once again by warlike countries, Harold emphasised:

There is no question that Germany and Japan, when defeated, could be readmitted to the comity of nations, before they have proved themselves fit to participate in the true spirit of sport.

. . . The Olympic Games can and must play an important part in building a structure of friendship and understanding between peoples of different nations. It is totally wrong to say they breed ill-feeling.

. . . There is no doubt that a friendship built up in sport is an enduring one, and the opportunity which international competitions provide for people to get to know one another is of very real value to the future peace of the world. Sport is one human activity of universal appeal, and we should surely cultivate to the utmost any activity which can so readily be shared by men and women of every nation and creed.

Let us hope therefore that all that the Olympic ideal stands for – the ideal of the common humanity of all men – can be revived as soon as is practicable. It is what we have been fighting for, for over five long years. It would indeed be most fitting that London, the centre of the British Empire which stood almost alone at one period of the war, should be the first city to celebrate the revived Olympic Games.

It was Abrahams at his most eloquent, using his legal brain to mount one argument after another in favour of an Olympic Games in London in 1948. These arguments proved conclusive.

Helsinki had not been forgotten, and in 1947 Abrahams was among those who ensured that the Finns were awarded the Games for 1952. But London had won the right to take the movement forward, and it was generally accepted that the English capital was best disposed to provide the facilities and stability required.

Later Harold was able to write, 'Soon after the end of the war, the IOC decided that it would be possible to hold the XIVth Games in 1948 and, in early 1946, the Games were allotted to London. It is no exaggeration to say that the decision to apply for the Games in the circumstances of the aftermath of nearly six years of war was a most courageous one.'

For many, food shortages and psychological scars were enough to cope with in the aftermath of horrific war. The last thing on their minds was an Olympic Games. Many ex-servicemen struggled to come to terms with what they had seen and done. One of these was Tony Abrahams. He had been Mentioned in Despatches while fighting in Greece, yet the 22-year-old had paid a price for his heroism.

When I came back from the war I wasn't well because I had been wounded in the head. And they put me in a hospital in Mill Hill. This was about September 1945. They were giving me electrical treatment daily, that nowadays they never will, and you move like hell when you are given it. I was in a pretty bad way at the time. I was depressed.

Harold was a very good uncle and he came to see me one day in the hospital. He was sympathetic in a way that neither my father nor my Uncle Adolphe was. I can't remember the words but Harold said something to the effect of 'I went to see a very good man once and his name's so and so and I jolly well recommend him'.

Anyway the chap came to see me in hospital – a nice fellow, and I said to Harold, 'How come you know him?' and he said, 'I had to use him on occasion.' This psychiatrist examined me. He came twice actually. And then he suggested that they stop the electric treatment because he didn't think it was suitable. And he also said that I didn't need the other sort of treatment that was being advocated, to sit on a couch and pour out your life story.

He said that I obviously had had some difficulties in the war and also I'd got a bit of metal in my head. He conferred with the Mill Hill doctor and reckoned that it would be alright for me – and it was alright. I went up to Cambridge in January 1946.

In effect, Harold had used his own psychological suffering before the war to help save a relative from treatment that might have resulted in permanent brain damage. Abrahams would do everything in his power to help those who were suffering around him to rebuild their damaged lives. And pretty soon that meant extending his adopted family.

Sue Pottle explained, 'Harold and Sybil had moved to "Great Jenkins" from "Whiteladies" in Rickmansworth in 1945. My natural mother, Florence Hodge, had come to work for them there, and I'm told she wanted to emigrate. But she couldn't do so if her child did not have its father's name on its birth certificate. So Harold and Sybil adopted me in 1946, when I was nearly three.'

Her new brother Alan remembered her arrival. 'The maid, her mother, came in with her and left. And Sue stayed behind.' Heartbreaking as that must have been for Sue at the time, her new surroundings were at least stimulating and spectacular. She explained, 'Great Jenkins was a large, rambling Tudor farmhouse, with half-moat. We kept chickens in the stables and had lots of cats.'

These were stories from just one family in a nation trying to heal itself. Millions of families were trying to find a semblance of normality, after the confusion and pain to which they had been subjected. It was a strange environment in which to plan for an Olympic Games. Yet life had to go on, and Harold Abrahams believed the London Olympics could be part of the healing process.

With his personal life happy and harmonious, Harold threw much of his energy into athletics administration. Harold wanted to ensure that he had influence when decisions were being made in the build-up to the Olympics. So in 1946 he became Assistant Treasurer to the British Amateur Athletic Board, of which he had been a member since its inception. On July 2 of that year, at an Executive Meeting of the Organising Committee for the London Olympics, Harold was appointed Chairman of the Technical Committee. That gave him full responsibility for seeing that the equipment and various venues conformed to the rules of the IAAF. He was also due to oversee the smooth staging of the track and field events at Wembley Stadium.

Absurdly, the Civil Service, which had insisted that Harold stay on after the war, were reluctant to give Harold enough free time to fulfil his

Olympic duties. Where Harold was supposed to have found the time to act as treasurer for the 1948 Games – as Janie Hampton suggested in her book *The Austerity Olympics* – is a mystery. Abrahams had to break the bad news about his limited availability to his friend Lord Burghley, who in turn told an Organising Committee meeting on August 29, 1946. The minutes of that meeting were brief. 'The Chairman explained that Mr Harold Abrahams would not have time to serve as Chairman of the Technical Committee but he would assist on the broadcasting side.'

In fact he was willing to lend his expertise to all media matters through the Press and Publicity Sub-Committee. But Abrahams soon had to tell Lord Burghley that the chairman of this sub-committee, C.B. Cowley, was abusing his position on the Organising Committee to make unilateral decisions on Press and Publicity too. Harold warned that the Press and Publicity Sub-Committee would stand down if it wasn't granted the power it had anticipated. Burghley felt obliged to call Harold's bluff and disbanded it, though it was to his credit that Abrahams continued to give advice when it was asked for.

Despite the problems he faced as the Games drew near, Harold was determined to give his heart, soul, and every spare moment to the London Olympics. After all, the Games he had helped to win presented a unique opportunity to right the wrongs of 1936. Abrahams explained:

> The Berlin Games were such a spectacle that something very vital was missing. I came away having watched a wonderfully organised but rather mechanical and inhuman exhibition. How to combine world record achievements with the spirit of amateurism is a problem which becomes more and more acute each year. We have a grand opportunity to make the first post-war Olympic meeting the starting point for something really worthwhile.

Sportsmanship would be more important than ever, something he was able to convey to British athletes from the moment he was appointed as one of their Assistant Team Managers. Harold also knew better than anyone the sort of problems athletes faced at such a major event, and how to solve them. And his influence as a journalist was just as significant in this regard. Through a series of public and private pronouncements, the Olympic legend flexed his muscles in the right places. By doing so, he helped to ensure that the athletes were going to be provided with everything they needed. It was their party, after all.

In January 1947, he wrote, 'As a former competitor, I'm delighted above all to see that every consideration is promised to the needs of competitors. They are after all the most important people at the Games – and too often in the past they have had just complaints against the arrangements made for them.'

At London '48, there would be new gadgets to help those athletes – including starting blocks that would propel Olympic sprinting into the modern era. The days of digging holes with trowels at the Games were over. Many models of starting blocks had been used at athletic meetings prior to 1948; but none of them had proved altogether satisfactory. Early in Olympic year, Harold was able to bring to public attention an inventor he had known for decades, a man called Henry Rottenburg. This was the same Professor Rottenburg who had made the 'Abrahams long-jump measuring gauge' back in 1923. Now aged seventy-two, Rottenburg still worked for the London Instrument Company; and he had come up with the best starting blocks yet. Athletes could slide their launch-pads back and forth, so that each individual could settle into their most comfortable and effective position, ready for an explosive start.

There was also to be remote-control starting equipment, equidistant from each athlete, activated by the starter in his usual position. That way there was no delay in hearing the gun if you were furthest from the starter. Harold also drew attention to a special 'photo-finish' camera, which ensured accurate decisions from the judges. By taking pictures of each athlete as they hit the tape, then providing the definitive result within ninety seconds, there could be no doubts about the finishing order.

The technology was ready. Now the athletes were invited to put the horrors of war behind them, and start serious preparation for the great sporting spectacle. There were pre-Olympic trials at the White City in August 1947, which took the form of a match between the Combined Services and the British Amateur Athletic Board. Harold looked smart enough as he did the announcing in his jacket and tie. But as the midday rays began burning into his bald head, he protected himself with an outrageous floral sunhat. It was so floppy and incongruous that photographers forgot the track action and began to photograph Abrahams, the Assistant Honorary Secretary of the BAAB, in his strange attire.

Picking up her newspaper the next day, Christina McLeod Innes – or Christina Morley as she had been known for the past twenty-two years – was amused to see her old flame looking so comical. Highly strung as a young man at Cambridge, he had only rarely relaxed enough to let people laugh at him. Even then it had required something irresistible to make him swallow his pride – the opportunity to perform a Gilbert and Sullivan song on stage, for example. Now he didn't seem to care how bizarre he looked in public. Christina, who had spent the war as a nurse on the other side of the Atlantic, hadn't seen fashion-conscious Americans try the jacket, tie and floppy hat combination too often. Looking at Harold's picture, it was easy to see why. She cut it out of the newspaper and saved it for a rainy day.

Meanwhile Harold was studying newspapers too, for the recent form of all the athletes he could find. As the leading British authority on his sport, he had been given the important task of deciding the seeding for the track and field events at the 1948 Olympics. In addition to the reports he already had in his own post-war files, he knew just who to ask for some up-to-date information on the world's best post-war performers. Roberto L.

Abrahams at the pre-Olympic trials, August 1947.

Quercetani was a brilliant Italian statistician, passionate about athletics. His knowledge of the sport from a global perspective was second to none; and he was only too happy for Harold to draw upon his wealth of facts and figures. Quercetani recalled, 'I first got in touch with him in 1948, when he used the inaugural *Olympic Handbook*, edited by Don Potts and myself, for the seeding of Olympic events at Wembley.' With Quercetani's assistance, Harold made sure those seedings were as fair as humanly possible.

Even more important, as the countdown to the Games began, was public opinion. Abrahams continued to shape it by setting out a clear and simple objective for the athletes and spectators of the host nation. In June he spoke about the dangers of becoming too obsessed with victory through specialisation in a single event. He hinted at the mental problems such self-imposed pressures had caused him. Victory – and sometimes even defeat – often came at a price. Without being judgemental, Harold reminded his audience that a healthy perspective was going to be essential at London's Olympics, coming as they did so soon after the war. It was all about getting the balance right:

> I should be the first to recognise that the modern trend of intensive specialisation contains dangers and problems; but it is much wiser to acknowledge and solve these than to condemn or ignore them. How can we, with such a prize at stake, still retain our sense of proportion? How can we strive to win without minding too much when we lose? If we solve that problem, we gain all that is best in international competition . . . What does matter is that those participating and watching should unstintingly appreciate the brilliance of achievement, no matter from what country the performer comes.

Alan Abrahams once said of his father:

> The film *Chariots of Fire* was very accurate in terms of what it said about the kind of person my father was when he was younger. Later in life he wasn't like that at all. He did a lot of work for international athletics and he was also very good at conciliation – he saw everyone's point of view. He was a good chairman. The point I am trying to make is that he was massively different later in life to the person he had been. Somewhere along the line there was quite a sea-change of personality. I can see though why the psychiatric treatment

he received in the mid-thirties might have worked for him, and was the 'tipping point' in his becoming more relaxed. He had obviously been extremely competitive – a classic Type A personality. Perhaps that wasn't really him.

In part that change had been prompted by Harold's enforced retirement from active competition. It also came about through the personal crisis he suffered in 1936, when he realised the dangers of excessive intensity in all areas of life. But perhaps the sea change in Harold came in the run-up to London '48. With his pre-war and post-war perspectives on the Olympic movement, Abrahams knew just what had to be done differently this time around. Winning should never again matter as much as it did to the Germans on a nationalistic level in Berlin or, for that matter, as much as it had to him on a personal level in Paris. There had to be an end to the madness of excessive sporting ambition. Ambition without balance was dangerous, both individually and collectively. Harold hadn't lost his personal drive. But he had left behind the blinkers of his sporting prime. And his new-found wisdom was perfect for London '48 – even necessary.

Lord Burghley captured the mood when, as Chairman of the Organising Committee, he made a wonderful speech at the Opening Ceremony, setting out the significance and objectives of the Games. Addressing a packed Wembley and King George VI, Burghley said:

Your Majesty, the hour has struck. A visionary dream has today become a glorious reality. At the end of the worldwide struggle in 1945, many institutions and associations were found to have withered and only the strongest had survived. How, many wondered, had the great Olympic Movement prospered?

In 1946, the clarion call went forth to the athletes of the world bidding them to gather here in London to celebrate the XIV Olympiad. Here today, in this vast arena are assembled 6,000 competitors, the cream of the youth of the world drawn from sixty-one nations, who have answered this call. This is the answer to that question, and here is the proof of the inherent strength and vitality of the movement . . .

The eyes of the world today, and for these next fourteen days, will be on London. Your Majesty, we are deeply honoured that you have consented to come here today to declare the Games open. Forty years ago your royal grandfather, King Edward, in 1908, opened the Olympic Games of London, the Games which were carried through under the leadership and genius of that great British sportsman, Lord Desborough. This is indeed a memorable occasion, and in asking you, sire, to carry out this task, I speak for all when I say, not only are we deeply grateful to you, but it is our firm belief that you are kindling a torch, the light from which will travel to the uttermost corners of the earth; a torch of that ageless and heartfelt prayer of mankind throughout the world for peace and goodwill amongst men.

As he witnessed the scene and sensed the enormity of the moment, Harold Abrahams was inspired to find words which were no less powerful than Burghley's. Harold wrote, 'After long years of almost unending national and international strain and stress, here was the light of a flame which crossed a continent without hindrance, caused frontiers to disappear, gathered unprecedented crowds, and lit the path to a brighter future for the youth of the world.'

It didn't matter that the star of the Games wasn't British – just that the Games had a star. Harold wrote:

In track and field events there is almost always at least one competitor whose performances are automatically brought to mind whenever the particular Games is mentioned. For example Paavo Nurmi in 1924 and Jesse Owens in 1936. Without doubt Fanny Blankers-Koen of the Netherlands, the 30-year-old, is the headline for 1948. She had competed in the 1936 Olympics at the age of 18, and in 1938 had equalled the world's 100 yards record. During the war in occupied Holland, she set up world records for the 100 yards, high and long jumps and equalled that for the 80 metres hurdles, while in June 1948 she added the world's 100 metres record to her quiver. At Wembley, she broke the tape 11 times (including a heat and final in sprint relay), her victories in the two sprints being clear, her only struggles being in the 80 metres hurdles and the relay.

Had Blankers-Koen entered the long jump – won with a leap which fell almost two feet short of her world record – she would almost certainly have won that too. And she had begun to change Harold's mind about women's athletics, for which he had previously shown no great respect or affection. Of the eighth day of London '48, Harold wrote, 'In the women's sprint relay Fanny Blankers-Koen brought her total medals up to four by a brilliant "anchor" run which brought victory for her country over Australia almost with her last stride.'

Britain was still searching for her first gold, and it seemed tantalisingly close later that evening, in what Abrahams described as 'one of the most thrilling duels imaginable'. He explained, '. . . Most of the crowd stayed to watch 28-year-old Dorothy Tyler of Great Britain in what seemed an endless duel against a coloured American high jumper, Alice Coachman. Twelve years previously Dorothy, a 16-year-old schoolgirl, had gained second place in the Berlin Olympics . . . At 5ft 6¼in Alice Coachman took several minutes to make her first effort and then cleared it first time. Dorothy Tyler failed, but got over second time. Neither could clear 5ft 7in. Miss Coachman won because she cleared the height at her first effort.

Of the fifty or so countries taking part in the track and field events, thirteen had winners. Great Britain was not one of them. No matter. The true triumph of London 1948 was that GB – and not least Harold Abrahams – had ensured the survival of the Olympic movement by striking the right tone.

He was able to write, 'In this, the first Olympic meeting after World War Two, Great Britain was given the opportunity of setting a new standard of sportsmanship of which we might all be justly proud. I am sure that this was achieved, and that the XIVth Olympiad can fairly be regarded as a model for all time.'

Financially it was also a success, which was almost as important. Any obvious loss would have caused an outcry among the suffering British public. Abrahams assured them:

> Despite the enormous difficulties produced by shortage of materials, rationing and so on, the organisation met with universal approval. Improvisation was the order of the day – a special track was laid at Wembley stadium for the athletics . . . Expenditure [for the Games] amounted to under £600,000 which included something in the range of £200,000 for temporary work at Wembley and other venues and services provided by Government Departments. The income provided from 'gates' – on many occasions there were over 80,000 spectators at Wembley – meant that overall there was an excess of income over expenditure of between £10,000 and £20,000.

No wonder Harold Abrahams had now been promoted to Honorary Treasurer of the British Amateur Athletic Board. He was also elected a Vice President of the Amateur Athletic Association that same year. These honours justly reflected the role he played in reigniting the Olympic flame.

Having worked so hard, perhaps he was entitled to one careless moment. Looking back on his life in front of the microphone, Abrahams reflected, 'I never had a real disaster – except in the Olympics in 1948, when I said there was a hold-up because the girls were taking their shorts off, when I meant tracksuits.' Back in 1948, that was not an acceptable image to evoke. But he got away with it. And since he had been commissioned to add commentary to the official film of the Games, he was able to redeem himself, and help shape the way the Games would be viewed in retrospect.

Many others were credited with the organisation and success of the 1948 Olympics. But who best personified the spirit of the Games, and helped to take athletics to new audiences at home and abroad? Harold Abrahams.

Christina Morley couldn't have failed to notice the affection the British public had for her former fiancée, or his importance during such a vital post-war year. As 1948 came to a close, she may have felt he needed taking down a peg or two. So when Harold opened a card with seasonal greetings 'from Christina and Francis Morley', and recognised the familiar handwriting, he also noticed that she had attached to the card a newspaper clipping. It wasn't some glowing tribute to Harold and his hard work at the Olympics. It was the photo from 1947 of Abrahams, the great athletics hero, looking faintly ridiculous in a floral, floppy hat. She didn't comment on the photo, preferring to let it speak for itself. She was teasing him, fondly; and the card survives to this day, as proof that there were no hard feelings between them for the break-up which had come before Harold's 1924 Olympic triumph.

By then Harold would have welcomed any light-hearted distraction. As soon as the Games had finished, he had begun re-writing the athletics rulebook, a process which took three long years. Finally, in 1951 he was able to announce that, 'after a great deal of coming and going and very much burning of midnight oil, the task is done and the new rule book will in due course see the light of day'.

The process of starting a race – something close to Harold's heart – had been changed:

Much bad starting has in the past been due to raggedness, caused, I believe, by the irregularity with which runners 'get to their marks'. A new rule states that in all races up to the half-mile there shall be an 'assembly line' 10 feet behind the starting line and that from this line the starter will tell the competitors to 'get to their marks'.

. . . At the other end of the race, it has been strongly recommended that the 'photo-finish' camera should be in use, and, along the same line of thinking, electric time-keeping is now to be 'officially recognised'. Experiments have shown that human timekeeping on the whole favours the runner, so we may expect that, in sprints particularly, records in future will be harder to beat.

Later that year he put further pressure on his IAAF colleagues by asking publicly, 'Ought we not to time more scientifically with electrical timekeeping always in use?'

No wonder Harold Abrahams was described by athletics historian Peter Lovesey as 'the architect of the modern laws of athletics'. There were many more changes to track and field rules, too numerous and technical to mention here. But there was one more of great note, given what Harold was to witness and be part of in the next few years.

A new rule regarding world records determined that records in running and walking races could only be acknowledged if made in scratch races. This ruled out specially concocted handicaps but did not rule out a pacemaker who dropped out after two or three laps.

Pacemakers would remain controversial, though the mere mention of them conjures an image of one magical race in particular from the 1950s. And that was a race where one of Harold's closest young friends was destined to take centre stage.

PART III

BANNISTER TO CHARIOTS

CHAPTER ONE

BANNISTER

' I've been asked many times if I think a mile will ever be run in inside four minutes. I always answer, "Not in my lifetime."'

Even as Harold Abrahams said it, the boy who would change all that was starting to grow up. Roger Bannister was lucky to survive the war after his house was bombed in Bath. Bannister and his family sheltered under the stairs in the basement and avoided injury.

Harold met the teenager for the first time on Saturday, March 22, 1947 at the White City. 'It was the day before he was eighteen,' pointed out Harold. 'He was a lanky, rather uncouth youngster.' He was also quite highly strung, a characteristic that reminded Harold of an athlete he had always admired – himself.

It was a cold, wet Saturday – but a vital one on the university calendar all the same. Oxford faced Cambridge in the Varsity sports. Bannister wasn't expected to set the world alight, but suddenly destroyed the field to win by 20 yards. 'After that I realised I could develop this talent,' Sir Roger said later. Harold always marvelled at the way Bannister had almost stumbled on his chosen sporting path. He said, 'It was rather by chance that he took seriously to running at all.'

After his Varsity victory Bannister met Jack Lovelock, and shook the legend's hand 'so vigorously that I upset his glass'. Bannister was at the same Oxford college where Lovelock had studied – Exeter. They struck up an easy rapport, and were joined by the man who had immortalised Lovelock's Berlin triumph. In *The First Four Minutes*, first published in 1955, Bannister wrote:

Another great British athlete and former Olympic champion I met for the first time that evening was Harold Abrahams, who has made such a great contribution to the popularity of athletics in this country, both by his writing and broadcasting. On this occasion he noted my promise, and it was the beginning of a close friendship which has continued throughout my athletic career. His advice has been invaluable to me on all occasions when important decisions have had to be made.

Tragically, Lovelock wasn't able to act as a mentor. After a riding accident, he suffered from headaches and dizzy spells, which surely played a part in his death towards the end of 1949. Having left work in New York one day because he felt unwell, Lovelock never made it home. Sadly he lost his balance on a railway platform, fell onto the track and was hit by an oncoming train.

Harold and Sybil were devastated by the news, and it fell to Abrahams to pay tribute to the hero of Berlin. On December 28, 1949, Harold broadcast a personal message to the nation: 'How difficult it is suddenly to have to speak of the tragic and premature death of a friend. John Edward Lovelock – but millions of athletic fans will always think of him as "Jack" – was one of the greatest runners the world has ever known.'

At least Lovelock's athletic prowess had been immortalised through Harold's chaotic commentary in Berlin. And in Bannister, Abrahams saw a young man with no less potential. He knew Roger needed time, and defended him when early races sometimes went wrong. Support, inspiration and improvement; these were Harold's aims for his favourite young athlete. In the early spring of 1951, Harold tried to illustrate Bannister's potential by comparing him to two greats of times gone by: the Mighty Atom and former mile world-record holder, Sydney Wooderson of Great Britain – and Lovelock:

Take Wooderson first. At 18 he had run a mile in 4:29.8, and Bannister had done 4:24.6. At 19 (to be accurate, within two or three weeks of his 20th birthday) Wooderson's best was 4:13.6, and Bannister's was 4:17.2. At 20, Wooderson had done 4:12.6, Bannister 4:11.1 sec; at 21, Wooderson did 4:10.8, Bannister 4:09.9. At 22, Wooderson 4:06.4, Bannister – we shall see. Lovelock did nothing, so far as I know, until he had passed 21. He was 23 when he set up his world mile record of 4:07.6.

Of the three, Bannister is by far the most powerful, with a long, raking and some may think an almost lethargic stride. He has not the astonishing acceleration of Wooderson, nor the beautiful relaxation of Lovelock. He is not so dynamic as Wooderson, not so aggressive as Lovelock, who, for all his apparent calm, possessed plenty of explosiveness underneath.

But Bannister probably has greater potential power than either. What he now requires is confidence in his own ability. Modesty, a characteristic of Wooderson, in Bannister amounts to an almost complete reluctance to acknowledge his greatness. He has the brain to plan and dominate a race as Lovelock did at Berlin in 1936. To beat the world – and I believe he can, all being well, at Helsinki in July next year – he must cultivate a purposeful aggression.

Roger took on board Harold's constructive criticism, and duly announced himself as a serious force on the world stage in the Benjamin Franklin Mile at the Penn Relays Meeting in Philadelphia. It was Saturday, April 28, 1951, and 40,000 people were waiting to see the big race. Bannister had already astonished the American press by explaining that he didn't have a coach because he believed the athlete should coach himself as far as possible. One reporter wrote, 'No manager, no trainer, no masseur, no friends! He's nuts – or he's good!'

'I don't know about having no friends,' was the way Sir Roger reacted to that quote when it was read back to him in 2010. He seemed to have no argument with the rest of the description; and it was unusual for British athletes to travel to such events unaccompanied. Sir Roger later suspected that Harold had seen to it that his solo trip received approval from the appropriate athletics authorities.

Harold previewed his friend's big test against quality American opponents like this:

> Roger Bannister, one of the best milers Britain has produced, is to compete against America's Don Gehrmann, Fred Wilt and Stewart Ray at Franklin Field, Pennsylvania this afternoon . . . The time could be fast, round about 4min 5sec, but that depends on how the race is run. Roger's chief aim will be to win, not to break any records. He says: 'I'm going to run against my opponents, not the watch.'

He didn't just run against them, he demolished them. After stalking the Americans for three slow laps, Bannister showed his rivals a clean pair of heels to win by 20 yards in 4:08.3. Abrahams wrote, 'His last lap, which he did in 56.7sec, is phenomenal, and must have left the opposition spellbound. So far as I am aware the only man who has ever run a lap at this sort of speed in a mile is Gunder Haegg, the Swede, who in the first lap of his world record mile of 4:01.4 did 56.6.'

So Roger's was the fastest last lap ever seen in a mile race up to that point in time; and it sent shockwaves through America. Harold added, 'Bannister's chances of an Olympic win at Helsinki next year have increased considerably. He is taking a leaf out of Lovelock's book in learning all there is to know of his probable opponents.'

Harold had demanded 'a more purposeful aggression', and Bannister had responded. In his book *The First Four Minutes*, he explained, 'Having great respect for Harold Abrahams' judgement, I hoped that I was beginning to show a little of the necessary aggression. The possibility of the four-minute mile was again mooted. I was full of doubt, but it costs nothing to talk about such things.'

And he talked about such things with Harold Abrahams, who was beginning to reconsider his previous claim that no one would run one in his lifetime. But the first target had to be a medal at the 1952 Olympics. And there was ample opportunity for Harold and Bannister to discuss that dream too. Sir Roger explained later, 'I used to go and stay with Harold and Sybil for the odd night.'

On July 26, 1951, Roger wrote to Sybil after staying with the Abrahams family for the weekend. The letter shows how much affection Bannister had for them all.

Dear Sybil,

May I say how much at home I felt with you and Harold all weekend. From the moment I arrived you were kindness itself to me and did your utmost to see that I had just the sort of rest I needed. I am most grateful. Harold's friendship and my friendship with you which has grown out of it are good reasons why I should be thankful to have taken up running but I hope I shall continue to cherish them long after my spikes are hung up on the wall.

I hope you will have lunch with me when you next visit Alan and the Dragon School.

With best wishes,

Yours ever

Roger Bannister.

Harold's daughter Sue still has a wonderful photograph of Roger, stripped to the waist and riding a motorbike towards the camera on a sunny summer's day. It is a snapshot of a young man clearly pleased to be able to do something fun and just a little dangerous without fear of recrimination. He is getting away from the pressures of competitive athletics.

The 'L-Plate' on the motorbike suggests that he is a novice. Indeed, Sir Roger admitted in 2010, 'I hardly ever rode a motorbike. It is definitely me in the picture, but I cannot remember exactly where or when. The only time I remember riding a motorbike was later in the Royal Army Medical Corps; but on that occasion the weather was far too cold to be stripped to the waist like that.'

The photograph is taken either on the country roads around Great Jenkins, or on holiday with the Abrahams family in Cornwall. The history of athletics might have been very different had Roger's lack of experience led him into trouble on that motorbike. Such concerns didn't appear to worry the young Bannister as he rides towards the camera; he looks as though he is having the time of his life.

Another photograph shows Sybil and Sue Abrahams with Roger and friends, relaxing with a picnic on some rocks at Polzeath or Porthcothan in Cornwall. Again the sun is shining and the group couldn't have looked happier. Sue explained: 'We were guests of some of our friends; and my father brought Roger down for a few days. I remember he used to go out for long runs and drink a lot of milk. I'm not sure exactly what year it was, but he was already recognisable, because I remember some people saying, "Oh look, Roger Bannister!"' For someone so shy, it couldn't have been easy when strangers pointed and stared. To be in the trusted company of Harold Abrahams, a man who knew the pressures of athletic fame, was helpful and reassuring.

Of course, Harold still had to write objectively about Bannister in the newspapers. And he wouldn't spare his young friend from criticism if he felt it necessary to point out a few home truths. The key was this: his criticism was always constructive, something greatly appreciated by Roger's father. On August 7, 1951, Ralph Bannister wrote to Harold to thank him for getting tickets for an athletics meeting at the White City stadium in London. He ended the letter by saying, 'We take this opportunity of thanking you also for the encouragement and advice which you have given to Roger. We have detected your keener critical faculty on occasions passed unnoticed by other observers.'

A little later Harold told the nation about those parents and what the family were having to deal with at their home in Harrow on the outer edge of London:

> His father was a civil servant and both his parents could properly be described as – in the nicest sense – extremely simple folk. I think they have been a little appalled at the worldwide publicity accorded to their son during the last few years, for ever since Roger became 'news' – as he did the day before his eighteenth birthday – he has been unceasingly in the public eye. Mercifully he is not on the telephone, but reporters have never been deterred from turning up at all hours of the night and day for 'copy'.

They would have had no luck later in August, because Roger and Harold were away fulfilling what proved to be an unusually demanding race schedule for Bannister. Abrahams remembered, 'I got to know him really well in the summer of that year when he went with a British team to Yugoslavia, Greece and Turkey. Roger ran himself to a standstill in a 1,500 metres race at Belgrade and was so exhausted that I wondered if he had done himself a permanent injury.'

Mercifully there was no lasting damage, though he was defeated and less than fully fit. Roger wrote to Abrahams from Harrow on their return. 'My dear Harold, I enclose the cheque for tour expenses. I cannot really thank you enough for your many kindnesses to me on the tour. I am sure that even "gippy tummy" will in time become a pleasant recollection I can look back on. I have decided to go away to Scotland for a rest because as yet my mind refuses to work at medicine. Please give my kind regards to Sybil and the children . . . Yours ever, Roger.'

No wonder Bannister felt like escaping the pressures of England before a new academic year started at Oxford University. Harold remembered, 'By this time people were beginning to tip Bannister as a probable winner of the Olympic 1,500 metres at Helsinki in 1952. It was obvious that in so far as anyone can be said to have a chance of winning an Olympic title, Bannister had that chance.'

But journalists wanted to know what Roger was going to do in order to build up his competitive strength for Olympic year. They didn't understand his shyness or his stubborn streak, which prevented him from performing like a puppet for the benefit of others, and always would. Harold understood, though. And he wasn't going to put pressure on this very special young man like the others did. He would be there to offer advice when appropriate; and more often than not Bannister listened. Sir Roger said in 2010: 'It wasn't advice in relation to training, because he was a sprinter and I was a middle-distance man. It was more to do with tactical planning in relation to when to run and when not to.' Bannister was determined to pick and choose carefully. He explained later, 'I reached a position in which I was being criticised in the press for not racing often enough. They said, "Here's this chap. We think he's good. We want to see him." I said, "Well, no. I run if I want to run. There is nobody paying me to run. If I think that five races a year is the right number for me, and I feel that I'll work up towards a peak in the middle of the season, that's what I'm going to do."'

Harold explained how the media reacted when Roger stuck to his guns:

> Unfortunately his very personal methods of training, his refusal to accept any 'official' coaching, and his deliberate policy of avoiding publicity, led to much criticism from the British press. But Roger, though extremely sensitive to criticism, particularly when he felt it was so unjust, deliberately followed his own policy and prepared for the 1,500 metres. He has never put himself in the hands of a professional coach because he prefers to do his own thinking. A devotee of the late Jack Lovelock, he held the view that a runner could only have one or at the most two peak races in a season. He planned to be at his peak in Helsinki, and consequently refused to race week after week against strong opponents as many other great middle-distance runners do.

There was little Harold could do but help to choose Roger's key races. Then came the bombshell. Bannister had dreamed of emulating Lovelock by winning the 1500 metres gold medal at the next Olympics in Helsinki in 1952. Previously, the heats had been scheduled to allow a day or two's rest before the final. 'That was what I was planning for and I could have coped with it,' insisted Sir Roger later. But just three weeks before the Olympics, the technical director in Helsinki decided that Bannister and his rivals would have to race on three successive days. 'It was said afterwards that there had been a rather deliberate attempt to change the programme because I was the favourite,' Bannister recalled.

Asked whether he had been 'nobbled', Sir Roger replied, 'I can't make that claim, but what happened favoured one of the other competitors, Josy Barthel, who was a hard racer trained by Woldemar Gerschler.'

Abrahams explained, 'Bannister had planned his peak for a heat and a final at Helsinki with one day's rest in between. Unfortunately the organisers – in my view quite unnecessarily – inserted an extra round, which meant three days racing in succession.' Sir Roger picked over these words many decades later and concluded, 'Harold understood why I was dismayed at the change in the programme, with the extra race introduced.' Note that he says, 'in my view quite unnecessarily'. He was right. There were no more qualifying competitors in Helsinki than there had been in London.

The change threatened Bannister's gold medal chances; and Harold seemed as distracted by the unwelcome news as the athlete himself. As he prepared to follow Roger's fortunes and those of another top British athlete of the day called Chris Chataway, he was involved in an unusual road traffic accident. Norris McWhirter, who was also a victim, explained, 'When in Helsinki being driven to the stadium by Harold Abrahams, who five Olympics earlier had become the first European to win an Olympic 100 metre gold medal, we were hit by a tram.'

A tram, by its very nature, runs a defined and careful course through any city on rails in the road. Therefore one can only assume that the accident must have been Harold's fault, partly due to his lack of familiarity with his surroundings. His friend Norris played the incident down by adding, 'Apart from a bruise on my forehead where I struck the windscreen and Harold being a bit shaken, no damage was done other than to the unfortunate hired car.'

On July 22 Harold's wife Sybil wrote, 'My Darling, It was so good to hear your voice after the 800 metres commentary, and to know that you are still alive and kicking! The message about your accident reached me just after lunch – and I couldn't help feeling alarmed in spite of assurances that you were only "resting" . . . Give Roger every kind of good wish, won't you? – and Chris Chataway!'

But Chataway was destined to trip on the kerb and fall in the last lap of the 5000 metres. And all the good wishes in the world couldn't improve Roger Bannister's frame of mind before he tried to win gold in Helsinki. Harold Abrahams said of Bannister during these difficult pre-race days, 'He was like an actor who had thoroughly worked himself into a part, only to be faced on the opening night with an extra scene which he hadn't rehearsed at all.' Sir Roger didn't dispute that analogy. 'By the third day of these successive races, I knew in my heart that it was a virtually impossible task for me. And it all went disastrously wrong when I came fourth instead of winning. There were no British track and field gold medals in Helsinki.'

As supportive as ever, Harold said, 'That he finished fourth and himself beat Lovelock's Olympic record by two seconds, was a great achievement. And to me, knowing intimately just how seriously the extra race had worried him, it was proof positive that he was, potentially, the greatest runner in the world at one mile.' Even so, it was Barthel who collected gold. Perhaps he should have given his medal to the man who changed the schedule and inserted that extra, killer round. 'It favoured the man who won, Barthel,' repeated Sir Roger.

Lord Coe was interesting when he joined the debate about what qualities should be demanded of an Olympic champion. He pointed out that such changes to schedules can work both ways. 'In 1984 they changed the number of 800 metres races an Olympic athlete was required to run from four to three. It is no longer an endurance event. It gives the advantage to athletes with a sprint base, not an endurance base.' That was the other side of the coin, and highlighted the fact that feats of endurance are also something to admire in championship middle-distance running. Reflecting on Helsinki 1952, Lord Coe added, 'Sir Roger Bannister did some high-quality work, as good as some do now, but he didn't come from a big endurance base. I think he ran about twenty miles a week.'

From Bannister's perspective, of course, the point was that the Helsinki goalposts had been moved almost at the last moment, giving him no time to prepare properly for the nature of the new Olympic challenge.

One way or another, Helsinki had been a miserable experience for Harold, Roger and most of the British party. Yet in some ways it was a blessing in disguise, because Bannister often said he would have retired had he returned with Olympic gold. As it was, there was unfinished business. Therefore Roger licked his wounds and vowed to come back even more determined. Sure enough, within a year, he was beginning to build towards something that became even more historic than an Olympic triumph.

CHAPTER TWO

STOPWATCH ON EVEREST

At the start of the 1953 athletics season in the UK, Harold wrote a clever little introduction to an article on athletics:

> The photographers of my youth used to try to disperse that expression of restless distrust so usual on the part of a victim confronted with a camera, with the words 'Smile, please! One minute, please!' Today keen followers of athletics say to middle-distance runners: 'Mile, please; four minutes, please'.
>
> Will 1953 produce the first four-minute mile? That possibility is brought a little nearer by Saturday's performance of Roger Bannister in shattering the British record with a time of 4:03.6. Earlier in the year, unaided by any real opposition, John Landy, of Australia, had run the mile in 4:02.1 and 4:02.8.
>
> In the whole history of athletics two men only, the Swedes, Gundar Haegg and Arne Andersson, had shown better times than this 22-year-old Australian.

Haegg's best came closest to the four-minute barrier – in 1945 he clocked 4:01.4. Bannister was now moving up into the big league. You could sense the excitement building; and more than half a century later, Sir Roger Bannister still remembered something else Abrahams did to intensify the hype and add a new dimension to the quest for glory. Roger didn't have to explain it, because Harold did so very clearly at the time:

> Recently, I plotted all the world's best miles on a 'target', with 4 min

as the bullseye. I called 4:02.4 an inner; 4:04.8 a magpie [a middle-ranking, white ring on a shooting target]; and 4:07.2 an outer. The first outer ever was scored by Glenn Cunningham (USA) with his then world record time of 4:06.8 in 1934. The Swede, Andersson, gained his first magpie with 4:02.6 in 1943, and also gained the first inner with a time of 4:01.6 in 1944.

All in all, three men have gained inners, eight magpies, and 12 outers. In 1952 alone we have had five men scoring magpies, four more scoring outers, and, of course, Landy's inner. Surely with these men – and they do not include Bannister, with his new record, 2.8 seconds better than Wooderson's best – the bullseye should be hit this year.

In June the 'Kentucky Cowboy', Wes Santee – largely overlooked in Harold's analysis – retaliated by running a mile in 4:02.4. In a year of supreme human endeavour and achievement, the race for the first sub-four minute mile had just taken on a new urgency. By the summer of 1953, Harold had begun to use a fresh and fitting metaphor for the sporting challenge which Bannister, Santee and Landy faced. Following Sir Edmund Hillary and Sherpa Tenzing Norgay's conquest of the highest spot on earth on May 29, it was only natural that the most formidable mountain of all would start to symbolise all great challenges.

In 2010, Sir Roger pointed out, 'The year 1953 was when Everest was climbed. So I think the expression "the Everest of athletics" was used by quite a few people, and Harold was certainly one of them. And it was in that year of 1953 that I made my first attempt on the four-minute mile. It was at a time-trial event, not in full competition.' The event took place almost in secrecy on June 27 – a month after Hillary's moment of triumph. Harold, who was in on the secret, described Bannister's attempt:

Roger Bannister, at Motspur Park, where nearly 16 years ago Sydney Wooderson set up a world record of 4:06.4 for the mile, made a sterling bid to try to bring to Great Britain the Everest of Athletics – the four-minute mile.

With a British record of 4:02.0, he missed this goal by less than one per cent with a time which is the fastest for eight years, and has been beaten only by the Swedes, Haegg and Andersson. Bannister's time was only three-fifths of a second outside the world record and he beat his own British record made eight weeks ago by 1.6 seconds.

This was a planned assault on the four-minute mile, dictated by the knowledge that in the United States Championships to be held a few hours after his own run, Wes Santee, who recently ran a mile in 4:02.4, was set to accomplish 4 minutes.

What Harold neglected to mention was that Chris Brasher – who much later founded the London Marathon – deliberately ran so slowly that he was almost lapped and therefore shouted encouragement from Bannister's front. The time – achieved under the camouflage of a Surrey Schools meeting – was the third fastest to that point in history. As Harold had pointed out, it was a British record on the face of it.

Yet even Bannister felt the day had been too artificial to be called a race at all. And he suspected the time would be rejected by officialdom. Conversely, he also knew he was one step closer to achieving his goal. Closer, it seemed, than his American rival Santee, who on the same day showed less promise by slipping back to 4:07.6. The elusive four-minute barrier held firm.

Sure enough, after due reflection, the British Amateur Athletic Board felt it necessary to refuse Bannister's time official recognition. Harold may even have worded the BAAB statement himself. As a friend of Bannister's and a journalist, he praised and hyped the young man's running. As a defender of the integrity of truly competitive racing, he felt compelled to act otherwise:

> The Board, having very carefully considered the circumstances connected with this performance, regret that, although it has no doubt that the time was accomplished, it cannot recognise the performance as a record. It has been compelled to take this action because it does not consider the event was a bona fide competition according to the rules. The Board wishes it to be known that whilst appreciating the public enthusiasm for record performances, and the natural and commendable desire for athletes to accomplish them, it does not regard individual record attempts as in the best interests of athletics as a whole.

This was the tightrope Harold had to walk, his loyalties split by his various roles. One moment he wrote boyishly in a way that could only increase the public demand for that historic record and the general sense of expectation. The next, as a sober administrator, he shared the concerns of the establishment, which focused upon the long-term dangers of a mania for records – a mania which Harold, by his own admission, had helped to create. To keep the sport pure, races had to be genuine. To keep the sport popular, the public mood also had to be reflected. Nowadays it would be easy to conclude that Harold was suffering from a clear conflict of interest. Back in the 1950s, he simply tried to play his various roles as well as he could.

And all the time he wanted to be a good friend to Roger Bannister, with whom he identified so strongly because of their similar temperaments. Abrahams wrote:

> At this time I was seeing Roger very often for lunch when he could spare time, for generally it was in the luncheon interval between lectures that he did his training on the nearby track. And he was coming frequently to spend the weekend at my country house where he was always so welcome as a guest and used to consume literally gallons of milk.
>
> I know much of the workings of his mind – my own experience in top-class competitions over a quarter of a century earlier made it possible for me to show some sympathy for his own nervous psychology. Athletes to be any good must be highly strung; but they must learn to accept the nervous tension of pending competition and to understand that anxiety before an event is a natural and useful thing.

As Sir Roger examined these words in 2010, he agreed, 'That's fair enough. He was highly strung and I don't pretend that I wasn't highly strung too – all top track and field athletes are highly strung – it doesn't apply to other fields of sport. Harold was a benign and helpful advisor.'

In the autumn of 1953 an Austrian called Franz Stampfl was coaching Brasher on Friday evenings; Bannister began to go along to these sessions in order to benefit from Stampfl's expertise too, and Chris Chataway joined them at weekends.

Sir Roger explained, 'Franz Stampfl was coach to Chris Brasher, had been for a couple of years, and I went to the Duke of York Barracks, where Stampfl had a group of athletes one day a week. Chris Brasher was going to be a pacemaker when it came to the attempt on the four-minute mile, and so was Chris Chataway . . . We were a group of friends, Chataway, Brasher and I. We worked together, and Stampfl had a great personality, he was enthusiastic and extremely helpful.'

Stampfl had been a 22-year-old javelin thrower when he went to Hitler's Berlin Olympics of 1936. He recalled, 'But I saw the militarism and brutality of it all at the time. And I made up my mind I would go over to England.' Abrahams was waiting. Stampfl arrived as an art student in 1937, and decided that he wanted to stay on. 'I made an application to the Home Office, and the Home Office said to me, "I'm afraid you can't stay here unless you do a job which no Englishman can do." So I went to the Amateur Athletic Association and asked for an interview, and asked them to give me a chance. Oddly enough, the person who interviewed me was Harold Abrahams, who won the 100 metres in the Olympic Games.'

By then Harold was Assistant Honorary Secretary of the AAA. He felt sympathy for Stampfl's situation, having seen for himself the evils of the Nazi regime. Stampfl talked enough sense about coaching to make Harold sit up and listen. But he was only twenty-five years old, with little practical experience of the craft beyond a previous job as a ski instructor. Abrahams was also slightly concerned about the prospect of letting a would-be coach with harsh Germanic characteristics loose on British athletes. He did not want the finest young British talent to be subjected to anyone who might adopt a dictatorial approach to coaching. He appears to have said so, and Stampfl was not best pleased at what Harold seemed to be implying.

Later Stampfl said, 'During my first interview with the Amateur Athletic Association, when I was seeking an opportunity to coach, a moment of indignation forced me to crystallise a policy to which I have always adhered. "I am not a German coach," I told them, "and I do not force anyone to do anything. There are no laws to control athletes."' This remark was the clincher, for Harold Abrahams would always remain wary of coaches he felt were controlling.

Stampfl was in. And although he was cruelly shipped to Australia during the war, he was back in good time to play a part in Bannister's story. Abrahams had used his contacts to help Stampfl make a post-war living by coaching around Britain. Now the Austrian was ready to inspire Bannister, just as he was already inspiring Brasher.

Interval training became Stampfl's calling card. Athletes were timed repeatedly; their pulse rate was measured during periods of lesser intensity, as they prepared to push themselves harder yet again. The fitter the athlete became, the greater number of repetitions Stampfl gave him – and the less recovery time he was allowed. These routines were gruelling but wonderfully informative. The Austrian may have laid claim to the concept of interval training; but Sir Roger pointed out, 'It had come in with the Swedes, Gundar Haegg and Arne Andersson during the war. I did it all my life. The difference with Stampfl was that, instead of racing monthly on my own on grass, this training was on a track. And at the Duke of York's we did careful trials of exact pace.'

To an extent Bannister remained at the mercy of his rival from down under, John Landy. While the Englishman had failed in his summer attempt, the quest for the four-minute mile continued where the weather was warmer. Harold recalled, 'During the autumn and winter of 1953–54, Bannister was training harder than he has ever trained before; and this despite the fact that he was working at the time for his medical finals. Anxiously, almost daily, we scanned the papers for the performances of John Landy in Australia and Santee in the United States.'

Harold didn't just read the newspapers, he wrote for them too. With the onset of the northern winter, the spotlight fell on Landy and his efforts down under. One of Harold's stories carried the headline 'BID FOR FOUR-MINUTE MILE – LANDY'S THREE RACES'. Harold wrote:

> Will next Saturday see what may be described as the athletic conquest of Everest – the four-minute mile? Now it is the chance of the Australian, John Landy, who is scheduled to make the first of three attempts on December 5 . . . The four minute mile seems to me a certainty in the near future. I cannot help hoping that this distinction will fall to Roger Bannister who, in my admittedly biased opinion, is potentially the finest middle-distance runner in the world.

These were nervous times back in Britain, as Bannister and Harold watched to see whether the Australian would steal the glory. Abrahams recorded, 'Four times during the winter Landy was inside four minutes three seconds and Roger was powerless to do anything about it.' But he could still train; and he worked with Stampfl until he was finally able to run sets of quarter-miles in 59 seconds. The question was this: could he combine four of them, or at least come close enough to doing so, and break the four-minute mile? There was no time to lose. Harold warned Bannister towards the end of April 1954 that Landy had left for Europe with the avowed purpose of breaking the four-minute mile in June or July in Scandinavia. In the United States, Wes Santee was joined by the Olympic 800 metres champion and world half-mile record holder, Mal

Whitfield, who announced that four minutes was child's play almost and really his for the asking.

Sir Roger recalled, 'Harold Abrahams always knew what was happening with the other athletes.' The news may have been unsettling on one level, but it also provided motivation on another. Bannister's competitive streak has been much underestimated down the years, and he was determined to be first through that mythical barrier. Harold recalled, 'Quietly Roger Bannister laid his plans. He knew that he was nearing physical perfection. He was attuned in mind and body as never before, and he had had the advantage of training throughout the winter with his great friend Chris Chataway.'

Interestingly, Abrahams had exchanged letters with Chataway too, prompted by the athlete's careless revelation that he was a smoker. Chataway revealed, 'Harold Abrahams, "Mr Athletics", wrote me a letter saying, "Once you have given up [running] you have the rest of your life in which to smoke."' Chataway was contrite in his reply: 'I think there is nothing worse than the pretence that one never trains, and spends one's time smoking and drinking. Apart from being extremely arrogant, it strikes me as being so unfair to the less successful chaps.'

Fortunately the preparatory training for the daunting assault on the four-minute mile had been much heavier than Chataway's smoking. Bannister and his friends were now ready to make their hard work count. They targeted May 6, 1954. Oxford University were to take on an Amateur Athletic Association team at Iffley Road. The idea was for Chris Brasher and Chataway to set the pace in the selected race. Then, when the time was right, Bannister would finally make the break for glory.

'Harold wasn't involved in the tactical planning,' Sir Roger pointed out. But the older man did provide Bannister with a welcome refuge from the increasing pressure during the build-up to the big race. Roger went to stay with the Abrahams family at their country home at Great Jenkins, an enchanting place which Sybil thought to be an old Tudor hunting lodge. There was space and peace in the farmhouse and fields beyond. Bannister spent much of his time playing with Harold's adopted children, Alan and Sue. There was one serious moment of competition, when Roger and Alan faced each other in deadly combat to establish who had the better balance and nerve. 'They indulged in slow cycle races,' Harold revealed later, 'a fitting prelude to the fastest mile in history . . . Roger is in his element with children and that seems to me to give a sound indication of the man's real character.' Cycle too slowly and Roger would fall off. One can only assume he avoided too many risks at such a crucial time, and let the boy have his day in the sun.

Soon it would be Roger's turn. The British athletics community was buzzing with the growing belief that Bannister could be on the verge of something special. This was the picture Harold painted of his young friend in that key month of May:

He is now just twenty-five – a serious-minded medical student due to take his finals in September of this year. He stands six foot one and a half inches in height but weighs only eleven stone and, with exceptionally long legs and small body, is the coach's dream for a middle-distance runner . . . with a mop of untidy sandy-coloured hair and an extremely intelligent face. He is exceptionally modest though he has a real understanding of his ability to succeed.

Harold's faith in that ability was considerable; and if history was to be made, he wanted his son Alan – minus his bicycle – to be there. Everything felt right – until the key players drew back their curtains on that all-important day. No one could guarantee the weather, least of all in England. The elements appeared to be playing a joke on Bannister and his supporters. When the man of the moment boarded a morning train from London to Oxford, conditions were poor. It seemed there would be no chance to do any record-breaking after all. A slightly forlorn Roger opened a carriage door, 'and there, quite by chance, was Franz Stampfl inside. I was delighted to see him . . . Franz understood my apprehension.'

The Austrian understood it, but he was not prepared to accept it. Here was a man who had been on a boat in the Atlantic during the war when it had been torpedoed. He had survived for nine hours in the cold sea when others had died. He had then endured appalling conditions on another boat to Australia, when he had been treated as an enemy alien during the war. Stampfl explained later, 'If ever there was any wavering doubt in my mind, the war convinced me that the mind, body and soul must be cultivated into one dynamic force to achieve sporting greatness. I discovered that physical hardships could be overcome if there was a burning desire from the mind to produce complete mental control.'

The Austrian had faced and fought off death itself on more than one occasion. All Bannister had to deal with was some wind in Oxford. Yet Stampfl knew better than to pour scorn on the young man's under-standable concerns. Instead he spoke positively, with the underlying conviction that 'with the proper motivation, that is, a good reason for wanting to do it, your mind can overcome any sort of adversity'. Then, Franz said something which really hit home. 'In any case,' he asked Roger, 'what if this were your only chance?'

Bannister found Stampfl's pep-talk inspirational; but the best-chosen words in the world couldn't calm that infernal Oxford wind. When they reached Iffley Road, Roger watched anxiously as the afternoon gusts swayed the trees. Harold Abrahams remembered it like this: 'The day was hardly propitious. There was a high wind and showers, and half an hour before the scheduled time of the start, Roger was doubtful if the attempt was worth making.'

Stampfl claimed more bluntly, 'Bannister didn't want to run. It was very windy and freezing and he told Chataway and Brasher that he didn't want to run.' Stampfl could have spoken to his friend again, but he had already said his piece on the train. I told Brasher and Chataway to go and persuade him to run. They came back to me, one by one like a relay, and I told them both to tell him that if he didn't run then, he'd never do it. Later they told me he ummed and aahed.'

It looked as though the assault on Everest was to be thwarted by the lack of a weather window. Harold remembered what happened next. 'But miraculously the weather improved, and more important still, Roger regained the feeling which he had temporarily lost that this was to be his day of days. Just before the race he said to me: "If the wind holds off I believe I can do it." He said it in no boastful spirit; it was the remark of a man who had trained as much as a human being could train, and who knew what his perfectly attuned body was capable of doing given half a chance.'

If Roger Bannister was going to do it, Harold Abrahams had to be part of it. This was part of Harold's genetic make-up. He liked to be at the centre of everything, or as close as humanly possible. In this particular case, it meant finding a place for his stopwatch at the top table. The timekeepers listed in the programme for this particular athletics meeting were as follows: W.A. Findlay, C.S. Hill, R.G. Hudson, L.R. Richards and W.J. Burfitt. But that wasn't the line-up by the end of the day. Abrahams appears to have used all his power within the sport to muscle his way into the group of men whose watches would determine whether Bannister's name would feature for all time in athletics history or not. That, of course, assumed that Roger would decide that a record attempt was feasible.

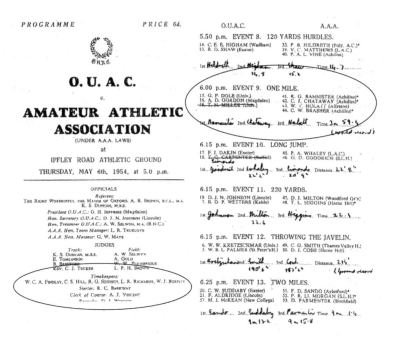

PROGRAMME   *PRICE 6d.*

O. U. A. C.

v.

AMATEUR ATHLETIC ASSOCIATION

(UNDER A.A.A. LAWS)

at

IFFLEY ROAD ATHLETIC GROUND

THURSDAY, MAY 6th, 1954, at 5.0 p.m.

OFFICIALS

Referee:
The Right Worshipful the Mayor of Oxford, A. B. Brown, B.C.L., M.A.
K. S. Duncan, M.B.E.

President O.U.A.C.: G. H. Jeffries (Magdalen)
Hon. Secretary O.U.A.C.: D. J. N. Johnson (Lincoln)
Hon. Treasurer O.U.A.C.: A. W. Selwyn, M.A. (B.N.C.)
A.A.A. Hon. Team Manager: L. R. Truelove
A.A.A. Hon. Masseur: G. W. Mays

JUDGES

Track: *Field:*
K. S. Duncan, M.B.E.   A. W. Selwyn
E. Tomlinson   A. Gold
R. Bashridge   W. W. Plumbridge
Rev. C. J. Tucker   L. P. H. Brown

Timekeepers:
W. C. A. Findlay, C. S. Hill, R. G. Hudson, L. R. Richards, W. J. Burfitt
Starter: R. C. Barkway
Clerk of Course: A. J. Vincent

O.U.A.C.   A.A.A.

5.50 p.m. EVENT 8. 120 YARDS HURDLES.
14. C. E. E. Higham (Wadham)   33. P. B. Hildreth (Poly. A.C.)*
13. R. D. Shaw (Exeter)   39. V. C. Matthews (L.A.C.)
  40. P. A. L. Vine (Achilles)

1st *Hildreth* 2nd *Higham* 3rd *Shaw* Time *14. 7*
14. 9   *15. 2*

6.00 p.m. EVENT 9. ONE MILE.
15. G. F. Dole (Univ.)   41. R. G. Bannister (Achilles)*
16. A. D. Gordon (Magdalen)   42. C. J. Chataway (Achilles)*
~~18. T. N. Miller (Univ.)~~   43. W. T. Hulaff (Alfreton)
  44. C. W. Brasher (Achilles)*

1st *Bannister* 2nd *Chataway* 3rd *Hulaff* Time *3m. 59. 4*
(world record)

6.15 p.m. EVENT 10. LONG JUMP.
17. F. J. Dakin (Exeter)   45. P. A. Whaley (L.A.C.)
18. T. G. Carpenter (Balliol)   46. G. D. Goodrich (S.L.H.)

1st *Goodrich* 2nd *Whaley* 3rd *Carpenter* Distance *22' 8"*
22' 1"   *20' 9"*

6.15 p.m. EVENT 11. 220 YARDS.
19. D. J. N. Johnson (Lincoln)   47. D. J. Milton (Woodford Gr'n)
7. B. D. P. Wetters (Keble)   48. T. L. Higgins (Herne Hill)*

1st *Johnson* 2nd *Milton* 3rd *Higgins* Time *22. 5*
22. 6

6.15 p.m. EVENT 12. THROWING THE JAVELIN.
6. W. W. Kretzschmar (Univ.)   49. C. G. Smith (Thames Valley H.)
5. W. B. L. Palmer (St. Peter's H.)   50. D. J. Cosh (Herne Hill)

1st *Kretzschmar* 2nd *Smith* 3rd *Cosh* Distance *214'*
190' 6"   *187' 6"*   *(ground record)*

6.25 p.m. EVENT 13. TWO MILES.
20. G. W. Suddaby (Exeter)   51. F. D. Sando (Aylesford)*
21. F. Aldridge (Lincoln)   52. P. R. J. Morgan (S.L.H.)*
57. M. J. McKean (New College)   53. D. Parmenter (Birchfield)

1st *Sando* 2nd *Suddaby* 3rd *Parmenter* Time *9m. 14*
9m. 13. 2   *9m. 15. 8*

Conspicuous absence: Proof from the match programme that Harold Abrahams is NOT listed among the official timekeepers on the day of Roger Bannister's sub-four-minute mile.

Just another race? 'Event 9, One Mile'. Roger Bannister, Chris Chataway and Chris Brasher became household names after that historic assault on the 'Everest of Athletics' – unlike W.T. Hulaff of Alfreton.

Still there was doubt, almost until the very last moment, though Bannister rejected the notion that he had his arm twisted by anyone. Roger never did respond to unwelcome pressure from others. Instead he insisted, 'The decision was mine alone, and the moment was getting closer. As we lined up at the start I glanced at the flag again . . . Yes, the wind was dropping slightly. This was the moment when I made my decision. The attempt was on.'

Harold's son Alan remembered that moment too. 'I was up on the balcony of the clubhouse. I was ten or eleven at the time.' Six men started, but pretty soon only three mattered. Chris Brasher became the first pacemaker, taking Bannister along at a lively pace, with Chataway tucked behind in third. Abrahams kept an eye on the clock as the tension built steadily over the first half of the race. 'Paced well over the first two laps, Roger reached the half-mile mark in one minute fifty-eight point three seconds – just one fifth second faster than Gunder Haegg's intermediate time in his famous mile record of July 1945.'

But Brasher had begun to gulp like a goldfish, and halfway round the third lap Chataway realised it was time to take the strain. Bannister stayed in second as Chataway moved up from third to first. The reshuffle cost precious fractions of a second. Was Bannister too relaxed? Abrahams claimed, 'In the third lap he took a breather and reached the bell in a time which required that he should do the last lap in fifty-nine point three seconds if he was to achieve four minutes.'

That elusive sub-four-minute mile, previously within touching distance, seemed to have disappeared behind the clouds. Chataway gave it everything he could from the front; but less than halfway round the final lap he began to puff out his cheeks in distress, knowing he could do no more for the star of the show. Bannister sensed as much and hit the front, gliding away like a being from another planet. Now it was all down to how much he had left, and how much he wanted his place in history. Harold watched, spellbound, as time threatened to sweep his young friend off the mountain like an avalanche. 'Throwing in every ounce of energy and driving along his flagging body, he approached the tape. I glanced at my watch as the relentless second hand sped towards the four-minute mark.'

A thousand pairs of eyes did the same, some with more responsibility than others. In all the commotion, photographs show that Abrahams isn't acting like an official timekeeper at all. He isn't even on the finishing line as Bannister blazes down the home straight. As Roger prepares to break that tape, Harold is pictured at least five yards short of the line instead of level with it, as any timekeeper should have been. Therefore it is difficult to see how he could have taken a reliable official time, despite his wealth of experience, since he couldn't clearly have witnessed the precise split second at which Bannister's partially shielded torso hit the tape. 'I can't comment on that,' said Sir Roger in 2010 when asked about Harold's irregular position. Bannister justifiably pointed out that he was a little busy at the time to be making a mental note of where everyone was standing.

'I find it hysterical that Harold managed to muscle his way onto the list as an official timekeeper,' said the former *Times* athletics correspondent Neil Allen. However he managed it, Harold and his stopwatch took a prominent role as Bannister reached the point of oblivion. Abrahams may not have been where an official timekeeper should have been; but more than a quarter of a century of expertise apparently helped him to press down on that button at the right moment. 'All the times were identical,' emphasised Sir Roger in 2010, when it was explained to him that doubts had recently been expressed about Harold's positioning.

As he hit the tape feeling like 'an exploded flashbulb with no will to live', Bannister had no idea what the stopwatches showed. He remembered collapsing 'almost unconscious, with an arm on either side'. One of those supportive arms belonged to Franz Stampfl. Harold might have provided the other had he been any closer; instead he was still staring at his stopwatch. One number dominated his brain. And it wasn't a four.

We can assume that the other men who mattered – the chief time-keeper, Billy Findlay, and the third timekeeper for the race, Charlie Hill – were more appropriately placed than Abrahams to record the precise instant that Bannister crossed the line. At least one of the other time-keepers listed in the programme – Hudson, Richards and Burfitt – must have been instructed to time the winner originally. It isn't clear at what point that man was relieved of his duties by the influential Abrahams. But he must have been surprised, since the convention of the day was for timekeepers at big races to be placed on a raised platform on the outside of the track, level with the line. Conversely, judges of the finishing order were generally on the inside of the track; but they were supposed to be 'in line with the finish' according to IAAF rules. Therefore Harold wasn't on the right side of the track to be a timekeeper. He was on the judge's side of the track, and not even in the correct position for that task, either.

Abrahams must have moved quickly away from his flawed vantage point once the race had finished, because Norris McWhirter later wrote, 'The timekeepers, Bill Findlay, the 70-year-old Charlie Hill, R.G. Hudson, L.R. Richards, W.J. Burfitt and Harold Abrahams were in a huddle. The three taking the first place timing recorded identical times and it was this which I now had to announce.'

Again, such 'huddles' would subsequently be outlawed in the IAAF rulebook, which by the 1970s was stipulating that 'each timekeeper shall act independently, and without showing his watch to, or discussing his time with, any other timekeeper'. That later addition was clearly designed to act as a safeguard against collusion.

Back in 1954 Norris kept the Iffley Road crowd in suspense for as long as he could. Bannister amusingly described him as 'a person who was very punctilious in the management of facts and information'. At any rate, McWhirter's announcement went like this:

> Ladies and gentlemen, here is the result of event number nine, the One Mile. First, number 41, R.G. Bannister of the Amateur Athletic Association, formerly of Exeter and Merton Colleges, with a time which is a new meeting and track record, and which, subject to ratification, will be a new English native, British national, British all-comers, European, British Empire and World's Record, the time, three minutes . . .

CHAPTER THREE

THE FALL-OUT

Very few people heard the next words, which were 'fifty-nine point four seconds'. Alan, watching from the pavilion balcony, described the scene. 'The whole place below me went mad. It was very dramatic. I wasn't sure what had happened, or why.' Even Harold was overcome. 'The record caused me more emotional disturbance than any event I have ever seen in nearly forty years' association with athletics,' Abrahams confessed.

Had Bannister's achievement really moved him more than Jack Lovelock's Olympic win back in Berlin? It was an extraordinary claim. How could he have been more emotional – hysterical even – than he was in 1936? We can only assume that he had to fight back the tears in Oxford, as he realised the enormity of what Bannister had done. Abrahams said at the time, 'I feel as though an atom bomb has gone off.'

The athletics world would never be quite the same again. The four-minute barrier had been broken. And Harold Abrahams, Roger's great friend, had been among the first to know. He felt pleased to have shared the day with Alan, and told the nation a few days later, 'I was there – and perhaps more important my 11-year-old son was there too. He and Roger are great pals.' To Alan, this had seemed like any other race. Suddenly his playmate seemed to be everyone's hero. 'I remember going back to school in Oxford at the time and one of the masters explained to me what had happened and suddenly it made a lot more sense.'

Perhaps Alan's father didn't have time to explain the significance of what they had just witnessed, because he still had so much work to do. Bill Findlay, Charlie Hill and Harold Abrahams registered precisely the same time with the referee, Sandy Duncan; and there has never been any argument about their findings. In due course they also had to fill in the IAAF world record application form. Under the heading 'Timekeepers Certificates', the wording went like this: 'I, the undersigned official timekeeper, of the event above mentioned, do hereby certify that the time set opposite my signature was the exact time recorded by my watch, and that the watch used by me has been certified and approved by my National Association'.

Damning evidence: Harold Abrahams has signed – and been confirmed – as one of three timekeepers for Roger Bannister's 3:59.4 mile, despite his dubious position when Bannister hit the tape.

The application form was signed by Sandy Duncan and the three official timekeepers: Bill Findlay, Charlie Hill and Harold Abrahams. All registered 3 minutes 59.4 seconds, and Findlay also signed the following statement: 'I confirm that the above timekeepers exhibited their watches to me and that the times as stated are correct.' The other signature on the form was that of the starter, Ray Barkway.

Kevin Kelly, athletics historian, commented, 'I find it amazing that Harold Abrahams is described as a timekeeper on an official form when he quite clearly was not.'

Yet there was no rule in the old AAA Handbook or IAAF handbooks stating categorically that timekeepers must be in line with the finish. It was commonly accepted that they should be, of course; an unwritten rule that almost went without saying. But since the rule itself only came in later, Harold's poor positioning apparently represented no official transgression. But what would have happened in the modern era, if a huge cash prize had awaited the first man to smash the barrier? How would Landy and the others have reacted, if given the chance to challenge the validity of Bannister's time on a technicality? Could legal action have followed anyway – despite the absence of a firm ruling on the positioning of timekeepers – due to the fact that Harold wasn't supposed to have been a timekeeper at all and wasn't even listed as a reserve?

Mercifully none of Roger's rivals tried to question the validity of Abrahams' signature on the official certificate. They weren't there; they didn't know anything more than the undeniable fact that they had been pipped to the post in the race to break four minutes. After all, the widely accepted time was 3:59.4 – not 3.59.8 or 3.59.9. So it would take a very determined conspiracy theorist to conclude that Bannister never actually smashed the four-minute barrier that day.

The intention here isn't to discredit Bannister; rather to expose the irregular way in which a genuine feat of sporting excellence was handled by those who really should have known better. The little boy in Abrahams had become carried away, beyond all reason and logic. Just as he had contributed so much to Bannister's story, so Harold could have jeopardised its climax. Fortunately, Roger's glorious moment survived the carelessness.

No one noticed the timekeeping anomaly until experts and historians matched photos to certificates in September 2010, during the course of research for this book. And even if Bannister's rivals had been told back in 1954 that something was amiss with the administrative technicalities at

Iffley Road, it is doubtful whether Landy, Santee or the others would have tried to take advantage. Chivalry still counted for something back then.

To an extent, however, Harold had played with fire that day. Why was he allowed to become 'official' at the last moment? It seems that Harold simply couldn't bear the thought of having been there on what turned out to be such an historic day, with nothing to link him forever to the big moment. So he put that right at the drop of a hat, in a move which said everything about the huge amount of power and influence he could wield in his sport.

In time, Abrahams would be remembered as the only significant timekeeper on the day. The process started almost immediately. Even though Findlay was chief timekeeper, Harold allowed the McWhirters, Norris and his brother Ross to list the timekeepers in alphabetical order in an *Athletics World* report. That put him first among equals: 'Abrahams, Findlay and Hill'.

There may have been rumblings of discontent behind the scenes. The McWhirters felt compelled to carry the following lines of clarification in *Athletics World*, with regard to those who were on Harold's side of the track: 'We have been requested to point out that the cluster of stopwatch holders round the finish post at Oxford on the occasion of the four-minute mile were NOT officials but undergraduates. The AAA timekeepers were situated on the other side of the twelve-lane-wide track.' Indeed they were; yet Harold was to be found on the side of the undergraduates, press men and enthusiastic professors. Had someone noticed and felt aggrieved that Abrahams had assumed an official role after the race? And had that person subsequently made a complaint about Harold's 'promotion', and seen fit to fire a mischievous shot across his bows? We will probably never know.

Abrahams was 'Mr Athletics', and he probably considered himself above any such objections; besides, his work that day was far from done. In addition to writing a newspaper report, he had to record the television commentary for the race. Strangely, however, when he dubbed that commentary over BBC footage a little later, the depth of his emotion didn't come across. Since his commentary wasn't live, neither could it be truly spontaneous. Unlike Bannister, the man with the microphone hadn't quite hit the heights of the Lovelock era.

His commentary calling card would always be Lovelock and Berlin. But his 'think-piece' on what he had seen at Iffley Road was fascinating, because his reflections were driven by something more than pure joy for

Roger. Within twenty-four hours, Harold had tried to offer some perspective on what they had been through. 'I was lucky enough to be present at Oxford yesterday and see Roger Bannister's great performance. I was in fact one of the official timekeepers and I watched that second hand as it crept all too quickly towards the four minutes and Bannister came gallantly towards the tape.'

He explained to radio listeners how the record had moved him more than any other moment in all his decades in the sport; but he added:

> I keep on asking myself why. Let's look at the facts calmly if we can. A runner ran a mile just two seconds faster than anyone else had ever done before. The mile record has been beaten many, many times in the history of sport, but never has a record caused so much excitement. All, really, because that record moved from one side of the whole number four to the other . . . Whole numbers have a curious fascination in athletics . . . There can be no doubt at all that for all time people will remember that Bannister was the first man to run a four minute-mile.
>
> I can remember that as I looked at my watch yesterday and saw that record coming to Britain, my first thought was 'Thank goodness that is over at last', followed by the feeling 'Well, where do we go from here?' It's natural to be elated at such a great achievement by an athlete from Great Britain, and make no mistake this is one that Roger Bannister richly deserves. No man could possibly have trained harder; no man used his brain to study and plan to greater advantage. But we should be on our guard against making sport too much of a stunt. Bannister himself has said that we shouldn't sacrifice the value of healthy competition, of racing that is against one another, for the clamour of faster and faster times, with the watch mattering so much more than the victory. The best contribution that sport can make to a troubled world is the fine example of athletes from different nations sharing in the stimulus of rivalry, and the true appreciation of great athletes no matter what their nationality.

Deep down Harold didn't regard Bannister's four-minute mile as a proper race. As far back as 1938 he had said, 'Well, some people are rather opposed to what I may call staged records. I must confess I like a record that just happens.' Of course, there was no way the British Amateur Athletic Board was going to try to rob the world of this human achievement on a technicality. The arguments they used for rejecting the Motspur Park British record were swiftly brushed aside in Oxford, because there was at least an attempt by all the racers to finish. Sure enough, Bannister's record was ratified.

Always perceptive, Abrahams understood the significance of the achievement immediately, and the sporting immortality it would afford the young student. Within days Harold told Britain:

> There are some names in sport that become really famous – Suzanne Lenglen and William Tilden in Lawn Tennis; Jack Dempsey in boxing; Bobbie Jones in golf. And in athletics – Jesse Owens, Paavo Nurmi or Marjorie Jackson [Australia's sprint queen]. At almost precisely four minutes past six o'clock last Thursday evening, Roger Gilbert Bannister achieved lasting athletic fame by being the first man to run a mile inside four minutes . . . His securing of the four-minute mile for Britain, which after all is the real home of middle-distance running, has been I think something of a crusade – a mission to prove to himself that he could do something which had been ordained he possessed the ability to do.

Harold marked Bannister's achievement in style. Sir Roger explained, 'He gave me a stopwatch and eventually I presented it to Pembroke College, Oxford.' It wasn't just any old stopwatch – it was *the* stopwatch. Sir Roger added, 'It says, "From Harold Abrahams, time-keeper, presented to Roger Bannister on the occasion of his four-minute mile".'

Bannister was thrilled to receive the Omega Chronometer, stopped at 3 minutes, 59.4 seconds. He couldn't have known how much controversy Harold's watch might have caused, had the timekeeping at Iffley Road been subjected to the scrutiny of the modern journalistic age. So Roger penned the following note from his Harrow home:

> My dear Harold,
> Your wonderful surprise arrived this morning and I quite literally don't know how to thank you. (I can hear you saying 'Don't try!') You have played such a large part in any success I have achieved – as my guide, philosopher and friend – that it is difficult for me to say enough of what I feel. All I can hope is that we can continue to remain as close when my running days are over!
> My father will be using the new watch this afternoon – though at

the moment I think he feels it's too precious to touch. I expect I shall see you before you read this but I wanted to write immediately to say how much I was thrilled by your present.

Yours ever,

Roger

After hearing that letter read back to him in 2010, Sir Roger acknowledged, 'I was extremely moved that he gave me the stopwatch – that was the one from the four-minute mile. It was a very generous gesture. I think my letter reflects my gratitude and was a gesture of friendship in return for his gesture of friendship.'

What part had Harold Abrahams played in Sir Roger's historic achievement? First and foremost this was Bannister's triumph, though the runner was always first to acknowledge that he had broken the four-minute barrier due to a team effort involving Brasher and Chataway. Yet aside from the timekeeping issue, Harold's contribution to the story was not without significance. Using his own painful experience from thirty years earlier, he had helped a highly strung young man cope with his nervous nature and the pressures of fame and big-time racing. He had helped to choose the few races Bannister agreed to run. He had been a mentor and a supporter. And originally he had given Britain – and therefore Bannister – the gift of the inspirational Franz Stampfl.

In his own small way, Harold had also been a reassuring presence on that unforgettable day; but his positive influence had been a factor from much earlier in Roger's athletics career. Abrahams had advised him, encouraged him and above all believed in him. 'Guide, philosopher and friend,' Roger had said. That summed it up rather nicely.

Before very long, however, Harold Abrahams was wondering what sort of a monster he and Roger Bannister had created. 'I remember saying to Roger Bannister, "You know you did the biggest disservice to athletics in the world by the four-minute mile." And one is half-serious. And I've contributed as much to that as anybody with my mania for the statistical side.'

Later Abrahams sometimes referred to Bannister as 'the first man to run one thousand seven hundred and sixty yards in under two hundred and forty seconds'. It still smacked of statistical mania, but at least it wasn't so dangerously catchy. Harold complained, 'Records, records, records! School, Club, County, Match, District, English Native, British National,

British All-Comers, European, Olympic, World!! It seems to me that unless we do something to curtail this mania for records, we shall ultimately destroy amateur athletics in this country.'

'The Four-Minute Frenzy', as Harold called it, had led to Bannister's historic achievement. Some would say it created an unstoppable momentum, which led all the way to professionalism. Abrahams wanted track athletics to return to its purest form – racing for the thrill of competition. To be fair to Sir Roger, he did his best to lead the sport back to its competitive roots within months. He did so by taking part in one of the greatest head-to-head races of all time. His next big showdown wasn't about statistics or times at all. It was man against man, a duel in Canada.

To stand a chance of beating John Landy at the Commonwealth Games in Vancouver later in that summer of 1954, Bannister knew he would have to run the race of his life. Just forty-six days after Roger's barrier-busting race at Iffley Road, Landy shattered the Englishman's time. On June 21 in Turku, Finland, he ran a mile in 3:57.9, which was rounded up to 3:58.0 under the IAAF rules of the day.

Landy had a style so relaxed, compact and economical that he barely seemed to have any contact with the track at all. He was smaller than Bannister, seemingly weightless, a man who could float through a mile with ease. The Englishman, graceful as he was, couldn't match the quiet harmony of Landy's action. But Bannister's longer arms and legs helped him to flow with such power when he ran all out that he became a force of nature. So who was the greater runner? The clock said Landy, the economy said Landy, the limbs said Bannister, the spirit said Bannister. The answer was about to come in the most dramatic, gladiatorial track battle imaginable.

By the time Landy and Bannister met on August 7, for what became known as the 'Miracle Mile' or 'Race of the Century', the public appetite for the rivalry had reached fever pitch. A broadcast audience of 60 million joined 35,000 in the Empire Stadium. The sunshine was warm but not oppressive, a gentle breeze no more than refreshing. When the runners lined up, all but two were bit-players – and they must have known it. This was always going to be about Landy in green and Bannister in white, with the red bar of England streaking across his chest.

Landy floated round the first lap in fifty-eight seconds. Roger followed, but the Australian was gliding effortlessly. Landy increased his speed in a clear attempt to break his rival. He was flying, and Bannister was faced with a decision: respond immediately or let Landy go and try to reel him in later. Roger took a terrible gamble and decided to wait. He watched patiently as his opponent took a fifteen-yard lead in the backstretch of the second lap. Suddenly Bannister wasn't even in touch any more, and that decision to let Landy go seemed deeply flawed. 'It was a frightening thing to do,' Roger admitted, looking back. 'But I believed he was running too fast. I had to save energy for my final burst and hope I could catch him in time.'

It required exceptional nerve to decide that the fastest miler in history had somehow misjudged his race. At the halfway mark, Landy clocked 1:58, his adrenalin taking him to new heights. But during the third lap, almost imperceptibly at first, Roger responded. He began to eat into that seemingly insurmountable lead until, with a lap left, the race was back on again. The roar of the crowd reached fever pitch as Landy kicked for home with a soul-destroying burst on the backstretch of the last lap. The Australian said later of his rival, 'I had hoped the pace would be so fast that he would crack at that point.' In such sparkling form, he felt confident that no one could live with him. But how much damage had he done? He used the start of the final bend to check back. He looked over his left shoulder, hoping to see a broken man a safe distance behind. At that precise moment, Roger flashed past his right shoulder, seizing the lead before Landy realised what had happened. The Englishman hadn't been broken at all. And in a grim fraction of a second, as Landy looked ahead again and saw his rival streak away, he said to himself, 'I've had it.'

Bannister was in full flow, unstoppable now. This was for Helsinki, this was for all those who said he didn't have the mental toughness to beat another man in track combat. It was for the hours of training, the mental anguish, the obsessive desire to fulfil his potential. And as he hit the tape, he knew he had proved himself, not just as a runner but a competitor too. His time of 3:58.8 wasn't a world record, but that wasn't the point. Both men had broken four minutes in the greatest duel of all time; and Bannister had come out on top.

An understandably proud Sir Roger reflected later: 'Harold Abrahams didn't like pacemakers. Well, there was no pacemaker for my greatest race of all, against John Landy.' That said it all. The achievement put an end to any doubts his friend Harold had ever raised about Bannister's track record. At the start of the summer, Roger had clocked the most famous sporting time in history. Now, before the end of that same extraordinary season, he had triumphed in the most memorable race. Unlike Harold, who had never faced Liddell over 100 metres, Bannister had taken on his greatest rival over their strongest distance and won. He had proved himself completely; a fact merely confirmed when he won the gold medal in the European Championships in Berne towards the end of the season. Now he could retire early and gloriously.

Harold explained:

> To some people this outstanding success might become a perpetual millstone around their necks. But I don't think this will prove to be the case with Roger Bannister. Running has never been his be all and end all. He is the typical British amateur, with no thought of capitalising the fame which his prowess has brought to him.
>
> His main concern now is to lead a really useful life, and I believe that he will one day be as famous for his skill at and contribution to medicine as he is in sport. He has never allowed sport to dominate him. In September he takes his finals to become a doctor, and it seems likely that he will then find it necessary to abandon first-class athletics.
>
> . . . He is far too intelligent to rate sporting ability too highly. He has far too many other interests to be one-sided. He loves reading, for instance, and he writes – not only articles on athletics and medical subjects – but also about the many things he has seen in his travels to all parts of the world.
>
> The six foot two inch young man of twenty-five is one of the nicest personalities I have ever been fortunate enough to know so well. To be with him is not only to share in the success of a great athlete, it is to experience the fine comradeship of a really good mind.

Unfortunately, Bannister's 'Miracle Mile' was very nearly the last piece of satisfying athletics Harold ever saw. The prospect of a routine operation seemed harmless enough. And on September 25, 1954 the *Manchester Guardian* reported, 'The condition of Mr Harold Abrahams, the former Olympic Games 100 metre champion, and sports broadcaster and writer, who had an abdominal operation in Westminster Hospital, was stated yesterday to be "fairly comfortable".' The following day the *Sunday Times* echoed, 'Mr Harold Abrahams is making satisfactory progress.'

But then Harold's condition took a turn for the worse, and *The Times* of September 28, 1954 reported, 'Mr Harold Abrahams, the former Olympic Games 100 metre champion, has had a relapse after a recent abdominal operation in Westminster Hospital. A bulletin issued last night stated that his condition "gives rise to some anxiety".' Reading between the lines of such a sober announcement, Harold's condition was life-threatening. Jack Crump, Abrahams' closest associate in British athletics administration, revealed later, 'Harold had been desperately ill . . . so ill indeed that not until I was diplomatically approached by the *Daily Telegraph* to be ready to supply an obituary did I realise the seriousness of the situation.'

Like the fighter he had been since the day of his premature birth, Harold rallied, and the next day the *Manchester Guardian* was able to report, 'MR ABRAHAMS IMPROVING. Mr Harold Abrahams had a "very comfortable day, and is going on satisfactorily", it was stated at Westminster Hospital last night.' Unfortunately he wasn't quite well enough to pay personal tribute to Roger Bannister at a glittering event in London. His eldest brother was, and a *Daily Telegraph* correspondent filed the following report for the September 29 edition.

> With characteristic modesty, Dr Roger Bannister received the Silver Pears Trophy in London yesterday for running the mile in 3:59.4. At the ceremony I talked to Sir Adolphe Abrahams, medical advisor to the British Olympic teams since 1912. He was emphatic that today's athletes are no better physically than 50 years ago . . . Sir Adolphe was able to give encouraging news of his athlete brother Harold, now a little better after a relapse following an operation.

Harold emerged from hospital with the scar from a large incision down the abdomen. But you couldn't keep a good man down, and a few months later he was announcing new rules to bar promoters from advertising events as 'record attempts' and to ban the use of pacemakers in the breaking of track records.

Abrahams warned, 'The British Board intends to invite the International Federation in Melbourne [1956] to adopt the British rule. I cannot, of course, say whether the IAAF will do so, but certainly the general opinion at recent meetings of its Rules and Records Committee, of which I am a member, was against all paced records.'

Harold maintained that under the new rule 'Bannister's 3:59.4 mile would certainly have been barred'. His record had been beaten since then anyway, and they weren't talking about the retrospective erasure of past achievements from the record books. Therefore it hardly seemed to matter. Even so, Bannister and Chris Chataway quickly spoke out against the new rule. Even in 2010, Sir Roger defended pacemakers. He told me, 'Yes, I would still agree with them. For example, when you are in a team against another team, such tactics are justified.'

Back in the mid-1950s, Abrahams countered Roger's argument like this:

> I would like to put the following questions to Roger Bannister and Chris Chataway, each of whom has criticised the new rule. First, are 'paced' records in the best interests of athletics as a whole? Second (to Roger): In your heart of hearts, do you think that your 3:58.8 mile in that wonderful Empire Games in Vancouver did far more good, and was far more in harmony with the best in amateur sport, than your first '4-minute' performance?
>
> 'If 'paced' records should be recognised as a valuable part of amateur athletics, why not go the whole hog and introduce 'mechanical' pacing? What better, as a 'stunt', than having a wax model of a runner made, and arranging for it to traverse the track at even pace which will result in its completing a mile in 3:55? Announce this to the crowd and let them witness the runner against time.

He didn't seriously want to see that happen. It was just his way of illustrating a point he made in a later interview: 'I'm very conscious that one's got to get the proper balance between the athlete and the spectator, and it is all going the spectator's way. The interest in records is spectator, isn't it?'

Yet the journalist in Harold couldn't stop talking about records and new barriers. And when Harold and Roger took part in a radio broadcast later in their lives, Abrahams made an outrageous claim. 'I don't think a three-minute mile is necessarily impossible; you see, if you could run at 220 speed you would do 2:56. When those doctors [find a way to] produce enough Oxygen [for] you, why shouldn't you do 2:56?'

Bannister, a doctor himself, poured scorn on the notion. 'Well, I think that is actually impossible,' he said.

'You probably don't like to be contradicted, Roger, that's the trouble,' quipped Harold, quick as a flash.

On some issues they would simply have to agree to disagree. But it would be wrong to portray the pair as friends who became enemies in the aftermath of the four-minute mile. On the contrary; when Roger and his wife Moyra had their first child – a daughter called Erin in February 1957 – they asked Harold to be her godfather. Naturally, Abrahams was only too delighted to accept the role.

Yet Harold and Roger didn't stay as close as they might have done. Bannister explained the increasing distance between the two men like this. 'There was no falling out; it was simply that our paths diverged. I concentrated on medicine; he remained in athletics among other things.' Sue Pottle believes that Bannister's decision to distance himself from athletics for a good number of years had caused frustrations on her father's side. Sue explained, 'He seemed to think that Sir Roger should have been putting more back into athletics after he stopped running, but my father probably didn't realise just how much time and energy a junior doctor has to put into medicine.'

Yet their paths did converge again later. Sir Roger pointed out, 'For about seven years, when he was the *Sunday Times* [athletics] correspondent I also wrote for the *Sunday Times*, and he was very easy to work with. There were no problems at all.' Harold's daughter Sue felt less easy when she recalled, 'I'm not sure my father was too thrilled when Sir Roger took over from him as *Sunday Times* athletics correspondent, but that's life.'

On the other hand, Abrahams must have been genuinely delighted when, as Chairman of the Sports Council in the mid-1960s and early 1970s, Bannister pioneered the testing of sportsmen for anabolic steroids. Harold may have taken a little strychnine in that 'Easton's Syrup' back in 1924, but he was certainly no cheat. No one wanted to see the modern-day drug-takers caught more than Abrahams. The common ground he and Roger shared on the growing problem of drugs in sport was surely more important than the differences they had over how much funding the Sports Council should or should not be setting aside for athletics. 'We didn't always run on parallel lines, but there was a mutual respect,' Sir Roger concluded gracefully.

Looking back, the friendship between Harold and Roger was at its height during that extraordinary period in the early 1950s, when a sub-four-minute mile became more than a distant dream. As the letters and newspaper articles show beyond question, they were lucky to have each other in many ways.

Abrahams had played the fame game and knew what a unique talent Roger was. He did his best to be supportive and protective, and he benefited both personally and professionally from their relationship. By claiming to have timed that first sub-four-minute mile as an official, Harold perhaps benefited more than he should have done. His enthusiasm and even his ego took over at Oxford that day. For all that, he meant no harm.

And, mercifully, Bannister wasn't harmed. So Roger could reflect upon how he was able to face the music at Iffley Road partly because he had spent years listening to Harold and learning how to cope with the limelight while sticking to his guns. When everyone wants a piece of you, it is good to have a friend who has been there and done it. Roger responded with warmth, enthusiasm, and two very different miles, which will always stand out in athletics history.

CHAPTER FOUR

MIRROR IMAGE

For a man who did so much to popularise athletics, it was extraordinary how unpopular Harold Abrahams became among many athletes and coaches towards the end of the 1950s.

'Harold actually became the living embodiment of the things he had fought in the 1920s,' Lord Puttnam – producer of the movie *Chariots of Fire* – pointed out. 'There is quite a rich vein for you as Harold's biographer, if I may say so.'

You ignore David Puttnam at your peril; and, as we shall see, he had a point. Yet in one case at least, when Harold championed a cause he had previously undermined, he emerged with great credit.

In 1928 Abrahams had written, 'I do not consider that women are built for really violent exercise of the kind that is the essence of competition. One only has to see them practising to realise how awkward they are on the running track.' Just before World War Two he added, 'I confess to a deep-seated opposition to women's athletics'.

By March 1955, however, Harold had changed his tune so drastically that he was writing in *World Sports* 'as a sporting suffragist'. The journal even carried a cartoon of Harold holding a placard which read, 'Equal Rights for Women.' He also served as the Women's Amateur Athletic Association's legal advisor.

What sparked such an emphatic defence of women in the 1950s was a claim by a group of Belgian doctors that they should no longer take part in competitive sport. Harold replied:

I write as one who used to have considerable doubts on the subject –

pretty forcibly expressed, too, a quarter of a century ago. It is nonsense to suggest that women shouldn't take part in competitive sport, and I challenge the Belgian doctors, or other medical men, to produce any real evidence to support this contention . . .

Competitive sport for women has come to stay, and it will need something more impressive than a few pompous utterances to stop it. Some of the most charming women I know are first-class athletes.

One of the women Harold surely had in mind was an athlete called Valerie Ball, whom Harold described as 'one of the best middle-distance runners Britain has had – and a most attractive personality both on and off the track'.

She seemed to capture his imagination as much as Bannister in her own way. The fact that her best events, the 400m and 800m, were not in the Olympic programme increased Harold's sense of injustice. By the time Valerie Ball had finished with athletics, Harold was virtually a sporting feminist. She had done as much as Fanny Blankers-Koen to change his way of thinking.

What helped Harold temper his chauvinistic ways was the fact that Valerie Ball was feminine; so feminine, in fact, that she was regarded as a pin-up girl in sporting circles and beyond. In 2010 she told a funny story about an official athletics gender test she had to undergo, which was supposed to involve a full medical examination. 'I had to go to a doctor to get a certificate to say I was a woman,' she said. 'He just looked at me and signed it.'

Harold tried to offer Valerie Ball coaching advice, but she wasn't his most dedicated pupil. She admitted, 'I was young and I was already winning just about every 440 race I ran. I don't think I appreciated how clever he was, or the fact that he wanted to help me. He was fascinated by the clock. The stopwatch was his god. Even when I was running about 57 seconds, he said that if I could learn to run at an even pace I could do better.'

Harold began to wax lyrical about Valerie in the newspapers. Fortunately, Sybil warmed to Britain's most glamorous athlete too. They had music in common, as well as the more obvious link through Harold. 'Music was more important to me than athletics,' Valerie explained. 'I was studying at the Royal College of Music, playing the violin and piano.' The younger woman brought out Sybil's caring side. Valerie recalled later, 'In January 1952 I had glandular fever and for a couple of weeks I convalesced at Harold and Sybil's home. Sybil was a lovely lady, so kind to me, she was very friendly and she was so warm that she must have made Harold very happy.'

The following month Valerie went to see England's rugby team play Ireland in the snow, and met her future husband, England star Chris Winn. Now, on top of her commitment to her music, Valerie suddenly had another distraction. Neither the courtship, nor the violin or piano could ruin her Olympic chances, though. The bigots who ran international athletics had done that already. When Roger Bannister, Chris Chataway and the rest headed for Helsinki in 1952, Valerie Ball was left at home – for no better reason than the fact that she was a woman.

'I'd have liked to have been in the Olympics, I must admit,' she said wistfully in 2010. 'It's difficult to explain to people. They come and say, "You were in the Olympics, weren't you?" I say, "Not exactly." I'd have loved to run in the Olympics; but I didn't protest or complain – I just took it. It all went back to 1928 when the women ran the 800 at the Amsterdam Olympics and collapsed at the end. That's why it was no longer included.'

Some female competitors had been so distraught that they had been in tears at the finishing line in Amsterdam, leading to unfair claims that women simply weren't suited to gruelling events. Since then perfectly capable women hadn't been allowed to compete over two Olympic laps at all, and that was the real crying shame.

In summer 1952, Valerie was powerless to do much more than follow Harold's reports on the indifferent progress of the British Olympic team. But all the time something was building inside her. On the evening of September 17, 1952, the moment came to unleash it. Valerie was racing under floodlights, which always put her in the mood. 'Floodlights were fun,' she recalled, 'it gave an athletics meeting an exciting air.' She always had a strong will to win; but the floodlights pumped a little more adrenalin into her toned body as she started her two-lap race round the track.

A little over two minutes later, barefoot by then and wrapped in a blanket, a beaming Valerie knew she had made history. One report announced, 'Valerie Ball, 23-year-old daughter of Sir Nigel Ball, set up a new world record of 2:14.5 for the women's 880 yards run during last night's floodlit international athletics meeting at White City, London. After the race Miss Ball said: "I was most surprised by my performance; I had no thoughts of a world record attempt either before or during the race."'

The injustice of Valerie's Olympic exclusion while still in her prime stayed with Harold somehow. By early 1957 the former male chauvinist was really getting somewhere in his fight for women's equality in athletics. He wrote proudly, 'European Championships have been extended from five days to six, and a women's 400m race is to be added to events. The International Olympic Committee is to be asked to include an 800m for women and a women's pentathlon in the 1960 Games.'

The likes of Dame Kelly Holmes, Jessica Ennis and Denise Lewis would have reason to be grateful for the pioneering pressure Harold Abrahams exerted on their behalf back in the 1950s.

Yet the male athletes were furious with him during that same decade and beyond. They blamed him for slowing the march towards professionalism. And his stubborn fight to prevent the inevitable is interesting, if only because it seemed to contradict the younger Harold so comprehensively.

Lord Puttnam seemed saddened by the way Abrahams changed. 'My interpretation is that ironically Harold became the mirror image of the very things he had once opposed.' He was quite adamant about Harold's shortcomings. 'He became the establishment; he became the person who blocked advances, in training, in what he termed as professionalism.'

Tom McNab, who trained the actors and worked as a historical consultant on the film shared that view. 'Abrahams was a poacher turned gamekeeper. In his athletic days he had a professional coach and often went against the mainstream of athletics thinking. But when he became part of the establishment he undermined professional coaching and became reactionary.'

Had he really become the mirror image of what he had once been? The truth isn't quite as simple as Puttnam's conclusion suggests. Sir Roger Bannister, who knew Abrahams so well, understood his motivations better than most. 'Harold felt that coaches were becoming too big for their boots. He felt there was a danger they were becoming too dictatorial. He felt that the athletes' personality had to be protected and respected.'

Harold tried to remind everyone that his own involvement with a coach had never compromised his independence:

> I was not just being trained; I was being helped with my training, which is a vastly different thing. Well, a lot of these modern people regard a coach as a wet nurse or a Svengali. I didn't. I thought for myself. I argued with Sam Mussabini. If I differed with him I said so.

If he recommended something I almost invariably asked 'why?' . . . I think a lot of the modern coaches are just hangers on, frankly. I don't think they know much about it and you can be over-coached.

The battle over coaching in the UK caused ill feeling for years. During the mid-1950s, two camps were close to war. On one side were Harold and his British Amateur Athletic Board colleague, Jack Crump, who acted like officers. On the other side was Geoffrey Dyson, more of a sergeant major in his ways. Dyson had been appointed AAA chief coach in 1947; and it was Dyson who enjoyed the support of most of the top athletes.

Tensions rose when Harold and Crump took a British athletics team on a ground-breaking trip to Trinidad and Jamaica without a coach in February 1956. The move was considered provocative and they were criticised for it, because Crump's wife and Sybil went too. Harold and Sybil both worked hard on the trip, which was paid for by Simon Vos of the Regent Oil Company, then British owned. Sybil revealed how she worked for Trinidad radio while out in the Caribbean: 'I was bounced into doing a half-hour programme – songs and documentary sketches – and on that occasion I roped Harold in as "commentator" – he had to do the linking up.'

Abrahams wasn't there just to sit back and enjoy the Caribbean sunshine. None of the British party was. Harold explained:

Soon after our arrival in Trinidad we were all hard at it, for the basic idea behind the trip was not so much the actual competition as the general encouragement to athletics which the visit of some of our leading competitors could give. [They] gave a series of 'clinics', or coaching sessions, which were tremendously popular. Jack Crump showed a number of films, and I gave a talk, illustrated by slides of most of the leading past and present performers, to an audience of about 200 . . . A particularly fine slide of Jesse Owens had a tremendous reception. I talked for the best part of an hour and then came many and various questions . . . One of my audience asked me whether, when running, you should breathe through your nose . . . I pointed out that the mouth is a much more rapid source of supply. I added, rather hesitatingly, that you should keep your mouth shut when you have won – and was most relieved when they were on to it like a shot!

Harold concluded, 'The trip was thoroughly worthwhile, and I hope it may be repeated in the not-too-distant future . . . There is great enthusiasm and much hidden talent in the West Indies.' He wasn't wrong, as the world now knows. Yet this innovative trip attracted condemnation for its alleged opportunism.

Tensions escalated further still towards the end of the year, when John Disley, who had been 1952 Olympic steeplechase bronze medallist, led protests against the lack of coaches with the British Olympic party in Melbourne. Harold was there as assistant manager and found himself in the firing line. Disley wrote, 'We could see that where other teams had half a dozen coaches to cast a critical eye over training workouts, the British only had one, supplemented by the willing but uninformed assistant team manager.'

Disley added, 'We were not receiving the unofficial daily cash allowance enjoyed by many other teams. After agitation we were given limited free postal facilities, but this measure did little to restore our pride. It appeared that the Swedes, who had started a fund for the hapless Hungarians, were even contemplating doing something for the "poor" British!'

It seemed so wrong, because back in October 1948 Abrahams had revealed how he had used an IAAF Congress that year to try to end such resentment once and for all. 'The British proposal advanced the suggestion that no athlete should be prevented by any financial embarrassment from representing his country in international competition, and a man's governing body should be allowed, in proved and suitable cases, to see that he suffers no financial loss from international selection.'

Abrahams had also been the brains behind a British Amateur Athletic Board presentation to that same IAAF Congress, showing how it would be possible to redraft the rulebook without using the word 'amateur'. But that didn't mean Harold wanted the sport to turn professional; he simply preferred the term 'non-professional'. He also despised any rule-bending practice which smacked of professionalism – the sort of underhand compromise the national boards of some other countries often indulged in quite unashamedly.

The storm raged on towards the next Olympics, as Abrahams tried to keep professionalism at bay. But Harold's own earnings from the sport never did strengthen his case. An athlete called Derek Johnson, the 1956 Olympic 800m silver medallist, pointed out:

According to I.A.A.F. and AAA laws an athlete must obtain permission if he wishes to ask payment for writing an article in a newspaper or magazine, or for taking part in a television or radio broadcast. Permission is invariably withheld if the subject of the article or broadcast is directly connected with athletics, unless the athlete can show that writing is an integral part of his livelihood . . . But many of these officials, among them Jack Crump and Harold Abrahams, write or broadcast regularly.

This cynical attitude towards professionalism is, in my opinion, the biggest single cause for the bad feeling that has so long disgraced our sport; and until we have one law that applies equally to everybody – whether it allows or prevents us all from writing or broadcasting for payment – I can see nothing of real value being achieved towards healing the breach.

It was a powerful argument. And Harold's privileged position in journalism had already aroused the wrath of the unions. The National Union of Journalists had long argued that Abrahams should be banned from writing for newspapers. He was not a full-time, trained journalist – and not a union cardholder either. Besides, as an athletics administrator he was operating from an insider's position of unfair advantage. On one occasion, Harold even broke a press embargo, writing in detail about a freshly selected British athletics team on a Monday, when the news was not meant to come out until Tuesday. On more than one occasion union members refused to handle his copy in newspaper offices.

But Harold wasn't going to give up writing or broadcasting for anyone – not for the unions or the athletes. He defended himself against Johnson's attack with a hint of irony:

The growth of athletics in popularity since 1946, a progressive trend which occurred doubtless in spite of the officials, has led inevitably to the sport becoming 'news' . . . The real question is not, so it seems to me, 'Should officials write for payment?' but rather: 'Should those who write for payment be appointed as officials?' It is apparently forgotten that officials cannot obtain their appointments except by favour of those who have the power to appoint . . .

Those who believe that the actual personnel of the Board is wrong should make their voices felt not in the press but in their clubs. If the opinion against members of the Board is strong, their change could be achieved . . . Criticism always suggests frustrated energy, particularly destructive criticism. We have got to find a way to harness this energy, and this we shall never do if athletes and officials keep one another at arm's length. The problems to be solved require the best combined efforts of athletes and officials; there is really no time for either party to add to these problems.

Unfortunately the ill feeling was hard to eliminate when the man most British athletes looked up to, Geoff Dyson, was being treated so shabbily in their view. In 1957, for example, during an end-of-season, two-match tour to Poland and West Germany, Dyson travelled as team coach; but by the time he arrived, Crump and Abrahams had already picked the team. It was a similar story when a replacement had to be found quickly for an injured relay runner. This time Crump made the decision unilaterally.

A furious Dyson asked to be flown home. Harold acted as peacemaker. Crump explained, 'I told Harold Abrahams of Dyson's request and of my decision to book him home the next day. He pointed out to me that Geoff was an employee of the Amateur Athletic Association and that John Turner, who was with the team, was the AAA's chairman . . . [Harold] had a two-hour discussion with Geoff . . . Finally I was told that Mr Turner had instructed Dyson that he was to stay with the team, which was travelling on to Germany two days later, and that finally Dyson had accepted to do so.'

With skilful mediation, Abrahams had helped avert a worse crisis. But from that moment on, the coach's days were numbered. In 1959, the BAAB appointed a lawyer to undertake an independent enquiry into the state of coaching in British athletics. The lawyer was Harold Abrahams' nephew, Tony. 'That was inappropriate,' claimed Mel Watman, former editor of the magazine *Athletics Weekly*, much later. And it is hard to justify the appointment of a leading administrative figure's relative for any kind of independent judgement. Nevertheless, Tony Abrahams always insisted that he was entirely impartial in the way he conducted his enquiry. He concluded that Dyson was paying too much attention to elite athletes and not enough to grass-roots coaching.

This seemed to reflect Harold's view, because he didn't seem to care very much about medals any more. 'In the Olympics, I feel that the important thing is not so much to win as to take part,' he had begun to insist. 'This is the ideal behind the Olympics, and is still common sense.' It was also the complete opposite of Abrahams' attitude towards the Paris Olympics, for which he had seen fit to be coached intensively for nine months. According to bronze medallist Porritt, Harold felt he 'simply had to win the final and win it he did'. Now he was denying the latest generation of athletes the chance to satisfy similar ambitions, and the opportunity to benefit from a similar intensity of professional coaching. Now he valued the amateur ethos above all – and seemed to be advocating the same, relaxed attitude to athletics that he had criticised as a younger man. This is why men like Lord Puttnam talked about mirror images, and Harold as the living embodiment of all he had fought.

Two things had changed. First of all, having suffered too much as a young man because of his sporting ambition, Abrahams now had the wisdom of an older man's perspective. Secondly, there was now a more general threat to the competitive purity of athletics, one which hadn't existed in his day. The latest crop of athletes seemed to want payment for their competitive efforts. One of Dyson's athletes, Arthur Rowe, won gold at the 1958 European Championships, but was widely believed to accept illegal appearance money on a habitual basis. Harold had never done that when he was an athlete. Rightly or wrongly, he saw Dyson as part of the new, infected way of thinking, someone who focused on the very best at the expense of the others. Harold's opponents in the argument preferred to condemn the rigid rules which in their view had created the necessity for such 'shamateurism' in the first place.

Sir Arthur Gold, who later took over from Crump, recalled, 'There was a clear personality clash between Harold and Geoff Dyson and they argued over who had responsibility . . . Harold would get Dyson to justify everything he said and there were problems between them.'

The AAA soon decided to scrap the differential in salary between the Chief Coach and the other national coaches. This, apparently, was the final straw. Dyson left. Many still believe that represented a severe loss to British athletics. And Dyson soon proved his value on the other side of the Atlantic. First he wrote a brilliant and definitive work on training and coaching called *The Mechanics of Athletics*. Then from his new base in Canada, he influenced some of the top figures in North American athletics. And when Carl Lewis won four gold medals at the 1984 Olympics in Los Angeles, his coach Tom Tellez waved Dyson's book at reporters. 'This is my Bible,' he explained. 'I owe it all to him.'

Harold Abrahams may well have underestimated Dyson's value to British athletics. Peter Radford, a British sprinter who became 200 metres world record holder in 1960, revealed, 'Geoff saw him as an obstacle, a man who couldn't see sense. I was on Geoff's side, on the side of the future, whilst Harold was fighting for the past of the sport. Geoff saw

Harold as a man who was not at all interested in the future of the sport.'

But on that last point Dyson couldn't have been more wrong. Harold was desperately worried about the future of the sport, and determined to ensure that it remained pure, so that it could be enjoyed by athletes at all levels. Despite the enormous natural ability he had enjoyed as a young star, he was now fighting for the rights of those with far less talent. This certainly wasn't the same man who had complained in 1924 that elite athletes might suffer at the Games if money was spent instead on those with no hope of making the finals.

Hypocrisy? Make up your own mind. In some ways Abrahams really had become the mirror image of the man he had once been. Yet there was also a consistency underpinning everything. He was always passionate about athletics, and he was always determined to do what he thought was best for athletics. As times changed, so, in his view, did the best course of action. He was fearful of what professionalism might mean for the integrity of his beloved sport, and he reacted accordingly. Sometimes he was right, sometimes he was wrong.

Lord Puttnam, with his wonderful eye for dramatic twists and turns, has enough evidence to support his thesis. Yet it is also true that most people change as they grow older. And in 2010, Puttnam analysed his own journey through life, using Abrahams and Liddell, the central characters in *Chariots of Fire*. 'For the first twenty-five years of my career – certainly until I left the film industry, really – there was more Harold than Eric about me. And I sincerely believe or hope that the last fifteen years have been more Eric than Harold.'

In Puttnam's mind, Abrahams still seemed to stand for naked ambition, Liddell for altruism. The real Harold Abrahams was slightly different, and he too tried to make the trek from one pole to the other. Even so, we can be fairly sure that, had Puttnam's film covered Harold's entire life, Abrahams would not have come out favourably. 'Did she marry someone nicer than Harold?' Puttnam asked hopefully when he was given some details about Christina McLeod Innes in 2010.

Abrahams could be extremely nice. But in order to protect the ethos and spirit of the sport, he could also be ruthless as he tried to crush rebellion or mere dissent in some cases. Neil Allen, the former athletics correspondent of *The Times*, recalled, 'He was always prepared to think that he knew best – and many times he did. He had an extraordinary conceit. He would say, "Let's think things out. Let's look at it logically." That meant let's look at things his way.' When Allen stood his ground on various issues, he was subjected to some typical Abrahams wit, as Harold played merrily with his adversary's first name. 'To quote Shakespeare, "Kneel, you bastard, kneel,"' Abrahams quipped in one after-dinner speech with Allen present. Neil endured the inevitable ripple of laughter, but took some revenge later that evening. 'We have heard so much about Harold's great victories,' Allen acknowledged in a speech of his own, '. . . much of it from him.'

Former *Athletics Weekly* editor Mel Watman sometimes witnessed Harold's heavy-handed tactics at the Annual General Meetings of the Amateur Athletic Association. He admitted:

> Harold could be quite cruel at these meetings. Most of the people speaking were volunteer officials with no training in public speaking and they would make their points falteringly. And Harold, who was trained as a barrister and had a tremendous command of the English language and a wonderful voice, would demolish them. I always felt uneasy about that side of him. But to me he was like a second father. I could see two sides to him. Charming . . . but you wouldn't want him to be your enemy. He was ninety-five per cent positive but he was also a little too authoritarian at times.

You didn't have to be a little guy to be withered by the Abrahams put-down. Sir Arthur Gold confirmed, 'Harold did not suffer athletic fools gladly. His ability to examine, cross-examine and re-examine a suggestion and then, if necessary, subject it to the cold douche of reason earned him the respect of his colleagues from many countries in the fields of athletic administration.'

Lord Coe, 'Mr London 2012', was fascinating as he explained how a leader's natural desire to be liked cannot always be allowed to prevail – especially when there is only a limited amount of time to ensure that important things are done his or her way. Seb explained, 'Harold Abrahams left no one in doubt over who was in charge. But one of the qualities of leadership is that sometimes the decisions you make are not particularly popular, not with everybody. It's a question of finding a route through – because no one gets everything entirely right. The main thing is to make sure that you are shaping events, rather than the other way round.'

Abrahams habitually shaped events and refused to be shaped by them. Opponents said he was living in the past. And sometimes, quite unashamedly, he was.

CHAPTER FIVE

Drawing Up The Future

Harold Abrahams was a picture of concentration in the Stade Colombes, Paris. He remained oblivious to the crowd, which was filling the arena to catch the best of the action. Abrahams, the tall Englishman, waited for his chance. Timing was everything; Sam Mussabini had taught him that. In this stadium, he was used to being kept waiting. No matter, he was focused on two things only: the report of the pistol and the tape. No one else could hear the pistol or see the tape. But Harold could.

Peter Radford witnessed the priceless moment. 'It was an international meeting between Great Britain and France at the Stade Colombes in 1958. It wasn't during the height of competition; the crowd was still coming in. Harold had gone to the start of the 100 metres. To me he was already an old man. He looked down his lane, standing quietly. No one was talking to him.'

Had they tried, Harold probably wouldn't have heard. The pistol, the tape; when he heard one, he was to run like hell until he reached the other. Shut out everything else. This time Abrahams had done something really special. He had managed to shut out time itself. Harold heard the pistol and reacted.

Radford said, 'Slowly, steadily, he began to move.' Harold didn't try to sprint. He didn't need to. Even in his prime, Abrahams had been a master of slow motion, until he perfected the right steps and body-shapes. That's how he had learned his technique under Mussabini's guidance. They had even used slow-motion film. So Abrahams was in no hurry now. Not when he already had that supreme feeling of moving just a little faster than the others.

Radford added, 'He walked the lane very deliberately, all the way to the end.' Reliving every inch of the race, he could probably hear the 1924 crowd's roar all over again, as the rivalry with Charley Paddock and the others reached its climax. Radford, the up-and-coming teenager, watched transfixed. 'I sensed that, as he neared where the tape would have been, there was a slight, almost imperceptible dip of the shoulders. It happened on his final stride . . . then he walked away.'

Most people concluded that Harold Abrahams had just run the 1924 Olympic final all over again. But it might have been an action replay of the finest piece of running he ever did – in the semi-final.

Either way, Harold Abrahams never stopped feeling grateful to Sam Mussabini, architect of his success in both races. Radford recalled:

> One time I remember an athletics meeting at the White City and the East German girls were running. Harold came up to me terribly enthusiastically, and said, 'Sam was right! It's all in a shoulder-shrug!' The point he was making was that the shoulders have to rise to their high point when the knees are most forward in a sprinter's action. At the time I thought that so much had changed, and to me Harold was already an old man; therefore he couldn't possibly know everything about sprinting. But now, looking back, I wish that I could have got into his head and shared his ideas.

Abrahams was a brilliant man, but a lot of people in British athletics had stopped wanting to listen to him. Fortunately, just as he faced mounting hostility in the sport so close to his heart, he became increasingly celebrated in a very different domestic field. Throughout the 1950s and early 1960s, the beauty of Britain provided the perfect escape from the ugliness of athletics politics. Harold Abrahams played a leading role in the setting up of Britain's National Parks, and left the country a lasting legacy.

Curiously, the National Parks project was something he fell into by chance. Harold seemed to have a commendable sense of the absurd as he recalled how his post-war path was determined by a typically British combination of daft bureaucracy and old school tie. Abrahams wanted to go back to the Bar but the Civil Service wouldn't release him and offered him a job at the Ministry of Town and Country Planning instead. Harold declined initially, but then remembered that he knew the Establishment Officer in that department and reconsidered. With a chuckle he explained, 'I went there initially to help out with an Act of Parliament, which I never in fact did help out with, and I liked it there and stayed on.'

After a year representing the Ministry in his beloved Cambridge, he became Secretary of a new body called the National Parks Commission. It was the perfect opportunity to preserve what was best about his native landscape. 'The British Isles was the best in the world for him,' said his daughter, Sue Pottle. 'He was absolutely patriotic, all for king and country.' Harold once summarised his task like this:

> The National Parks Commission was set up primarily to designate National Parks. We've got ten of them. Lake District, Peak District, Pembrokeshire Coast, Dartmoor, Exmoor, Northumberland and so on, with the idea that those are areas where the public can enjoy beautiful scenery and get sufficient recreation. It is a frightfully lucky job to have because it brings one into contact with so many people. Local authorities manage the Parks. I go down to Park meetings and help with problems. You've got a great conflict. You've got a limited amount of land in this country. How is it to be used? Are you to have recreation or are you to have a power station? I am essentially a person who believes that the only way in life is compromise. It doesn't mean giving way on things that really matter. There are precious few things that you can be absolutely certain about. I enjoy enormously trying to bring together two conflicting interests and trying to sort it out . . . and get those people thoroughly dissatisfied with the result!

Harold could afford to joke, because his negotiation skills brought stunning results and new National Parks. 'I would say the Cornish Coastal Park was 99 per cent down to Harold,' his daughter claimed. The job brought out the best in him. Rosemary Warne, his last great companion, explained:

> He had a superb way of dealing with people, a charm about him and a lovely laugh that made you feel relaxed. He saw the ridiculous not only in others but in himself, which made you feel good because he wasn't too pompous. He would have been incisive about what he wanted to do in the National Parks and he loved his team and the people he worked with. That came over hugely in his recollections of that phase in his life. He set up the Lake District, I think, and a

difficult one on Dartmoor where he crossed swords with a Lady Sayers but charmed her. He negotiated land from owners and things like that.

Harold knew how lucky he was, and after around a decade in the role, he enthused, 'I've got a lovely job, one of the nicest jobs I could ever have run into . . . I've seen more of England in the last ten years than I saw in the first fifty.'

The reward for his good work was announced on the BBC in 1957: 'Among those made Commanders of the Order of the British Empire was Mr Stanley Matthews, who was honoured for services to Association football. Other CBEs include Mr Harold Abrahams, Secretary of the National Parks Commission, and a well-known sporting commentator and journalist.'

Harold Abrahams, CBE. It had a ring to it; but with brothers called Sir Adolphe and Sir Sidney, Harold wasn't going to rest there. He continued to give everything he could to athletics, both nationally and internationally. To an extent he applied the same principles as he did in the National Parks. The fact that he wanted to preserve the best of the past didn't mean he was reluctant to make the future better too.

Despite his obstructive approach to elitist coaching and pro-fessionalism, Harold could also be extremely forward-thinking. He liked to work at the cutting edge of progress when it came to international athletics administration. And you didn't persuade people to change rules if you came across as unpleasant. Sir Roger Bannister readily acknowledged, 'Harold was highly intelligent and he was a lawyer who understood how to coordinate meetings. He was able to steer his colleagues towards making difficult decisions in a diplomatic way.'

Sometimes his patience was pushed to the limit. In 1957, Harold explained, 'Every two years, the Rules and Records Committee of the International Amateur Athletic Federation meets to discuss new rules for competition, or alterations to old ones, and to make recommendations on them to IAAF Congress. I have been lucky enough to be a member of this committee for more than twenty years, and I have always been interested in these matters.'

He had become Chairman of the IAAF Technical Committee in 1956, a post he was to hold for twelve years, patiently chipping away each year until the IAAF listened to and implemented many of his suggestions. It wasn't always plain sailing. Since 1954, he had been pressing for a new system of qualifying standards for the Olympics. At that time he had written about 'a proposition from Britain', – which meant him – for limiting the number of athletes for each event. He explained, 'My view is that entries should be limited to one per nation, with an option of two more, provided they reach a strict standard.'

Two years later the IAAF still hadn't seen sense, so Harold tried again. He explained, 'In 1956 we proposed – I did most of the advocacy – that the Olympics had become so large that there should be what was called a qualifying standard and which is now rightly called an entry standard.'

The IAAF procrastinated and delayed. 'Still no progress,' Abrahams complained in 1958. But Harold remained the driving force for sensible change, and in the summer of 1959 he was able to announce on radio, 'We've got to the stage now with over ninety countries in the Olympics, we must cut the number of competitors down, and what they're doing now is they're allowing one entry from each country, and two more if they reach a certain standard.' Those first standards came into effect on October 1, 1959. It had been a five-year fight but his Olympic vision had become reality.

There was another personal triumph for Abrahams at around this time, as he continued to push for sensible rule changes in athletics. The catalyst, Neil Allen recalled, was the 1958 European Championships in Stockholm, on which he reported. 'At the start of the 800 metres, they all began in a line across the track and rushed for the inside. Britain's Mike Rawson took at least two strides on the infield and then went on to win, but they disqualified him.' Harold Abrahams fought for his fellow Brit. Allen recalled, 'After a long meeting which I listened to on tip-toe outside the window, it was decided that Mike hadn't gained enough of an advantage to warrant disqualification, and that the field caused what he did, and the field had not subsequently been disadvantaged by what happened.'

So Rawson was reinstated and awarded his gold medal. But there was a widespread feeling that something had to be done in the long run in order to prevent those chaotic and potentially violent starts. Allen added, 'Harold was the man who persuaded them to change it, so that the draw for the 800 metres now takes place in lanes. It was definitely Harold who did that.' The following year the IAAF ruled that the first 300 metres of the race should be in lanes. Later that became 100 metres in major championships.

Sebastian Coe – now Lord Coe – thought he probably benefited from the new ruling:

Putting in lanes was certainly the right thing to do, because it protects people from being bundled off the track. Probably on balance, with the kind of style I had, that was a good thing for me, though I seem to remember that some of my early races were not in lanes, and personally I was never worried about mixing it in a race. Skills of self-preservation didn't play such a heavy part after the lanes came in for the start.

The lanes added to the complexity of the sport, because you have to be aware of what is going on ahead of you and behind you as you move in from the outside to the inside after the staggered start. It is the most complicated race to get right, there is nothing more demanding than the 800 metres.

Abrahams virtually wrote the IAAF rulebook, using the abiding principle of common sense over absurd technicality. He explained:

Time and again one is apt to get bogged down in words, unless one stops to inquire 'What are the rules trying to achieve?' Rules are made, not to hamper competition, but to ensure that it takes place on a fair basis. Many officials are influenced too much by the actual wording of the rules instead of trying to understand the reasons for them. They seem to think they are considering an Act of Parliament. How often is a perfectly wise rule abused by a pernickety official!

Norris McWhirter, who later became famous for his appearances on the hit television show *Record Breakers*, built on his previous tribute to explain, 'Against the stolid petty opposition of senior office-holders, both in the AAA and the IAAF, who were often athletes *manqué*, he managed by sheer force of personality – and with very few allies – to improve not only the national status of our sport but also the world status.'

Partly thanks to Harold's common sense over decades, athletics still makes for such an enjoyable and thrilling spectacle today. Roberto Quercetani pointed out, 'As a track legislator, Harold was for a long time a leading wheel in the IAAF Technical Committee, and his lucid reasoning, partly the result of his training as a lawyer, was often reflected in the rulebook.'

Harold had always possessed an innovative streak. He was equally quick to endorse others who were similarly brave enough to start something new and worthy. He did just that in 1958, when a bunch of young athletics enthusiasts formed a group known as the National Union of Track Statisticians – or NUTS for short. Mel Watman was one of the NUTS, and didn't expect an athletics legend like Harold Abrahams to befriend his group quite so readily. Watman explained, 'We were treated with suspicion, but all we wanted to do was to organise more comprehensive and accurate British ranking lists. Harold saw that and he became our first president. He was really hands on, attending all our committee meetings. With his BAAB treasurer's hat on, he also managed to finance some of our publications.'

'NUTS' was a British version of a like-minded international group called the Association of Track and Field Statisticians. Harold became a founder member of that too, after the idea for the ATFS was first mooted in a Brussels cafe in 1950. His standing as a pioneer track-statistician was reflected when he was appointed the ATFS's first Honorary President. No wonder he became known generally as the Father of Modern Statisticians.

Abrahams loved figures. Numbers were wonderful; numbers brought order to a chaotic world. You could show off using them; he couldn't get enough of them. But the older and more eccentric he grew, the more obsessive he became, until his love affair with numbers bordered on an illness. Harold was almost defensive about his preoccupation with statistics. 'Well, they don't mean a lot to me emotionally,' he once said. 'It is a bit of a narcotic, this record business. When I'm tired and depressed, and quite frankly I'm not often tired and depressed, I find it helps to do a sort of mechanical thing.'

It was an asset to his athletics broadcasting, particularly in an Olympic year, when he would prepare a list of the best performances of British athletes ever in the Games. 'It delights me to be able to throw away a line and then for people to say, "Good Lord, how did he know that, doesn't he know his athletics well?" One's got it all in front of one.'

Harold's obsessions with time, distance, speed – and just about anything quantifiable – had begun in his childhood. There was the compulsion to jump further than his age; then there was an account Abrahams gave of his voyage to the USA while at university. He wrote, 'The journey took six days, nine hours and 48 minutes. The most we ever went in one day was 542 miles, the least 454 miles. The average speed was about 24 miles per hour.'

This was before he became immersed in the science of athletics, which he studied carefully with Sam Mussabini. The number of strides, the length of stride, maximum speed and the time it took to reach maximum speed . . . numbers were everything and it stayed that way. In 1935 he described statistics as 'my pet lunacy'. He collated them during the war at his Ministry; he carried on in peacetime.

People were baffled as Harold took his love of statistics into the wider world. Instead of telling one astonished interviewer about the highlights of a round-the-world trip he had just completed with Sybil, Harold revealed, 'The last lap from New York yesterday took nine hours, 23 minutes, 57 seconds. I took all the timings from take-off to landing – throughout the 45 days of the trip. And we've done 21,900 miles in the air, 77 hours and 49 minutes, 49 seconds.'

'I'm afraid he is maddening!' admitted Sybil, perhaps only half-joking. Harold freely admitted to his addiction:

> I time almost everything. Speeches at dinners, going upstairs, overs at a Test Match, the number of rallies at Wimbledon. It amuses me, but I think there's more than that in it. I once handed my stopwatch to a dentist, when I was going to have my tooth out, and I said, 'Would you mind?' Because I had tried to time having a tooth out before from start to finish and I had unfortunately gone under before I could. And this time he did it and when I woke up I asked how long it had taken, and he said, 'Four minutes and eight seconds', and I said, 'Oh, world record!' I think again this is a pattern. The statistics are solid and unemotional.

Rosemary Warne admitted, 'I did find the timekeeping thing infuriating. It did used to jar on me at times, when I found it unnecessary. It was all part of his psyche; the obsession of time was just part of him. I remember him saying, "I just did a minute pee," and I thought, "So what?" I thought. "You're getting a bit desperate if you're timing that."'

Rosemary and Harold's nephew Tony agreed that nine months of time-intensive work with Sam Mussabini might have left lasting scars on Harold. 'Could be,' said Tony. 'He was obsessed with time. He always wore two watches – one stopwatch. He timed going to the loo and going out for a walk.'

He would infuriate people by taking off his watch and putting it in front of them, especially if he suspected they were going to be long-winded. Then he would punish them with statistics afterwards. Tony recalled, 'Some politician made a speech which went on and on. "Do you know how long you spoke for?" demanded an irritated Harold. "About five minutes," came the reply. "You spoke for the amount of time it took Zatopek to win the 10,000 metres," Harold told him.'

Abrahams also became obsessive about the precise location of tube exits on platforms. Tony recalled, 'He wrote something to show which carriage stopped opposite the exit at any station he used from Edgware to Morden or Camden Town. It's all detail. In sprinting, time is all detail.' Some might say these were further symptoms of a form of post-traumatic stress, after all his painstaking preparations as an athlete and the mental anguish on race days. By the time he stopped running, he had almost tried to turn himself into a machine. Therefore there were bound to be repercussions, and sometimes he sounded like an overloaded computer.

One letter he sent read as follows:

Dear Sir,

I am rather puzzled by the interesting advertisement in yesterday's *Sunday Times* Magazine. The statement is that in the Rowing Eights over 2,000 metres, the win was by 7/100ths second, which represents three centimetres.

My calculations might of course be wrong, but I make the position as follows:

Olympic record for Eights over 2,000 metres 5 min 45.02sec.

In 345 seconds boat travels 2,000 metres.

In one second boat travels 5.797 metres.

In 1/100 second say 5.8 centimetres.

In 7/100 40.6 centimetres.

Please, am I wrong?

Yours faithfully,

HAROLD M. ABRAHAMS

It was typical Harold. Maddening, pedantic, usually right. And he stayed sane in spite of his obsession, because he loved people. He loved athletes and wanted them to help him unite the world in a common love of the sport, and not become poisoned by money. He was an idealist; he saw athletics as a wonderful agent for peace and harmony. He had a vision for an Olympic medal ceremony that would prevent countries from using his beloved Games as a vehicle for nationalism. He wanted the Olympic theme played instead of the national anthem, and the Olympic flag flown above that of the winning country. The gold medal winner would be introduced as 'Your Olympic Champion' and his nationality mentioned only coincidentally. If thirty-six different countries won a medal each, that was Harold's idea of Utopia.

Later in his life, Harold went even further. He said, 'I would arrange that different events took place in different cities – possibly in the same country but perhaps even in different countries.'

It almost sounded like John Lennon imagining there were no countries – it isn't hard to do. Harold added:

> I believe that any common experience that can be shared, which doesn't depend on nationality or language or anything else, is something to be encouraged. I mean the obvious thing to speak of is music. You don't bother about the nationality of a composer unless you are an expert musician; you just enjoy the music. And I would like to feel that one can enjoy the athletic performance of a great athlete not thinking about where he is from. I don't think that one thought during a race that Nurmi was a Finn.

The concept transcended the accepted principles of international sport. It was way ahead of its time. And yet he had an eye on history too. 'I feel that the important thing is not so much to win as to take part. This is the ideal behind the Olympics, and is still common sense.' It wasn't the ideal he had followed in 1924. But now Abrahams was older and wiser. Was there anything wrong in that?

Whether he was looking at the rulebook, statistics, the past or the future, it was his love of the sport and the world athletics community that gave Harold Abrahams such energy. His influence was founded on that love, and he gave more to athletics than he received. Considering the way he protected and resurrected the Olympic movement at various critical moments in its history, you could argue that there has never been a greater British Olympian.

'He is right up there,' said Lord Coe. 'Certainly up there.'

CHAPTER SIX

TRAGEDY STRIKES

Harold Abrahams had to absorb some terrible body blows as he fought his battles for the soul of athletics. One twist of fate was so cruel that many men would never have recovered.

It was hard enough that Harold faced the 1960s without his favourite brother, Sidney Solomon – S.S. – Abrahams. When Solly died in 1957, Philip Noel-Baker, who had been an Olympic colleague to both brothers in his time, best summed up the loss. He wrote to Harold, 'He will be deeply missed; and to you to whom he was an immensely successful track-mentor who started your really great career, as well as a very devoted and admiring brother, it will be a most poignant break.'

Christina McLeod Innes – Christina Morley as she now was – knew it too. She wrote to Harold from the Quaker village of Jordans, Buckinghamshire, on May 15, 1957, to offer her condolences.

'I do want to tell you how sorry I am to hear of your brother's death. He had of course a very distinguished career, and must have been a remarkably able man . . . I have an idea he was a favourite of yours: and I do sympathise with you in this loss.'

After recalling with affection Solly's visit to her parents' house in Cambridge during their university days, Christina added, 'Please give my love to Sybil: I do wish you and she would find some reason to come in this direction occasionally – It would be so very nice to see you, but somehow it is a rather tiresome journey between your part of the world and ours. With love, Yours ever, Christina P.S. What an inadequate letter; but you will know how truly sorry I am and only wish I could express it better.'

Though Harold doubtless appreciated the letter, visits to Christina's house with his wife Sybil remained few and far between. Harold's daughter Sue thought she knew why. 'I had been to Christina's with my mother before. I remember going there because Jordans was quite near where I went to school. But I would have thought Mum was a bit overpowered by Christina's intellectuality, and a bit nervous of her. That's just my feeling. Sybil was softer than Christina.'

The other reason why Harold and Sybil rarely visited Christina during this period was that he barely had a spare minute in his average day, let alone a spare day in his average week. As *Desert Island Discs* presenter Roy Plomley had pointed out at the end of the fifties, 'I know that you're also a J.P. [Justice of the Peace] in your town, and I don't know how you find time for all these activities?' Harold replied, 'I don't do any of them as well as I should like, but I have found in life that if only people would let alone, one's got plenty of time to do lots of things.'

Harold didn't want to be 'let alone' too much, because above all he loved doing things with Sybil. He would help out in any of her dramatic productions if invited to do so. He would meet each artistic challenge as best he could, given his lack of natural talent. Abrahams freely admitted that his enthusiasm far surpassed his ability. 'I love Gilbert and Sullivan. My wife was in D'Oyly Carte; I've taken part in amateur productions. Not leading parts, unless you call the Executioner in the *Yeoman* a leading part. I was jolly good as the Executioner – I brought the axe down exactly at the right moment on the right note. I took the part of Mr Bunthorne's solicitor, and I sing in choruses. I never know quite what my voice is, nor does anybody else, and I dropped a fan at the critical moment in *The Mikado*.'

His own musical limitations helped Harold to appreciate his wife's talent even more. On *Desert Island Discs* he complained to Roy Plomley, 'Well, you told me I would be unable to take a record of my wife singing. I should love to have done that. [But] I accept that and I'd therefore like to take a record of somebody singing a song which she herself sings so beautifully, and which I'd like to be reminded about. It's the "Eriskay Love Lilt" and I've chosen the record sung by Lois Marshall.'

The last thing Harold wanted was to be without Sybil; especially after they had worked so hard to conquer his demons in the mid-1930s. That personal victory had won them many years of happiness.

By the early 1960s Harold and Sybil were friends to the stars, too. He had been a member of the famous Garrick Club in London since 1953. Acting friends he made there had helped create a link between Harold's world and theirs by forming the Film Industry Sports Association. During his turn on the *Desert Island Discs* programme, Abrahams was able to say, 'I've chosen Stanley Holloway, who I'm proud to number amongst my friends, singing "A Little Bit of Luck" [from *My Fair Lady*].' His daughter Sue Pottle also recalled, 'Harold was also friends with Norman Wisdom – he came to White City sometimes. Sybil would get people like Diana Dors to come and open fetes. He knew the footballer Billy Wright, and his singer girlfriend Joy Beverley [the Posh and Becks of their day] too.'

It was a lovely life and Harold lived it to the full. His nephew Tony Abrahams remembered one strange occasion at the Garrick Club, where the rule was that you had to converse with your neighbour at the dining table. Some, Tony recalled, made more effort than others:

> Harold was with Alec Guinness and me. Sitting next to us was an old chap, a master in lunacy at the High Court. Harold was asking Guinness which film he most enjoyed playing in and Guinness thought for a moment and said, '*Kind Hearts and Coronets* because I played several members of the same family, including one woman.' At this point the dear old thing on his right, who was taking his soup, looked up and said, 'Are you a civil servant?' and Guinness said, 'No, I'm not actually.' The chap just went back to his soup. He had respected the rules.

But no famous acquaintance meant as much to Harold as Sybil, the woman who had made him complete at a time when meaningful relationships had seemed way beyond him. By the time they celebrated their 25th wedding anniversary in late 1961, they had taken to calling each other 'Mr and Mrs Punk' – a daft but endearing family nickname. Harold recorded a mock radio broadcast to mark the anniversary. There was a drum-roll, and then the pips you normally heard before the top of the hour, the news headlines or a major announcement. Harold's voice was heard next, playing the role of an excited broadcaster battling to keep his tone within the confines of BBC formality:

'This is the BBC Home Service. Here is the news. Today, Friday December 22, is the 25th anniversary of the wedding of Mr and Mrs Punk.' The announcement was accompanied by a fanfare of trumpets playing 'The Wedding March'. Then he went on, 'We offer them our affectionate greetings on this historic occasion. We should like particularly to congratulate Mrs Punk on her remarkable tolerance and stamina. For 9,131 days, she tolerated Mr Punk. For 219,144 hours, or if you preferred it, 78, 891,830 seconds, she's put up with all his faults. Mr Punk has asked us to say – without prejudice – that he's a jolly lucky chap. Hail, Punks!' The broadcast ended with a further trumpet fanfare.

There were those statistics again, the ones Sybil found so maddening. It was hardly the most romantically worded tribute ever composed by a husband to his long-suffering wife. Yet the message was brilliantly delivered and still sounds funny even today. It was full of love and driven by a frivolity worthy of a man forty years younger. Sybil had to love him for that. And everyone knew just how lucky Harold was to be loved by her.

Then, in the summer of 1963, tragedy struck. Sybil thought she was suffering from mild food poisoning, and in a telephone conversation with her daughter Sue she put her 'tummy upset' down to a meal they had eaten in a local restaurant together the previous day. What had really happened was that a poisonous virus from garden manure had entered her bloodstream. The doctors later said there was nothing they could have done to save her by that stage, even if they had known the precise nature of the problem.

Bravely, Sybil got up the next day to fulfil her obligations. It was mid-June and she was producing the local village play – A *Midsummer Night's Dream*. Her son Alan remembered painfully, 'I was there. It was extraordinary; we were in "Vicarage Garden" in Great Amwell. They had been rehearsing something in the church. We were having drinks, almost a cocktail party kind of thing, and it was very dramatic. She keeled over, fell to the ground and that was it. She had something. I don't know what it was. My mother's death had a devastating impact on my father.'

As Harold had said on *Desert Island Discs*, 'I don't like my own company very much. In fact whenever I am alone I indulge in athletics statistics, so that I'm not at all happy at the prospect of you marooning me.'

But Sybil's death had indeed marooned Harold, and in some ways he never recovered. All his life he had feared putting 'all his eggs in one basket' in case he lost the thing he loved most. He thought that someone had probably taken something away from him as a child, something he liked very much; and that his fears had spun out of control from there. Now someone – perhaps God – had taken Sybil away; and it left him feeling afraid and childlike all over again.

Harold had expected more time with Sybil. As their adopted daughter Sue put it, 'They had twenty-nine years together in all, which many people these days would regard as a long time. But in those days most marriages lasted even longer, and their time was cut short. It is a long time if you look at marriages that have broken down, but if you look at marriages that haven't broken down then it isn't, because a lot of them go on for fifty or sixty years.'

Harold knew that to be alone would destroy him. Norris McWhirter later revealed that Sybil's loss 'tested his fortitude to the uttermost'. Tony Abrahams helped Harold emotionally and practically in his hour of need, just as Harold had helped him after the horrors of war. Tony explained, 'After Sybil's death he came to live with us for a while on the top floor of the Goldsmith Building in Temple, central London.'

In a relatively short space of time, Harold did feel he could carry on – perhaps because he felt he had to for his own well-being. He returned to what remained of his normal world as quickly as possible, hoping to fill his days with his only other true love – athletics. Tony added, 'In the Temple he did a lot of work on his statistics in the library in the year after Sybil died.' Numbers were a numbing, neutral comfort – just as they had always been.

What didn't provide comfort at a most sensitive time were structural changes at the National Parks Commission. These signalled the end of Harold's career there after thirteen happy years, because he had reached retirement age. One distressed colleague wrote to Harold and said, 'In many ways you WERE the National Parks Commission.' He wasn't any more. And for lesser men, that would have been the final straw. For Abrahams, at least there was still athletics.

The one ray of light on the horizon was the fact that the following year was an Olympic year. As competition for places in the Great Britain athletics team increased, competition at the highest level of British athletics administration fell away. Age was therefore no barrier to Harold's pre-eminence.

The *Daily Telegraph* of November 30, 1963 carried the following story:

Abrahams is ready to take charge.

Officials retire next year.

The mantle of 'Mr Athletics', which has rested since the end of the war on the shoulders of Mr Jack Crump, 58, secretary of the British Board, looks destined to fall not on Mr Arthur Gold, 46, his successor, not on a younger man, but on Mr Harold Abrahams, treasurer of the British Board, who is 63 . . . After two serious operations he cannot, though, be considered from a long-term point of view . . . It is a pity that no really outstanding young personalities are coming into athletics officialdom.

Perhaps so, but Harold Abrahams still had at least as much energy to put into athletics administration as any younger man – perhaps more. The sport could save him after his bereavement, just as it had always saved him.

The Tokyo Olympics of 1964 brought Harold closer to joy than he had been for a year, because a British protégé of his struck gold. He had watched Lynn Davies jump 25 feet – the barrier Harold was never able to smash – when the young Welshman had competed as a youngster in Brighton. Davies, the man Harold described as 'Britain's finest long-jumper ever', took the Olympic title in Japan with a leap of 26ft 5¾in. A few years later, Lynn wrote to Harold acknowledging his contribution. Davies wrote, 'As one long-jumper of bygone years to another, may I thank you for your help and encouragement during the last decade.'

Abrahams sounded euphoric after Tokyo. He said, 'This has been the finest Games ever in every way. The superlative character of the arrangements rather terrifies me. I don't see how any country in the future can possibly live up to the standard which has been achieved here.' Later he added, without a hint of prejudice, 'Tokyo was the best organised Games with Berlin '36 a close second. The Tokyo Games were much more human because the Nazis were trying to prove their regime during the 1936 Games.'

The 1936 Games would always be a reminder of a time when Harold and Sybil had been trying to prove they could make it as a couple, their future in the balance. Now Sybil was gone; but Harold was determined not to let her memory die. Each year from 1964 the Duke of Edinburgh, President of the British Amateur Athletic Board, kindly agreed to present a cup called The Sybil Abrahams Memorial Trophy to the best British woman athlete at Buckingham Palace.

The first winner of Sybil's cup was Mary Rand, who also won long-jump gold at those Tokyo Olympics, silver in the pentathlon and bronze in the 4 × 100 metres. Would Rand have been able to achieve such stunning Olympic success had Harold not championed women's rights in athletics during the late 1950s, and helped broaden the range of events open to women at the Games? Probably not.

Meanwhile Harold set up a trust so that another award could be created, something closer to his wife's heart: the Sybil Abrahams Memorial Prize for Singing. It was a cash prize awarded to the best female singer in her last year at the Webber Douglas School of Singing and Dramatic Art. The prize was first awarded in 1965; and the practice continued all the way through to 1995. Every year for the rest of his life, Harold went to see a production of A *Midsummer Night's Dream* at the Open Air Theatre in London's Regent's Park. It was one of the places where she had most enjoyed performing, and of course the production was a poignant reminder of how she had died.

As one love affair came to a tragic close, another was about to begin. This time it was the turn of Harold's daughter Sue to become smitten; and the consequences on his life are hard to quantify even today.

Think of Harold Abrahams and you think of *Chariots of Fire*, or at least athletics. Few people think of an infamous spy called George Blake, a double agent who may have sent more than forty British agents to their deaths. Yet Harold's son-in-law helped Blake to escape from prison in Britain and live a long and happy life in Russia. Amazingly, Abrahams never knew about it. But others did, and Harold's chances of a knighthood were not helped by a chain of events so extraordinary that they almost defy belief.

Back in 1962, two peace campaigners – Pat Pottle and Michael Randle – had befriended Blake while they too were serving time. They had been imprisoned for conspiracy, following the occupation of an American air base at Wethersfield, Essex, by supporters of a group called 'The Committee of 100', a breakaway organisation with previous affiliations to the Campaign for Nuclear Disarmament (CND). Pottle and Randle believed Blake's forty-two-year jail sentence to be outrageous and inhumane. Even if the spy had betrayed forty-two British agents, they reasoned that he had been politically motivated. After all, the British Secret Service was trying to infiltrate rival spy-rings by turning enemy agents into double agents. So what right did they have to doom a Communist to forty-two years simply for doing his job better than they had? Pottle asked Blake if he had ever thought of escaping. The spy admitted that the idea had crossed his mind many times. 'Well, if you can think of any way I can help you get out, let me know,' said Pat.

Once Pottle was released, he proved as good as his word in helping Blake to lasting freedom. It was October 1966 when an Irish criminal called Sean Bourke broke Blake's fall as he escaped over the wall of Wormwood Scrubs prison using a rope ladder. Though the success of the escape itself sounded fantastically unlikely, the chances of Blake remaining at liberty were even more remote. He would need friends who were as cool and careful as Bourke had been courageous and outrageous.

Pottle did most to hide Blake when the heat was really on. He housed the fugitive in his own home while MI5, MI6 and Scotland Yard mounted one of the greatest manhunts of all time. Holding his nerve, Pottle defied them all, before Randle hid Blake in a secret compartment in a camper van, and drove the spy to the safety of East Germany. Blake soon made it on to Russia, where he remained beyond the clutches of the British authorities. However, the well-meaning Pottle and Randle were still vulnerable as they resumed their normal lives back in London. Only a handful of people had known the part they had played in Blake's escape at the time; and Sue Abrahams wasn't one of them.

She recalled, 'When I first met Pat, it may actually have been at the time of the escape; but we didn't really get to know each other and he certainly didn't talk about that. I was going out with someone else, or I was on the back of someone else's scooter, anyhow. Pat and I met properly at a dinner party in March 1967. I didn't know about the escape at the time, and I had nothing to do with it, though some people have tried to claim since that I helped to finance the escape. It isn't true.'

Sue would soon know some of the details, though. Pottle was an intensely charming and witty man, with beautiful blue eyes. One thing led to another at that dinner party, and Pat and Sue became lovers. Within weeks, Pat confided to Sue the part he and Randle had played in George Blake's escape. Sue would never forget the moment. 'I was a bit flabbergasted. Amazed. Struck dumb. But I thought it was quite an admirable thing to do. I thought the sentence George had got was totally wrong. So I was amazed and also rather proud, really, that I knew these two gents, Pat and Michael. But if Pat and I had already been married with a couple of children, I would have been very worried.'

They did marry – within months. 'We married on June 30, 1967,' explained Sue. 'Arthur Gold, Harold's boss on the British Amateur Athletics Board, sent me a baby-weighing scales and a baby photo book. As far as he was concerned, we couldn't possibly be getting married for any other reason. Casper, my eldest son, arrived in April 1970 so it was a long gestation period!'

When Harold walked his daughter down the aisle to where Pat Pottle was waiting, he didn't know that he was welcoming into the famous Abrahams family, the man who helped to spring George Blake.

CHAPTER SEVEN

MEDALS

'Harold had absolutely no inkling of what Pat had done,' insisted Sue. 'I don't think he ever knew. Pat wouldn't have told him. I certainly didn't tell him. I can think of no one else who would have told him. Pat told Alan but I'm sure Alan wouldn't have told Dad. Alan confirmed, 'Pat Pottle was quite a character and my father liked him, but he didn't know Pat had sprung George Blake, even though Pat's politics were well known. Pottle told me about springing Blake, he told me the whole story. It sounded incredible but it happened. Harold possibly wouldn't have known.'

Sue wondered how Harold Abrahams, famous ex-athlete and establishment figure, would have reacted, had he known the truth about his son-in-law. 'Harold liked Pat, he liked his spirit and Pat was witty, a good conversationalist with good humour at the dinner table. He could talk to Dad. My father liked someone to talk to and they talked about all kinds of things. Harold would definitely not have approved of springing Blake, even though he probably thought the sentence was too severe.

'Had Harold found out that his son-in-law had sprung Blake, would he have turned Pat over to the authorities? He might have gone to Pat and said, "Look, perhaps you ought to turn yourself in," especially if he had found out before we had children. But with the children? I don't think my father himself would have gone to the authorities. He might just have kept the secret. I think he would have been interested and amazed by how they did it.'

As those closest to him continued to pass away – his 84-year-old brother Adolphe died on December 11, 1967 – Harold enjoyed the addition of Pottle's sparkling intellect to family occasions. Had Harold known the link between Pat and George Blake, however, he surely wouldn't have involved his son-in-law in his beloved world of athletics – not even indirectly. Tony Abrahams explained, 'Pat had a printing business and Harold arranged for all the AAA's printing to be done by his firm. He rather liked Pat Pottle, who was a gentle person. He didn't approve of all his views. He didn't think he was a Communist, he thought he was an Anarchist. But he thought Pat's printing was good and he was always polite and interesting. He used to refer to him as "Pottle Printer" to me.'

So Pottle's company was sometimes a comfort – at a time when past sources of strength, such as the Olympic Games – were offering Harold less and less cheer. After sixty years, he had finally fallen out of love with the Olympics. In fact, Abrahams felt he had helped to create a monster.

In 1968, just before he left for the Mexico Games, Harold explained, 'I'm seventy next year, I'm setting out for the Olympics and this will be my tenth (I missed Los Angeles in 1932). It has become much more important to people since 1936 in Berlin; and then of course from 1952 onwards, television has played its part. The whole aspect of the significance of the Olympics has changed so much that I wonder whether dear old Baron De Coubertin would recognise it at all.'

Then Harold was asked if he would miss the Olympics if they didn't exist. For one who had served the movement almost all his life, Abrahams gave a poignant answer. 'Well, I think you are absolutely laying my soul bare, aren't you . . . If you said to me, "Would the world suffer if there weren't the Olympics?" the way they are going I'm not sure.'

Just as well something incredible happened at those Mexico Olympics, enough to rekindle the flame in any lover of athletics, a feat so extraordinary that it is still remembered and celebrated today. An American long-jumper called Bob Beamon had only qualified for the final with the last of three attempts. Harold could scarcely believe what he saw next:

He sailed into the stratosphere with his first jump of 8.90 metres or 29ft 2½in. In doing so he added 55 centimetres or 21¾ inches to the previous world record. He won the competition by a margin of 71 centimetres or 28 inches, easily the biggest margin ever. The long jump of Bob Beamon was almost literally 'out of this world'. As the

1964 winner of the Olympic long-jump title Lynn Davies observed: 'How can one compete against a man who goes into orbit?'

Beamon knew instantly the enormity of his achievement. He continued to bounce as he left the pit, the spring in his legs seemingly infinite. Harold felt he had watched something almost superhuman. He still remembered his astonishment when his fellow competitor Ed Gourdin had shattered the world long-jump record back in 1921, with a leap in excess of 25ft. But what he had just witnessed in Mexico was beyond belief. How could anyone jump 29ft 2½in? Beamon was only twenty-two. Talk about jumping your age in feet! Under Harold's system, the American had just given himself seven worry-free years!

On December 21 of that Olympic year, Harold gained a fitting reward for his lifelong commitment to his sport. He became Chairman of the British Amateur Athletics Board. The *Guardian* claimed that his appointment proved 'that he is almost as durable as General de Gaulle'. He was almost as prickly too. When asked how the BAAB – which was in debt at the time – proposed to pay for a certain item, Abrahams replied, 'By cheque.' He did not intend to lose a single verbal skirmish, however minor, now that he was in full control.

All seemed well in what was left of the Abrahams family too. By then the dust had settled on the Blake escape, which was widely accepted to have been the work of the KGB – the Russian Secret Service. That suited Pat Pottle just fine. Then Sean Bourke, the main organiser of the Blake escape, took it upon himself to write a book about it.

Sue Pottle recalled, 'When that book came out in 1970, I was very worried and I drove straight up to London and bought a copy.' She found that Sean had only thinly disguised the identities of his accomplices. Michael Randle's name was changed to 'Michael Reynolds' and Pat Pottle was 'Pat Porter'. One look at a list of fellow prisoners during Blake's time behind bars in England – particularly those with political motivations – would reveal their true identities. Sue Abrahams, by now Sue Pottle, said, 'The security services knew who had done it as soon as Sean's book came out. They knew who Michael Reynolds and Pat Porter were.'

But to arrest Pottle and Randle wouldn't bring Blake back – or Sean Bourke for that matter, because he had escaped to Moscow on a passport provided and altered by Pottle. Bourke had eventually flown back to Dublin, where the Irishman had been granted political asylum, and would die a few years later. To drag Blake's English accomplices through the courts now would make the authorities look very foolish indeed, since they had in essence been outwitted by a bunch of amateurs.

As Harold's son, Alan put it, 'The idea that a couple of "chancers" who had slipped off the radar had accomplished it was too embarrassing.'

Sue explained what happened next: 'The Special Branch sent a letter to MI6 or MI5 asking "do we want to prosecute the small fish when the big ones have got away?" It looked better if it seemed that the Russians had sprung Blake rather than two guys from CND. If the truth were known, it would really look a massive cock-up by the British security services and the police and prison services. I mean, everyone would have been asking how these so-called "nutters" got Blake out of the country with that lot trying to hunt them down.'

But the George Blake time bomb was ticking. The only question was whether or not it would explode in Harold's lifetime. If the scandal was linked publicly to his family, the embarrassment for Harold would have been immense. By now he wasn't just known for athletics broadcasting. He pointed out, 'I did a series of BBC programmes on the Victoria Cross, the George Cross, the Order of Merit, the Nobel Prize.' He even did the odd television show, including one with ex-miler Sydney Wooderson; but Harold never moved across to TV in a major way. It was that velvety Abrahams voice that had made him so perfect for radio. And his was now the voice of the establishment too. His son-in-law, on the other hand, represented anarchy.

It would have been easy to put such marked differences down to the generation gap, except that one of Harold's closest friends in the final years of his life was a woman almost half a century younger than he was. Abrahams first met a vivacious 23-year-old teacher called Rosemary Warne in 1969, when she picked him up at Felixstowe station as a favour to a friend. 'He is a BBC broadcaster and he lost his wife a few years ago, have you heard of him?' asked Elsie Eaton, a fellow singer in the Felixstowe Amateur Operatic Society. Rosemary admitted that she hadn't, though the gentleman who introduced himself at the station cut a striking figure. Rosemary remembered:

> This very tall, balding man – like Mr Pickwick stretched – with very bright blue eyes which seemed to sparkle. He wore a light blue shirt, bright blue blazer and similar bright blue trousers with brown shoes which I thought were most incongruous.

We had a very entertaining lunch. He was funny, a good raconteur, very amusing. I laughed a lot, I can remember, and so did Elsie and her husband Will. Harold was a very likeable, easy person. We both adored Gilbert and Sullivan, and from the age of ten I had been a member of the D'Oyly Carte Trust. I had all the magazines, and when he told me his wife had been second soprano that was it – smitten.

They developed a close but platonic relationship, and there were times when both would need a boost to their morale. In Harold's case, such a moment came in early 1970, and centred on his Olympic 100 metres gold medal. It had been mounted in a frame and surrounded by the signatures of his fellow 1924 finalists.

The *Daily Telegraph* of March 3, 1970 carried a headline: 'GOLD MEDAL STOLEN'.

'Harold Abrahams, the only British athlete to win 100 metres in an Olympic Games, has had his gold medal stolen, in a weekend raid on his London home.'

It wasn't so much a raid as an inside job. Harold's sister Dorothy had married a man who turned out to be unfaithful. He had a child by their maid, and Dorothy bravely agreed to adopt the baby. The boy was called Kim, and he turned out to be even worse than his father. He began to steal from the family whenever he could. 'At some stage "Cousin Kim" went round and stole the medal from my father's house,' said Sue Pottle. 'I think there were even fingerprints and a confession.'

'When Kim stole his gold medal Harold was very upset,' said Tony. 'Kim was already nicknamed "Convict 99" within the family because he had been convicted for other offences. Harold used to visit him when he went inside. He was always a great supporter of prisoner rehabilitation. Kim never served more than eighteen months at a time.'

On December 2, 1971, Harold was able to write to Tony, 'I expect that you may have been told that "Convict 99" was caught last week. I don't know where he has been taken. Apparently Dorothy was present at the arrest, and Kim first of all denied his identity, but there was no struggle.'

There was also no medal. It had been sold on, or perhaps worse. 'Dad always suspected that Kim had dropped it down the drain out of spite, because my father was protective of his sister Dorothy, and had shopped Kim to the police before for selling family possessions,' Sue explained. Kim was spared another conviction for the latest offence; but his story didn't end happily. Tony revealed, 'In the end he drowned himself . . . or at least he drowned. A sad business.'

The only brighter aspect to a sad story was the fact that Arthur Gold had another Olympic gold medal made for Harold, a commemorative one which was also engraved. 'He was quite pleased about the new medal,' said his daughter Sue. But of course it could never replace the original, complete with all his competitors' signatures.

Nothing seemed the same to Harold any more. The Olympic movement was hijacked horribly in 1972, when eleven Israeli athletes were murdered at the Munich Olympics. Harold felt that to abandon the Games almost before they had begun would play into the hands of those behind the atrocity. It was typical Abrahams to argue that the Olympic show must go on, however strong the opposing argument.

Back at home, the anti-Semitism which had driven Abrahams as a teenaged athlete still made an unwelcome return at times. Sue Pottle explained, 'When my father and Arthur Gold were running British athletics, they used to get anonymous letters talking about "you and your kind" and how it was all "brother to brother" among the Jews. He never knew whether it was from people within athletics who resented him, or whether it was from anti-Semitic groups.'

People were forgetting that Harold hadn't been Jewish in his thinking for half a century. Yet even friends didn't always understand. Norman Cuddeford, a co-commentator, recalled how a BBC producer called Geoff Dobson overlooked Harold for the sort of role he had been fulfilling since before the Second World War. Cuddeford explained, 'The Dobsons had a daughter born in 1968. Joan Dobson said to Harold, "We would have asked you to be godfather, but being Jewish . . ." And Harold replied, "I'm not Jewish".'

His dearest friends, such as Rosemary Warne, his trusted new confidante, and Christina, his former fiancée, weren't Jewish either. Christina's daughter, Sue Smithson recalled a very happy reunion at around this time. 'Harold came to my parents' house in the early Seventies and my son Robert would have been about ten. He was running around the garden and Harold was there with his stopwatch, timing him. He gave Robert a medal. He said he would rather give them to someone than to have them stolen.'

Robert still had that medal in 2010. Inscribed on the front, alongside the American and British flags and a runner, were the following words: 'OXFORD-CAMBRIDGE-PRINCETON-CORNELL'. On the back was written: 'TRACK AND FIELD MEET JULY 28, 1921 – TRAVERS ISLAND, USA'. And then there was the following inscription: 'Run Broad Jump Winner H.M. Abrahams CAMBRIDGE 21ft 8in'.[1]

Was it really just a coincidence that Harold had chosen to give Robert, an Anglo-American by birth, this particular medal rather than any other? Was it by chance that he selected a medal which he won at the very height of his romance with Robert's grandmother Christina, when they were engaged to be married? Perhaps. Whatever the truth, it was a poignant moment.

Not that Christina and Harold were spending much time looking back. They didn't really regard themselves as old at all, and they were still looking forward to the future. Sue Smithson revealed, 'My mother had gone out on her seventieth birthday and bought herself a bicycle.' She still enjoyed cycling, just as she had done half a century earlier, when she had acted as Harold's pacemaker. As for Harold, he still had more than enough energy to remain an important figurehead in the increasingly turbulent world of athletics.

Seb Coe still remembers meeting him as an up-and-coming middle-distance runner. He said, 'I did receive an award from him at one of the junior races at Crystal Palace. There was no mistaking you were in the presence of a very serious player in the sport. We knew and he knew who was in charge. I can remember that people were familiar with his story, were aware of being in the presence of someone quite extraordinary in the sport.'

In January 1974, a broadcaster called Jim Manning wrote to Harold to tell him, 'I mentioned you [on *Sports Report*] and said that in my view you had done more than anyone to popularise athletics. I did not have time to add that you have been given little gratitude by those who earn a living from athletics – either the competitors themselves or some of my colleagues.'

Abrahams still did the odd turn on BBC Radio, and thus completed an extraordinary fifty years in broadcasting. 'I'm not sure that there is anyone else who has worked quite that long for the BBC,' he remarked with understandable satisfaction. And there was soon another half-century to celebrate; his first love, Christina, was about to mark fifty years of marriage to Frank Morley.

[1]'Run Broad Jump' stood for 'Running Broad Jump', since not long before, athletes did standing broad jumps – to see how far you could jump without a run-up.

Rosemary recalled, 'Harold did mention Christina, and I think he mentioned her as an "an old love", and that he was very much looking forward to going to the fiftieth wedding anniversary of "dear old friends" and that he gave Christina a medal. It was a warm feeling that he was expressing.'

Frank and Christina returned that warmth, and their daughter Sue remembered some of the good-natured banter. 'Harold and Christina; it was always a family joke – "You might not have been here. You might have been Harold's daughter." Both my parents used to say that. Everybody was very relaxed about it and there was never any awkwardness.'

In that same summer of 1975, another social gathering required Harold to play a major role. The McWhirter twins, Norris and Ross – of *Guinness Book of Records* and *Record-Breakers* fame – had lived for half a century. Harold was called upon to give a witty speech to mark the occasion. Norris wrote to Harold with thanks for the part he had played.

'This is to try to express our appreciation to you for so characteristically contributing the high point of the evening at our celebratory party. We have always thought that the principle that people are the greatest experts on themselves held good but in this case we never knew what was coming next – that was not research, it was quarrying!'

It was the last birthday celebration the twins would enjoy together. On November 27, 1975, Ross McWhirter was murdered on his doorstep by two members of the Provisional IRA. Ross had offered a reward for information leading to the arrest of those responsible for recent bombings in London. His killers were members of the Balcombe Street Gang who were responsible for the bombings.

As much as he could do so, Harold helped the surviving twin, Norris, to cope with his loss. Abrahams was in his mid-seventies, but was living a life in which he never quite knew what was going to happen next.

CHAPTER EIGHT

TALKING MOVIES

Rosemary Warne was ushered into a corner of the Garrick Club and told to keep a wonderful secret. She recalled:

> Jack Willis, a judge, took me aside and said, 'You might be pleased to hear that a number of people have got together of importance and they are putting Harold up for a knighthood but you are not to tell him, he is not to know, but watch out.'
>
> I think he would have loved a knighthood. And he would have loved it a little bit more had Sybil been alive. I think it would have been the icing on the cake. He would have been thrilled that people thought enough of him to have given him that honour. Then nothing happened and one felt very sad and you couldn't say to him, 'You haven't got a knighthood.' I think it was a great shame that didn't happen.

There are many possible reasons why Harold didn't receive the knighthood two of his brothers were awarded. First of all he may have been perceived to be on the wrong side of the political fence. This was 1976, the year of Prime Minister Harold Wilson's so-called 'Resignation Honours'. Abrahams was known to be against the isolation of South Africa, despite the evils of apartheid. Indeed he had welcomed South African athletics officials to London the previous May, the month he stepped down as Chairman of the British Amateur Athletic Board, having accepted the first Life Vice-Presidency in the history of the Board.

The thorny issue of South Africa's participation in world sport would dominate the headlines again in the summer of 1976 – at the Olympics in Montreal. Perhaps Harold Wilson foresaw this. When the time came to debate the South Africa question at the 1976 IAAF Congress, only Harold stood up to be counted as a friend of the country where so many of his relatives still lived. A newspaper report revealed: 'Harold Abrahams of Great Britain, the only delegate to speak in support of continued South African membership, said he opposes apartheid but did not believe expulsion would improve the situation. "If you want to change the laws of South Africa, certainly you will not do it if you isolate South Africa. What good would you be to the coloured athletes in South Africa by excluding them from international competition?"'

Many would argue that history proved Abrahams wrong. But he loved athletics too much to approve of it being used for anything – even a wider good. And it is far easier to dismiss Harold's argument with the benefit of hindsight. Harold's view was quite widely held; there were 145 votes against South Africa's expulsion, defeated by 227 votes in favour. So 144 voices stayed silent; presumably because they could see which way the wind was blowing. Harold saw no reason to follow suit, because he was presenting a reasoned argument. And anyone who tried to accuse Abrahams of racism would be laughed out of the room. His friendship with Jesse Owens and his great respect for an early black British sprinter such as Harry Edward were well documented.

Feelings were running high when the Olympic Games started on July 17. By the following day they were almost in tatters. Around thirty African and Arab countries had walked away in protest at the IOC's failure to take action against New Zealand, who were playing rugby against South Africa at the time. Abrahams was disgusted and reflected later, 'I have often wondered whether Baron Coubertin would ever have started the modern Olympics, if he would have seen just exactly how they would develop. In the past fifty-six years I have been to twelve Olympics and I have watched with increasing sadness and concern the effect of Nationalism, professionalism, political interference and commercialism.'

But it was the politicians who decided on the knighthoods. And the Wilson Government may have thought that any honour due Abrahams was better delayed indefinitely; especially if they had been briefed about the Blake escape. Did the security services already know about the family link to Pat Pottle? Almost certainly; they had read Sean Bourke's book along with everyone else. And once they realised that 'Pat Porter' was Pat

Pottle, it would only take five minutes to check the culprit's family background.

Sue Pottle admitted:

> It has crossed my mind that when they put any proposed knighthood through whatever channel it has to go through – to be OK'd or vetoed – perhaps the security services were aware of that connection, and thought it might come out at some stage, so they vetoed it. It may have been that, I hope not.
>
> I've always thought that it was something else that affected his knighthood. I'd like to think it was something else, anyhow, because he would have liked his knighthood. He did say he would have liked it for Mum. Sybil would have liked to be Lady Abrahams. I think he would have quite liked to be Sir Harold too; of course he would. It would have put him on equal footing with his brothers.

Rosemary Warne didn't rule out the possible negative effect the Blake escape may have had when the establishment were considering Harold for a knighthood. 'It may have been affected by the family association with the George Blake affair. That, however, would seem unfair, as Harold, as an individual, was a man of such rectitude. It would have been extremely unlucky if he had been the victim of the resultant fall-out. I suppose if there was enough smear going on behind the scenes, it might have dented his chances. Or there may have been someone in an influential position who didn't approve of him.'

Tony Abrahams believed that Harold had enemies in high places – but not because of Blake. 'There was an element in certain parts of the establishment – I understood from my father – that found him a bit cocky. And I think the other element was the fact that they thought, "Well, he has got a CBE, he can mix it up with athletics."' Being awarded a CBE didn't stop Sir Stanley Matthews from being knighted, though.

In his book, *British Olympians*, Ian Buchanan pointed out, 'Abrahams was not universally popular within the sport and his sometimes brusque manner became rather more pronounced in his later years, but many people can bear witness to the gentler and more generous side of his character. Somewhere within the differing aspects of his personality probably lies the answer to the question as to why he never received any official recognition for the enormous amount of voluntary work he undertook on behalf of the sport.'

It was a shame, because there is no doubt that Harold valued recognition. When living legends were invited to give away medals to the winning athletes at Crystal Palace one summer's day in 1976, Abrahams was hurt by his treatment. He received no proper introduction to the crowd, and the organisers saw fit to have him present the medals for hammer-throwing, instead of the 100 metres which had preceded it. Harold was understandably grumpy when he tape-recorded a message for Rosemary, who had joined the army and was often away. 'To be asked to give away the "Hammer", when before that was the 100 metres! I would have liked the crowd to know – ninety per cent of them had never heard of me – that this bald old bugger had won a gold medal fifty-two years ago.'

But some recognition for his efforts came Harold's way after all. In November 1976, Harold was made only the sixth President of the Amateur Athletics Association since it began in 1880. After a lifetime's service to the sport, Harold followed in the footsteps of such illustrious names as the Earl of Jersey, Viscount Alverstone, Sir Montague Shearman, Lord Desborough and his friend the Marquess of Exeter, whose presidency had lasted some forty years. 'This is certainly one of the proudest moments of my life,' he said. 'To have been elected President of one of the oldest athletic associations in the world is a great honour – thank you very much.'

Sybil was no longer around to enjoy Harold's proud moment, but at least Christina was. And she saw him for the last time in 1977. Early in June, Harold made simple reference to this meeting in a taped message to Rosemary, who was in Germany. 'I think you know I'm going to see Christina for the day,' he said in a matter-of-fact way.

There was plenty to talk about, and not just Harold's AAA presidency. She would have been thrilled for him, and also excited about a forthcoming trip to Moscow and Leningrad that she had planned with her daughter Perry. Finally, she could see the place she had studied through historical books and literature more than half a century earlier at Cambridge. Remembering her enthusiasm for all things Russian, Harold must have been happy for her.

For all that, he would have loved to be able to share his old age with Sybil. Instead she had been dead for fourteen years. He continued to visit her final resting place, marking each anniversary of her death. Abrahams recorded a message that summer to Rosemary, describing his feelings about these journeys back to Great Amwell:

> I went in the afternoon to visit Sybil's grave. It's funny because in a sense one doesn't know why one does it, because it isn't the only day of the year one thinks about Sybil. I think one rather has the feeling that she may know one's doing it, although that doesn't at all agree with my feeling that when one's dead, one's dead. It's a weird thing, you can't really contemplate extinction, and in a way nothing in this world can be destroyed, it merely changes its form. But I like to go out there in some ways and I took some flowers from the garden and I like to think that perhaps she knows one's doing it, but of course it isn't the only time of the year I think about her.

These words prove once and for all that Harold did not have the rock-solid faith of a man who had supposedly converted to Christianity from Judaism. Sue told me, 'In his last years Harold told me he believed that in the end you go back to being what you were. He said that he thought that when we die, we very likely go back to our original religion, or words to that effect.'

But the truth was that Harold Abrahams was neither a committed Christian nor Jew in the second half of his life. If he firmly believed in anything, it was that he didn't want religion to restrict him in life. He never had let it. At best he was a 'hoper' for an afterlife. And he wouldn't have to wonder about such issues for much longer. Within eight months, his remains would join those of the greatest love of his life in that same graveyard.

At Crystal Palace on July 22, 1977, it was Harold's duty and pleasure as President of the Amateur Athletic Association to read out the following royal message: 'I have been asked to convey to all the athletes and officials of the A.A.A. the warm thanks of the Queen for their kind and loyal message of Silver Jubilee greetings, which Her Majesty much appreciates. As patron of the Association, the Queen sends her best wishes for the success of the Nationwide Building Society Silver Jubilee A.A.A. Championships to all those taking part in them.'

It was a grand way to leave the public arena, sixty-seven summers after his first appearance on one of the great stages of English athletics, at Stamford Bridge as a 10-year-old. But he would dearly have loved to see three more summers, so that he could lead the celebrations for the AAA Centenary in 1980. He had plans for those celebrations. Among other things, there was to be a definitive book – which he had already begun to research with its eventual author, Peter Lovesey.

Yet Harold Abrahams had already achieved so much. Lord Coe, Chairman of the London 2012 Organising Committee, summed up his admiration for Abrahams and all he gave athletics with the following memorable line: 'Respect is not a strong enough word, actually.'

Behind the scenes Harold wasn't finished just yet. He was ready to fight to the death, because he had recently been made aware of 'all these payments in athletics that are pretty extensive. I'm determined to do something to curtail them if I can, because it really is getting . . .' Harold couldn't seem to find the right word because his feelings were running so high in a recorded message to Rosemary. But he vowed, 'I'm going to have a crack at it, dear, because I think it is the only way in which we shall save athletics from being a very unpleasant thing.'

Harold's worst fears regarding the abuse of the amateur rules had been confirmed when he travelled to Turin for an athletics international between Italy, England and the USA. His Italian friend, the statistician Roberto Quercetani, met him there and recalled, 'The match was degraded by the absence of many leading athletes, attracted elsewhere by more fruitful commitments. Referring to promoters who would leave nothing untried to secure the best "stuff" available for their invitational meets, Harold jokingly asked: "Do you think they would pay $15 for an Abrahams vintage '24?"'

Though he had paid Sam Mussabini, Harold had never been paid or even asked for payment. He had run to win, not for money. How times had changed. No wonder he still had affection for a bygone era. And a few weeks before Harold Abrahams died, he wrote to Brian Marchant, Mussabini's grandson. It seems probable that early research on the *Chariots of Fire* project by Colin Welland had been the catalyst for contact between Abrahams and Marchant.

Harold wrote on November 23, 1977, and expressed his gratitude towards old Sam Mussabini one last time. He sent Marchant a copy of that scarcely legible Mussabini note, sent from one Parisian hotel to another before the serious action began in that unforgettable summer of 1924. As considerate as ever, Harold added a copy of what Mussabini had written in block capitals so that Old Sam's grandson would not mistake a single word. Abrahams, of course, knew the contents of that note off by heart.

Clearly heartfelt and beautiful in its simplicity, Harold's note represented the last words he ever wrote on the most momentous time of his life.

Meanwhile Mussabini's note was so full of controlled passion that Welland used it for the movie *Chariots of Fire*. Sam's words are worth recalling here, one last time.

HOTEL FRANKLIN
RUE BOUFFAULT
PARIS

JULY 7th. 1924

DEAR MR. ABRAHAMS,

YOU MUST PLEASE PARDON MY NOT COMING TO SEE YOU, MUCH AS I WOULD LIKE TO DO SO.

HOWEVER - I BELIEVE AND HOP YOU WILL WIN THE 100 METRES.

GO OUT DETERMINED TO DO YOUR BEST AND DON'T FORGET TO GO DOWN AT THE FIRST STRIDE.

A SPONGE AND SOME COLD OR PREFERABLY ICED WATER USED AROUND THE NAPE OF THE NECK, AND UNDER THE EARS AND AT THE WRISTS AND ELBOWS WILL BRACE YOU UP.

GET NICELY WARMED UP AND THEN RE-ACT TO THE GUN.

I SHOULD USE THE SPRINGY OLD 6-SPIKED SHOES.

ALL THE BEST OF LUCK FROM
YOURS TRULY
S.A.MUSSABINI

P.S.

PLEASE WISH FRED GABY GOOD LUCK FROM ME.

The letter proves that Abrahams kept Mussabini's original note for more than half a century.

42, Orpington Road,
London. N. 21 3PG
November 23rd., 1977

886 6472

Dear Brian Marchant,

I enclose a copy of the note which your grandfather sent to me the day before the first round of the 100 metres at Paris, together with a "translation". I can assure you that even after 53 years, I still have appreciation for all his help.

With kind regards,

Yours sincerely,

Harold M. Abrahams

HAROLD M. ABRAHAMS

When Lord Puttnam saw this letter for the first time in 2010, he became quite animated and declared, 'It is exactly as we had it in the film! Word for word! Colin must have got this from Harold. It must have come from Harold, because we didn't have any dealings with the Mussabini family, I'm ninety-nine per cent certain.'

Originally it wasn't so much Harold's story that had fascinated Puttnam as Eric Liddell's. Puttnam explained later, 'I was looking for a theme about someone doing something which was extraordinary.' As it turned out, Puttnam stumbled across exactly what he was looking for by chance. He told me in 2010:

> It was rather embarrassing, I had rented a house in Pacific Palisades on the coast outside LA, from a guy who was a fanatical yachtsman. I was ill and I couldn't leave the house, so I was suddenly thrown back on what he had in his library.
>
> Every book seemed to be on sailing and navigation and I found the one book that wasn't – by Bill Henry. It was the official history of the Olympic Games. So I started reading it and I got back to 1924. And I just found this extraordinary paragraph, not about Harold but about Eric Liddell refusing to run.
>
> And that's the bell that rung and I thought, 'Could you get the audience to accept the fact that someone couldn't run in the Olympics?' And that's where it started. But I also saw Harold Abrahams in the story and more people. The original title for the film was *Runners*. And it was about a group of men, it was always intended to be about a group of men. From Day One I knew that Eric's story wouldn't hold a movie on its own. It's too thin. It's a one-line plot. So it was always going to be about relationships. And the film would have been a thin brew without Harold Abrahams.

His writer, Colin Welland, went to work quickly, and Puttnam remembered, 'Colin definitely did have a conversation with Harold. It must have been in the autumn of 1977.'

It appears that Harold and Colin connected, and this made Abrahams all the more enthusiastic about the idea of being 'immortalised' on the silver screen. To use Harold's words, suddenly everyone was going 'to know that this bald old bugger had won a gold medal' more than half a century earlier. To use Puttnam's words, 'And there was never for one moment any concern that Harold was not going to be happy about the project at all.'

The reason that Welland and Abrahams clicked was that Colin also felt he had been the victim of prejudice. And as he listened to the older man, he would have drawn parallels in their respective stories. That's one of the reasons why Lord Puttnam still feels lucky, all these years last later, that he commissioned Welland. He explained, 'In a way Colin was a masterstroke because it allowed Colin to say things about being a northerner in the south; things that I think he felt deeply about. Where I "lucked in" was that the Jewish outsider, Harold, became the northern outsider, Colin, in the sense that in the film Harold said what Colin felt.'

Rosemary Warne recalled, 'Harold told me that he'd got some interesting news to tell me in 1977 for Christmas and then he didn't tell me anything. I found myself thinking, "Come on, what is this interesting news?" and he said, "No dear, I'm not telling you." I think he was probably going to tell me about it before the news came out. I think it was *Chariots of Fire*. He was very chuffed and bubbling because something was happening.'

It was ironic that Harold would end up paired for all time in the public imagination with Eric Liddell, the Scotsman he never faced over 100 metres. Puttnam revealed, 'We were aware they had raced over 220 or 200, and there was a reason why we changed the race to the 100 in the film. It was very simple: we didn't want to confuse the audience. With regard to Liddell's story, 100 to 400 was a clearer distinction than 200 to 400, which was less of a stretch.'

A stickler for accuracy, Harold might not have liked the distortion. But in that initial, exploratory conversation with Welland, no such intention would have emerged. It was the uncompromising nature of the two characters, Abrahams and Liddell, that was becoming so irresistible to Welland. Eric in his prime wouldn't compromise his religious beliefs by running on a Sunday; and Abrahams in his prime wouldn't compromise either, because he was so determined to produce his very best, whatever the casual conventions of the day. Both men stuck to their guns, in Harold's case despite the undertones of anti-Semitism.

Part of Harold must have known that the film would give him a kind of sporting immortality. Maybe he even sensed that, just when all seemed lost, his own story would help to preserve something of the purest spirit of athletics. The movie would become a monument to an era when athletes ran for no other reason than because they felt a fire in their bellies. But what would they call it?

CHAPTER NINE

CHARIOT FOR
'MR ATHLETICS'

Time was short. Harold Abrahams had one Christmas left and he spent it with Rosemary in Bielefeld, Germany, where she was stationed. 'He seemed in very good form,' she recalled. 'We spent some of the time with Lieutenant-Colonel James Haswell (who went on to become the first insurance ombudsman) and his family. Harold found their roundness of thought and worldly understanding a joy, and was happy at their home during his last Christmas.'

On his return to Winchmore Hill, where he was living with Alan and his wife Phyllis, Harold went back into battle one last time for the future of athletics.

There was no obvious cause for concern, since this was normal behaviour. 'He had just turned seventy-eight but he was still fit and would go on mile-long walks,' Alan explained. 'Right until the end, he kept working. Always busy, always with something to do. That's the way he liked it.'

On January 4, the last night of his conscious life, Harold called Robert Stinson, Honorary Secretary of the British Amateur Athletic Board. Stinson was a much younger man, and Abrahams had overseen his rise through the administrative ranks of athletics. At the same time Harold had become a close friend of the Stinson family, and on one occasion had even taken Robert's wife Sue to the D'Oyly Carte theatre to see *The Mikado*.

But this call was probably about a British hammer thrower named

Barry Williams. Two articles in the *People* newspaper in 1976 had given the impression that Williams had taken anabolic steroids. As a result he had lost his international eligibility. In a damage limitation exercise, Williams and the BAAB were in the process of retracting his previous remarks.

On December 30, 1977, Stinson had written to Harold, 'I would be grateful if you would find time to call me at home with regard to the Barry Williams problem.'

The Williams case probably confirmed all Harold's fears; that the march towards professionalism was already turning athletics rotten; that drug use was bound to be the consequence of appearance money. Of course people were going to cheat if they thought they could get rich by cheating. All Harold and Stinson could do once the Williams case had been addressed was to try to ease the pressure on the floodgates. If they burst open, professionalism threatened to swamp the sport completely. By relaxing amateur rules where they could, so that athletes at least had money to train and travel, they might keep more competitors on their side.

Harold had already seen to it that athletes the world over could tap into trust funds – he called them 'subventions' – set up by their national governing bodies. His colleague Arthur Gold recalled, 'How well he prepared his speeches is best indicated by his submission to the IAAF Congress in Montreal in 1976 of the BAAB proposals on the new amateur rules – proposals he had played a large part in drafting. He spoke for more than an hour and at the end of the ensuing debate the proposals were carried almost "in toto" with only minor amendments to qualifying phrases.' Subventions were in, and athletes therefore had a little less reason to complain.

Stinson wondered whether there was anything else that could be done to make British athletes feel more valued, without giving way to full-blown professionalism. The athletics writer Mel Watman pointed out, 'Probably more than most people, Robert Stinson was responsible for the liberalising of the amateur rules. And Harold was still forward-looking, even though he was tied to the amateur ethos of the day.'

As they talked on that night, Abrahams and Stinson knew they were fighting a desperate rearguard action. Those floodgates still looked set to burst. Soon they would; and Harold's bid to protect the purity of his sport would be swept aside by the materialism of modern-day athletics. 'I think we should endeavour to retain the spirit of the old, while abandoning habits of thought and actions derived from a society that no longer exists,' Harold always said quite reasonably. You could almost hear him saying it one last time that night.

He may have sounded like King Cnut, defiant as the water crashed in around his legs. But he had to do something to restore some sanity to his sport. Track and field athletes poisoned the world over by drugs and money; the very idea was too much for Harold to bear.

Sue Stinson recalled, 'Robert suggested that Harold should go to bed because of the tiredness he could hear in his voice.' The voice of athletics was weakening slightly, as its owner tried to plot a course through the latest mess to somewhere beyond. Robert Stinson said soon afterwards, 'Harold was the living embodiment of long-term progressive thought on athletics. I count myself fortunate that I was talking to him only thirty minutes before he suffered the stroke which proved fatal.'

His son Alan remembered the moment he realised something was seriously wrong. 'We had finished dinner and he had gone upstairs to his office. We heard a crash. It was similar to my mother, the way he suddenly collapsed. He'd had a stroke.'

Harold was taken to Chase Farm Hospital in Enfield. Rosemary was informed almost immediately. Alan hoped she might hold the key to his recovery. Rosemary explained, 'Alan rang me, maybe on the fourth of January, told me the sad news and asked if it would be possible for me to come over, because they thought that familiar voices might assist in bringing him to. I managed to get compassionate leave and came over on a boat. When I reached the hospital I talked to him about everything and played music. It is funny because you have a body lying there and you are not sure what they know, what they can hear and what they can't hear.'

Sue Pottle recalled, 'Many of us visited my father at his bedside, we sang him Gilbert and Sullivan and chatted about this and that – but no reaction.'

Rosemary remembered the underlying despair:

It was very hard for me and the family. It was hard for all of us. I shaved him, because one of the things he was always so meticulous about was that he was always clean-shaven whenever one met him. He was meticulous about how he looked, personal hygiene and so on. And when I arrived, he hadn't been shaved for two or three days and he had got this awful stubble around him. And I thought maybe if I did that it would help because it was really quite soporific sitting around there. I think he had an electric shaver and I tried, I was probably pretty awful at it but I thought he looked a little better and I thought maybe that would make him feel a little better. If it got through. One didn't know. That was it really. There wasn't a lot else one could really do. He got pneumonia I think I'm right in saying. He was certainly very chesty. He didn't come to.

By now Alan had given up hope. 'After the first forty-eight hours, my view and that of my wife was that we kind of hoped he didn't wake up again. If you can get the patient back to consciousness within forty-eight hours there is a good chance of success. After that it is less likely.'

There was to be no awakening for Harold, and Alan pointed out, 'He was dead before he hit the ground in all but name. In practical terms he was dead. He had made it clear he didn't want to be a vegetable and wanted to go quickly. He didn't want to hang around. That was one thing he was scared of.' Alan's sister Sue explained, 'I don't believe he would have wanted to awake in a paralysed state, because his brother Adolphe had been like that for about six months at the end of his life, and it had been very difficult.'

Harold Maurice Abrahams had come into the world early. It might be said that, following his collapse, he left a little late – even for his own liking. He died on January 14, 1978.

Poor Rosemary Warne, whose army commitments had forced her back to Germany, scraped together enough money to head back to England again, following her heart. 'I remember going with the family from 42 Orpington Road. They very kindly let me ride in the car or one of the cars. We went to Enfield Crematorium. I don't really remember very much after that, I felt a bit miserable.'

Norman Cuddeford remembered the scene. 'It didn't seem to be a Jewish funeral. Nobody was wearing Jewish garb, it was a Christian funeral.' 'The funeral was private – almost just family. Ross McWhirter's widow was there, and Ken Gardner, who my parents had fostered during the war. Tony was there too and a few others,' Sue Pottle explained.

Harold would have been tickled that one of his former work colleagues captured the essence of his spirit as his once-athletic body finally returned to the elements. Cuddeford explained, 'Geoff Dobson, Harold's BBC radio athletics producer, was there. As the service came to an end, the coffin began its journey through the curtains. When it had disappeared, Geoff Dobson showed me his stopwatch. "That was 47.3 seconds. I think

Harold would have been pleased with that.'"

Robert Stinson, who had heard Harold's last impassioned words on this earth, reflected sadly, 'Perhaps because he has been regarded as immortal, I fear too many of us had taken for granted the thoughtful influence that he has exercised in the sport behind the scenes over the years.'

At least Harold never lived to see the day when athletics went fully professional.

Christina Innes seems to have grieved privately. She kept all his obituary notices, doubtless reflecting upon how close she had come to sharing most of that action-packed life with him. As a friend she had done so, despite long interludes when their lives had followed different paths. Christina isn't listed among those who attended Harold's Memorial Service, which took place at St Bride's, the 'journalists' church', just off Fleet Street on February 20, 1978. But then again there were too many there to list each one.

Norman Cuddeford recalled:

> I was an usher at the Memorial Service and it was packed. The music was beginning to fade away and the service was about to start when there was a kerfuffle outside and an old boy on sticks who was also deaf came in. I could see there was a small gap up in the choir stalls by Harold Evans of *The Times*, so I directed him there. As we made our way, he said loudly, 'Can I tell you a story about Harold?' I told him that he could tell me if he could be a little quieter but he was deaf as I say, so he still spoke loudly as he began, 'We always used to meet once a year for lunch. I was at Oxford, Harold was at Cambridge and we used to race. Harold, I'd tell him, I knew your backside better than your front side because I could never keep up with you.' A lot of people in the church heard him and they all laughed.

It summed up Harold's excellence on the cinders rather nicely.

Looking back, it was the fact that the church was packed out which said more about Harold than any particular religion. The Marquess of Exeter represented the Duke of Edinburgh; Sir Roger Bannister was there, and Harold's fellow-medallist from 1924, Lord Porritt, read the lesson. But there were so many others who wanted to pay tribute to 'Mr Athletics'. Norris McWhirter delivered the eulogy and began like this: 'To deliver a remotely adequate address on the life and achievement of Harold would require an inordinate amount of time. In his life Harold timed everything and everybody. He quite unfortunately specialised on sermons and on addresses at memorial services . . .'

McWhirter later talked of the 'profound sense of loss' felt by 'all those whose lives were sometimes touched, sometimes transformed by the many kindnesses and the warmth of his feeling, particularly to those who through youth or inexperience, or straitened circumstances lacked the wisdom or the substance of which he could and did so generously give.' Then he reminded everyone of Harold's 'immense achievement' in ensuring 'that track and field athletics today has the status of a national sport.' 'It was a feat,' he insisted, 'which so assuredly must have been marked by the family's third knighthood had he lived to complete the final act in his lifelong service to athletics as President of the AAA – a body whose centenary history was latterly engrossing him and which he was uniquely qualified to write . . . Harold's memorials range from the permanence of his place in Olympic history to the near permanence of the IAAF rulebook, which he virtually wrote, to the transience of so many wonderful after dinner speeches.'

'In giving thanks for his life and achievement of the incomparable Harold at the last we may all say as surely Harold can say, "I have fought the good fight, I have finished my course, I have kept the faith."'

Harold's life was over; yet in a way his story was just beginning. *Chariots of Fire* soon brought his sporting passion to many millions of people, thanks in no small measure to a performance of extraordinary depth by the actor who played him, Ben Cross.

Tom McNab had knocked Cross into shape before filming; so the actor looked the part too. McNab had coached genuine British athletes at a time when he felt that Abrahams the administrator had been determined to block all progress. Poor Ben took the brunt of McNab's bitterness during the pre-shoot training. 'I used to make him do extra press-ups,' admitted the coach years later. 'Ben asked me why he had to do more than anyone else. I just looked at him and said, "I hated you, Harold Abrahams."'

Meanwhile in the film itself, Sybil seemed to show disdain for Harold too at one point – or at least for his temporary weakness. 'If I can't win, I won't run!' says a petulant Harold. 'If you don't run, you can't win,' says Sybil sharply. No one would have guessed that Harold didn't meet the real Sybil until nine years after he had stopped running – or that she was more understanding of Harold's weaknesses than anyone else alive.

As for Christina Innes, it was as though she had never existed. Rosemary Warne claimed, 'He would have hated the fact that Sybil was portrayed as being involved with him at university because it wasn't true.'

'We had to play a lot of games with time,' acknowledged Puttnam. 'We did know that Harold had a girlfriend during his running days. I never knew her name and I didn't know they had been engaged; I just knew there had been someone and he had been involved with her at the time. But the attraction of Sybil for us was this Mikado thing, and the notion of this exotic woman. Irresistible, frankly.'

Other inaccuracies caused unease. The film had Harold running round the courtyard in Cambridge, beating the chimes as though no one had ever done it. Abrahams never achieved this feat or even tried, though one of his best friends did – Lord Burghley. Puttnam knew this; but he made Harold the successful courtyard runner for dramatic effect. Had he been alive, Harold would undoubtedly have refused to take the credit for something a good friend did. Rosemary insisted, 'I think if Harold had seen the film he would have been very upset about being given the credit for David Exeter's run. They were great friends.'

Then the movie portrayed Harold's Cambridge University elders as anti-Semites, rushing to condemn Harold's use of a professional coach, Sam Mussabini. In reality, Harold wasn't trained by Mussabini while he was at university. That came before, when he was just fourteen, and shortly after, when he was twenty-three. Rosemary claimed, 'I think they overdid the anti-Semitism. I didn't feel – certainly not in his later years – that he was at all fussed about it.'

This was a commonly held view among friends and family; yet Harold said in numerous interviews that anti-Semitism had indeed motivated him. And Lord Puttnam insisted, 'The anti-Semitism is not exaggerated in the film. I am not suggesting he was repeatedly victimised but it did exist and it was a factor.'

The movie-makers could have stuck rigidly to the truth in all areas of Harold's story. But the Oscar-winning screenplay writer, Colin Welland, was a master dramatist; and by not sticking strictly to the truth he created something truly beautiful. Some of the reasons behind the film's power and resonance lie in the subtle changes he made to the real story. This book will not condemn *Chariots of Fire*. There is still so much about it to celebrate.

Sir Roger Bannister told me, 'It was one of the greatest films about sport. It took America by storm. If [Hollywood] are determined to make a film, they change the names and make it anyway. I don't think you can stop them as such. It is a film portrayal and you would expect the producer to make some changes. I think Harold Abrahams would have enjoyed it and been interested in it.'

Had he survived a few more years, perhaps Harold might even have been tempted to take Christina to a private viewing. But Harold was gone, and so, by then, was Christina's husband Francis. Sue Smithson confirmed, 'My father died in 1980, not long after Harold, really. My mother must have been relatively newly widowed when *Chariots of Fire* came out. But she was absolutely determined to go and see the film. She would have been about eighty and we went up to London by train and by bus to the cinema. My mother and I went to see *Chariots of Fire* in a cinema in Regent's Street.'

Yet you had to wonder how Christina Innes felt, watching Harold's story unfold in that West End cinema. Many a woman in her shoes would have been jealous at the way Sybil's character had usurped her place in what was fast becoming a nationally-celebrated story. Christina reacted quite differently. As she gazed at the screen, she became defensive on Sybil's behalf, because the actress who played Harold's future wife was nothing like her. Sue Smithson remembered:

> My mother found it interesting, even though she said she didn't find
> it entirely true to what had actually happened. I remember that my
> mother said they could not have chosen an actress who looked less
> like Sybil to play the part. I think Sybil was always blonde and that
> was what upset my mother so much – because the girl who portrayed
> her in *Chariots of Fire* was definitely brunette. I remember my
> mother saying, 'Ah, but that actress is nothing like Sybil was!' She
> certainly didn't like the actress who had been chosen to play the part
> of Sybil. She thought that was just crazy.

It almost sounded as though she was speaking for Harold; imagining perhaps what his own reaction would have been, had he been sitting right there beside her.

Sue Pottle had similar reservations. 'The lady playing my mother was in all aspects totally unlike her and she played her more as a harpy or perhaps even a femme fatale – neither of which she was. The real Sybil was given to gentle flirtation! Pat and I thought the film was a romanticised version of events but a great film that we enjoyed.'

The ticket for the Royal Film Performance of *Chariots of Fire* in 1981 shows that Her Majesty Queen Elizabeth The Queen Mother attended.

Meanwhile Christina at least acknowledged that the Harold she saw up on the silver screen was essentially recognisable as the man she had once loved. Sue Smithson explained, 'I don't think she had any objections or criticisms about the portrayal of Harold's character. I think the anti-Semitism was probably exaggerated.'

But then Harold had exaggerated the anti-Semitism in his own mind at the time, as he later admitted. And although certain aspects of *Chariots of Fire* would have irritated him, the common consensus is that Abrahams would have enjoyed many of the film's more accurate elements. Above all, he would have loved the sheer passion for athletics that 'Chariots' captured and generated.

The movie won four Oscars including Best Film, and became an international phenomenon. 'It is hard to imagine,' explained Sue Pottle, 'that Harold would not have enjoyed the chance to bask once more in the glory of his achievements. It would have been almost as good as receiving a knighthood.' Lord Puttnam put it like this: 'My guess is that Harold would have done what Jenny Liddell [Eric's sister] did. He would have gone along with the film, but retained the right to criticise after it came out. I think he would have been pretty thrilled with the Oscar, though. He liked prizes.'

And he would have loved the reaction of Eric Liddell's elderly wife Florence, who took the trouble to approach the actor who played Harold in the film at its premiere. Lord Puttnam recalled, 'Eric Liddell's wife came up after the premiere and said to Ben Cross, "Ah, Mr Abrahams, my husband spoke a lot about you." That was very moving.' Harold would have been delighted to think that Liddell spoke a lot about him, just as Abrahams spoke and wrote so much about Eric and his unfathomable talent. And Abrahams would surely have been gratified when his story was deemed so strong and so positive that a world leader used it to illustrate a new initiative for world peace. That's precisely what US President Ronald Reagan did on June 3, 1988.

Making a speech to emphasise that Mikhail Gorbachev, then president of the Soviet Union, was seeking 'serious reform' over in Moscow, Reagan summoned the required optimism like this:

> And here is a story, one last story that can remind us of what we are about. It is a story that a few years ago came in the guise of that art form for which I have an understandable affection – the cinema.
>
> It is a story about the 1920 [sic] Olympics and two British athletes: Harold Abrahams, a young Jew, whose victory – as his immigrant Arab-Italian coach put it – was a triumph for all those who have come from distant lands and found freedom and refuge here in England and Eric Liddell, a young Scotsman, who would not sacrifice religious conviction for fame. In one unforgettable scene, Eric Liddell reads the words of Isaiah. 'He giveth the power to the faint, and to them that have no might, he increased their strength . . . but they that wait upon the Lord shall renew their strength . . . they shall mount up with wings as eagles. They shall run and not be weary.'
>
> Here is our formula for completing our crusade for freedom. Here is the strength of our civilisation and our belief in the rights of humanity. Our faith is in a higher law . . . 'Come, my friends', as it was said of old by Tennyson, 'it is not too late to seek a newer world.'

CELEBRATIONS

In 1987, Pat Pottle and Michael Randle were named in press reports as the mystery men who helped George Blake escape twenty-one years earlier. Pat and Michael decided to take matters into their own hands, to get their motives out into the public domain once and for all. In 1989 they published a full account of their involvement in the Blake escape. It was entitled: *The Blake Affair – How We Freed George Blake – and Why*.

Prompted by none other than Norris McWhirter, Conservative MPs demanded that the case be reopened. Sue Pottle explained:

> Norris read the book and decided that a certain female who provided financial backing for the Blake escape, someone mentioned in the story but not named, was me. In fact it wasn't me, but Norris decided that Dad's money had effectively sponsored the Blake escape. He thought money originally belonging to his late friends Harold and Sybil had been 'misused' in this way, unknown to my parents. Then there was my husband Pat's admission in the book that he had played a major part in the escape. Norris was appalled and he decided to instigate an early-day motion in the House of Commons, urging that the people who had helped Blake be prosecuted. He didn't stop to think whether Dad would have wanted that trouble to land on his daughter's family – or if he did weigh it all up, he didn't seem to care enough.

It was decided that Pat Pottle and Michael Randle would indeed be prosecuted; and, in a move which was linked by some sections of the media to the funding of the imminent trial, Harold's medals were put up for auction and sold for £23,300 – double the estimate. Sue Pottle insisted, 'Alan initiated the selling of the medals in 1991; but it wasn't money for the trial. Pat and Michael had legal aid for that.'

The man who bought the medal collection was Mohammed Al Fayed, who had put up half the $8 million needed to finance *Chariots of Fire*. His son Dodi had been an executive producer on the film. Mohammed Al Fayed said, 'Abrahams was a man of great integrity. He was the victim of the worst snobbery and racial prejudice and yet triumphed over everything to win the gold medal in the 1924 Games. That is why I backed the film and bought the items. I was inspired by a man who was the victim of severe racial prejudice and yet by the strength of his own morality triumphed and won a gold for his country.'

Now the morality of Pat Pottle and Michael Randle came under the microscope. They admitted in court that they had helped to release Blake; but they argued that it had been justifiable on humanitarian grounds, due to the severity of his 42-year sentence. Incredibly, Pat and Harold's daughter were allowed to fly to Russia at this time, to see Blake himself. Sue Pottle revealed: 'We went during the trial, in 1990, to get evidence for the defence. The authorities hadn't taken our passports away. We went with our solicitors and got a statement from George. I can't remember whether they allowed George's evidence in the trial; but it was just him saying that these guys did it for best reasons and not for anything else. The first time I met George, he was at the airport with a hat pulled down and a long coat on. He was a very charming and attractive man as far as I was concerned.'

But the judge wasn't impressed by evidence gleaned from a double agent – and instructed the jury to find Pat and Michael guilty. Alan Abrahams recalled what happened next: 'My brother-in-law Pat and his co-defendant pleaded guilty; and yet the jury found them not guilty, because they were politically motivated.'

The verdict made legal history, and would have fascinated Harold as a former barrister, even if his family hadn't been involved. George Blake was delighted, and invited Pat and Sue back to Russia for another break. Christina Morley thoroughly approved of the jury's verdict. When Pat Pottle died in 2000, she carefully collected and preserved his newspaper obituaries, just as she had collected Harold's. Christina, the remarkable survivor from the *Chariots of Fire* era, finally passed away on February 28, 2003, when she was almost 101.

What would have happened if Harold Abrahams had married her? Would he still have made the sacrifices necessary to become Olympic champion? Without his 100 metres victory in Paris, Abrahams would probably never have become such a powerful voice in world athletics later in life. The Olympic movement might then have lacked the protection it needed to survive some of its worst post-war crises.

As the Games returned to London in 2012, Harold Abrahams and the principles he held dear became relevant once more. And it is hard to escape the conclusion that they will always be relevant, if we wish to preserve the true Olympic spirit for future generations. Though Abrahams was far from perfect, Lord Coe was right: respect really isn't a strong enough word; not for a man who lived his life to promote and protect the simple thrill of competition, in the hope that it might bring unity to a troubled world.

ACKNOWLEDGEMENTS

My thanks to His Royal Highness The Duke of Edinburgh for writing a foreword that gave so much insight into the pressures experienced by Harold Abrahams – as well as perspective on a lifetime of achievements. I have no doubt that Harold would have been absolutely thrilled to know that Prince Philip had contributed in this way to his biography.

Helping to make that happen was Prince Philip's good-natured Private Secretary, Brigadier Sir Miles Hunt-Davis, GCVO, CBE. The Brigadier couldn't have been more helpful in his final year in the role before his retirement at the end of 2010. I am still amazed at the speed and efficiency of the correspondence from Buckingham Palace, when there were so many more important things to consider on a daily basis.

Lord Coe very kindly made it clear that he would also have been willing to write a foreword for the book, which is further proof of the high regard in which Harold Abrahams is still held. My thanks go to Seb for this and the valuable thoughts he shared on Harold's standing in his sport. Similarly, Lord Puttnam made time for me and very generously gave my project his blessing. This was something that also meant so much, coming as it did from the man who captured the essence of the young Harold Abrahams so memorably by producing the wonderful *Chariots of Fire*.

Sir Roger Bannister, an intensely private man, allowed me to infringe upon that privacy on several occasions. The result was, I hope, accuracy in the telling of Harold's story where it coincided with his own. This happened for a few remarkable years, an era in athletics still celebrated today.

Mel Watman, doyen of athletics statisticians and a man who lives and breathes the sport, was astonishingly thorough in furnishing me with information I lacked on track and field. Newspaper cuttings, record books, early copy-editing, encouragement; Mel's enthusiasm and eagle eye never ceased to amaze me. Thank you so much, Mel. Peter Lovesey, that brilliant novelist and athletics historian, provided support and advice when I most needed it, as well as athletics magazine articles aplenty from the relevant era. He is a true gentleman, wise and insightful.

Kevin Kelly, another athletics historian of note, offered me the benefit of his own vast knowledge and use of some of the photographs he has collected over the years. His passion for athletics shone through at every turn. Neil Allen, a distinguished sports journalist and former athletics correspondent of *The Times*, furthered my education in the sport. He offered valuable perspective on Harold's personality from his personal dealings with Abrahams, and generously lent me some of his precious books. Mel, Peter, Kevin and Neil, you are the kind of warm-hearted experts an athletics newcomer dreams about. I will always be grateful. Mel's friend Andrew Huxtable provided the record of highlights of Harold's athletics career included here; no mean feat and further proof that the National Union of Track Statisticians can boast some serious brainpower. Thank you, Andrew.

Then there were members of the Abrahams family, who gave so much to make the book what it is. Sue Pottle, Harold's daughter, was the first to be approached for her blessing. She was an amusing, welcoming and helpful companion throughout this process. Moreover, Sue allowed me to use family letters in order to piece together the story of her parents' courtship. This couldn't have been an easy decision but helped, I hope, to do justice to their beautiful love story. Sue's brother, Alan also furnished me with his memories and perspective on his father's life, and did so with great dignity. One of the great tragedies of the build-up to publication of this book was that Alan lost his son Shane, to whom Harold had left his Olympic Games gold medal. Shane is respectfully remembered here.

Tony Abrahams, Harold's nephew, supplied a wealth of photographic material and no shortage of interesting opinions on what made his uncle tick. His charming wife Liz went beyond the call of duty with some superb research. Thanks to you both.

The Abrahams family also lent me books Harold had written, which offered a wealth of valuable source material. *Athletics*, published by George G. Harrap was one such book. *Training for Athletes*, written by Harold and his brother Adolphe and published by G.Bell and Sons, was another which provided a fascinating perspective from the 1920s. The fact that Harold wrote *Athletic Sportsgraph*, published by Young World Productions for the British Olympic Association, as late as 1972 shows just how many decades Abrahams was at work on his trusty typewriter. Thank you Harold, for all you left us.

Rosemary Warne, one of Harold's best friends in his final years, allowed me to use taped messages sent by Harold, as well as books, anecdotes and contacts. Above all, she offered patience and understanding when the going got tough. Major Warne really is a remarkable lady; and it is easy to see why Harold valued her company. The same can be said of Rosemary's friend and former athlete, Valerie Winn. Thanks to Valerie and her husband, ex-England rugby player Chris for their assistance.

The daughters of Christina Morley, Sue Smithson and Perry Morley, were also very helpful. They supplied fascinating photographs and memories of both their mother and Harold. Sue's husband John was equally reliable when it came to keeping open the channels of communication.

There are so many others to thank: James Cox, the archivist at Gonville and Caius in Cambridge University; and Dr Chris Thorne, a fountain of knowledge on the Cambridge University Athletic Club. Hannah Westall, the archivist at Girton College in Cambridge; Paul Willcox of the Achilles Club and his researcher-friend Marion Stevenson; John Bromhead, who interviewed Harold Abrahams shortly before his death; my thanks to you all for the support you gave me when the project was still in its infancy. At Repton School, Paul Stevens was an able historian; and other members of staff, from secretary to caretaker, were most kind during my unannounced visit there.

Many thanks also to Graham Ball and the *Sunday Express* for use of that newspaper's archive material. I am equally grateful to Jeff Walden and Joanne Cayford at the BBC. To Philippa Bassett, thanks and apologies for the many times I intruded upon her peaceful, ordered existence at the Special Collections department of Birmingham University in order to access the Harold Abrahams collection there. A big tribute goes to Dr Martin Polley, who might have written this book himself and so graciously stepped aside, yet still showed the generosity to offer valuable assistance. Gratitude and recognition should also be sent across the Atlantic to Rob Fouch, for the generous access he gave to his own Harold Abrahams collection.

I am also very grateful to the publisher at J.R. Books, Jeremy Robson, whose enthusiasm for the project from the outset was typical and vital.

To Tom McNab, Peter Radford, Sue Stinson and Anne Donaldson – more thanks for your memories and efforts. To all the others who helped to build the picture – but whose names I may have forgotten to mention – my thanks and apologies.

Last and definitely not least, thank you to my son Luca. His first sporting hero was Usain Bolt, and his enthusiasm for Bolt's exploits encapsulated the simple thrill of running fast for sprinters and fans alike. That is the feeling which drove Harold Abrahams to stardom, and that same feeling inspires so many of us to see how far our sporting dreams will take us.

It is a pleasure to thank so many. How very lucky I have been to receive your help. If the reader has found this book enjoyable, it is undoubtedly down to your efforts.

HAROLD ABRAHAMS CAREER STATISTICS – HIGHLIGHTS

By Andrew Huxtable1908

1908

Summer, Hunstanton Beach:

    50yd (Handicap) race: Won (Time unknown)

1909

Bedford Grammar School:

    100yd (Under-10): Second (Time unknown)

    220yd (Under-10): Won (Time unknown)

    440yd (Under-10): Won (Time unknown)

1910

Brighton Beach:

    Quarter-Mile (Handicap: Over-10): Won (Time unknown)

July, Stamford Bridge, London:

    Lotinga Cup (For relatives of London Athletic Club Members). Handicap off 31.25yd in 150yd Race: Won (Time unknown)

1911

April 3

    100yd: (Bedford Grammar School Under-13) Won in 14.0sec

July, Stamford Bridge:

    Lotinga Cup 150yd Race (Handicap 17yd): Won (Time unknown)

1914

April 4, St Paul's School, West Kensington, London:

    Long Jump: Won (4.73 m)

    100yd: Won (11.8sec)

    300yd: Second-equal (winning time 39.0sec)

1915

March 30, Repton School, Derbyshire:

    Long Jump: Won (5.52m/18ft 1½in)

    150yd: Won (17sec)

    440yd: Won (59.4sec)

1917

April 2, Repton School, Derbyshire:

    100yd: Won (10.8sec)

    220yd: Won (25sec)

1918

April, Repton:

    440yd: Won (56.6sec)

    Long Jump: Won (6.23m/20ft 5½in)

April 4

    100yd: Won (11.2sec)

    220yd: Won (24.0sec)

April 20, Public Schools Championships at Stamford Bridge, London:

    100yd heat: Won: (11.0sec)

100yd final: Won (11.0sec)
Long Jump: Won (6.19m/20ft 3¾in)
440yd: Third
1919
August 29, Aldershot:
Race against Willie Applegarth (Abrahams given 2-yard advantage). Won by 6yd
(10.0sec)
November 11, Cambridge University Freshman's Sports Day Two:
100yd Final: Won (10.2sec)
Long Jump: Won (6.48 m/21ft 3in)
440yd Final: Won (52.8sec)
1920
February 5, Cambridge University's Caius College v Oxford University's Magdalene
College:
100yd: Won (10.8sec, victory margin 4yd)
Long Jump: Won: (6.36m)
120yd hurdles: Won (19.2sec, victory margin 3yd)
440yd: Won (53.0sec, victory margin 3yd)
February 24, Cambridge University: Caius College v Emmanuel College, (Inter-
Collegiate Final):
100yd: Won (10.2sec, victory margin 2yd)
Long Jump: Won (6.69m/21ft 11½in)
High Jump: Won (1.65m)
120yd hurdles: Won (18.2sec, victory margin 5yd)
440yd: Won (53sec, victory margin 1½yd)
Caius wins the Rouse Ball Challenge Cup for the first time.
March 12, Cambridge University Sports:
100yd final: Won (10.2sec, narrow victory over Guy Butler)
Long Jump: Won (22ft or 6.70m)
March 27, Cambridge University v Oxford University at Queen's Club, London:
100yd: Won (10.0sec, victory margin 1 foot over Bevil Rudd)
Long Jump: Won (6.88m or 22ft 7in)
July 10, England v Scotland v Ireland in Crewe:
220yd: Heat: Won (24.2sec, REALLY SO SLOW?! victory margin 6yd)
220yd: Final: Won (23.2sec, victory margin 4yd)
Long Jump: Third (6.49m)
August 15, Antwerp, The Olympic Games:
100m: Heat 10: Won (11sec)
100m: Quarter-final: Fourth and eliminated: (Won by Charley Paddock in 10.8sec)
100m: Won (11.2sec)
Long Jump: Third (6.16m)
August 17, Antwerp, The Olympic Games:
Long Jump: Twentieth and eliminated before finals (6.05m/19ft 10¼in)
1921
March 19, Oxford v Cambridge 'Varsity Sports at Queen's Club, London:
100yd: Won (10.2sec – by two feet from Guy Butler)
Long Jump: Third (21ft 4in/6.51m, compared to winner L.St C. Ingrams' 6.72m)

June 25, London Stamford Bridge:

75yd: Won (7.4sec – breaking the world record by 0.2sec. But the track was discovered to be 8 inches too short)

July 2, London Stamford Bridge: The Amateur Athletic Association Championships:

100yd final: Second by half a yard to Harry Edward – who won in 10.2sec (heat and semi final statistics unavailable)

220yd final: Second by 1½yd to Harry Edward – who won in 22.2sec.

July 23, Cambridge, Massachusetts, Harvard and Yale versus Oxford and Cambridge:

100yd: Second (won narrowly by Ed Gourdin in 10.2sec)

Long Jump: Second (6.73m. Won by Ed Gourdin with a world record 25ft 3in/7.69m)

July 28, Travers Island, New York: Oxford and Cambridge versus Princeton and Cornell:

100yd: Won (10.4sec)

Long Jump: Won (6.60m)

November 28, Cambridge University: Inter-Collegiate Championship:

100yd: Won (10.2sec)

Long Jump: Won (23ft / 7.02m)

1922

March 25, London Queen's Club, Varsity Athletics: Oxford University versus Cambridge University:

100yd: Won (10.2 – by one yard from Guy Butler)

Long Jump: Won (6.70m)

1923

March 23, Cambridge v Oxford 'Varsity Athletics at Queen's Club, London:

100yd: Won (10.0 – the first man to win the Varsity 100yd four times)

Long Jump: Won (23ft 7¼in/7.19m – a British record)

440yd: Won (50.8sec) Beat W.E. Stevenson by 3yd

July 6, London Stamford Bridge, The Amateur Athletic Association Championship:

220yd: Heat 11: Won (22.4sec)

Semi-final: Equal-second with W.P. Nichol: (In 22.0sec. Eric Liddell won in 21.6)

Abrahams was given chance of a 'run-off' against Nichol for final place: Abrahams declined and withdrew.

July 7, London Stamford Bridge, The Amateur Athletic Association Championships:

100yd: Heat 8: Won (10.2sec)

Abrahams withdraws from next round complaining of sore throat.

Long Jump: Won (23ft 8¾in/7.23m – a new British record)

July 21, Wembley Stadium, London: Oxford and Cambridge v Harvard and Yale:

100yd: Won (10.0sec – margin of victory 3yd)

Long Jump: Won (23ft 2¼in/7.07m)

220yd (straight track): Won (21.6sec – margin of victory 7yd)

1924

June 7, Woolwich, London:

100yd final: Won (in a world record-equalling 9.6sec, although Abrahams doubted the time's validity due to Nichol's proximity – just one yard behind – and concluded there was a slight downward slope on the track)

Long Jump: Won (7.38m)

June 21, The Amateur Athletic Championships, Stamford Bridge, London:
  100yd: Final: Won (9.9sec – margin of victory 1½yd over W.P. Nichol)
  Long Jump: Won (6.92m)
July 6, Paris, The Olympic Games:
  100m: Heat 14: Won (11.0sec)
  100m: Quarter-final 4: Won (10.6sec – equalling the Olympic Record)
July 7 Paris, The Olympic Games:
  100m: Semi-final 2: Won (10.6sec – equalling the Olympic Record again)
  100m: Final: Won (10.6sec – equalling the Olympic Record for a third time. But on
  the 1/100th of a second watch he was timed even faster at 10.52sec)
July 8, Paris, The Olympic Games:
  200m: Heat 10: Won (22.2sec)
  200m: Quarter-final Race 4: Won (22.0sec)
July 9, Paris, The Olympic Games:
  200m: Semi-final 1: Third (21.9sec)
  200m: Final: Sixth (22.3sec, won by Scholz in 21.6)
July 12, Paris, The Olympic Games:
  4 × 100m relay: Heat 1: Won (42.0sec – a new world record)
July 13, Paris, The Olympic Games:
  4 × 100m relay: Semi-final 2: Won (41.8sec)
  4 × 100m relay: Final: Second (41.2sec, USA take gold in 41.0 – a new world record)
  GB Team: H.M. Abrahams, W. Rangeley, L.C. Royle, W.P. Nichol
July 19, London Stamford Bridge: British Empire v USA Relays:
  4 × 100yd: Second (USA wins by 1½yd in 37.8sec) British Empire Team: A.E. Porritt,
  E.W. Carr, W.P. Nichol, H.M. Abrahams.
  Long Jump: Second (7.07m – won by Ed Gourdin with 7.53m)
July 23, Queen's Club, London, Achilles Club v British Dominions:
  Long Jump: Second (6.96m – won by S.J.M. Atkinson of South Africa with 7.15m)
  100yd: Third (race won by Arthur Porritt)
August 9, Northampton, All English Championships:
  Long Jump: Won (7.21m)
1925
April 11, London:
  Long Jump: First (7.10m)
May 6, London Stamford Bridge: Bedfordshire v London Athletic Club:
  Long Jump: Second (6.70m – retired injured)

Acknowledgements: *Cambridge Review* (CR), *The Times*, Dr C.J.R. Thorne, G. Kobzos,
S. Hrnoir, H.F. McKendrick, C. Dean, W.B. Downing, J.N. Bromhead, I. Buchanan,
P.H. Lovesey, R. Magnusson.

INDEX

Figures in italics indicate captions.